Hitch-hiker's Guide to Europe

Ken Welsh was born in Australia. After serving in the
RAAF and working as a staff TV comedy writer he
sailed for Europe where he still lives. After several
months on the road he conceived the idea for *The
Hitch-hiker's Guide to Europe*, which has been in print
for fourteen years and is considered 'the road-bum's
bible'. Though married with three children, he remains
an insatiable traveller, paying his way with his work as
a professional photographer. He estimates that during
the last seventeen years he has travelled over three
hundred thousand miles. Ken Welsh is also the author
or photographer, or both, of six travel books about
Spain and one on Malta, and has published five novels.

Ken Welsh

Hitch-hiker's Guide to Europe

How to see Europe by the skin of your teeth

revised and updated for 1985–86

Fontana Paperbacks

First published by Pan Books Ltd 1971
Ninth edition first published by Fontana Paperbacks 1983
Second impression February 1984
Tenth edition February 1985

Copyright © Ken Welsh 1971, 1973, 1974, 1975, 1977,
1979, 1981, 1983, 1985

Set in 10 on 11pt Linotron Times
Reproduced, printed and bound in Great Britain by
Hazell Watson & Viney Limited,
Member of the BPCC Group,
Aylesbury, Bucks

For Ann, who came too.
And for Ben, who came also.
And for Marcos and Carina.

Contents

Introduction 9

Invitation 10

Hitcher stuff 11

The most your pound is worth 21

1 **On the road** 23

2 **How to hitch** 26

3 **What it will cost and how to get it cheaper** 44

4 **What to take** 57

5 **How to survive** 65

6 **The British Isles and Ireland** 83
England 84
Wales 110
Scotland 111
Northern Ireland 118
Ireland (Eire) 120

7 **Europe** 131
France 132
Belgium 158
The Netherlands 165
West Germany 176
Luxembourg and the Small Countries 191
Switzerland 198
Austria 207
Italy 215
Spain 232
Portugal 251
Greece 259

8 Scandinavia, Finland, and Iceland 276
   Denmark   280
   Sweden   288
   Norway   295
   Finland   303
   Iceland   309

9 The Communist countries 315

10 Morocco and North Africa 334

11 Turkey and the Middle East 350

12 Working in Europe 383

13 Photography 396

14 Weights and measures 399

15 Language 401
   French   401
   German   403
   Spanish   405
   Italian   407
   Dutch   409
   Swedish   411

Calendar 1985–86   413–414

Introduction

This book is designed to show you how to get around Europe for about £90 ($126) a week – cheaper if you're tough enough.

Although it's called *Hitch-hiker's Guide* and is aimed at people on a hitch-hiking budget, van and car travellers will also find it useful because it lists facts which someone with his own wheels can use just as well as someone who's moving around on temporarily borrowed wheels.

For every guidebook which is written, three-quarters of its readers can do better than it. That's because they are guidebooks and not at all holy. This book is no exception. And it's certainly not sacred.

Hitch-hiker's Guide gives you a rundown on Europe, Scandinavia, the Middle East, North Africa, and the Communist countries, telling you some of what there is to see and enjoy and giving you an indication of what it would normally cost. But I haven't experienced it *all*. There's lots more and plenty of it will be better than the stuff listed.

I ask those wandering souls who have already covered their first ten thousand miles on the road to skip the section which deals with the practical aspects of hitch-hiking. It certainly wasn't written for them.

Invitation

If you find a deal in eating and sleeping, or a way of saving money in any of the major cities covered in *Hitch-hiker's Guide* you are invited to send your find to me care of the publishers. Your hint and credit will be included in the relevant chapter.

Write to: Ken Welsh,
Hitch-hiker's Guide to Europe,
c/o Fontana Paperbacks,
8 Grafton Street,
London W1X 3LA

Thanks . . .
. . . to all hitchers who have responded to my invitation and written in with reams of interesting tips. Mail was so heavy during 1983–84 it was impossible to answer letters personally. So thanks to everyone, and thanks again. Keep those letters coming.

Special thanks for assistance in preparing the *Hitch-hiker's Guide* are owed to: Davi Isaacs, Noreen Wells, Isla Stone, Peter Stone, Allen Harbinson, Lynn Kersh, Ginney Ashton and Thea Braam – all good truckers.

Special contributors . . .
Alan Barlow – Iceland, Israel
Martin (Mel) Brook – France
Patrick Connolly – England, Scotland, Ireland
Simon Hayman – Switzerland, Austria, Jordan, Syria, Cyprus, Czechoslovakia

Hitcher stuff

Definitions for hitchers
'*Hitch-hike*: travel by begging lifts from passing motor vehicles. (Fifteenth century, of obscure origin: partly synonymous with Scots *hotch*, move by jerks)' – *The Concise Oxford Dictionary*.

'*Hitch-hike*: to travel by getting free automobile rides and sometimes by walking between rides' – *The Random House Dictionary of the English Language* (unabridged edition).

'*Wander*: rove, stroll, go from country to country or from place to place without settled route or destination' – *The Concise Oxford Dictionary*.

Opinions for hitchers
'When I see so many young people thumbing lifts these days I feel depressed. Have they no pride at all? I can't imagine anything more humiliating than standing at the roadside like a tramp, begging. I always thought that the great thing about young people today was their high principles, independence and determination to make a better job of the world than their predecessors did. But I just can't equate that picture of healthy, intelligent young people, with the deplorable one of cringing, cadging hitch-hikers swarming the roads in their thousands' – *opinion in the letters column of a women's magazine*.

Records for hitchers
The world record for hitch-hiking (as recorded in *The Guinness Book of Records*) is claimed by Devon Smith who, from 1947 to 1971, thumbed 291,000 miles.

Are there aspirants for the title amongst *Hitcher's Guide* readers? If you qualify, write to me (see address opposite) briefly detailing your travels and enclosing letters from three different people willing to back your claim. I will then approach the editors of *The Guinness Book of Records* to see if they can accept your accomplishments as a world record.

Each year readers write in with their record attempts in the following categories of hitching:
1 Longest hitch in one vehicle (excluding aeroplanes and ships).
2 Most miles hitched in any 12-month period.
3 Most miles hitched in any 24-hour period.
4 Slowest hitch between two points (include distance, time and brief reason for slowness).
5 The world's craziest lift.

Last year's winners in categories 1, 2, 3 were not beaten. I have added this year's best efforts to the 'honourable mentions':
1 (Longest hitch in one vehicle) *David Donkin, Leeds, UK*, is still the winner in this category. He covered approximately 3000 miles in a VW van, driven by two Aussies, through northern Europe, taking 12 days.

Honourable mentions go to *Joker, Baerum, Norway*, who hitched about 2000 miles in a German car from Chiclana (near Jerez in south-west Spain) to Munich, taking three days, and to *Graham Hopkinson, Gateshead, UK*, whose longest single lift in Canada was 1750 miles between Ottawa and Regina.
2 (Most miles in any 12-month period) Nobody has yet beaten *Alan Barlow, Cheadle, England*, who zigzagged 15,700 miles from northern Sweden to Sicily and Greece and back to the UK.
3 (Most miles in any 24-hour period) The record is still 1200 miles from Medicine Hat, in Alberta, Canada, to east of Thunder Bay, Ontario, held by *Ashok Gupta, Delhi, India*.
4 (Slowest hitch between two points) *Ruth Cleece, Preston, Lancashire, England*, rolls to victory. She hitched a lift on a steamroller in St Ives. A half-mile journey uphill took about 45 minutes!
5 (World's craziest lift) Plenty of challengers. Two of the zaniest: *Stephen Morgan, Poole, Dorset, England*, hitched a lift on the back of a bike pedalled by a Dutch schoolgirl and pulled his luggage behind on a shopping trolley. They covered 11 miles to Meerkerk in Holland. And *Chris Schelin, Kauniainen, Finland*, rode with a bunch of Italian farmers in a truck with no brakes, horn, signals or lights. 'Every time we came to an intersection or a curve, we all had to honk like geese. When we turned, the honking was accompanied by everybody pointing right or left. And when it got dark everybody shone flashlights on the road ahead.'

Honourable mention for *Ian Gunn, Ashburton, Victoria,*

Australia, who was given a lift in a bloodstained riot truck in Taumarunu, New Zealand.

Can you better these efforts? If so, let's hear from you. No testimonies are needed. Just tell me the facts. No prizes. Just brief glory.

Limericks for hitchers

There was a young hitcher named Bright
Who travelled much faster than light;
He went out one day
Thumbed in a relative way
And got home the previous night.
– *with apologies to the late Prof. A. H. Reginald Butler FRS*

A hitcher living in Staines
Is inventing with infinite pains
A new type of thumb
Which he hopes when it's done
Will travel him faster than planes.

Graffiti for hitchers

'Eurail, we hitch!' – *Patrick Hine, Oxford, England*

'Orange: such a beautiful place you can't leave it!' – *spotted by Mike Waldie of Shenfield, England, on the sliproad by the Orange péage, France*

'A hitch in time saves a fucking long walk!' – *scrawled on the railings at the autopista entrance near Gerona, Spain*

'Dear God, just let me get to London tonight and I promise I'll be a good little freak' – *seen near Oxford*

'Sandra L. is one slick hitch bitch . . .'
and beneath that
'She goes slumming in Lamborghinis . . .'
and beneath that
'So would you if you were built like her . . .'
and beneath that
'This is male chauvinistic rubbish!'
and beneath that
'Bullshit. Sandra's my girlfriend.' Signed, Lois.
– *seen on the A11, near Norwich, England*

'Rucksacks suck!' – *seen near Frankfurt, Germany, by Robert T. Duncan, Aberdeen, Scotland*

'Chuck bricks – that stops the bastards!' – *seen near Barcelona, Spain, by Keith Harvey, Haywards Heath, UK*

'Never give up – next thing you know you'll be voting' – *contributed by Yid, Flensburg, West Germany*

'If God had meant us to hitch-hike, he would have given us bigger thumbs' – *contributed by Doug Bissell, UK*

'Better a terrible ride than an easy walk' – *seen near Göteborg, by 'Slow' Archie, Netherlands*

'Don't spit – you might need it' – *seen one hot summer in Spain, by Paul Hinckley, Birmingham, UK*

'Hope you like the view because you've got plenty of time to see it' – *seen at Stillhorn services, Hamburg, by Mark Naisbitt, Darlington, UK*

'Welcome to the Black Hole – nothing leaves here, not even night' – *seen near Warrington, by Mike Eal, Solihull, UK*

Any more hitcher limericks, or hitcher graffiti? Send them in and I'll try to include more examples in the next edition. Include your name and address for a credit, and in the case of hitcher graffiti, where you saw it.

Quotes for hitchers

'When you get there, there's no there' – *Gertrude Stein* (1874–1946)

'Q: What *are* you rebelling against?'
'A: Wadda ya got?' – *Marlon Brando* in *The Wild One*

'What is the answer?' (*I was silent*)
'In that case, what is the question?' – *last words*, from *Alice B. Toklas, What is Remembered*, by *Gertrude Stein*

'The more corrupt the state, the more numerous the laws' – *Tacitus* (55?–130?)

'I am one individual on a small planet in a little solar system in one of the galaxies' – *Roberto Assagioli*

'The race advances only by the extra achievement of the individual. You are the individual' – *Charles Towne*

'A fanatic is one who goes through life with his mouth open and his mind closed' – *Dr Lawrence J. Peter*

'To enjoy freedom we have to control ourselves' – *Virginia Woolf*

'Freedom is nothing else but a chance to be better' – *Albert Camus*

'The journey of a thousand miles starts with a single step' – *Traditional Japanese saying*

'It's not worth while to go around the world to count the cats of Zanzibar' – *Henry David Thoreau* (1817–62)

'Travel, in the younger sort, is a part of education; in the elder, a part of experience. He that travelleth into a country before he hath some entrance into the language, goeth to school, and not to travel' – *Francis Bacon* (1561–1626)

'The use of travelling is to regulate imagination by reality, and instead of thinking how things may be, to see them as they are' – *Samuel Johnson* (1709–84)

'The denunciation of the young is a necessary part of the hygiene of older people' – *Logan Pearsall Smith*

'The real lost souls don't wear their hair long and play guitars. They have crew cuts, trained minds, sign on for research into biological warfare, and don't give their parents a moment's worry' – *J. B. Priestley*

'To travel hopefully is a better thing than to arrive . . .'

'Give me the young man who has brains enough to make a fool of himself . . .'

'For my part, I travel not to go anywhere, but to go. I travel for travel's sake. The great affair is to move' – *Robert Louis Stevenson* (1850–94)

'You will do foolish things, but do them with enthusiasm' – *Colette* (1873–1954)

'Adventure is something you seek for pleasure . . . but experience is what really happens to you in the long run, the truth that finally takes you over' – *Katherine Anne Porter* (1890–1980)

'If you don't risk anything, you risk even more' – *Erica Jong*

'I do want to get rich, but I never want to do what there is to do to get rich' – *Gertrude Stein*

'He travels fastest who travels alone' – *Rudyard Kipling*

'Every absurdity has a champion to defend it' – *Oliver Goldsmith*

'He who is impatient waits twice' – *Mack McGinnis*

'An adventure is an inconvenience rightly considered. An inconvenience is an adventure wrongly considered' – *G. K. Chesterton*

'Life as a hitcher is like being a pubic hair on a bog seat! Sooner or later you get pissed off' – *Wally Hughes*

Poetry for hitchers
There is no solace on earth for
 us – for such as we –
Who search for a hidden city we
 shall never see.
Only the road and the dawn, the sun,
 the wind and the rain,
And watch-fires under stars, and sleep
 and the road again.

Books for hitchers
Here's a list of books useful to hitch-hikers. Some are American editions and hard to find in Europe; some are out of print and will only be found in public libraries or secondhand book stores. To assist you in locating titles, I've included the date the book was first published:

Hitch-hiking in Europe – An Informal Guidebook by Ed Buryn. Hannah Associates, PO Box 31123, San Francisco 94131, USA (1969). This is the first hitcher's guidebook I know of. Ed had published his while I was still gathering info together for mine, which first appeared in 1971. My copy is autographed by the man himself. Extremely rare.

Vagabonding in Europe and North Africa by Ed Buryn. Random House Inc., 201 East 50th Street, New York, NY 10022 and The Bookworks, 1409 Fifth Street, Berkeley, California 94710, USA

(1971). Ed's second, much more substantial book went through several printings. You might find a secondhand copy if you're lucky.

The Hitchhiker's Road Book – A Guide to Traveling by Thumb in Europe by Jeff Kennedy and David E. Greenberg. Doubleday and Company, Inc., 245 Park Avenue, New York, NY 10167, USA (1972).

Rule of Thumb – A Hitchhiker's Handbook to Europe, North Africa and the East by Paul Coopersmith. A Fireside Book, Simon and Schuster, 1230 Avenue of the Americas, New York, NY 10020, USA (1973).

Europe – A Manual for Hitchhikers by Simon Calder, Colin Brown and Roger Brown. Vacation-Work, 9 Park End Street, Oxford, UK (1980).

Travellers Survival Kit Europe by Roger Brown, revised by Simon Calder. Vacation-Work, 9 Park End Street, Oxford, UK (1976).

Hitchhikers Manual Britain by Simon Calder. Vacation-Work, 9 Park End Street, Oxford, UK (1979).

Alternative England and Wales, published by Nicholas Saunders, 65 Edith Grove, London SW10, UK (1975).

Alternative London, edited by Georganne Downes with Kathy Holme and Max Handley. Otherwise Press. Distributed by Wildwood House, Gloucester Mansions, Cambridge Circus, London WC2, UK. This incredible book on how to use London was first published by Nicholas Saunders in 1970. Georganne publishes it now and you can find the tome in most decent bookshops.

Nicholson's London Guide, Robert Nicholson Publications, 24 Highbury Crescent, London N5, UK. For me, it's the best pocket guide to London on the market. Great value for money. Updated regularly.

Africa for the Hitchhiker by Fin Biering-Sørensen and Torben Jørgensen. Bramsen and Hjort, 12 Vestergade, DK-1456 Copenhagen K, Denmark (1974).

Travellers Survival Kit to the East by Nigel Clarke. Vacation-Work, 9 Park End Street, Oxford, UK (1979).

Asia for the Hitchhiker by Mik Schultz. Bramsen and Hjort, 12 Vestergade, DK-1456 Copenhagen K, Denmark (1972).

The Asian Highway – The Complete Overland Guide from Europe to Australia by Jack Jackson and Ellen Crampton. Angus and Robertson, 16 Ship Street, Brighton, UK (1979).

Asia Overland – A Practical Economy-Minded Guide to the Exotic Wonders of the East by Dan Spitzer and Marzi Schorin. The Stonehill Publishing Company, 10 East 40th Street, New York, NY 10016, USA (1978).

Latin America for the Hitchhiker by Mik Schultz. Bramsen and Hjort, 12 Vestergade, DK-1456 Copenhagen K, Denmark (1974?).

In Strangest Europe – A Cabinet of Curiosities, Rarities and Monsters by Peter Ratazzi. The Mitre Press, Sardinia House, Kingsway, London WC2, UK (1968). Weird facts about Europe, and weirder destinations.

Summer Jobs Abroad edited by David Woodworth. Vacation-Work, 9 Park End Street, Oxford, UK. Published annually.

Kibbutz Volunteer, Vacation-Work, 9 Park End Street, Oxford, UK (1978).

Whole World Handbook – A Guide to Study, Work and Travel Abroad by Marjorie Adoff Cohen, revised and edited by Margaret E. Sherman, of the Council on International Educational Exchange. Elsevier-Dutton Publishing Co. Inc., 2 Park Avenue, New York, NY 10016, USA. Published annually.

Wandering – A Walker's Guide to the Mountain Trails of Europe by Ruth Rudner. Photographs by James Goldsmith. The Dial Press, 750 Third Avenue, New York, NY 10017, USA (1972).

Backpacking by Peter Lumley. Teach Yourself Books, St Paul's House, Warwick Lane, London EC4P 4AH, UK (1974).

Stay Alive in the Desert by K. E. M. Melville. The Jerboa Press. No address in book, but printed by Grafiche Trevisan, Castelfranco Veneto, Italy (1970).

A Traveller's Guide to Health – A Guide to Prevention, Diagnosis and Cure for Travellers and Explorers by Lt Col. James M. Adam,

RAMC. Sphere Books, 30–32 Gray's Inn Road, London WC1X 8JL, UK, in association with the Royal Geographical Society (1968).

The Book of Survival by Anthony Greenbank. Signet, New American Library, 1301 Avenue of the Americas, New York, NY 10019, USA (1970).

The Complete Traveller by Joan Bakewell. Hamlyn Paperbacks, Astronaut House, Feltham, Middlesex, UK (1977).

International Youth Hostels Handbook, Volume 1 (Europe and Mediterranean) and *Volume 2 (Africa, America, Asia and Australasia)* published annually by IYHF. Copies obtainable at 14 Southampton Street, London WC2E 7HY, UK.

Auf Achse – Tips für unterwegs by Jürgen Bischoff. Bund-Verlag GmbH, Köln, Germany. German-speakers will find this book full of real hitcher stuff. Jürgen spent a long, long time on the road and once published a regular hitcher's letter called *On the Road*. He also wrote many Hitchers' Tips and Comments for previous editions of *The Hitch-hiker's Guide to Europe*.

Work Your Way Around the World by Susan Griffith. Vacation-Work, 9 Park End Street, Oxford, UK. Yet another first-rate tome from Vacation-Work, and to the best of my knowledge the *definitive* book of its type. Three hundred-plus pages stuffed with facts and ideas on working all over the world.

The Traveller's Handbook edited by Ingrid Cranfield. A Futura book published in association with WEXAS International Ltd. Seven hundred pages of every sort of information about every form of travel, including expeditions.

Seven League Boots – the story of my seven-year hitch-hike around the world by Wendy Myers. Hodder and Stoughton (1969). The title explains it all. Hard to find now, but worth the hunt.

The Student Book edited by Klaus Boehm and Nick Wellings. Papermac, 4 Little Essex Street, London WC2. Updated regularly. If you're bombing around trying to figure out just what to study when lack of funds finally forces you home, this 'applicant's guide to universities, polytechnics and UK colleges' will help. Six hundred pages of easily assimilated info on study courses from accountancy to zoology.

Guidebook series

Let's Go Guides, Elsevier-Dutton Publishing Co., 2 Park Avenue, New York, NY 10016, USA. Half a dozen titles covering Europe, Asia and the USA, aimed at the budget traveller.

Hachette World Guides, Hachette, 79 Boulevard Saint-Germain, Paris, France. In-depth cultural guides covering Europe, North Africa and the Middle East. Heavy to carry and very expensive, but well worth having the book covering your favourite country.

Michelin Green Guides, The Dickens Press, 4 Upper Thames Street, London EC4, UK. Cover countries, areas and capital cities. Strong on what to see. Excellent city maps.

Berlitz Travel Guides, Editions Berlitz, 1 Avenue des Jordils, 1000 Lausanne 6, Switzerland. Cover over fifty world-wide destinations. Reasonably priced, pocket-sized, all-colour photography.

The Rough Guides, Routledge and Kegan Paul, 39 Store Street, London WC1E 7DD. Volumes available on Greece, Spain and Portugal, and more titles on the way.

The most your pound is worth

at the date of going to press

Algeria	6.17 dinars	Lebanon	9.65 pounds
Austria	26.00 schillings	Libya	.36 dinars
Belguim	74 francs	Morocco	11.33 dirhams
Bulgaria	1.3 leva	Netherlands	4.15 guilders
Cyprus	.76 pounds	Norway	10.72 kroner
Czechoslovakia	8.6 korunas – Tourist	Poland	151.5 zloty– Tourist
Denmark	13.3 kroner	Portugal	200 escudos
Egypt	1.45 pounds – Tourist	Romania	18.79 lei – Tourist
Finland	7.7 markkas	Soviet Union	1.05 roubles – Tourist
France	11.3 francs	Spain	206 pesetas
Greece	151 drachmas	Sweden	10.5 kronor
Hungary	60.5 forints – Tourist	Switzerland	3.04 francs
Iceland	40.9 kronur	Syria	9 pounds
Israel	606 shekels	Tunisia	1 dinar
Iran	112.5 rials	Turkey	502 lira
Iraq	.38 dinars	USA	1.22 dollars
Italy	2300 lire	West Germany	3.68 Deutschmarks
Jordan	.49 dinars	Yugoslavia	223 dinars

The sterling and dollar equivalents given throughout the book were correct at the date of compilation, but, with the fluctuations of international currencies, they will certainly change during 1985–86.

Warning! Inflation is rampant, currencies in turmoil. Which means big problems for guidebook writers and worse ones for you.

Because of printing schedules this book had to be researched months before it went to press. To allow for the inevitable process of inflation between the time I researched the book and the time you will read it, I have automatically upped every price in the book by 20 per cent except in Switzerland which, because of its apparently stable currency, I have raised only 10 per cent. But prices may rise even higher than anticipated. So be prepared . . . an extra £20 in the pocket might make all the difference.

'I think your "what your pound is worth" should be submitted for the International Joke of the Year Award!' – *Marcel Thomas, Horndean, England*

1 On the road

Once upon a time – well it was only eighty years ago – a young man with a romantic head could disappear into the wilderness of his dreams to seek his fortune and become a man of the world.

These days jumbo-jets have made us all men of the world – if we can find the air fare – and the seeking of fortunes starts more often than not in the London School of Economics or in the dollar-shaped halls of learning of American business schools. You don't stake claims any more if you want to make a fortune, you buy shares; and you don't disappear into the wilderness because the wilderness has been turned into real-estate.

Sometimes you can sense all this closing in on you and you know you have to escape. You must get right away and there ain't no more slow boats to China, man, and if there were you'd have to belong to the Seamen's Union before you could get aboard. But you have to get away and the place you can go is on the road, the infinite miles of tarmac and pot-holes which criss-cross the world, the magic ribbon which can lead to a thousand other worlds.

Get on the road and sometimes you get the feeling of what a non-computerized planet must have been like – or rather, what it was like when people *used* machines and didn't *depend* on them. Get on the road and the press-button-something-happens syndrome disappears. The action-reaction principle doesn't apply on the road, unless you count a car not stopping as a reaction to a thumb in the air. On the road you enter the world of pure chance, a world where mathematical equations mean nothing. Because the tenth car doesn't stop doesn't mean that the eleventh will. On the road you are in a world where time passes without the aid of a clock. On the road you even have time to think.

You wake up in the morning – be it in some cheap hotel or in a sleeping-bag beneath a tree in a field – and you get up and have breakfast if you can afford it and then make your way to the road; and the only thing you know for sure is that you *don't* know where you'll be that night. That's a strange feeling the first time it dawns on you.

The thing is that the road takes you. You can't dictate to the road. If you do you might as well be in a train. Hitch-hiking is the art of wondering what will happen to you between your starting point and your destination and taking from everything that *does* happen everything that you can.

And unless you really have to go somewhere, a destination is not all that important. You can set out from London to go to Rome and end up in Lisbon and what the hell? Rome will still be there next time around. And if there isn't any next time? Well, you've seen Lisbon – and it's a nice city.

Hitching is more than anything else an attitude to travel, not just a means of getting from point A to point B. If you look upon it purely as a means of getting to where you want to go, you'll probably get very bored very quickly. Hitch-hiking is a cumulative experience, a never-ending happening of unknown factors which contribute, with a little luck, to a memory of what real travelling is all about – not just the chance to say that you've been to a place, but the feeling that at one time, somewhere, even if only for an instant, you felt like you had become a part of the land through which you travelled.

Hitch-hiking involves you. It fulfils that need for occasional fast forward movement which seems to be built into the mind of the twentieth-century wanderer – a sense of the looming miles ahead being slashed aside by the roar of a powerful motor – and, at the same time, it deposits you five, six, seven times a day into the guts of a lonely landscape where the atavistic man who survives in some of us can be briefly at home. And by the very nature of the game it is impossible to avoid the citizens of the country through which you are moving. You become, in effect, a mechanized Marco Polo.

That's the bright side of the game, but there's a dark side too, and it comes when you're twenty-seven miles from nowhere in the middle of a black night with rain drenching you and when you have no tent and no cover. It comes when you're sick, it comes when you're tired. Mostly it comes when loneliness hits you like a dart and you've got to be with people and in a light place, a warm place. It comes when it's like that and the cars won't stop and those that do don't seem to making up the distance between where you are and where you need to be.

It's when the dark side comes that you discover something about who you are, because the hitch-hiker who moves alone is with himself for a long, long time each day – and not many of us are used to that.

What you do when the dark side comes depends on who you are. Some people invest their remaining money in a train ticket home and for them, that's the best thing. Other people just wait for something better to happen and it usually does. And some people just keep on moving, which is what it's all about.

The warning, for what it's worth, is given; you pay for what you get and the longer the road the bigger the toll because hitching can be hard travelling.

Mostly, though, it's good travelling, and a hundred miles split between walking, riding pillion on a motorbike, bouncing on the tray of a huge semi or sitting comfortably in the back of a Mercedes – a hundred miles covered like that on the little-travelled side roads of Morocco or in the hard mountainous terrain of Greece will give you more memories (and bruises) than any sports-jacketed tourist will find as he slumbers in the relax-back aeroplane seat of an air-conditioned bus trying to figure in his travel-fuzzed mind which day it is in his twenty-one countries in twenty-one days super-fantastic luxury tour of the world.

Hitchers' Tips and Comments . . .

A taster for anyone dubious about undertaking a first hitch trip in Europe: try reading *A Hitch in Time* by Ian Rodger in combination with the *Hitch-hiker's Guide*. Enough to give any prospective traveller itchy feet! (*A Hitch in Time: Recollection of a Journey* – by Ian Rodger; published by Hutchinson 1966.) *John Hoad, Eastbourne, England*

I'd never been abroad until I read your book – boy, you've got a lot to answer for! *Steve, Heckmondwike, England*

2 How to hitch

Hitch-hiking is a sport. It's like a motorized version of snakes and ladders, except instead of throwing a dice on to the board and automatically moving, you throw a thumb into the air and more often than not don't move.

As with all sports, hitch-hiking has its mythical heroes. You hear stories of guys who can dress like something out of a hippy musical, stand by the side of the road without moving a muscle and take their choice of the cars which screech to a halt in regimental lines on either side of them; cars which not only give them lifts, but which detour thirty, forty or fifty miles out of their way to land the magic men at a stated destination.

And you hear of others who can pick the car they want out of an approaching bunch and always make it stop; and it's always a big Citroën or a Porsche, and its owner always buys them a meal at an expensive restaurant.

It's a fact that if you're a good-looking woman hitching alone you can make this happen. I know a girl who came clear across Germany in one day and never stepped into anything lowlier than a Mercedes. She was also propositioned twice, middle-aged German businessmen being as fast, if not as smooth, as their chariots.

But if you're not a magic man, or if you don't have long blonde hair, you're left with the problem of stopping cars. The only thing on your side when you stand by the road and put up your thumb is that *some* drivers pick up hitchers. Sooner or later one of them will stop – though you shouldn't count on it. You might go the whole day without a ride and then get twelve the next day. What you must do then, is try and raise the odds in your favour and to do that there are some basic things which can be considered.

APPEARANCE Not many people in Europe have anything against beards, long hair or hip clothes these days, so there are no worries there. But if you think of the problem in terms of how many people will willingly stop and talk to you if you approach them in the street while you're wearing fancy-dress costume and when you haven't bathed for twenty-three days, you get a perspective on how many cars are going to stop for some dingy freak thumbing them from the side of the road. The majority of people who will be picking you up will be ordinary suburban types. Their own kids wear beards and gear, too, but they are 'nice kids'. Look like a nice kid and you can skid around pretty fast.

LUGGAGE Carry as little as possible. Try and keep it down to just your frame-pack, or at the most, one hand item as well. I know plenty of people who have hitched carrying a frame-pack, suitcase, camera bag and portable typewriter, but it's not a good general rule. A lot of cars won't stop because they simply don't have room for your luggage.

ROAD TACTICS This is the most important thing of all and while plenty of experienced hitchers might argue that you can get away with any sort of appearance because people *want* to pick up freaks for a kick, or that if a driver wants to stop to help you on your way he's not going to worry about extra pieces of luggage, they'll agree unanimously that you have to choose your thumbing position carefully.

First (and most obviously, though it's horrifying how many fools do it), *don't hitch on a bend*. There are three reasons. One, it's deadly. Cars cut through bends and you can get killed. Two, drivers are concentrating too much on the problem of getting through the bend to be worried about anyone trying to stop them from the side of the road. Three, even if the driver was stupid enough to want to stop on a bend, the law forbids him to do so.

Second, *choose your road edge carefully*. Drivers aren't inclined to stop in the middle of the road – it's too dangerous – so you must pick a position, when possible, which has a nice safe edge for them to run off on to, and the more of their car they can get off the road when they stop the more they like it. And the smoother the area the better. Drivers don't like running off the road into mud, or pot-holes, or into a puddle of water when they don't know how deep it is.

Third, *when you're trying for a ride, try properly*. My experience has been that I get rides when I'm standing up and looking like I want to go somewhere. You might get one when you're lying on

the ground with your feet up on your pack, lazily devouring a
bottle of wine, with a daisy stuck behind your ear and nonchalantly
waving your free hand up above the grass, but the odds are right
against you.

HOW TO CONQUER BOREDOM Half an hour or more without a ride
can leave you feeling a little lost. It's not so bad if you're with a
companion – especially one of the opposite sex – but if you're
alone you can start suffering from terminal boredom.

If you're into Zen or yoga then time is the air around you and
you have no problem. If you've got a decent novel, things are OK.
Paper and pencil lets you catch up on letters back home or allows
you to make paper aeroplanes complete with military markings.
Standard side-of-the-road games, equally suitable for one or more
people, include hurling stones at specified targets (hurl at leisure,
spin and hurl, five hurls in ten seconds, etc.), golf, played with a
suitable stick and assorted round stones (across the road on the full
counts as a hole in one), tin-can football (hard on the boots),
breath-holding, and standing on one foot.

One driver reports pulling up beside two gentlemen of the road
who were in the middle of a push-up competition. He offered them
a ride but they informed him that the loser was buying dinner and
asked if he could wait a moment. The driver – patient type –
watched in fascination as the two hitchers battled it out. The loser
fell on his nose after the forty-seventh push-up, while the winner
did five more just for the hell of it. The hitchers later told him that
they held the competition every day.

HOW TO WAVE THE CAR DOWN My technique depends upon my
constitution. Normally I use my thumb – always my right thumb
regardless of which side of the road I'm on – but when I'm feeling a
little poetic I sometimes change to a regal, floating wave of my
whole hand which, if the driver happens to be feeling in the same
mood, seems to work wonders. And then, of course, there's the
old two-finger wave which, if the car doesn't stop, can be
continued in one sweeping movement upwards to tell any
rear-view-mirror observer that you're suggesting up him for the
money or sending him on his way with peace. (Once, in Spain, a
field worker watched my thumb technique with interest for quite
some time. Eventually he inquired if I was trying to stop a car. I
said I was, that I was going to Granada. He said I was doing it all

wrong and when the next car came, wandered out into the middle of the road waving his hand like a policeman's halt signal. The car stopped and he lined up a ride for me. Not that the driver seemed too impressed with it all.) How *you* do it is your problem, but there's one trick you might try. Always smile, and always latch right on to the driver's eyes as he approaches and don't stop staring or smiling. You can psych some of them into stopping!

COUNTRY IDENTIFICATION This is purely a matter of choice. I've done one trip with the international AUS for Australia attached to my pack and two cars stopped specifically because the drivers had relatives in Sydney. The question is, how many cars *didn't* stop because of it? Lots of people carry small flags or national emblems and one friend of mine went through Europe like a rocket, dressed in a suit and carrying a small suitcase with a notice attached which simply read 'US student'. Perhaps you can approach the problem in terms of international political opinion. Try and figure how popular your country is in Europe before you mount a sign.

DESTINATION PLACARDS These are used by most hitchers purely as last resorts after a rotten day's hitching. You find an old piece of cardboard or paper and print in large letters the name of the city you're heading for. Generally you can't tell how successful the idea is, so it's a matter of choice. I do think a destination placard is worth considering, for instance, on the German autobahns. The only places you're legally allowed to hitch or walk on these, or any other superhighways, are at the entrance and exit roads and, because of the ring-road systems, a car heading north might only be doing so to get to an exit road to take him south. Which can cause the temporarily northbound car driver to decide not to stop for what looks like a northbound hitcher who, in fact, happens to want to go the same way as the soon-to-be-southbound car. (Get it?) German students seem to make a lot of use of placards for that reason.

WHAT RIDES TO TAKE Providing a driver isn't obviously bombed out of his mind, my rule is to take any car that stops which has its bonnet pointed even vaguely in the direction I want to go. I work on the simple premise that if the ride is only for five miles, I'm going to be five miles closer to my destination and the next car I want might be sooner or later coming out of a side road we pass during that short drive. Some hitchers prefer to refuse the small rides in the hope that they'll eventually catch the big one. To me, that's like throwing away ten cents in the hope that you'll find twenty-five.

WHEN A CAR STOPS A lot of drivers who have stopped for you are nevertheless in a hell of a hurry. Most drivers pull up fifty or a hundred yards beyond you. Never risk losing a ride by wandering to them. Run. Grab your bag and move! When you get to the car, just wish the driver a good day in his own language (if possible) and then tell him where you're going. If you can't pronounce the name of the town have a map ready to pull out and point at. From then on, whatever the driver says, just answer *oui, si, ja* or *yes* as the case may be. It doesn't matter what the driver has said – 'I'm going to Kassel', 'I'm in a hurry', 'It'll be a slow trip' – *yes* is the one word which is the nearest thing to an answer. And keep smiling. Your one objective is to get into the car. Once rolling you can work out a way of finding exactly how far the driver is going.

FAST DRIVERS If you make the mistake of getting in with a fast one who you reckon is taking you both on a one-way ride (and it happens just about every trip), politely indicate that you want out. If he won't stop or doesn't understand what you're trying to say, be a little more obvious and a little less polite and make sounds which suggest you're about to throw up all over his upholstery. That usually drives the point home. And perhaps saves your life.

FAST DRIVERS (OTHER TYPE) Very occasionally, through no fault of their own, lady hitchers find themselves being attacked by guys who give them a ride. What to do? If it's one man it's not so bad. At least he has to stop the car first, and if he stops it in a suspicious place you've got a lead on what might be about to happen. In that case a simple 'no' (politely offered) will probably work. If it doesn't and he's obviously not a psycho type, you can try putting on a sick act, telling him you're having your period, that you're pregnant, that you've just had a bad operation or that you've got some dreaded venereal disease. If he *is* a psycho type you've got problems and about all you can do is keep talking until you can see a way out. If there's more than one guy there's not a great deal you can do about it. Screaming will probably get you roughed up pretty bad, fighting back, pulling out the old hat-pin or kneeing somebody in the balls will have the same result. (The knee works OK with one guy, but make sure your aim is good and you get him first try.) Best advice to offer is this: if you are a lady hitcher then travel with a second person. If you must travel alone, just make sure you're on the Pill.

THE LANGUAGE PROBLEM A lot of timid souls I know tell me that they could never hitch-hike in a foreign country because they just wouldn't know how to handle the language barrier. Well, the excuse is understandable, but it's a pretty sad one. One of the first things any hitch-hiker learns is that lack of language is no barrier to simple friendly communication. English-speaking people who say they don't know one word of a foreign language are either stupid or have no imagination. To start with, *imagination, communication* and most other words which end in *ion* in English are roughly the same in Spanish, French and Italian – they're just pronounced a little differently. And how many people don't know the meaning of *au revoir*, or *vino*, or *grazie*, or *Fräulein*? The point I am trying to make is that anyone who speaks English automatically has a stock of words in other languages he can draw on either because they are the same words, or they have entered the English language through popular usage, or because they figure prominently in films and books. Of course he mightn't be able to pronounce them correctly, but at least he has them and it doesn't take too many words to find out someone's name, what they do, where they're going, or if they're married and have kids. And that's the sort of small talk you find yourself indulging in when you're zipping down the highways of Europe and when you don't have a mutual language with the driver.

If you happen to speak a second language you're in business, not just because many Europeans speak at least one other language after their own, but because people who speak two languages, even if they aren't mutual, know enough about word association to be able to make some sort of conversation.

But many Europeans do speak English and when you get rides with them, that's when hitch-hiking comes into its own. On a good day you might be picked up by half a dozen cars with each of the drivers speaking a little English. Those drivers will usually be a cross-section of their society – young, old, rich, and poor – and from them you can glean a first-hand word picture of their country's attitudes and feelings.

If you don't have a mutual language with your host, don't worry about it. If you try to communicate and he's not interested in playing word games, just practise sitting without talking. If the tension seems to be building (and it often does), break it by offering a cigarette or something to chew – it nearly always works.

As a generalization, I've found that the better educated and/or more affluent my host, the easier it's been for me to talk with him even if he doesn't speak English. I say it as a generalization because I've had some great rides with truckies – particularly Arabs – without exchanging a single word. And it was from rides like those that I learned that communication is not only a matter of utterances, but a willingness to share the pleasures (or discomforts) of a situation. At that basic level, things can get boring but, if it's the only level you have, you learn to make the most of it.

GETTING IN AND OUT OF A CITY This is the biggest bugbear of any hitcher. Towns and small cities aren't so bad because you can walk in or out of them in less than an hour. But try walking out of Paris or London! If your ride has let you off in the suburbs of a big city and you want to go to the centre, you can try to hitch, but the odds are right against you. People in a suburban traffic stream usually don't have the chance to stop for you even if they want to. I've managed to hitch in the suburbs of medium-sized cities, but I've never had any luck in the big capitals. If you don't have any money, then obviously you'll have to walk and try to hitch, but the only real answer is to take a train or bus. You'll save yourself a couple of hours of hard work and a lot of energy.

The only way to get out of a really big city, as far as I'm concerned, is to take a train to the nearest small village outside the city limits. This might cost a pound or so, but it's quick and puts you straight on the road you want and away from the traffic-congested areas. And on a long walk out of a city – maybe two or three hours – you usually end up spending 50p or 60p anyway on drinks and food to keep you going. You can only walk by so many French *pâtisseries* before you break down and step inside!

FINDING A ROOM European cities and towns are nearly always six or seven centuries old at least, and this rather obvious fact gives the clue as to how to find the cheapest rooms in a strange city. The

majority of large towns and cities were built either on rivers or
ports for purposes of trade and communication, around a castle
which was built for the defence of an area, or around a church
which was the religious seat of a parish. The old sections then, and
the cheapest, are often around a castle, a cathedral, or on the
river, or around the port area.

This doesn't apply so much to very large cities which continually
instigate building programmes to clear such areas, but more in the
smaller cities. Lisbon is an example of a city with a cheap 'castle
area'. Paris used to be an example of a city with a cheap 'river
area'. (The Île de la Cité was reputedly the first settled area of
Paris. The Marais, supposed to have been the second settled area,
is now one of the cheapest places in the city.) Restaurants in these
areas are generally very cheap as well.

In villages and towns you can find reasonably priced rooms in
private houses. These normally cost about the same as a cheap
hotel room except, being part of someone's home, they are usually
cleaner and better value for money. If you want one of these but
can't spot a 'Room Free' sign, ask at the local bar.

Special note: when you visit a city covered in the *Hitch-hiker's
Guide* with a **Where to sleep** section, and decide to try one of my
recommendations rather than taking pot luck hunting around, you
may find it worth investing a few pence in a phone call. Wherever
possible I've listed the hostel or hotel phone number beside the
address; thus you can check, before you go to the address, that
they have a room free, that their prices haven't gone up since this
new edition was published and, also, that they are open. Many
student hostels close at various times during the year and, because
closing dates can vary from year to year, it's hard to make the
listings in this book absolutely accurate. A quick phone call could
save a lot of trouble (and bus fare money).

TRAVEL ALONE OR IN COMPANY? This is an old argument amongst
veteran hitchers. Opinions break down like this: men travel fastest
by themselves, but not as fast as a woman by herself. Two women
travel faster than two men, but a mixed couple travels faster than
any other pair.

Many drivers are wary of picking up more than one person,
especially if they're men. Travelling alone is the ideal, anyway,
because when you're by yourself you move at precisely your own
speed – you don't have to worry about your partner's fitness or his

inclination to go two hundred miles out of his way to catch an exhibition of Russian icon art in Geneva.

A lone woman will travel very fast, but it mightn't be pleasant travelling – lots of wolves drive cars. I'm not Moses the Lawgiver, but I think girls are crazy to hitch by themselves. Think of all those stalwart gentlemen willing to accompany you, ladies. And if that doesn't appeal, remember that two girls are safer than one and the chances of catching a ride don't drop dramatically.

A man and a woman together is the ideal combination if you must travel in company. You don't get lonely on the road or off the road and you still get plenty of rides. Another real advantage of travelling as a couple is that you can share double hotel rooms and cut the cost per head considerably.

To try hitching in the company of *more* than one other person is crazy.

HITCHING AT NIGHT This is a curly one. Some people swear by night hitching. Others swear about it. Some people say they can always get to where they're going at night. Others say drivers just won't pick them up and, although occasionally I've had to move at night and done OK, I think of all the times I tried but didn't get anywhere, and agree that it's a slow game. Anyway, you miss the countryside.

If you like the idea of night hitching or find it necessary to make a night-time journey, the following hints are handy. First, try to get under a light (obvious) and try to pick a light which will allow the driver to see that it's safe for him to pull off the side of the road. Second, try for an all-night service station where you can, if necessary, wander over to stopped cars and ask if they can help you on your way. Third, if you are stuck somewhere without light, for God's sake find a straight stretch of road where cars can catch you in their beam from a fair distance; and carry a white handkerchief or a white something to help them spot you. If you've driven a car at night, you'll understand the sense of that.

HITCH-HIKERS AND THE POLICE If you listen long enough to some of the road-talk around Europe you start getting the idea that cops devote most of their energy to hassling hitch-hikers. But before you finally make up your mind, take a good look at who's doing the talking.

Cops often stop you and ask to see your passport. They blow

you up for hitching on an autobahn instead of from the entrance.
They tell you to stop eating your lunch on the municipal grass
(grass is for looking at, *not* sitting on!). They wake you up and tell
you to piss off out of public parks. They ask to see your rail ticket
when they notice you loitering in a lovely warm railway station at
three in the morning.

That's usually all they do. Some of those things might be stupid
– like so what, you're asleep under the mayor's favourite oak tree
– but you have to be pretty uptight to think a cop is hassling you if
he asks you politely (and *most* of them are polite) to abide by some
bylaw he's being paid to enforce.

Thing is, of course, that a lot of people who consider themselves
very cool are so uptight that their eyeballs are popping. A cop asks
them to do something, they start screaming and next thing the cop
is frisking them for drugs, asking how much money they've got,
wanting to see their return ticket to country of origin and all the
rest of it.

Take someone with more authority than you and rub him the
wrong way and odds are you'll have trouble on your hands. Cops
are no exception. Be nice to the police, ladies and gentlemen, and
they'll be nice to you. But when you get way down south and too
far east, don't take my word for it.

HITCH-HIKERS AND IMMIGRATION OFFICIALS Every so often it
happens that some hitcher trying to cross a border is asked to
produce a substantial amount of money (substantial from a
hitch-hiker's point of view) to prove he can support himself in the
country he wants to enter. This is something that happens from
time to time all over the world.

In Italy, Spain, Greece and other Mediterranean countries it
tends to happen most during summer when a lot of people are on
the road and the authorities are cracking down on genuine,
nasty-type bums. These countries do have problems in summer.
Organized gangs from all over Europe descend on holiday resorts
to mug, rob and plunder the visiting tourist population.

In Germany, Denmark and other northern countries you may
be asked to produce money or proof of being able to support
yourself at any time, depending on the whim of the immigration
official you approach.

In England, non-British travellers can strike trouble at
Heathrow or Gatwick airports where officials regularly ask where

you intend staying, the purpose of your visit, whether you are solvent and whether you have an outward-bound ticket.

There's not much you can do if you strike trouble at an airport, but when you're on the road at a frontier post you can at least start things off in your favour – provided you're not approaching a country where people of your nationality require a special visa, and you don't have it.

1 Remember that like the police mentioned earlier, immigration officials are only people doing their job, and are not inherently nasty or out to cause hitch-hikers trouble (yeah, right, there *are* exceptions!).

2 Before approaching an immigration post, make yourself look as respectable as it is possible for a road bum to be. Put on a clean shirt or blouse. Comb your hair. Clean your teeth. Brush your shoes. Ditch your hash. Remember – the object is to disguise yourself.

3 At the post, stay as inconspicuous as possible. Don't jump the queue. Don't flatten little old ladies with your pack. Don't play musical instruments or portable radios. Don't be amorous with your partner (particularly if your partner is of the same sex). Don't fart, scratch your balls or be otherwise uncouth.

4 After approaching the official, place your passport in front of him. Don't throw it. Say *good morning, buenos días*, or *guten Tag* as the case may be. Call him *sir, señor*, or *mein Herr*. Don't refer to him as pal, mate, buddy, man or cock. Answer his questions civilly, agreeing with him where possible. Smile politely all the time.

5 If all this works and you get your stamp, thank the official politely in his own language, retire quietly, get the hell away from the frontier before he changes his mind, and revert to your true personality.

6 If all the above doesn't work and you don't get your stamp, under no circumstances break or kick things, make dire threats or start bellowing that the official is a dumbhead, a jerk, a dago bastard or a lousy shit. Nod your head understandingly, look disappointed and concerned, and with downcast eyes retreat from whence you came. Hide behind a bush for eight hours and try again when the official's tour of duty is over and his replacement has relieved him. This time you'll probably make it.

Mainly, hitching is a matter of persevering. Keep the thumb up.

Keep working. You hear of hitchers striking bad luck and moving slowly but you rarely hear a hitcher who knows his business not getting to where he wants to go.

★ **International car identification letters** It's a good idea to learn a few identification letters. Especially useful when you're hanging around roadside cafés searching out a likely truck to take you on your way. Also interesting to know the nationality or diplomatic status of the guy who didn't pick you up as his tail-end disappears in a cloud of dust down the highway.

A Austria	EIR Ireland	NZ New Zealand
AND Andorra	EQ Ecuador	P Portugal
AUS Australia	ET Egypt	PE Peru
B Belgium	FL Liechtenstein	PL Poland
BG Bulgaria	GB Great Britain	RA Argentina
BR Brazil	GBZ Gibraltar	RCH Chile
C Cuba	GR Greece	RL Lebanon
CC Consular Corps	H Hungary	RM Romania
CD Diplomatic Corps	I Italy	S Sweden
CDN Canada	IL Israel	SF Finland
CH Switzerland	IR Iran	SU Soviet Union
CO Colombia	L Luxembourg	TR Turkey
CS Czechoslovakia	M Morocco	U Uruguay
CY Cyprus	MC Monaco	USA United States of America
D West Germany	MEX Mexico	Y Vatican
DK Denmark	N Norway	YU Yugoslavia
E Spain	NL Netherlands	ZA South Africa

Hitchers' Tips and Comments . . .

I note that you think it 'crazy' to hitch in numbers greater than two. I'd like to inform you that I have just arrived back from a holiday in which there were three of us – two females, one male. We travelled through Belgium, Luxembourg, Germany, Austria (Yugoslavia by train), Greece, Italy and Switzerland. The longest period we had to wait for a lift was 1·5 hours. Our luggage was also far from minimal as we had set out in a car which broke down in Ashford, Kent! *Christine Wade, Southampton, England*

Re your statement that it's crazy to hitch with more than two, I disagree. I have hitched all over in a threesome (all girls). I even know of a friend who was out walking with about twelve when they were offered a lift in a laundry van. Beat that! *Wendy Foulds, Orpington, England*
I can't. K.W.

Great book! A 'no wordy crap' tour of Europe!
Here's some stuff. Re country identification, I reckon I can attribute fifty per cent of my rides to the Union Jack plastered on to my pack.
Useful to know that in Europe 'hitching' is known as 'auto-stop'.
If one is desperate, and in the company of other desperados, it's possible to book a motel for two and occupy it with, say, six. Works out pretty cheap!
A useful end-of-season trick is to go to offices of international car-hire firms (except Hertz) and see if they need any cars returned to base – for instance, from Copenhagen to Amsterdam. Sometimes you'll get the job and you get paid expenses for your effort. Good way of travelling. *Mike Feeney, Haslow, England*

About carrying flags. It's worked for me. I've hitched all year with an Alaskan flag on my pack and drivers have stopped and picked me up to find out what country the flag belongs to. *David Fremon, Palatine, USA*

Here are a few tips: Union Jack attached to my pack got me at least half my rides in France recently – but it should be removable just in case. A torch is an essential item if you're camping or hoping to sleep in churches (which I have done successfully). Definitely agree with you that 'high' packs are more practical than 'wide' packs. Try getting a 'wide' into a 2CV Citroën! *Paul Houghton, Bristol, England*

Advise others to travel with someone else and not go off alone. I did and regretted it – I was as lonely as hell! *Walter Stiles Hoyt, Bristol, USA*

What's this about W. S. Hoyt getting lonely? Everyone can talk to themselves. *Peter Nash, Chelmsford, England*

I agree with Pete Nash. What's more, talking to yourself is sometimes the only way you can get into a decent conversation! *Andy (Citizen of the World), London, England*

I've taken to praying to cars on my knees. Works wonders if you're not too proud and can manage a brave smile. *Timmy Mallett, Altrincham, England*

Hitching in threes is quite feasible, and fairly easy. One man and two girls can travel as fast as two men. The largest number of people with whom I've hitched and got a lift is 14. *Simon Calder, University of Warwick Golden Thumb Club*

For those who can't afford hotels in the big cities, it's worth a few bob to lay the pack up in the left luggage on the main station and see the sights with just a bedroll and washing gear. *Marcel Thomas, Horndean, England*

A further comment on the score of women hitch-hiking alone: If there are two or more gentlemen in the car which stops, unless one has very good reasons for thinking otherwise, the answer is obviously 'no'. *Beth Parker, Neuenkirchen, West Germany*

I bought and learnt to play a small musical instrument, a flageolet (glorified tin whistle), and when no vehicles are in sight I sit down and start tooting away. Passes the time away successfully. Good gimmick for starting conversation with any local, too. *Mickey Hohel, Plymouth, England*

I've been hitching, mostly in Germany and Austria, the last two summer holidays and I found my greatest asset for getting lifts was the wearing of a kilt.

Some drivers stopped out of curiosity, others were bent double with laughter by the time they stopped, but since they always gave me a lift, this didn't bother me in the slightest.

So if you've got a Scottish connection, get yourself a kilt! *Andy Deans, Fife, Scotland*

Try some yoga. Read a book. Write a letter to ma. Construct paper planes. Throw stones. Play golf with a stick'n stones. Football with a tin can. Hold your breath. Stand on one foot.

For godzakes! *What* is that kindergarten stuff? And is *that* what people levitate themselves off their asses and creep'n crawl abroad for? *Pasi Punnonen, Savonlinna, Finland*

Hold up a card with PLEASE! written in the local language. You get a smile if nothing else. *Bernard Jennings, Brisbane, Australia*

I used a card saying ANYWHERE! Boy, did I hit some wild places. *F. J. Gooding, Birmingham, England*

I'm a great believer in signs. I don't mean signs that say 'Amsterdam' or 'Antwerpen', but things like 'I don't bite!', 'I wash!' etc. *Mike Plummer, Seaview, Isle of Wight*
   One girl I knew hitched in a T-shirt which carried the slogan So Many Men – So Little Time. *Man, she did Europe in a FLASH! K.W.*

Having hitched as a student, and now a car owner and giver of lifts, I was very interested in the *Hitch-hiker's Guide to Europe*.
   I feel you don't say enough about the importance of hitchers earning hitch-hiking a good name. One bad impression leaves one sour driver and one less who'll pick up the next hitcher. Dirty clothes and dirty boots means a soiled car. Also, dear hitch-hiker, earn your keep, tell us where you've been and what you've seen, otherwise you're more boring than the stereo-cassette player.
   I only pick up clean, interesting looking hitch-hikers, who are presentable and who will be good travelling companions – not out-of-work dustmen. In a word, 'get professional' and make yourself pick-upable. *C. N. C. Peters, West Hagley, England*
   OK you bums, you heard the man. Out with the tuxedos! K.W.

Two friends hitched from London to Bristol with a sign saying *Moscow*. While talking about signs, remember that when hitching in the southern hemisphere, all signs should be held upside down. *Karlos Van Pee, Bristol, England*

I think maps, or good knowledge of an area are essential for fast hitching. Just because someone isn't going exactly where you want to go is no reason to turn down a lift. I often reach my destination swiftly by approaching it from a completely unexpected direction. Flexibility is essential. *Alastair Simpson, Hatfield, UK*

The overwhelming advantage of youth hostels, in my opinion, is that they act as a forum for swapping info and moneysaving ideas between travellers. Especially useful for first-time hitchers during their first weeks on the road. *Alan Thatcher, New Zealand*

I met a hitcher who'd had all his gear stolen by a driver who gave him a lift. The driver had put the hitcher's pack in the boot. When the hitcher reached his destination the driver stopped and the hitcher got out and walked to the boot. Then the driver simply took off with this hitcher's kit. On consideration, you have to admit, this could happen at any time! The only way I can see around it is that if the driver insists on putting your rucksack in the boot, when you stop you ask him for the keys and tell him *you'll* get the pack out. *John Pilkington, Bristol, UK*

How to stop yourself from getting bored on a lonely road – practise eating spaghetti out of a frisbee with a Swiss army knife. *John Pilkington, Bristol, UK*

I hold my destination placard upside down, and when helpful drivers frantically gesture, I flip it over to show I KNOW written on the other side. *Ashok Gupta, Delhi, India*

Whenever you hitch in Holland always use a destination placard. The Netherlands is such a full, small country, with such an incredible cobweb of roads that most people won't stop to pick you up if they don't know where you're going. With a placard, hitching isn't too bad here. *Gys de Graaff, Breda, Holland*

Tricks I've used with great success are to hold up a placard with my destination spelled wrong, or to hold the sign upside down. Human nature being what it is, people stop to point out the error, and in I jump! *John Riordan,Vinderup, Denmark*

When hitching in the UK I use a placard which says, TEST YOUR BRAKES! Works wonders! Also, remember, if you're in a car or truck with CB radio try using it to line up your next ride. Finally, if you're having no luck and you're bored, paper and pen comes in handy. You can write long, dull letters to the *Hitcher's Guide. Doug Bissell, 'The Clydeside Rebel', Glasgow, Scotland*

Nobody likes the idea of a soaking wet stranger messing up his brand new car. So, when it's raining, get under cover and try and *look* dry. *Theo van Drunen, Oosterhout, Holland*

Did Norway to Italy by thumb with the *Hitcher's Guide,* but ended up with one hell of a neckache from looking behind for cars as I walked. Simple solution – fit an adjustable bicycle mirror to the top of the rucksack and, hey presto, you've got a panoramic view of all that's coming from behind without moving a muscle. The mirror can be folded away along the length of the bag when not in use. *Michael McLinden, Harlow, UK*

Tramping around cities for days on end and walking the roads between lifts is very hard on the feet and blisters are a problem. I advise anyone new to the game to rub the soles of their feet with surgical spirit for a couple of weeks before leaving home. This toughens them up. *Paul Hinckley, Birmingham, UK*

Secret of getting rides with trucks is to go to truck-stops, roadside cafés, etc., and *ask*! You'll get a lot of knockbacks, but there's enough good guys around who'll take you aboard. What's more, at the end of their run they often get you aboard a friend's truck to keep you moving. It's unreasonable to expect a guy to stop a 32-ton juggernaut on the road when he sees a hitcher. It costs him time and it's *dangerous. Ian Smith, Liphook, England*

When crossing borders, anyone carrying dope should, as a matter of principle, leave the car he's hitched a ride in and cross on foot. More chance of getting caught? Yes. But if you're caught in the car with the stuff, the driver who's been good enough to pick you up can be in big trouble. *Ian, England*

When hitching at night try wearing a reflective band on your hitching wrist. Apart from being a great safety device it also helps get lifts as motorists tend to slow down when they see it. *Aidan Murray, Athlore, England*

Many stations have lock-up lockers. Who wants to lug a backpack around when sightseeing? And anyway, many places won't let you in with them, especially museums and churches. *Mari Doyle, Godalming, Surrey, UK*

Your book has a lot of good tips but I do wish you would do something about your ridiculous attitude towards 'lady' (sic) hitchers. Why is your book full of hints for heterosexual males? Boring . . . *Fiona Graph, London, UK*

The Hitcher's Guide *is full of hints for everyone. If I suggest a place where hitchers may find company, I'm referring to all hitchers – male and female heterosexuals, homosexuals and lesbians. (I admit to eulogizing Scandinavian girls, but I happen to think they're incredibly beautiful. Can't help that. Sorry.) As to my ridiculous attitude towards 'lady' hitchers ('lady' is synonymous with 'woman', 'girl' or 'female', and it doesn't matter which word I use, I'll still be criticized by a minority of ladies – women – girls – females), I can assure you that it is not meant to be patronizing. Lady hitchers can, and do, get into very nasty situations particularly when travelling alone. And these situations are caused by men – boys – males who are definitely not 'gentlemen'. I have to stand by my ridiculous attitude. K.W.*

Carrying your national flag biases fellow countrymen towards you but can bias foreigners against you. To overcome the problem, have a flag by your side and hold it up whenever you see a car from your own country. *Simon Wadsworth, Shipley, West Yorkshire, UK*

I've got many rides wearing an army jacket and a crew cut. Many people have stopped because they thought I was in the forces. *Wally Hughes, Munich, West Germany*

Good places for catching lifts are at large supermarkets where lorries arrive and leave from almost everywhere. *Peter Walsh, Truro, Cornwall, UK*

3 What it will cost and how to get it cheaper

The beauty about a hitch-trip is that you can make it on precisely the budget you have. Some people have done it for nothing, working their way everywhere and relying on hand-outs from others.

Basically, though, there are three grades of hitch-hiking, each with its own cost structure, and they are discussed below.

1 HOLE-IN-THE-WALL HITCHING This is for the hitcher on the tightest imaginable budget. It's a rough way of travelling, but preferable to not travelling. It involves *always* sleeping out, *always* buying and preparing your own food, *always* visiting museums and galleries on half-price days and *always* sightseeing on foot. It means that you must always walk into and out of cities, that you *must* carry a tent and that you *must* carry some sort of cooking pannikin. The weekly cost structure for this sort of travelling breaks down something like this:

nil	*(nil)*	bed
£2·50	($3·50)	main meal with leftovers for breakfast
£0·50	($0·70)	cigarettes and/or coffee
£3·00	($4·20)	a day or £21 ($29·40) a week

To make a round figure, add £9 ($12·60) a week for fares and sightseeing and for this most basic and foot-weary way of moving it will cost only £30 ($42) *a week*! (And you'll be pretty fit at the end of it all.)

2 HOSTEL HITCHING This is the normal way of travelling and for those with an average bank roll. It involves sleeping out whenever the weather is good to save your money, sleeping in hostels, dormitories or dirt cheap hotels when the weather is bad or when

you're in the city, eating at hostels or cafeterias, and generally
making full use of student and hostel facilities wherever you go.
Costs should be approximately:

£3·50	($4·90)	bed
£3·50	($4·90)	main meal
£0·50	($0·70)	breakfast (fruit)
£1·00	($1·40)	cigarettes and/or coffee
£8·50	($11·90)	a day or £59·50 ($83·30) a week

Add, let's say, £20·50 ($28·70) per week for ferry fares,
sightseeing, bus or train fares around and out of cities and you
have, for what is an average hitch-hiking budget, £80 ($112) *per
week*.

3 HOTEL HITCHING This, without a doubt, is the best way to do it if
you can afford it. For the money you have the privilege of sleeping
in a cheap hotel without the bug of curfews which plague hostel
hitchers. You also eat at least one good meal a day in a cheap
restaurant. Moving this way you're completely your own man,
dependent on no one and subject to no rules or regulations. But it
costs. Below is a realistic price structure:

£7·50	($10·50)	bed
£4·00	($5·60)	main meal
£0·50	($0·70)	breakfast (fruit or inclusive hotel breakfast)
£1·00	($1·40)	cigarettes and/or coffee
£13·00	($18·20)	a day or £91 ($127·40) a week

Add, let's say, £34 ($47·60) per week for ferry fares and a general
good time, and for the most luxurious and enjoyable way of
hitching it costs you £125 ($175) *a week*.

How to get it cheaper
When you're travelling on a hitcher's budget every cent counts.
You have a certain amount of money and that money must get you
around your route. Tricks to make your roll last as long as possible
are important. Here are a few.

INTERNATIONAL STUDENT IDENTITY CARDS These things are

invaluable. In many countries they will get you into museums, galleries, monuments and theatres at half price – and that can save you a *hell* of a lot of money. In Paris, for instance, some central cinemas were offering 25 per cent reductions to holders of student cards as we go to press.

In some countries card holders were offered reduced air fares between international cities. (But no one these days pays the full air fare anywhere. To give an example: as we go to press, a scheduled return air fare London–Màlaga–London costs about £125. But if you're willing to stand the minor inconvenience of travelling on a certain day of the week and returning on the same weekday within seven weeks you can find the same trip for around £85. Check travel pages in local papers for full details.)

Elsewhere you get discounts on everything from jewellery to tape recorders. The company of Lillywhite Frowd, for instance, at 67 St Paul's Churchyard, London EC4, offers holders of student cards up to 20 per cent discount on all sports and camping equipment (no tents), while H. J. Cooper & Co., 19–21 Hatton Garden, London EC1, offers wholesale prices on items like watches and typewriters. That can mean a saving of around 30 per cent.

Obtain these cards, or the information on how to buy one, from your college or university. For Britons, or foreign students in Britain, who require an International Student Identity Card, contact:

The London Student Travel Bureau, 52 Grosvenor Gardens, London SW1W OAG (tel: 01–730 8111).

If you're not eligible for one of these magic money-savers, it's worth mentioning that there is a very healthy black market in them throughout most university cities in Europe. The cards aren't hard to pick up and aren't very expensive.

It's also worth mentioning – just in case you couldn't guess – that faked student cards are just as highly illegal as faked anything-elses.

YOUTH HOSTELS There are three main disadvantages about youth hostels. First, they are often so far out of town it takes you an hour or two to locate and get to them; second, they have curfews which are usually strictly enforced, and third, they have a completely institutional flavour about them (though in fairness it must be added that some of the new hostels are superbly designed and extremely well administered). The advantages of hostels are equally obvious. They guarantee you a clean bed for a very reasonable fee and they supply (in some countries) excellent meals for a fraction of what they would cost outside. And married couples will be pleased to know that if there is plenty of free space in the hostels (usually only during or towards the off-season) the staff will do their best to put you in a room together. In fact, off-season hostelling (when you can find them open) is great fun. You end up getting hotel conditions for half the price you'd pay in an hotel.

There are over 4000 hostels in 44 countries throughout the world and a large number of them are in Europe. There is no maximum age limit for hostellers except in Bavaria in southern Germany (27). However, priority will always be given to members under the age of thirty if beds are filling up fast.

The *average* cost of a youth hostel bed in Europe is £3·50 ($4·90). The *average* cost of a meal is £2·50 ($3·50) – and a good meal, at that. Cooking facilities are available in many hostels if you wish to cut costs even further by preparing your own food.

Full information on the location of all international youth hostels can be found in two volumes of the *IYH Handbook*. Volume 1 deals with youth hostels in Europe and the Mediterranean area, Volume 2 with hostels outside Europe and the Mediterranean. They cost about £2 ($2·80) each and can be obtained through any national youth hostel association.

The cost of joining the Youth Hostels Association is extremely cheap in view of what you gain by membership.

Addresses to contact regarding membership of YHA are:

ENGLAND AND WALES
14 Southampton Street, London WC2E 7HY.
Trevelyan House, 8 St Stephen's Hill,
St Albans, Herts AL1 2WY.

SCOTLAND
7 Glebe Crescent, Stirling FK8 2JA.

NORTHERN IRELAND
56 Bradbury Place, Belfast BT2 1RU.

REPUBLIC OF IRELAND
39 Mountjoy Square, Dublin 1.

UNITED STATES
1332 I Street NW, 8th Floor, Washington DC 20005.

CANADA
333 River Road, Vanier City, Ottawa, Ontario K1L 8H9.

AUSTRALIA
60 Mary Street, Surry Hills, 2010 NSW.

NEW ZEALAND
PO Box 436, 28 Worcester Street, Christchurch.

SOUTH AFRICA
PO 4402, Cape Town.

You can cut basic living costs by better than a half if you're a member of the YHA. So, if you think you can put up with the disadvantages mentioned, join!

Warning! Guard your stuff well in the hostels. There's a lot being ripped off. Leave valuables at the desk (if they have facilities) or take them with you. Careful of your watch when you take it off to shower!

FREE MAPS AND LITERATURE These days there is no need to buy maps of European countries. Most national tourist agencies will supply them for free if you ask. Failing that, many service stations in many countries offer free maps. These maps aren't as good as Michelin or Hallwag, but then they don't cost a pound apiece. They're certainly good enough to help you find your way between the major cities and points of interest.

Don't be afraid to ask for literature, either. Tourist offices have tons of it and it's there for only one reason – to give away. City maps, descriptions of the sights, just about any information you can imagine. But tourist offices are funny. They rarely give until they're asked. So ask. Nicely.

WHAT TO BUY WHERE You can save the odd pound or dollar by being aware of which countries sell which items cheaper than other countries and stocking up before you cross borders.

For instance, buy cigarettes on ferry-boats crossing international waters (where they are duty-free) or in Belgium, Luxembourg or Spain which are the three cheapest countries in Europe for tobacco. Even if you don't smoke you should always buy your quota for resale. If, for example, you carry 10 packets of cigarettes from Spain where 20 filter-tips cost 30p (42 cents), into Denmark where 20 filters cost around £2 ($2·80), you can reasonably expect to sell them for around £1 ($1·40) a pack and thus make a profit of about £7 ($9·80) – enough to keep you on the road for an extra two days. The same goes for bottles of spirits. Always buy your quota if you think you can sell it across the border at a profit.

Anyone thinking of camping out would do well to stock up with instant coffee in England before crossing to the Continent where, in many countries, it is more than twice as expensive. And the same goes for tea drinkers.

Hitchers with worn-out boots can buy the cheapest boots in Europe in Czechoslovakia or Poland. Those with worn-out clothes can find the best bargains in new clothes at sales in Germany or England. Those who want secondhand boots or clothes should head for the flea markets in any of the big cities. Amsterdam, Paris, Madrid, London, Rome all have big open-air markets where you can buy anything cheap if you haggle long enough.

SOMETIMES CHEAPER TO BUY A TICKET If you're in a big hurry to go somewhere for a specific reason, remember that it's sometimes cheaper to buy a bus or train ticket than to hitch. For instance, in Turkey, if you're in a hurry, buses are much cheaper than hitching. Sometimes it's even cheaper to *fly* than to hitch if you join up with a charter flight.

A big thing these days – especially in holiday resort areas on the Continent – is to buy the remaining half of someone's charter holiday ticket after they decide they don't want to go home. It means you might go, for example, from Corfu, Greece, to Luton airport, north of London, for only £50 or so. It's a great way of flitting around, but it's illegal, because tickets are not transferable. You've been warned! But usually if you can get by the baggage check and passport control of the airport you are departing from you'll be OK. There's not much they can do when you arrive at the other end. If someone nabs you, just plead ignorance.

As there's always a chance you'll be turned back from the airport you are trying to leave from it's not a bad idea to make some arrangement with the person from whom you're buying the ticket that if you miss out you get a refund.

BLACK MARKETS There aren't many black markets in money left in Europe these days, but you'll find them in the Communist countries, in the Middle East and also in Morocco, though that one's not worth worrying about.

Basic rules to follow when making a black-market deal are (1) know the bank rate of exchange on the currencies you are trying to trade, (2) always try to choose your own ground on which to make the bargain so that you make it harder for any would-be informer to arrange for the police to see the transaction, (3) try never to make a black-market transaction alone, but always in the company of a friend who can keep discreet watch for you, (4) haggle like hell because the first rate you'll be offered will probably be too low, (5) never exchange travellers' cheques on the black market because if there is any police crack-down and your man is picked up they may be able to trace you.

If those rules sound too James Bondish, just remember that when you play the black market you are breaking the law. Any black-market dealing is risky. If you're caught – and there are people who make a living by passing information to the police – you'll either be thrown out of the country (if you're lucky) or thrown into jail. Make sure the market is worth it before you play it. To get an idea if the market really *is* worth playing check through foreign exchange listings in magazines like *Newsweek*. *Newsweek*'s list has three columns: name of country, what the dollar is worth in that country under the heading Selling Rates Banknotes and what the official rate is in that country (under the heading Transfers).

TRAVELLERS' CHEQUES When you set out on your hitch-trip you'll probably have a fair wad of money. The safest way to carry it is in travellers' cheques which can be cashed just about anywhere in the world. The cheques cost a small amount to buy and you must pay a small commission when you cash them, but if you happen to lose your wallet or it gets stolen, you can make arrangements to cancel those cheques by going straight to a bank. It's a good idea, though, to keep a few dollars or pounds sterling in the pocket just in case you do want to play around on a black market.

RESTAURANTS Only go into restaurants (or bars) where you can check the price list first. If you go into a place without a price list and have an absolutely disgusting meal and they ask £6 for it, you're obliged to pay (if they can catch you). *Always* check!

HOTELS When you ask the price of a room and you are told, do not accept immediately. Try the downcast-face act and ask gently if there isn't a somewhat cheaper room in the house, for instance, on the top floor. It's surprising the number of times, especially in France, when you'll be offered something a fraction cheaper.

There are dozens of little ways of saving on your expenses. Always be on the lookout for them – youth hostels are where you hear of many – and when you discover them pass the word around. Help others travel cheaper, too!

Warning! If you want to buy a camera, radio, cassette recorder, etc., it's best to wait until you get to Switzerland or Germany where such things are cheaper. Better yet, wait until you reach a duty-free port or airport. But this is the warning . . . some so-called duty-free ports and airports offer very bad deals on some items. For instance, I have seen cameras at London's Heathrow airport with higher price-tags than you can find in a good discount store right in the centre of town. Don't be fooled by the words 'tax-free' or 'duty-free'. Check out prices.

★**For van vagabonds only** An easy way to save money is to know petrol prices in countries you plan to drive through. Four-star petrol in Belgium, for instance, may be cheaper than in neighbouring France, so by simply filling up in Belgium before crossing the border into France you can save quite a lot of money. In a van with a ten-gallon tank capacity it could be as much as £3 which stays in your pocket. For a current list of petrol prices around Europe write to The Royal Automobile Club (Foreign Touring Department), 49 Pall Mall, London SW1Y 5JG.

★Drivers should also know that in some countries (Czechoslovakia and Poland, for instance) tourists can buy petrol coupons at the frontier which offer discounts.

★Remember, also, to nurse ailing vehicles into cheaper countries where workers' wages are considerably less than in the north and where motor repairs can be a lot cheaper.

Hitchers' Tips and Comments...

On my last two trips to the Continent I discovered that the only places which would change money and travellers' cheques on Saturday nights, Sundays or public holidays were bureaux at railway stations, airports or hotels. Also, it's worth noting that most places will only exchange travellers' cheques from the most prominent world banks or travel agents. Anyone carrying cheques from minor banks can have trouble. *Sue Pyle, Geelong, Australia*

True enough, especially in outback areas. Perhaps best to stick to big names like Cook's and American Express. Also, I've noticed that trying to get rid of lesser-known currencies — like Australian dollars — is like trying to give away rocks . . . no one is interested. K.W.

Thanks to Sue Pyle for her advice. *But*, arrive early at railway stations — even queue in advance — or you face horrendous queues. The exchange at Gare du Nord, Paris, on a Sunday is mobbed. *Julia Butt, Glasgow, Scotland*

Try the hypermarkets on the outskirts of French cities where you can buy enough for a picnic meal dead cheap. *Steve Ireland, Belfast, N. Ireland*

You find these giant supermarkets outside Spanish cities, too. I've seen them between Málaga and Torremolinos and between Alicante and San Juan. At least 25 per cent cheaper than in the cities. K.W.

Re black-marketing. I found black markets in Russia, Poland, Czechoslovakia, Hungary, Romania and Bulgaria. Here are some tips. (1) Have dealers count the money into your hand. Some can count money so fast they'll count one note twice and you'll never know the difference. If every note hits your hand, you know what you're getting. (2) Ask higher than the going price. If the dealer offers to pay, forget it. He's up to something. (3) Don't accept old bills in Poland. Many are no longer in circulation. Insist on checking old-looking bills in a shop before accepting them. (4) Be careful. *Jim Henderson, Regina, Canada*

If you get stuck in the rain at night near parked trucks, check with drivers until you find an empty truck and ask if you can sleep in the back. Sometimes works and it gives you a dry night's kip. Happy hitching. *Phil Hardy, Leicester, England*

When I'm travelling anywhere in Europe, and it's time to sleep, I simply go to the nearest apartment block, press somebody's bell, then when the door opens, go in, go down instead of up, hide out under the stairs and roll out my sleeping bag. I'm always up and away by 8 a.m. to miss janitors, stair washers etc. *Danny Long, Saffron Walden, England*

An International Camping Carnet will get you discounts in many European camping grounds. *Alan Thatcher, New Zealand*

In France, Italy and Spain, always stand at the bar when taking coffee or drinks. If you sit down you get thumped with a whacking great service charge. *Alan Thatcher, New Zealand*
  Most bars have three price structures. As Alan says, it's cheapest to drink standing at the bar; sitting at a table inside is more expensive; sitting at a table outside on the terrace is more expensive again. K.W.

Travellers' cheques can be used as fake cash to convince immigration officials that you're loaded when you enter a country. Just go to a bank, declare all your TCs lost and you'll be issued with new ones. Now you can use the supposedly lost ones to wave in front of immigration officials' noses. Of course, don't try and cash the old ones or you'll be in *big* trouble! *Ashok Gupta, Delhi, India*

Couple of tips for fellow hitchers. If you *must* travel by train, always travel at night – it's cheaper and you save more money by having somewhere to sleep. And if you fly anywhere always keep the disposable cup and cutlery you get with meals – handy camping implements. *'Jock the Hulk', alias Jim Condron, East Kilbride, Scotland*

A possible chance for cheap train travel in foreign countries is to buy a ticket for the first station towards your destination and then board a train which only stops at big towns. When the conductor tells you that the train doesn't stop at the town on your ticket, babble in English, pull out maps, panic, etc., and odds are he'll shrug and leave you to work things out for yourself. I once travelled from Marseilles to Boulogne this way for 80 francs. *Paul Hancock, Salisbury, Rhodesia*

On the Newhaven-Dieppe ferry route I found I could save over 50 per cent of the fare by buying a *same day return*, instead of a one way ticket! But you have to hide your luggage until after you get the ticket so you *look* like a day-tripper. At the other end you can give the return part of your ticket to some hitcher who looks like she/he needs it. *Cathy Jurgen, Edinburgh, Scotland*

When changing money, check if there is a flat rate of commission on transactions, e.g., $1. If so, find a few likely looking souls and change all your money in one go, thus making the commission proportionately less than if the money was changed in several transactions. *Ian, England*

You make the hole-in-the-wall hitcher sound like a superhuman toughguy. It helps if you are, but anyone who can carry a tent can get by on the budget you suggest. There are advantages to hitching hole-in-the-wall style, too; you *never* have to worry about finding a bed in cities. City campsites are never full up like hostels. Further, you can recover some of your campsite costs because better off campers and caravaners often give you food, particularly when they're on their way back home. *Jon Glanville and Martin Elston, Bristol, UK*

The English 5p coin is the same size as the German 1-mark coin. Thus, feed the 5p into a 1-mark change machine on stations and hey presto, 25p. *Lesley Kountaff, South Africa*

Re Lesley Kountaff's tip about the English 5p being the same size as German marks. New machines detect whether the coin has a serrated edge (like the 5p) or not (like the German mark). Also, in Salzburg I met people who had been deported from Germany after being caught trying this stunt. They'd been fined, too. So be discreet! *Glyn George, Merseyside, UK*

The German Tourist Office (very helpful people) suggested that I was inciting people to commit an offence by publishing the information about interchangeable 5p and 1 mark coins. I'm not inciting anyone to do anything, I'm just reporting a fact. And right now I'll warn you that if you knowingly try to defraud a slot machine company by placing a 5p coin in a slot marked for 1 mark coins, and thereby profit, you will have committed an offence. Got that, all you happy truckers? K.W.

Ever noticed the similarity between the 10p UK coin and the French 5 francs? *Philip Attwool, Orpington, UK*

Ten French centimes works as 50 German pfennigs. *Iris Ollech, Gladbeck, Germany*

For coin-machine fiddlers: in Germany, a British 1p can be used as a 50 pfennig piece in luggage lockers and the like. Change machines can generally tell the difference between German and foreign coins, but it's worth trying 5 Austrian schillings, 5 Spanish pesetas and 2 Greek drachmas (the silver one with the king's head) for 1 German mark. In Switzerland I had smaller gains by using the following instead of 10 centimes: 1 US cent, 50 Austrian groschen, 2 West German pfennigs and 50 Belgian centimes. *Alan Barlow,Cheadle, UK*

On returning to England with lots of coinage, I set out to check coins against each other. Similarities are noted in the following list. There's no guarantee that these coins will fit slot machines, but it's nice to know that in an emergency they might be usable for various purposes:

use 10 groschen as 1 penny (tiny gain)
use 10 groschen as 10 French centimes (tiny gain)
use 50 Belgian centimes as 50 groschen (tiny gain)
use 1 Belgian franc as 20 lire (tiny gain)
use 5 Belgian francs as 5 schillings (tiny gain)
use 5 French centimes as 5 Swiss centimes (tiny gain)
use 10 French centimes as 1p (tiny gain)
use 20 French centimes as 200 lire (tiny gain)
use 1 Dutch cent as 5 French centimes (tiny gain)
use 1 Dutch cent as 5 Swiss centimes (tiny gain)
use 5 Dutch cents as 20 Swiss centimes (tiny gain)

use 20 lire as 1 schilling (tiny gain)
use 10 Swiss centimes as 25 Dutch cents (tiny gain)
use 1 peseta as 1 Belgian franc (tiny gain)
use 1 peseta as 20 lire (tiny gain)
use 5 pence as 5 Belgian francs (tiny gain)
use 5 pesetas as 5 pence (tiny gain)
use 5 pesetas as 5 Belgian francs (tiny gain)
use 5 pesetas as 5 schillings (tiny gain)
use 10 lire as 5 pence (good gain)
use 10 lire as 5 Belgian francs (good gain)
use 10 lire as 5 schillings (good gain)
use 10 lire as 5 pesetas (good gain)
use 5 pence as 5 schillings (good gain)
use 5 pence as 1 mark (good gain)
use 2 pence as 10 schillings (good gain)

Hope all this helps someone. *Pete Edwards, Manchester, UK*

Two friends of mine tried your trick of using the wrong coins in slot machines which one of them learned about while hitching in Germany. One was fined £350 and the other £200. Is it really worth it? *Fran, London, UK*

Army and Navy Stores. Good quality and cheap. Best for boots, knives and combat jackets. *Hinsh, Glasgow, Scotland*

4 What to take

The only sure thing that's going to happen on a hitch-hike trip is that you will get sick of lugging your pack around. It's an unavoidable millstone which is always too heavy.

Some hitchers are very aware of this and it's not unusual to see people wandering around Europe with a hold-all which has scarcely the capacity of an airline bag. When you figure it, all you basically need, apart from the clothes on your back, is a toothbrush, a change of socks and underwear, and a spare shirt. But that's pretty rough travelling and, for myself, if I'm hitting the road for anything longer than a couple of weeks, I like to carry enough stuff to keep me comfortable and reasonably clean throughout any situation I'm likely to encounter.

Any list of what to take on a trip – as with any other suggestion in this book – can only be a guideline to a plan you might finally adopt for yourself. The two lists which follow soon are based on what my wife and I carry when we set out.

The first thing you need, of course, is a pack. The only type worth considering, in my opinion, is a frame-pack with some sort of adjustable system which allows you to vary the tension strap, which sits just above your buttocks, so that a load, no matter what its weight, can be kept from digging into your spine. The shoulder-straps, also, should be adjustable so that you can find the most comfortable carrying position and they should be made of leather, rather than the cheaper webbing material, because the latter tends to crease and become very uncomfortable.

Examine the shoulder-straps well before buying because, if you're carrying any sort of load, it's your shoulders which will take the bashing for the first few days until you get fit. Some more expensive packs have canvas-encased sponge-rubber strips sewn to the inside of the strap. These are great. You can fit them on to a cheaper pack yourself.

Another important point to consider when buying is that there are 'wide packs' and 'high packs', meaning that the volume of the pack, when filled to capacity, comes either from the width or from the height. I favour the high pack because it's easier to carry through crowded streets without slaughtering people and, more important, it's less trouble to get through the door of a small car.

If you can't afford a frame-pack consider an army or navy duffel bag. You can usually rig them up fairly comfortably.

If your budget doesn't run to sleeping in cheap hotels, you'll need a sleeping-bag. (Even if you're sleeping in hostels, which charge a small fee for the use of bedding, you can save money by having your own bag.) The bag you should buy is the best you can afford for the conditions you expect to meet. If you've any sense you won't be considering sleeping out in anything close to freezing and therefore you *do not* need something like Hillary took to Everest. Any good camping shop should be able to give you a rundown on what is available. The minimum requirements are that the bag will keep you comfortable at freezing point, that it is reasonably water-resistant and that it is light.

If you take a sleeping-bag, then you need something to lay it on – a groundsheet of some kind. Don't buy a regular groundsheet because they cost money and weigh a couple of pounds. The best thing – and for free if you look around – is a six feet by four feet sheet of heavy-duty plastic (like factories encase new mattresses in) which is light, disposable and easily replaceable, and which doubles perfectly as a poncho if you're caught in the rain.

If you're a hole-in-the-wall hitcher (which means that to make your money last you have to sleep out every night and always prepare your own meals) then it might be worth investing in a lightweight inflatable air-mattress. You'll curse the extra weight by day, but bless the comfort it offers you by night. (Remember to take a puncture repair outfit along with the mattress!) If you reckon your shoulders can stand it you might consider taking the midget stove that the Gaz people make. You can buy refills in just about every European country. (Spain is the cheapest country I've found for refills.) It's cheaper to make fires, but also more hassle, especially if you're thinking you'd like a quick cup of coffee.

Suggested men's list
passport and money
6 passport-size photographs
good pair of light boots plus spare laces (you'll be walking quite a
    few miles a day)

sandals for city wear when you're resting up
2 pairs of trousers
2 shirts (drip-dry)
1 good jacket with plenty of pockets
2 changes of underwear
2 pairs of socks
3 handkerchiefs
sweater
toilet bag containing:
toothbrush and paste
small bar of soap (use other people's where possible)
toilet paper (most toilets on the Continent seem to be without it –
    stolen by hitch-hikers, no doubt)
nail scissors and file
sticking plaster (for blistered feet – very handy during first week)
½ dozen aspirin tablets
dozen anti-diarrhoea tablets
needle and cotton
pocket knife (doubles as eating knife and fork)
spoon
plastic cup
combination bottle-opener, corkscrew and can-opener (simplest
    type possible or it won't work)
notebook, pen and envelopes
reading matter
spare box of matches
maps of areas to be travelled through
if under 18 years old, a letter from parents or guardian stating that
    their permission has been granted for you to travel and
    hitch-hike alone

Suggested women's list
passport and money
6 passport-size photographs
good pair of tough shoes or light boots plus spare laces
sandals for city wear
2 pairs of slacks or jeans
3 blouses (drip-dry)
1 light crushproof, drip-dry dress
3 changes of underwear

3 pairs of socks
3 handkerchiefs
sweater
toilet bag containing:
toothbrush and paste
small bar of soap
toilet paper
small pair of scissors and nailfile
sticking plaster
½ dozen aspirin tablets
dozen anti-diarrhoea tablets
couple of sanitary towels or tampons (which can be hard to find if
  you're stuck in small southern European and North African
  villages; same goes for the Pill. Take them with you)
needle and cotton
pocket knife (doubles as eating knife and fork)
spoon
plastic cup
combination bottle-opener, corkscrew and can-opener
notebook, pen and envelopes
reading matter
spare box of matches
maps of areas to be travelled through
if under 18 years old, a letter from parents or guardian stating that
  their permission has been granted for you to travel and
  hitch-hike alone

Those lists, depending on your sense of proportion, will seem
impossibly long and stupid or the exact opposite. If the latter, you
can only be warned that every extra pound you carry in your pack
will be like lugging around dumb-bells. Don't be tempted to put in
too much else. If you are, try to dispense with some other item.
For instance, if you see the necessity for an extra shirt, try *not* to
see the necessity for the sandals.

Reading matter is something I was trapped into taking on my
first hitch-trip. I figured I'd have plenty of time to catch up on
some stuff I wanted to read and took six paperbacks. Well, I had
plenty of time all right – on some Portuguese back-roads – but I
never got around to reading three of the titles because I'd given
them away after the first day. Plus I was wishing to God I'd left
half my clothes home and had managed to subdue my camera-bug

to the extent where I'd taken a Kodak Instamatic instead of the heavy SLR I use.

(One item I *do* carry, mainly because it dispenses with several others, is a Swiss army knife. They are advertised as pocket workshops and it is an accurate description. The one I have has two blades, a screwdriver, a bottle-opener, a tin-opener, a corkscrew, a punch, a pair of scissors and a miniature wood saw which is strong and sharp enough to cut small branches for campfire kindling. I've lost count of the number of things I've managed to do with it when I've been on the road. There's a super *de luxe* version, incidentally, which even has a pair of tweezers and a plastic toothpick.)

Best rule is to pack only what you absolutely need and then get ruthless and dispense with 20 per cent of it. Remember that you'll probably pick up odd bits and pieces to take home and you'll need room in the pack – and the strength to carry them.

The tougher you are before you set out, the more you're going to like yourself when you're slap in the middle of what you just know is going to be a rideless day. One of those days when the only place you're about to go is where you get around to walking to!

★**Lifesaver** When I'm heading into colder climes – and that can mean just about anywhere in Europe during winter, including Spain, Italy and Greece – I've taken to carrying a heavy, woollen knitted scarf. I know this goes against everything I've written regarding bulk and weight, but I've found that the scarf has more value than an extra sweater when you're stuck on the road in an icy wind. You can wear it around your neck, open it up and cover half your upper body with it, wear it around your ears and head or wrap it around your face Arab-style. A scarf can be a lifesaver. Think about it. (But don't blame me if the sun shines the whole way and you never have to use it!)

Hitchers' Tips and Comments...

If your budget stretches to it, try 'sportsman's blankets' (sometimes called 'space blankets'). Indestructible, lightweight, plastic-backed foil sheets that reflect body heat and have many uses: blanket, poncho, windbreak, groundsheet. Also, when on long stretches in the backwoods, a water bottle is worth its weight in gold. *Kelley and Gail, Muswell Hill, London*

A few things I think a traveller should carry, but which you don't mention: International Driver's Licence, so you can help out drivers on long hauls; mini-radios, which can help conquer boredom on the road; clothes-washing materials, like a small ball of plastic string and a couple of pegs. *Daniel Kidren, Henzligger, Israel*

For cheap, comfortable sleeping, try a hammock. Do it in style, lads! *B. J. Brock, East St Kilda, Victoria, Australia*

Useful additions to the *Guide*'s list might be: a light plastic water bottle; one pair of woollen gloves – it gets damn cold in Switzerland even in September – a luxury well worth including; large felt pen marker for quick, easy destination placards; assorted tupperware food containers (tops double as plates); plus if you live in the UK as much cheap food as you can carry – it will save pounds in the first week on the Continent. *John Hoad, Eastbourne, England*

I strongly recommend getting hold of a 'survival bag'. I bought mine in an Army & Navy store. The bag, made by Karrimor, is plastic, and designed so you can put your sleeping-bag and luggage in it. Really keeps you dry. I've used mine for a year and it's still OK. As for Swiss army knives, I've had two ripped off. They've got everything else on them – why not a burglar alarm? *Dave P., Leeds, England*

One of the smartest things I did was carry a Xerox copy of the first page of my passport, and extra photos. It saved me a lot of time and expense in phonecalls when my passport was ripped off in Yugoslavia. Try cashing a travellers' cheque without a passport! *Jim Henderson, Regina, Canada*

A useful addition to my pack has been a couple of plastic, refillable cigarette lighters. They sell in Britain for about £1 and give 2000–3000 lights, and will work when it's wet or there's a strong wind. They have an adjustable flame which gives a blowtorch effect and will light even damp kindling. *Adrian Park, Preston, England*

If you want to carry a plate, take a frisbee instead. Great plate, yet useful for roadside games. *Mike Waldie, Shenfield, England*

If you're heading into cold areas, take a plain coloured towel, then it can double up as a scarf. I can't recall ever having needed a scarf and towel simultaneously. *Kevin Bilke, Southampton, UK*

Scandinavian Airlines (SAS) give away free 'pen portraits' of all major cities. These booklets cover tourist attractions, places to eat and stay (usually way above a hitcher's budget), plus other handy things to know like shopping hours, Tourist Information Centre addresses etc. Also an inner city map. Pick them up at SAS offices. *John Strachan, Toowoomba, Australia*

Instead of buying Karrymat rolls to sleep on, or other registered makes, go to an industrial supply place and ask for a sheet of 'Plasters Oats' cut to the required size. It's the same condensed foam you buy in the camping shops but about half price. *Mike and Sue, Leicester, UK*

I always carry several lengths of strong string. It serves as clothesline and replacement bootlaces, and once I was able to use it to repair a slash in the side of my pack. *Tommy Haig, London, UK*

Keep matches, salt, pepper, etc., dry in 35mm film cans. *Ian Bambury, Great Bookham, UK*

A better buy than Gaz stoves is a paraffin stove. It's heavier and a bit more expensive to buy but it's much more economical. You can even burn diesel in it, although this turns your pots black. *Nigel Clayton, South Africa*

An insulating pad such as Karrymat provides warmth, dryness, adequate comfort and protects your bag from rough ground. A cheap, compact, brightly-coloured cagoule keeps you warm in wind or rain and makes you more visible by the roadside. Freezer bags and tinfoil are great for carrying and cooking food in. Insulating tape, safety pins and thick rubber bands are useful for running repairs. Consider a second water bottle if you like wine. Packs with an *internal* frame are more comfortable and compact than the traditional framesack, and cheaper. *Paul, London, UK*

Sunglasses worth carrying, especially in Mediterranean area, North Africa or if you're heading into snow country. Keep on trucking! *Danny de Dude, Stanislaus, California, USA*

We were amused by Mike Waldie's comment about frisbees, but a better idea is to take a metal plate which you can use as a frying pan, a cooking pot lid *and* a frisbee! *Jon Glanville and Martin Elston, Bristol, UK*

Take a compass. Don't laugh: you don't need anything more elaborate than the type that comes out of a Christmas cracker but mine has saved me endless hassles in city streets. I never go to any town of which I have less than intimate knowledge without mine. It's been particularly useful in cities like London where much of the travelling may be done by underground railway: have you never come out of a strange tube station and wondered which way to go? *Stephen Morgan, Poole, Dorset, UK*

Ski belts available at all sports shops are marvellous for carrying valuables as they're bigger than purses, so take passports as well as a notebook, etc. (easier than fumbling in rucksacks and safer).

   Losing a passport is a lot of hassle as we found out. Worth having a visitor's passport (one year duration) as well as full passport if you're on a long trip. Needless to add – keep them separate! *Julia Butt, Glasgow, Scotland*

5 How to survive

FOOD If you're down and out for food, remember that the cheapest buys are always in the markets. In-season fruit will never cost you more than 15p (21 cents) apiece and if you're that broke you can find bruised pieces which the stallholder will probably give you. Also check the floors where you can often find edible wastage. Just cut out the bad sections and give what's left a wash under running water and you're all right.

Chinese restaurants – and just about every city in Europe has them – always serve plain boiled rice. Not the tastiest of dishes, but at 60p (84 cents) a bowl it's cheap, and if you splatter it liberally with the free soy sauce you can get it down.

Every country in Europe knows about potato chips. A big plate of these – and make it obvious that you need them! – won't cost more than 60p (84 cents) and they'll hold you together until you can figure something out.

Salvation Army and other religious organizations often have free soup kitchens. To locate them ask fellow hitchers or, in an emergency, ask the police. Don't freeload on them! Only use them if you have no alternative.

Bananas, apart from being nutritious, are about the most filling item weight-for-weight that you can buy. Two bananas and a small loaf of bread will keep you going all day. Cost? Around 45p (63 cents).

In country areas, try the old tramp trick. Approach farmers or house-owners, explain the problem as best you can and offer to do an hour's work for a good feed. You'll get a lot of knockbacks, but there are enough good people around to agree to such a simple bargain.

When you're a long way from home and the money's getting low you nearly always have to start cooking for yourself. This is not so bad if you balance your diet – though the whole deal tends to get a little boring after a while. I find that in such emergencies it's possible to eat fairly well for £1·25 ($1·75) a day, by eating only

one meal and watching what I buy. The following list is an example
of the type of hot, nutritious meal you can prepare:

couple of potatoes (bake them in the campfire ashes)
couple of eggs (boil in a tin can)
one or two sausages (barbecue them on the end of a stick or piece
    of wire)
loaf of bread (toast it)
couple of pieces of fruit
    (try stewed apple or mashed banana on toast)
coffee (boil water in tin can)

The two basic condiments that help make a meal worth eating are
sugar and salt. Salt is cheap anywhere, sugar not so cheap. Don't
be afraid to go into a shop and ask for only 100 grammes of sugar.
It's enough to last a dozen cups of coffee. (But don't worry if you
don't have any. Eating sugar is only a habit and your body
operates better without. Mostly, sugar just rots your teeth.)
    Fire-making isn't hard. The 'pyramid'-type fire is the easiest.
You put small sticks and any old paper you can find in the middle
and then build larger sticks in a pyramid shape over them, making
sure you leave plenty of room for the fire to breathe. Try to put a
low wall of large rocks on the down-wind side of the fire – it
reflects heat back into the fire and it's something of a safety
measure. Always, of course, cover the fireplace with dirt and
trample on it before you leave.

SLEEPING If you're a hole-in-the-wall or hostel hitcher you'll have a
sleeping-bag with you. You must have one to sleep out in Europe.
The nights can get chilly even in summer.
    Sleeping out on good nights is no problem. You just sack down.
Rainy nights are when you're in trouble and want to head for the
nearest hotel or hostel. But if you have no money, what do you
do?

In the country
If you're carrying a tent you can hole up in that, but if you haven't
you must start improvising. Plastic wrapping material is the stuff –
if you can find enough of it. You need enough to cover your
sleeping-bag completely and it has to be broad enough so that with
the aid of a stick you can erect a miniature tent over your head.
    You can sleep in the rain with a groundsheet and sleeping-bag,

but even waterproof bags (unless they are very expensive models) tend to forget their maker's claims and sog up. Two nights of rain spells the ruin of most bags unless you have the chance to dry them out properly.

If you don't have a tent, then your choice of action is limited. Bridges and culverts are good bets. Animal shelters in the fields are OK if you can get one to yourself without the company of a cow. Failing that, approach a farmer for permission to sleep in one of his outbuildings. Some will let you, some won't. (Southern Ireland is the place for that. I know many hitchers who have not only been given permission to sleep in the hayloft, but have been supplied with blankets *plus* breakfast the next morning!)

In the city
In towns and cities you have more chance of finding a dry place to sleep. There are railway stations, which are nearly always impossible to sleep in, but which at least are warm and where also, more often than not, you meet other people to talk to. (Of course, if you don't have a ticket for a train departing the next day you stand a good chance of being booted right back into the cold, cold night, but with luck you'll get by.) There are churches (particularly in France) which are sometimes left open. There are sites with half-constructed buildings which offer superb shelter (and the occasional watchdog to keep you on your toes). There are street foyers to large office buildings where you can at least find a corner in which to squat out of the wind. There are Salvation Army type relief places, the addresses of which you can get from fellow hitchers or from the police. And finally, particularly in smaller towns or city suburbs where the police are more easy-going, you can always beg the loan of a cell for the night. It's been done before, though for me that'd be the absolute last resort!

Warning! Sleeping out alone in cities is getting dangerous. (See letters by Hugh Darlington, Clive Gill and Hugh Dunne at the end of this chapter, and other letters elsewhere in the book.) There are too many stories like this in the pipeline for it to be a joke. It's happening all the time. And it's not just things getting stolen. There's often violence involved and I've met more than one girl who has either been raped or just managed to fight her way out.

Sometimes, because of the money problem, you just have to sleep out, so what to do?

Ideally, get with a group of people so that thieves will think twice about trying to sneak up to the camp. If you have to sleep alone, conceal yourself as well as you can (you should, anyway, to avoid visits from police, park guards and nightwatchmen). Always keep your passport, papers, money and travellers' cheques on your person, or at least in your sleeping-bag. Finally, if you're by yourself, keep a dirty great stick handy by your sleeping-bag.

If you're ever attacked – be it at night, as the result of a ride you've hitched, in a bar, anywhere – remember that the surest way of saving your skin is to run like hell and forget all about being a hero.

If you're cornered and you have to fight, fight dirty. Anyone who is attacking you will presumably have no hesitation in laying you out and you have to fight on those terms. Unless you're a trained boxer or at least a brown belt martial arts man, forget all about fancy holds and uppercuts. Only experts can defend themselves scientifically. Fight like an animal – go for your opponent's eyes, throat, plexus, genitals and knees – and *get out* of the vicinity.

If you are attacked by several opponents and can't escape you've got big problems on your hands. Safest thing is to give them everything you've got. That way you *might* save yourself a beating up. If you're convinced they're going to bash you even if you hand over your stuff, or if you decide to give it a go, the odds of you winning are slim. But with considerable luck you might be able to break through them and get room to run (and if you've got your money and passport on your person the loss of your pack isn't so important).

If you go down and you know there's no way you can get up again, all that's left is to save yourself from as much damage as you can. Lie on your belly to protect your crotch and get your arms up to protect your head. That leaves your kidneys and back exposed, but there's nothing else you can do; except play dead.

And, of course, during the brawl – whether you're fighting one man or five – scream at the top of your voice for help. You *might* get some.

MEDICAL The worst thing that can happen on the road is that you might get ill. If you're moving with someone, it isn't so bad – you've got moral support. But just one day alone on the road when you're physically ill can be hell. You feel like you're never going to make your destination.

The only thing you can do is keep moving and if it's some ordinary little thing which any doctor can fix, stop off at the nearest village, search around and find someone who can speak your language (bars and cafés or the police station) and enlist their aid to help you out. If you find you can't pay the doctor, all you can do is give him your name and address and promise him that you'll send him the money when you have some. If he won't buy that you might have to give him something as collateral. Give him anything except your passport! Most doctors, though, like most people, aren't going to strike a rotten bargain if they see you can't pay.

APPENDICITIS is one of the most dangerous things that can hit you while you're on the road. If it should happen when you're in a city, present yourself to the nearest tourist information office and convince them to take it over from there. (Play it sicker than you are if you have to, because they'll be able to get you to a decent hospital faster than you can yourself.) If you're out in the country, get yourself to the nearest town or village and let the police take over. Wherever you are, the best rule for something as serious as appendicitis is to somehow put yourself into the hands of a person or organization that has the facilities to act for you while you rest. If you can get straight to a hospital, well and good, but they usually take some time to locate and it is important that you should move as little as possible. The effort you'll put into flagging down a ride, if you're on the road, is going to take all the strength you can afford.

A SPRAINED ANKLE is something which can quite easily happen to you on the road. What you must do is bind it tightly and keep off it as much as possible. It may mean holing up in a hostel or somewhere for a few days. While resting you can bathe it in hot water. If you even vaguely suspect it might be more than a sprain, hobble along to the nearest chemist and let him take a look. That way you get a qualified opinion for nothing. If he thinks it is something more serious, *then* you can spend money at the doctor's.

Remember that whatever you think you might have, providing it's not obviously serious, a chemist can give you an opinion and prescribe simple drugs and medicines much cheaper than a doctor will.

DIARRHOEA is something which will attack just about every hitcher if he stays on the road long enough or does enough trips. For that reason I always carry a couple of dozen tablets which a doctor friend once prescribed for me. They are the sort of tablet you take *after* you get the attack. There are other prescriptions you can take to fortify your intestines *before* you go into an area (like Morocco or Turkey) where you might pick up a bug. Talk to a chemist before you start on your trip. Take something with you – it's worth the effort.

If, however, you are on the road and are suddenly stricken there's nothing you can do but wait it out. Eat as little as possible – dry biscuits and black tea without sugar seem OK – and rest.

(A friend of mine once got an attack in Algeria. He was in the middle of nowhere and he reckons he was in a bad way. He had no paper except one book which he hadn't read. He tells of sitting on the side of the road, frantically reading page after page so he'd have a backlog of paper to see him through his next attack. The book? Richard Aldington's *Death of a Hero*.)

If you're convinced your stomach will give out when you hit the wilder regions there are a couple of things you can do to lessen the chances of complete tragedy . . . Don't drink tap water but stick to bottled drinks like local mineral water, beer or Coca-Cola. Don't eat uncooked vegetables and only eat fruit which you peel, like oranges and bananas. (Human dung is used as fertilizer in some Arab and Eastern countries.) Eat only meat which is well cooked. (Long cooking won't save you if the meat is bad before it's cooked, but at least it'll destroy any lurking kitchen germs.)

TOOTHACHE, of all things you can get on the road, is probably the least dangerous and yet the hardest to live with. The methods of holding the pain down while you get yourself to a dentist are legion. My favourite is to buy a bottle of whisky or cognac and to hold mouthfuls of the stuff over the offending tooth. Each mouthful usually holds the pain down for five minutes or more. It's a nice way of handling the problem if you can afford the luxury, and after a couple of hours you're so pissed you don't give a damn about anything anyway. Mouthfuls of cold water held over the tooth sometimes help for very brief periods of time. All you can do is stay sane until you reach a dentist. (See Simon Barry's letter at end of this chapter.)

SELLING BLOOD Blood is one thing that everyone has and which plenty of people need and in several areas in Europe it is possible to sell it at rates which vary from £1·50–£4·80 ($1·83–$5·85) a half-litre (about a pint). The biggest markets are, at the moment, in Greece, Turkey and Spain. Whether they will remain the markets is another question. Information on which countries and which hospitals in those countries are buying can always be picked up on the road from other hitchers and in youth hostels. The facts are continually changing so I am not listing any places here.

The idea of selling rather than *giving* blood may be repugnant to plenty of people and I agree, but this chapter is to do with survival, and selling your blood is a more honourable way of making a dollar than some others I can think of.

If you decide you have to hawk your blood, keep a very close watch on what is happening to you, particularly if you're in some out-of-the-way-type country and some backwoods hospital. Check, for instance, that the needle is clean and make sure they don't take more than half a litre from you. When you leave the hospital go and sit in a café or bar and have a coffee and something to eat and generally relax for half an hour. *And don't, under any circumstances, give blood more than once a month!*

SELLING AND PAWNING OTHER THINGS It's remarkable the number of people you meet on the road who will moan, 'Christ, man, I'm stony broke.' And sitting on their wrists is a £25 watch. It reminds you of the motorist who dies of thirst in the desert because he forgets to moisten his lips from the water in his car radiator.

Most big cities have pawn shops and even if you can't find one there are plenty of other shops which will buy your gear. Sleeping-bags, tents, cameras, watches, wallets, rings, even haversacks (bundle your stuff into something else) are all items which are easy to sell, although you'll only get a fraction of what you paid for them. Youth hostels are great places to unload tents and sleeping-bags to people looking for a bargain. You'll also get a better price there than you will from a shop or outdoor market. (At outdoor markets set up your own pavement stall – but be ready to scoot when the inspector comes and make sure you don't set up on a local's pitch.)

In effect, you're never really down and out until you're down to the clothes on your back and your boots. And a good pair of boots are worth a few dollars to anyone!

Survival is purely a matter of common sense and imagination. Use both and there's no problem.

★**Money belts** When you're on the road you can afford to lose everything except your passport, money and any return tickets you have. You should always keep those three items on your person wherever you go. A good way to do this is to buy one of those old-fashioned money belts, or make one from light canvas or suede. A cheaper alternative is to sew a deep pocket on to the *inside* of your trousers. If you do that, just make sure you don't move too far away from your trousers.

Hitchers' Tips and Comments...

Re your invitation to offer information . . . The buy of my life has been a small gas burner. They're light, compact and foolproof. Refills are cheap and give you a good week's cooking. A pan and a plate and you're set for a feed anywhere. If you can take the weight, a kilo of spuds and onions doesn't go astray either.
Here's a good recipe. Vegetable stew. Use a packet soup for a base, boil up spuds, onions, carrots, salami – anything that looks a fair thing – and eat with plenty of bread. It's not the best eating in the world but it's a lot better than starving to death and I've had some nights that have changed my life sitting around the burner in cheap pensions with a bit of good company. (Find a freak with another burner and you're getting into a two-course feed!) *Frank Scahill, Punchbowl, Australia*

Dear Sir: Stuff the *Hitch-hiker's Guide to Europe.* I've had three copies ripped off in hostels in as many months! *Peter Lane, London*

Don't leave cameras, radios, etc., in hostel rooms. My mini-radio was lifted in Rome. Check them in at desk. *Mike Feeney, Haslow, England*

It's worth a mention that people who wear glasses should always carry a spare pair with them. *Dave Williams, Birmingham, England*

It's probably worth carrying your optician's prescription with you, too. K.W.

You have plenty of instructions on how to keep dry (plastic bags, etc.) but have made no mention about protection from the sun. Sunburn can be one of the most distressing and painful afflictions to affect the hitcher. So how about a hat and sun glasses and a light, plastic tube of barrier cream?

And how about a packet of vitamin pills to keep the pecker up when food is scarce? *Dr Ivy Garnham, Salisbury, Rhodesia*

Lomotil pills are the best cure for diarrhoea. *Unsigned, South Kensington, London*

Watch out for national holidays all over Europe. You can get stuck without bread because you can't cash your travellers' cheques or pawn things. You can change money at the big hotels, but the rates are a bloody rip-off.

Last summer I took along a tube of Steratabs, which are water sterilizing tablets, and also seem to have a gut reinforcing effect after a couple of weeks' use. (Very handy in North Africa.)

Definitely forget about dossing out in a big Spanish town. I got a truncheon in the ribs one night. Stations, subways, everything is patrolled. If you sleep sitting upright on a park bench you're OK (preferably with your eyes open!). Watch out for the 5 a.m. high-pressure street hosing all over Europe. *Clive Gill, Birchington, England*

If you need food really bad, pick a big and busy self-service place. Join the line and just buy a cup of coffee. When you pass the cash register pick a table where three or four people have just left after a big meal, sit down and get stuck into their leftovers. *Paul Rush, San Francisco, USA*

I write as a fellow traveller who has found the *Hitch-hiker's Guide* most useful. I did, however, come unstuck and will give you a brief account of my fortune and misfortune.

I left England with the intention of hitching to Istanbul and then taking the overland route through the East to Australia. My second lift landed me in Paris for two days and then I made a château near Orleans where I stayed for a further seventeen days. I hitched in Spain for a couple of weeks and then back to Marseilles and asked at the dock about a boat for Italy and was immediately put in touch with a guy delivering a brand new yacht to Genoa — three days on the Med with all expenses paid!

I finally ended up in Rome (after Venice), having spent six fantastic weeks travelling on a minimum budget, having met the kindest and most generous people imaginable. I then referred to your book and headed for the Borghese Gardens where I crashed out in my sleeping-bag for free. I woke at four in the morning to find my pack had been stolen. It contained my entire kit, including my addresses, diary, maps, books and all the hints I had collected from people *en route*. Also my contact lenses and worst of all . . . my *trousers*! Fortunately I had my wallet and travellers' cheques in my sleeping-bag and my passport and papers in a bag around my neck.

I met a Belgian a couple of days later who, in the same park, had been forced to hand over his pack to a bunch of thugs on the threat of his life.

I ask you to suggest that people don't crash out alone in Italian parks! *Hugh Darlington, Oxford, England*. PS My copy of the *Hitcher's Guide* was in the bag. Got a spare one?

Selling blood in Greece, you've got to be over 21 — they check your passport for all particulars. *Dave Martill, Leicester, England*

Check out coin return slots. Telephones are an obvious place, but also in the endless banks of automatic lockers in airline terminals. Best place to panhandle is at an international airport. Hit US tourists returning home for the odd foreign coins they got stuck with and couldn't change back into dollars. *Len Tower, Bay Shore, New York*

Great places for sleeping rough are football stadiums and sports grounds. They are usually easy to enter and it's not necessary to be up and away too early in the morning. I've also had good kips in grounds beside open-air swimming pools. For late autumn and winter when nights are freezing try underground car parks (easy once you slip by the attendant) and under the stairs in foyers of office and apartment blocks. *Danny Long, Saffron Walden, Essex, England*

I sold some blood in Spain, but if you have any North African stamps in your passport it's no deal.

I always buy plenty of packet soup before leaving on a big hitch. Mixed with macaroni or rice it really sticks to the ribs. Follow that with bread and cheese and coffee and you can tackle Mt Everest! *Dennis Clubb, Bletchley, England*

If you're stuck in coastal towns on the Continent and can't find the price of an hotel, try the Missions to Seamen. These are really for seamen, but most of the padres in charge are kind-hearted blokes and many let you kip on a couch in the TV lounge. *J. P. Ridley, Falkirk, Scotland*

If you are crashing out (roughing it) take something for the mosquito bites – 'cause whatever you do these crazy goddamn creatures get you. *Capt'n Clem, Bristol, England*

In cold weather try the old tramp trick of keeping warm by putting two thicknesses of old newspaper between your shirt and jumper. *C. J. Major, Cambridge, England*

Easy money: collect empty coke bottles from dirt bins or especially along beaches and claim the deposit. I know someone who kept himself for six weeks in Torremolinos, Spain, this way. *Lesley Kountaff, South Africa*

One of the most useful items I packed was some fishing tackle. Just some line, a few hooks and float – nice way of passing time on any coastline, lake or river in Europe. Camping rough it provides food or even offers an afternoon's pleasure while waiting for a ferry ride somewhere.

What I've often resorted to (e.g., hitched from Athens to Luxembourg city with *no* negotiable money) is going into bakeries in the morning and asking for yesterday's leftovers. Often got a fresh loaf; often got yesterday's pastries. Was rarely refused totally. *Roger Brown, author of Travellers Survival Kit Europe* (published by Vacation-Work, Oxford)
   Roger: Great book! K.W.

Stay clear of Persian drivers if possible – we crashed outside Munich after several heart attacks. They are far worse than the Belgians. *Jonah, Neath, South Wales, GB*

I had all my luggage ripped off from a *locked* left-luggage locker in Gare du Nord, Paris – on the last day luckily.

Fortunately it was insured and I've been able to replace it all with better stuff – except the photos which are the only thing I regret losing. *Dave, Southampton, England*

For those who get their *Hitcher's Guide* ripped off – try a plain paper cover! *Marcel Thomas, Horndean, England*

Spain is still good for selling blood, but you must weigh over 55 kg otherwise they won't take it. *Unsigned*

A few lines to all would-be travellers going camping or hiking abroad. To cover you for medical care write to your local Social Security for an E111. This is an exemption form for medical costs abroad. *Miss E. Reed, Peterborough, England*
  I understand that Britons carrying this form in EEC countries don't have to pay for medical services. Brits should check at their Social Security office. K.W.

Medical Insurance form E111 is *not* available to students – only those paying National Insurance, or unemployed, or under 19! *Avril Horton, Leeds, UK*

For Brits only: when applying for form E111 from the Social Security, ask for leaflets SA 28 and SA 30. These tell you which countries have reciprocal health agreements with Britain, and thus where you can get treatment free or at reduced cost. *Alan Barlow, Cheadle, UK*

One thing you don't seem to mention is travel insurance. Luggage, money, medical and personal accident can all be covered with a good company very cheaply. *S. Derrick, Southampton, England*

Appearance: I try to save a clean shirt (at least) for the journey home and keep my face, hands and nails clean if I'm broke. Then I *look* OK even if I stink. *Bernard Jennings, Brisbane, Australia*

For toothache: even better than booze is a packet of dried cloves available from most chemists or health food shops. Just let them dissolve over the offending tooth and the ache vanishes. Warning: don't chew them or have more than two at a time, unless you want a hole burnt in your throat. *Simon Barry, Isle of Man, GB*

Your advice about knocking on farm doors for food works. I did that in Germany, after being dropped off on an autobahn, and even though they didn't speak English and I don't speak German, I got food and blankets for the night. *Alan Smith, Sunderland, England*

If you do this, remember to offer to do an hour or so's work the next day. It keep the image up. K.W.

If you need tomato sauce or mustard for home cooking visit self-service restaurants with a plastic bag. *Thrifty, Israel*

Plainclothes cops dressed like freaks mix in cafés, bars and discos all over Europe whenever city fathers decide to do a 'clean-up'. They're after smokers and other 'undesirables'. Watch it! *J.D., Notting Hill, London*

I read it in your book, and I've been warned a thousand times – 'beware of thieves in Italy'. One always thinks, it can't happen to me! I was parked outside a youth hostel in Rome for ten minutes. When I returned to the car, I found it had been broken into. My jacket, money, radio and camera had been pinched. I'd like to warn fellow travellers to be that extra bit careful whilst travelling in Italy. *Gary Sogot, Johannesburg, South Africa*

These things don't happen only in Italy. They happen elsewhere, too. Never let your gear out of your sight. Never leave anything of value in your van. Look at it this way: your pack with clothes, camera and the rest of your stuff is worth maybe one hundred, two hundred pounds. Would you leave two hundred quid's worth of bank notes on a bus-stop floor while you went for a coffee? Or on the front seat of your van? These thieves don't see a rucksack or a camera – they don't need rucksacks or cameras. They just see money sitting there waiting to be ripped off. K.W.

Consume plenty of vitamin C. It'll save you from lots of minor ailments. *C. D. Cook (New Zealander), London, England*

Vitamin C is particularly important in the daily diet. You find good quantities of this vitamin in brussels sprouts, parsley, cabbage, cauliflower, oranges, lemons, mandarins, silverbeet, etc., so look for these fruits and vegetables when you shop in markets. Because money circumstances so often force you to eat badly when you're on the road, I reckon Dr Ivy

Garnham (see page 73) hits it on the button when she says take along a pack of vitamin pills. Look for a pill that contains both vitamins and minerals. Avoid junk food whenever possible. If you have a choice between a hamburger joint and a workers' café offering good, simple food, take the latter every time. Junk food wrecks you. K.W.

If you're on the road and you walk by a garbage tip or rubbish dump, get your ass in there. People throw away really good stuff. I once found a chair I sold to a junk shop for enough money to buy me food for a day. It was tough hitching to get the chair back to town, but at least I got to sit on it while waiting for a ride. Roll on baby. *Steve L. Mannheim, Los Angeles, United States*

If you're sleeping out in a city it's advisable to leave your gear in a locker in the main railway station. This lessens the risk of robbery (though it doesn't guarantee it). If you enter a park at night with a pack on your back, you'll attract the attention of muggers. *Hugh Dunne, Dublin, Ireland*

For males only. If you fall on hard times in Israel, it's worth knowing that most big hospitals have sperm banks. If you can overcome your embarrassment, and also pass a blood test, you can earn around £5 sterling per contribution. *Ray Tout, Israel*

Anyone know if European hospitals seek contributions for sperm banks? K.W.

A Eurocheque card (and your cheque book, of course) can be very handy in case of an emergency in Western Europe. You can't normally get money on the card, but you can buy air and boat tickets. Remember, if you lose the card and the cheque book you're giving a forger the licence to do you for a lot of cash. *Nigel Roberts, Prescott, England*

Pavement drawings are a way of making a few coins anywhere in the world. If you can't draw, find some abandoned picture on the pavement and touch it up. You should earn something off the tourists. But keep an eye open for the original artist!

Flowers picked from municipal parks during the night sell well on the street the next morning. *Jez, Hemel Hempstead, England*

If you're stuck for a place to sleep in a large city, try the national departure lounge of the main airport. *Paul Dowrick, Andover, England*
   Good toilet facilities, but very expensive meals and coffee. Take your own food. K.W.

My funds were running low in Corfu and I was thinking of heading for home when I heard someone in a bar say they were desperate for a haircut. I'd never cut hair before, but I took a chance. It worked out OK (thank God) so I became a hairdresser charging 100 drachmas a trim. My new-found skill kept me on the island another month. *Janet Pawlter, Chelmsford, UK*

Forget the Mediterranean coasts in July and August unless you enjoy fighting your way through millions of tourists and spending hours looking for rooms and then paying rip-off prices. Go to Scandinavia, Scotland or Timbuktu, but don't go to the Algarve, the Costa del Sol, the Riviera, or Greece, etc. If you *must*, be warned, take a tent. It will save you a hell of a lot of money and time. *Alan Thatcher, New Zealand*

Big supermarkets, department stores, etc., often have good, clean toilets with *hot* water! Don't hesitate to discreetly take advantage, though don't go as far as two guys I saw in the Corte Ingles store in Málaga, Spain. Rucksacks and gear all over the floor, dirty plates and clothes soaking in sinks, and them stark naked soaping themselves all over. Nuff to give us bums a bad name. *Jerry Jakes, Plymouth, UK*

Dehydrated packet food is light, doesn't take much space and is reasonably cheap. Just add water and heat for a while on a small gas burner. Use small single portion packets from camping shops. With bread it's a good meal. *Andrew Price, Torquay, UK*
   I think fresh food is always better than dehydrated food, but if you decide to go that route it would be cheaper to buy the food in large commercial packs like those used by restaurants. With a group of friends splitting costs you could save as much as 50 per cent. K.W.

Eat muesli, the type without sugar that you buy from health stores. Pour milk or juice over it. A cupful at breakfast will keep your stomach happy until it's time for dinner. Also, it's extremely nutritious. *Paul Henning, Hillsborough, Florida, USA*

I've made money on the road during the Christmas season by painting Christmas scenes on café windows with poster paints. It's easier to do than it sounds. Buy a kid's colouring book with Christmas scenes, rip out a suitable page and tape it on the *outside* of the window. Back inside you trace a black outline of the picture and then colour it in. By the way, my present well-thumbed *Hitcher's Guide* has been heavily used despite the plain brown paper cover which reads *Terra Firma Classicus*. I can leave it lying around in hostels and no one so much as opens it, much less thinks of nicking it. *John Riordan, Vinderup, Denmark*

Liked John Riordan's tip about calling his copy of the Hitcher's Guide *Terra Firma Classicus*. Mine now reads the same with '*Essays on the Early Latin Classics*' by K. W. Welsh. Nobody even touches it. *Mark Naisbitt, Darlington, Durham, UK*

To stop condensation in survival bags punch small holes on top: small enough to keep rain out, big enough to let air in. *Patrick Fitzgerald, South Lopham, England*

You can get ample pickings from fish markets along the Mediterranean coast. Go to the quaysides after the stalls have closed down and you'll find plenty of fish lying around. OK, they may look dirty, but give them a quick wash in the sea and you've got yourself a free meal. *John (Tight-fist) Morton, Amersham, England*

When short of cash anywhere in Scandinavia, a highly nutritious and affordable commodity is tinned mackerel or sardines. Also, many shops sell bananas and apples at a reduced price because they're bruised. Day-old bread can also be bought cheap. *Jeff Moore, England*

When looking for a place to crash, keep an eye out for bandstands. They provide perfect cover. *Philip Attwool, Orpington, UK*

About thieving in hostels: it's not just obvious valuables like cameras or radios that disappear. Some people will nick *anything*, like towels or clothing hanging on radiators to dry. Some hostels provide lockers but these shouldn't be regarded as absolutely secure. A girl with a set of skeleton keys was caught red-handed in Munich hostel helping herself to cameras. Italy in particular seems to be bad for thieving so don't ever turn your back on your gear or it might not be there when you turn round again.

All French wine bottles with stars around the neck have deposits and can be cashed in. *Alan Barlow, Cheadle, UK*

Nostalgia made me pick up your book and leaf through it. Without making a fetish of hitch-hiking I did it for a few years when I first arrived in England (from New Zealand) because I couldn't afford to travel there any other way and was quite literally dazzled by Europe.

What strikes me about your book is the emphasis given to your hitch-hiker being 'ripped off' by Europeans and yet you proceed to give space to people proclaiming ways and means of 'ripping off' these same Europeans. I don't in fact wish to be holier than thou, but I can't see anything particularly admirable about picking municipal flowers and then selling them; or defrauding foreign public transport systems; or exploiting the loneliness of migrant workers by abusing, in my view, their hospitality. I should think that the average hitch-hiker today is a good deal better off than the average migrant worker.

To say that your book is offensive is probably pitching it a little high as I'm sure a lot of the tips in it, places to stay, restaurants, etc., are very useful. It's just a great pity that you are encouraging a brand of rather unpleasant, parasitic travellers. *H.D., London*

For one pound just nip into one of the following railway stations: Venice, Toulouse, Basel and Hamburg. You can take your pack into the cubicle and spend a good 15 minutes soaking. *Mari Doyle, Godalming, Surrey, UK*

Need a bath or wash? Motorway service areas in France and Belgium have showers for truckers. Warm water and free. Desperate for a kip? You can crash in them, too, but don't make your bed until 11 p.m. when it's quiet. The cleaners will wake you at 6. *A. P. Kik, Middlesbrough, Teesside, UK*

Learn to play a musical instrument, such as the flute or trumpet, and busk your way around Europe. In Munich I played the flute for two hours one rainy night in the city centre and made £20! *Pete the Freak, London*

6 The British Isles and Ireland

Most Australians and North Americans use England as the base
for their European trip for one of two reasons – one sound and the
other unfashionable. The sound one is that if you can get the
correct papers (see chapter on **Working in Europe**) you have more
chance of working in England than in any other European
country. The second reason, the unfashionable one, is that
England remains in a manner of speaking the object of an Oedipus
complex. It's the Motherland and even if most of her sons have
long since left, via means of secession, revolution and diplomacy,
or have just wandered off uninterested, she still offers the solution
to the most puzzling question of all: where did our families come
from?

Plenty of people find the answer a little disappointing. The tiny
island crammed with over 55,000,000 people is hardly the green
field of yesteryear which grandmothers and grandfathers back in
the old ex-colonies talk about so fondly. England can present a
mean face. Many of her people rarely see whatever green fields
are left because they can't afford the train fare. Her gasping cities
are grimed and blackened by industry. Too many Britons are
literally fighting for survival amidst overpopulation. It's not
unusual to find city children who have never seen a cow, much less
the cow in its green field. And that sad observation is, of course, as
true of New York as it is of London.

But have no fears. London is a great city and a load of fun, even
if it never did swing with quite the momentum *Time* magazine
would have liked to believe, or if Antonioni's *Blow-Up* turned out
to be as much a blueprint for London to fashion itself by as
London ever was an inspiration for the movie. But it's all fun if
you can enter into London's idea of fun which, along with its
discotheques and cinema clubs and thousand lifestyles is also the
place where you try to convince yourself that your 10×10, dirty-
floored bed-sit is the next best thing to a palace (in London it is,
unless Daddy is supplying you with a nice fat allowance each

week); and that the solid wall of bus, lorry, car and train fumes which you breathe is as healthy as the next cubic mile of poison. And not to mention the noise. Take a walk in Hyde Park one day, around midday. Stroll a hundred yards in from Park Lane and stop amongst the green silence and listen to the dragon of sound flowing around beyond you.

But when you finally leave the big city, there *are* places you can go on that tiny island. One of them is northern Scotland, way up in the damp Highlands where you can walk for hours and never see a person and where the only noise is that of continuously falling rain – clean rain – and where the smell is of pure air and not of nearly pure carbon-monoxide.

And then, just a little way across the water is Ireland, especially southern Ireland where the people are just a fraction wild and where the landscape is a fraction wilder, and nearly as beautiful as the people. Southern Ireland, like northern Scotland, is a place you can absorb, which you can let run over and into you – not like the Midlands in England where even though you may be living it up and enjoying yourself you have to keep it all at arm's distance in case it kills you with an overdose of claustrophobia.

But don't get me wrong. Dirty, cancerous, black-faced London is one of the most exciting and one of the greatest cities in the world and you may find that the diminishing green countryside of which it is capital harbours more than a handful of memories for you.

England

population	46,000,000
size	50,053 square miles
capital	London, population 7,212,000
government	Constitutional monarchy
religion	Protestant Episcopal
language	English, with very little of anything else spoken or understood
currency	*Pound Sterling* One *pound* equals 100 *pence*. Coins of ½, 1, 2, 5, 10, 20, 50 *pence* and £1. Notes of 1, 5, 10, 20 and 50 *pounds*

England is stacked with sights to see. But where to start? From

1. N.W. Highlands
2. Grampians
3. Southern Uplands
4. Cheviots
5. Pennines
6. Cambrian Mountains
7. Cotswolds
8. Dartmoor
9. Mourne Mountains
10. Wicklow Mountains

John o' Groats
Thurso

Ullapool
SCOTLAND

Gairloch
L. Maree
Inverness

ATLANTIC
Loch Ness
NORTH

OCEAN
Fort William
Balmoral
SEA

Mallaig
Ben Nevis
Braemar
2

Glen Coe
Dundee

Loch Lomond
Crieff

Glasgow
Stirling

Clyde
Edinburgh

Abbotsford
Melrose

Alloway
Ayr
3
Selkirk
Jedburgh

4
Carter Bar

Londonderry
Dumfries
Hadrian's Wall

Donegal
Carrick Fergus
Stranraer
Carlisle
Newcastle

Larne
Keswick
Durham

N. IRELAND
Belfast
Lake Windermere

Sligo
9
Haworth

IRISH
5

SEA
Blackpool
Manchester

Galway
Liffey
Conway
Liverpool
Chester
Grimsby

EIRE
Dublin
Caernarvon
Bangor
Lincoln

10
Harlech
Trent
Nottingham

Limerick
WALES

Adare
Kilkenny
Birmingham
ENGLAND

Tralee
Cashel
Aberystwyth
Kenilworth
Warwick
Norwich

Killarney
Clonmel
6
Stratford-upon-Avon

Blarney
Cork
Cardigan
Abergavenny
Stow-on-the-Wold

St. David's
Severn
Oxford
London

Carmarthen
Monmouth
7
Thames

Cardiff
Bristol
Westerham
Canterbury

Bath
Windsor
Battle
Dover

Stonehenge
Amesbury
Winchester
Chichester
Brighton
Hastings

Salisbury
Portsmouth

8

Lands End

CHANNEL ISLANDS
FRANCE

0   50   100   Miles
0   50   100 km

London, a trip into the South and South East is a great introduction to Britain. Some twenty miles south of the capital is the town of **Westerham** and near it is **Chartwell**, the country home of the late Sir Winston Churchill (open March to October) where you can see a collection of the statesman's paintings, the study where he wrote many of his books, and amongst many other things, the famous wall which he built with his own hands and which looks exactly like a wall.

Heading farther south is the village of **Battle**, one of the crucial landmarks of English history, for it was here that in 1066 the Battle of Hastings was fought. An Abbey was built on the site by William the Conqueror after the conflict.

Canterbury, on the A2 if you're heading to Dover on your way to the Continent, is worth a stopover for its cathedral. It's a classic and famous as the scene of Thomas à Becket's assassination in 1170. The city's worth a look, too.

Heading west along the coast through **Rye, Winchelsea** and **Hastings**, and then along the South Downs through **Brighton** (one of England's most popular seaside resorts), you eventually come to the old walled cathedral city of **Chichester**. Next is **Portsmouth** where, in the naval dockyards, you can see Nelson's flagship the *Victory* in dry dock. You can board the 180-year-old ship and look over all its decks. Also in Portsmouth is the house in which Charles Dickens was born. It is now a Dickens museum.

A little to the north is **Winchester**, ancient capital of Saxon England and famed for its superb Norman cathedral.

Salisbury is yet another city with an outstanding cathedral. It and the Close which sit on the river Avon make for one of the most often painted and photographed scenes in all the British Isles. By following the pretty road through Woodford, along the Avon, you join the A303 at **Amesbury** and you're within a couple of miles of **Stonehenge**, the mysterious stone circle possibly connected with the druids of ancient Britain. Stonehenge is worth the visit, but because of past vandalism the monument is roped off, and can only be seen from a distance. (If you want to wander among megalithic stones take the A345 north to **Marlborough** and then the A4 to **Avebury**, a picturesque village encircled by two sets of standing stones.) Also in this area (if you have spare cash for the admission fee) is **Longleat**, home of the Marquess of Bath, yet another titled gent of England who has to make ends meet by

turning his family seat into a profit machine. The marquess does it
by having lions and other wild animals roaming in his grounds.
   Devon and **Cornwall** to the west are best reached via the M5.
In **Exeter**, see the Cathedral, ancient buildings and what is left of
the Roman walls. The M5 and A38 trunk route will take you
rapidly down to **Dartmoor** and Cornwall, but if you have time take
the slower, northern route A39 through beautiful **Exmoor** and
along the spectacular **north Devon coast**. Cornwall has an even
grander coastline on the north, stormswept by the Atlantic, and a
more peaceful but equally lovely subtropical south coast. While in
the area don't miss **Glastonbury** (legend says that this is Avalon,
resting place of King Arthur and the Knights of the Round Table).
Visit Glastonbury Tor and see the ancient Zodiac pattern set out
in the surrounding fields. The beautiful cathedral city of **Wells** is
also worth a visit if time is plentiful, as is the **Cheddar Gorge**.
   Whilst in the West Country, do not miss **Bristol**, England's
greatest medieval port, with its wealth of history and interest. And
see **Bath**, with its Georgian architecture and Roman baths, a city
renowned for its spa where you can take the piping hot natural
waters. From Bristol on the A466 you pass **Tintern Abbey** and
then it's up the beautiful **Wye Valley** to **Monmouth**, passing the
Forest of Dean which still has oaks planted by Nelson in case
England ever ran out of wood for her ships!
   Starting from London again, you can head out to **Windsor** with
its huge castle which is still used by the British Royal Family (you
can wander in the grounds and the castle when the Royal Family
are not in residence) and nearby **Eton** – where there is a school on
whose playing-fields (some people would like to believe) the battle
of Waterloo was won.
   Cambridge can now be reached by the M11 from London –
named from a bridge which crossed the river Cam in ancient days –
and since the thirteenth century one of England's great seats of
learning. Peterhouse College was founded in 1284. Prominent
Britons who were educated at Cambridge included Newton,
Darwin, Macaulay, Milton and Byron. See King's College Chapel
and, just beyond, a classic English scene, green slopes leading
down to the river Cam where punters drift in peaceful waters.
   From Cambridge it's the A11 to **Norwich** with its Castle
Museum complex, cathedral, and medieval streets. It is also the
gateway to the **Norfolk Broads**, a popular destination for boating
holidays, and it's worth the effort to try hitching boats to

picturesque Broads villages like **Potter Higham** or to the east coast resort of **Great Yarmouth**.

South-west sits another of England's great educational institutions and Cambridge's famous rival, **Oxford**, which has been a student centre since the twelfth century. Have a look at Magdalen College and Merton College (founded in 1264), walk down the High Street (so *very* English), see Christ Church which was founded by Cardinal Wolsey and try and get in to see the very important Bodleian Library which contains 3,000,000 volumes and 50,000 manuscripts.

Continuing north on the A34 you are skirting the **Cotswolds**. Short detours will take you through quaint villages with such outlandish names as **Stow-on-the-Wold**, **Chipping Norton**, and **Shipton-under-Wychwood**, until you finally reach **Stratford-upon-Avon** – Shakespeare country. Shakespeare's birthplace is worth a visit but watch out for rip-offs. Anything around the main attractions will be expensive and street vendors should be avoided.

In the town (if you can fight your way through the busloads of tourists) you can see Shakespeare's birthplace, Anne Hathaway's Cottage (she was the playwright's wife), Hall's Croft where Shakespeare's daughter lived, and three miles out of town is Mary Arden's House – she having been his mother. All of these places are worth seeing if you're at all interested in Shakespeare or Elizabethan architecture. Two other places to visit are Holy Trinity Church where the man was baptized and where he is buried and the Royal Shakespeare Theatre where from March to January performances of his plays are held. Booking is usually well in advance if any well-known actor like Alan Howard is playing. To be thoroughly English in Stratford, try hiring a punt and poling yourself around the river for an hour or two.

Just eight miles north of Stratford is **Warwick**. The castle, though expensive, is in my opinion well worth the visit. Warwick Castle recently sold off many of its treasures so it might not be such good value for money as it was in the past. And five miles farther north is **Kenilworth** with the ruins of the castle which Sir Walter Scott wrote about. The jousting grounds outside the walls make a nice camping area if you're at all romantically inclined.

From Kenilworth you are on the way to **Worcester** and **Hereford** and the remote and unspoiled Welsh Border country.

But you may prefer cities and their associations, in which case from Kenilworth you move on through **Coventry**. North of Coventry is **Birmingham**, England's second largest city. It's your classic urban jungle, but contains a wealth of theatres, galleries, museums, and nightlife. From Birmingham take the M6 and M54 to **Telford**, where Abraham Darby first used coke to smelt iron in the 1700s and so began the Industrial Revolution. The event is commemorated both by the preservation of the world's first iron bridge and in the **Iron Bridge Museum**.

Back on the M6 your next stop could be **Stoke-on-Trent**, home of the pottery industry. Stoke, too, is something of an urban mess but the Wedgwood Village, Gladstone Pottery Museum, Chatterly Whitfield Mining Museum, and City Museum are worth a visit for those interested in such things. From Stoke the M6 goes north and the A54 leads to the **Peak District National Park**, containing lovely, lonely moorland and hills, and old mineworkings now open to visitors.

Peak District towns like the spa centre of **Buxton** are worth visiting. South to **Nottingham**, the city around which the legendary Robin Hood is said to have operated. There's scarcely anything left of Sherwood Forest these days, but if you care to travel out to **Edwinstowe** you can see the church where they say Robin married the Maid Marian. Nottingham Castle, from where the Sheriff hatched his plans against Robin, is now a museum and art gallery. Two of England's oldest public inns are in Nottingham – the Trip to Jerusalem (twelfth century) and the Salutation Inn (thirteenth century). Those interested in theatre should have a look at what is becoming one of England's best, the Nottingham Playhouse.

East from Nottingham, the A46 takes you to the underrated city of **Lincoln**, dominated by a spectacular cathedral which houses one of the few remaining copies of the Magna Carta, and surrounded by Roman and medieval remains.

The route north takes you through the ancient counties of **Yorkshire** via the M1, or **Lancashire** via the M6. Both are heavily industrialized but offer masses to see and do, excellent motorway links, lovely surrounding countryside and, above all, some of the friendliest folk in England.

The M1 will take you to **Sheffield**, a city famous for its steel and cutlery industry, sitting amongst the lovely rolling moorland of South Yorkshire. Among many sites of interest, visit the Worsburg Mill Museum at nearby **Barnsley**, and Abbeydale Industrial Hamlet, Conisbrough Castle and Roche Abbey near

Sheffield itself. The M1 takes you through West Yorkshire, and **Leeds** with its fine medieval remains and a certain lingering Victorian splendour. At **Halifax** (on the M62), set in the lovely Calderdale Valley, visit the nearby Shibden Hall Folk Museum. Camera freaks will enjoy **Bradford**'s National Photographic Museum. The A650 will take you north to **Keighley** and then to **Haworth**, famed as Brontë country, where the extraordinary Misses Brontë lived in the local parsonage and wrote *Jane Eyre* and *Wuthering Heights*.

North of Haworth and you reach the **Yorkshire Dales National Park**. Hitching here may be slow, but it will be peaceful and you'll enjoy great scenery. Best route is the A684 through the heart of **Wensleydale**. If you have time, check out picturesque villages like **Sedburgh**, and **Hawes** with its **Hardrow Force** waterfall.

To the east lies **York**, which embraces nearly twenty centuries of history, and remains England's most medieval looking city. Four gates still open through the three miles of Roman walls which girdle the city. Visit the incredible York Minster which took 250 years to build and still dominates the city. Don't miss the 2500 square feet of stained glass which comprise the Great East Window. Photographers will love the lurching buildings in streets with names like Whip-ma-Whop-ma-Gate, the Shambles and Goodramgate. See also the Castle Folk Museum, housed in an old prison, which features reconstructions of York streets, and the National Railway Museum where you can board the *City of Truro*, the first 100-mph train in England.

York is surrounded by some lovely old towns, including **Beverley** and **Harrogate**. South of Ripon stand the ruins of **Fountains Abbey**, once among the largest in Europe until Henry VIII fell out with the pope! Next try the **North Yorkshire Moors National Park,** where you can walk on rugged Rosedale moor or visit the ruins of **Rievaulx Abbey**. The abbey is set in a magical valley where you can wander in peace and forget the world a while. East again takes you to **Pickering** with its castle and the North York Moors Steam Railway, and then to the east coast.

Heading north on the A1(M) you reach **Durham**, an important medieval city dominated by a magnificent Norman cathedral. It also offers a host of other attractions for the culture vulture: a castle, the Gulbenkian Museum and the County Durham Open Air Museum.

North yet again on the same route and you find **Newcastle**, with its warm, hospitable people (Geordies), speaking the most unintelligible dialect in these islands! Asking directions *can* be confusing. You might get the reply: 'Gan reet doon this lonnen', i.e., 'Go straight down this long road'; or someone might say 'Howay, mar' which means 'Come on, friend'; 'nee' means 'no'; 'neet' is 'night'; 'summick' is 'something' and so on, everything spoken in a lovely deep lilting accent. The city displays a wealth of attractions: Roman sites, galleries and museums are all easily reached by a cheap and efficient metro system. Of special interest to culture addicts is the Shakespeare season at the Theatre Royal. The Royal Shakespeare Company takes all its productions (four each from Stratford and London) to Newcastle for two weeks each year in February and March.

Farther north on the A68 and you are in wild Northumberland where the introspective can walk alone for hours in the **Border Forest Park** and the Cheviot Hills, before crossing into Scotland.

The other route is the M6. Follow this and you can choose from two of the most important cities in England, **Manchester** and **Liverpool**. Manchester is England's northern capital and it shows. Here you'll find excellent theatres (including the famed Royal Exchange), three first-rate galleries, famous libraries, and museums covering subjects like Air and Space, Industry and Transport, and the history of the city. The city also boasts splendid Victorian architecture, including a stupendous Gothic town hall.

Liverpool, too, has a lot to offer. Great buildings like the Town Hall and the Liver Building, the Walker and Sudley galleries and two superb cathedrals are worth visiting. No football freak should miss the opportunity of visiting the stadiums of Anfield (Liverpool) or Old Trafford (Manchester United) – the experiences are unforgettable.

South of Liverpool is **Chester**, a great town for a whiff of the Middle Ages. Two miles of walls enclose the city and its streets are riddled with architectural leftovers from medieval times. The city was known to the Romans as Deva and in the Grosvenor Museum is an excellent collection of Roman artifacts. The Chester Zoo is famous for its pachyderms.

Next stop is **Lancashire**. The M6 will take you to **Lancaster** and then to the **Trough of Bowland**, an area of moorland and forest, wild and lonely enough to blow the city grime from your hair.

North-west again and you're in the English Lake District, a spectacular and beautiful area, very easy to take after the smog and bustle of the great industrial cities of the Midlands. Here there is a lot to see in a small space and if you are an English literature fan a trip along the A591 will take you by **Lake Windermere** and along to the tiny village of **Grasmere**. It was here that William Wordsworth lived for many years in Dove Cottage which is now the Wordsworth Museum. The poet is buried in the Grasmere churchyard. After Wordsworth moved out of Dove Cottage, Thomas De Quincey (*Confessions of an Opium-eater*) – perhaps the first turned-on Englishman – set up house there for twenty years. **Keswick**, just a dozen miles farther on, is a town in which Lamb, Keats, Shelley, Scott, Carlyle, Tennyson and Ruskin all stayed at one time or another.

The southern lakes get very crowded in summer, so if you want to experience a little of what Wordsworth was about then head for less visited northern lakes like **Crummock Water** and **Buttermere**. A word of warning: sea beaches in the area have been polluted by discharges from the Sellafield (Windscale) nuclear plant!

Carlisle, a city of 71,000, boasts an eleventh-century cathedral, a museum featuring Roman remains, and a castle in which Mary, Queen of Scots was imprisoned in 1568. From here also, you can find your way out to **Hadrian's Wall** – although a better place to see it is near the village of **Wall** just north of **Hexham** which is on the A69.

North of the Roman wall and you've made Scotland.

★**Annual events and customs** England is a great country for celebrating its own history and customs. It seems that just about every village and town has some celebration some time in the year. For full details of what's happening where and when, you'll have to check at tourist offices, but here's a sample of the type of thing to look for: *Pancake Day Race* at Olney, Buckinghamshire, on Shrove Tuesday (February). *Cheese Rolling* at Cheltenham, Gloucestershire, in June. *Brick Throwing and Rollingpin Throwing Contest* at Stroud, Gloucestershire, in July (this is an international event amongst Strouds from England, Australia, Canada, and the USA). *Shakespeare Birthday Celebrations* in April and *Shakespeare Season of Plays* at Stratford-upon-Avon, Warwickshire, from March to January. *Bottle Kicking and Hare Pie Scrambling* at Hallaton, Leicestershire, at Easter. *Manchester to Blackpool Veteran and Vintage Car Run*, in June. *Southport Music Festival* at Southport, Merseyside, in September and

October. *Wassailing the Apple Trees* at Carhampton, Somerset, in January. *The Hot Penny Ceremony* at Honiton, Devon, in July. *Annual Carnival and Rolling of the Tar Barrels* in November, at Ottery St Mary, Devon. *East Kent Morris Men Hop Hoodening Tour of Kent*, in September. *Isle of Thanet Ploughing Match* at Margate, Kent, in October. *Bonfire Celebrations* at Lewes, East Sussex, in October. *The Appleby Horse Fair* at Appleby, Cumbria, in June, which is a gathering of gypsies for a horse fair. *Guy Fawkes Celebrations* all over the country in November. *Oxford v Cambridge University Boat Race* from Putney to Mortlake every March or early April.

★**Cigarettes** Tobacco and alcohol are tremendously expensive in England, so if you're a smoker and you're entering the country, don't forget to pick up your maximum quota of everything from duty-free shops on ships or at airports. These shops will have lists posted telling how much you are allowed to import free of tax.

★**Hitching in England** Hitching is OK except around the tremendously congested and built-up areas. It's best to clear those by bus or train – but one tip, when in big cities (and this applies all over Europe), is to go to the central markets very early in the morning, say 4 or 5 a.m., and try to pick up a ride from the scores of lorry drivers who have delivered produce. They'll be heading home in every direction. You can pick up some long, long lifts. Hitching is fast on the big highways. It's much, much slower on the small roads –and considerably more pleasant, too. No hitching is permitted on motorways, only on entrance and exit roads, and at service stations – very fast.

★**The Islands of the British Isles** For information write to the following addresses:

Isle of Wight Tourist Board at 21 High Street, Newport.

Orkney Islands Tourist Association Information Centre, Kirkwall.

Isle of Skye Tourist Association at Meall House, Portree, Isle of Skye.

Jersey Tourist Information Bureau, Weighbridge, St Helier.

Guernsey Information Bureau, PO Box 23, St Peter Port.

Isle of Man Tourist Board at 13 Victoria Street, Douglas.

★**Money savers** If you anticipate doing a lot of sightseeing around the British Isles it's well worth buying special passes which are available. One allows you to visit all sites administered by the government including musts like the Tower of London and Stonehenge. Another, more expensive, gains you entry to all of those plus many of the National Trust properties around the country. The Open-to-View ticket is available from the London Tourist Board at Victoria Station Forecourt, and from the British Tourist Authority. For full information, write to the British tourist office in your country.

★**Van vagabonds** If you feel like hiring some wheels for a week or two on the road, the cheapest way you can do it is by hiring a Dormobile. In fact, if you can get together with, say, four other people you can probably drive cheaper than you can hitch! Considering that four bodies can sleep in the van (take it in turns to sleep in the annexe tent) and that you can cook on the premises, it works out pretty cheap. (Of course, if you're planning on van vagabonding for more than two weeks you're better off buying a beat-up heap so you can sell it later and recover some of the money.) The only problem with Dormobiles is that the minimum age for insurance is 25, 'unless people are able to transfer their own vehicle policy to the satisfaction of the Hire Operator'. (Whatever that means.)

★**Travel Club** Hitchers from the United States, Australia, New Zealand, South Africa and Canada might be interested in contacting the London Colonial Club at 20–22 Leinster Square, Bayswater, London W2 (tel: 727–4364). Amongst its services, the Club specializes in overland adventure tours, car and van hire, baggage storage and shipment and also offers a mail service. If you pay the overseas membership fee – which means that you pay *before* you land in London – you are entitled to a free transfer from London's Heathrow Airport, or from Victoria Station if you land at Gatwick, to a Club hotel where you have two free nights' accommodation. You must be between 18 and 35 years old and travelling on a non-British passport.

London: where to sleep

Many hitchers make their base in London, and for anyone staying there for a fortnight or more the only answer is to hook up with another person and find a room in bed-sit land. (You can find singles, but doubles usually work out much cheaper per head.) Two good central areas to do this are Notting Hill and Earls Court – although both areas are getting more and more expensive. These areas have two advantages. One, they are within twenty minutes of just about everything and, two, they are crawling with students, travellers, and kindred souls.

Single bed-sits cost from around £35 per week. Doubles start from £45. The advantage of taking one, even for a short period of time, is that you can save a small fortune by doing your own cooking on the two-ring burners which come with the room. If you only intend staying two or three weeks, best you don't tell the landlord that. He's looking for long-term tenants. Mutter something under your breath about being in London for three or four months, or that you're studying. Work it out from there. You'll be expected to pay a week in advance and may have to put down a returnable deposit against your key and against possible damage of furniture and fittings in the room. (Seventy-five per cent of London landlords seem to think that anyone under age thirty is automatically going to destroy the entire building or, failing that, hold wild orgies and opium parties on alternate nights. They're not always wrong.)

There are two basic ways of finding a room. The cheapest is to check the noticeboards around the Earls Court or Notting Hill Underground stations (ask anyone to tell you where the boards are located) and see what is being offered. Make a note of the telephone numbers and ring up to make an appointment to see the room. This costs phone money but saves a lot of time and shoe leather because many of the rooms are gone within minutes of the notice being put on the board and the void notice will stay there for days.

The second method is to go to an accommodation agency and pay them a fee to locate a room for you. The agencies advertise in newspapers or on the same noticeboards as the landlords. It'll take you longer to find the room by yourself – especially in autumn and winter because of the influx of university students – but it'll work out a few pounds cheaper. Beware of some agencies who are rip-off artists! *Time Out* magazine often runs exposés on these people.

For serious room-hunting, and particularly if you're going to be staying in London for any length of time, it's worth buying a copy of *The A to Z Atlas of London* published by Geographers and selling for around £1·50. This 270-page book is indispensable for finding your way around the 30,000-odd streets of London and its environs. The free Underground map supplied at Tube stations is the weapon needed to tackle the more than 250 Underground stops.

The London Tourist Board at Victoria Station Forecourt will supply information about hotel and student accommodation. They place bookings in hotels and guest houses at prices as low as £7. Visit the centre in person on the day accommodation is required, or write in advance to the London Tourist Board, 26 Grosvenor Gardens, SW1.

For casual beds in Youth Hostels Association hostels (you must be a member) prices are from £2·95 to £4·50, with meals from £1·75 to £2·25. (For addresses of individual hostels, tel: 836 8541.)

Holland House Youth Hostel at Holland House, Holland Walk, Kensington, London W8 (tel: 937 0748).

Youth Hostel at 38 Bolton Gardens, Earls Court, London SW5 (tel: 373 7083).

Youth Hostel at 84 Highgate West Hill, London N6 (tel: 340 1831).

Youth Hostel at 36 Carter Lane, London EC4 (tel: 236 4965).

Salvation Army Red Shield Centre for men and women at 66 Buckingham Gate, London SW1 (tel: 222 1164).

Salvation Army Red Shield Centre for women (and married couples) at Cambria House, 37 Hunter Street, London WC1 (tel: 837 1654).

The Salvation Army Hostel for Men at 18 Great Peter Street, London SE1 (tel: 222 1546) and at 263 Waterloo Road, London SE1 (tel: 928 4591).

The Salvation Army Hostel for Women (Hopetown) at Old Montague Street, London E1 (tel: 247 1004).

Susan Lawrence Hostel at 170 King's Cross Road, London WC1 (tel: 837 5919).

Ambrosden Hostel at 1 Ashley Place, London SW1 (tel: 834 1451).

Youth Travel Bureau dormitories at 34 Cranley Gardens, London SW7 (tel: 370 2842). Men only (16–26).

Hood's House at 358 Finchley Road, London NW3 (tel: 435 6147).

Gayfere Hostel at 8 Gayfere Street, Westminster, London SW1 (tel: 222 6894). Students only at tel: 222 1402. Dormitory.

Saney Guruji Hostel at 18a Holland Villas Road, London W14 (tel: 603 3704). Dormitory. Book in advance if possible. No meals but cooking facilities.

YWCA and **YMCA** For complete information write to YWCA, National Offices, 2 Weymouth Street, London W1N 4AX (tel: 631 0657), or to YMCA, Metropolitan Region, 31 Craven Terrace, Lancaster Gate, London W2 3EL (tel: 723 0071).

There are YWCA hostels at:
Central Club, 16 Great Russell Street, London WC1 (tel: 387 3378).
Alexandra Residential Club, 13 Lloyd Square, London WC1 (tel: 837 5711); also at 2 Devonshire Street, London W1 (tel: 580 5323); and at 2 Weymouth Street, London W1 (tel: 580 6011).
Ashley House, 14 Endsleigh Gardens, London WC1 (tel: 387 3378).
Victoria, 32 Warwick Square, London SW1 (tel: 834 1089).
Park House, 227 Earls Court Road, London SW5 (tel: 373 2851).

There are YMCA hostels at:
YMCA, 112 Great Russell Street, London WC1 (tel: 637 1333).
The Barbican YMCA, Fann Street, London EC2 (tel: 628 0697).
The German YMCA, Lancaster Hall Hotel, 35 Craven Terrace, London W2 (tel: 723 9276).
The Indian Student YMCA, 41 Fitzroy Square, London W1 (tel: 387 0411).
Waltham Forest YMCA, 642 Forest Road, London E17 (tel: 520 0931).
King George's House YMCA, Stockwell Road, London SW9 (tel: 274 7861).
Hornsey YMCA, Tottenham Lane, London N8 (tel: 340 2345).

Lower priced hotels are from around £7 per night, these prices sometimes include breakfast. A selection follows:

Hotel Melita at 76 Fordwych Road, London NW2 (tel: 452 1583).

Deaconess Guest House at 90 Holland Road, London W14 (tel: 603 3773). Women only. It's run by Lutheran sisters, but is open to anyone of any religion. Good bargain but big disadvantage is that it locks up at 11.30 p.m.

Howard Hotel at 64 Princes Square, London W2 (tel: 727 6062).

Mrs Garnet's Hostel at 23 Estelle Road, London NW3 (tel: 485 3734). Cheap, very nice. But also very small. Absolutely essential you ring first.

Alliance Club at Newington Green, London N16 (tel: 226 6085). Men only. Special rates by the week.

Concord House at 49–51 Leinster Square, London W2 (tel: 229 7388). Long-term ladies only.

Albert Hotel at 191 Queen's Gate, London SW7 (tel: 584 3019).

(With most of these listings costing £7 or over, they might seem like budget-breakers. But remember that in England most hotels give you bed *and breakfast* – which makes the pain a little easier to bear.)

The Greater London Council has a chain of about a dozen hostels for men and women. Prices are reasonable. For full information write to Director of Housing, County Hall, London SE1 7PB (tel: 633 7736). Write to the International Students House, at 229 Great Portland Street, London W1 (tel: 636 9472), who have rooms at their residences in Great Portland Street and 10 York Terrace East, NW1.

If you have your own tent try **Hackney Camping**, at Millfields Road, London E5. (Tube to Liverpool Street Station, then bus 22A to Mandeville Street at Hackney Marshes. Walk over the bridge.) Costs around £2. If you don't have a tent, but would like to sleep in one, try **Tent City** at Old Oak Common Lane, London W3. (Tube to East Acton and ask from there.) There are 400 beds in sixteen tents – men's, women's and mixed – plus space for private tents. Free hot showers and baggage store. Costs around £3. For more information write to Barnaby Martin at 11 Ellesmere Road, East Twickenham, Middlesex TW1 2DJ (tel: 01–892 3570). Barnaby is doing a great job, but he can only keep these two places open if people pay him. So don't expect free beds!

For sleeping rough, there are plenty of hide-away spots in Hyde Park or Kensington Gardens. The police make checks, but these are very big parks. Also, the city is dotted with greens and churchyards (as are most big cities) where you can kip down if you're quick enough getting out of sight and quiet enough after you do.

Warning! Travellers arriving at Victoria Station by train, *avoid the hostel agents*. Some of these touts try to con you into vans, then drive you off to some woe-begotten flea-pit. If you need help, ask the London Tourist Board staff at Victoria. They dress in uniforms, but they're OK people. They have lists of cheap, decent places to stay. Just insist that you want somewhere *really* cheap. The tout warning applies to Liverpool Street Station, too, but that station has no LTB office.

London: where to eat

A good filling meal in London usually comes out at around £2·50. You get this deal by choosing carefully at the chain restaurants. Names to look out for are *Wimpy, McDonalds, Pizzaland, Burger King* and *Kentucky Fried Chicken* restaurants. But Indian restaurants – and there are plenty of them – are without a doubt the cheapest places to eat, and they aren't plastic like the chains. (The Indian Embassy, Bush House, Aldwych, WC2, serves rice and curry lunches for about £1·95.) An Indian meal will rarely cost you more than £3 and that's for as much as you can eat. If you're on the cheap, remember that you can buy plain rice dishes for around 60p and you can liberally sprinkle the rice with the free, nutritious soy sauce you usually find on the tables.

An invaluable little book is **The Good Caff Guide** by M. Fletcher (Wildwood, £2·50) which lists 120 fairly cheap London cafés.

In all big cities, wherever you find a big concentration of offices and office workers, you find a proliferation of cheap eating spots. In London, in these areas, you can eat as cheaply as anywhere in Europe. Examples:

The Stockpots There are two of these in London and they offer very good food at a very good price. Addresses are: 50 James Street, W1; and 6 Basil Street, SW3. **The Chelsea Kitchen** at 98 King's Road, SW3, is run by the same people.

Bedford Café, 43 Bedford Street (off Strand), WC2. Good, hot meals.

F. Bennett's Fresh-Cut Sandwiches at 14 New Row, WC2. A take-away sandwich bar.

The Market Snack Bar at 15 New Row, WC2.

Apollo Restaurant at New Row, WC2, gives excellent value for money. Right opposite is **The Regency**, a very small place and a favourite with theatre types from the nearby New Theatre. It's a trifle more expensive, but good value.

Ye Olde Round Table in St Martin's Court (just across from New Row) and at the side of Wyndham's Theatre. Try their pub lunch.

Summit Sandwich Bar in Lisle Street, WC2 (in Soho and off Wardour Street). It's unnumbered, but beside the Falcon Pub.

At 25 Lisle Street is **Chan May Mai**. Very popular with the local Chinese. A few doors up is the **Mirama Chinese Restaurant**, also very popular with the locals.

Nelson Restaurant in Whitcomb Street, WC2, has a top-value daily special every lunchtime. The place has no number and is up on the first floor.

Restaurant Casali at 6 Maiden Lane, WC2, gives you a really good feed at a decent price.

Avery's Salad House in Hind Court (off Fleet Street, EC4) on the way up to Doctor Johnson's House.

Ludgate Sandwich Bar at 31 Pilgrim Street – just off New Bridge Street at Ludgate Circus, EC4, and on your left.

Mick's Café at 148 Fleet Street, EC4 (open day and night). Rough and ready and *very* cheap. Opposite is

Lieto's Café at 39–40 Whitefriars Street, EC4. Simple British food – so good that even the journalists eat it!

On the corner of Apothecary Street and Blackfriars Lane (just off New Bridge Street) health buffs will find the **Food for Health Restaurant**. The owners are authors of a book, *The Home Book of Vegetarian Cooking* (Faber & Faber), and they claim that they want to prove that vegetarian meals need not be a drag. They have a health food counter where you can buy things like live yoghurt and pure sugars.

Other vegetarian restaurants are **Cranks Health Foods Restaurant** at 8 Marshall Street, W1, with branches at 196 Tottenham Court Road, W1 (upstairs at Heals), and Oxford Circus (upstairs at Peter Robinson); and **Sharuna** at 107 Great Russell Street, WC1 (which specializes in Indian-style vegetarian cooking).

The India Tea Centre on the corner of Woodstock and Oxford streets sends you on the big tea trip. Fantastic range: Darjeeling, Assam, Nilgri, lemon, orange, spiced and, in summer, iced. But it's 60p a glass!

Most of the workers' tiny cafés, for instance around the side streets between Ladbroke Grove and Portobello Road, or around the Petticoat Lane area, in short, any of the poorer areas, serve reasonable meals for around £2·50. A feed of take-away fish 'n' chips can be had nearly anywhere in London for £2.

There are thousands of pubs in London and a fair proportion of them sell food of one kind or another at lunchtime. Some might only offer snacks like sandwiches or sausages, others put on proper hot meals. The point is that pub food offers one of the best deals to be had in London. Check with people in your area for the pubs which offer the best value for money.

If you take a bed-sit and decide to do your own cooking, the cheapest places to buy supplies are those that buy in bulk and sell under their own brand-name. Consequently, many items are a little cheaper.

London: what to see and do

TOWER OF LONDON at Tower Hill. Entrance charge. Great if you're a history fan. Ten centuries of England staring you right in the face. See the crown jewels (extra charge), the armoury, the rooms where Raleigh was imprisoned, site of the old chopping block, and lots more.

ST KATHERINE'S DOCKS beside the Tower of London first harboured ships in 1827. The docks are now restored, and in them you can see the Maritime Trust Collection of Historic Ships. Particularly beautiful is the three-masted schooner *Kathleen and May*, built in 1900.

THE MONUMENT in Monument Street. Cheapest way to get a good view of London. The column, which is 202 feet high and was erected the same number of feet from where the Great Fire of London started in Pudding Lane in 1666, was designed by Wren. You can climb to the top for a small fee.

ST PAUL'S CATHEDRAL on Ludgate Hill. Free to enter, but it costs to go into the upper galleries. Worth paying, though, because from the Golden Ball on the top (only one person can enter the ball at a time) you get a great view. You can also look straight down through a glass panel a couple of hundred feet to the cathedral floor. All sorts of people buried in the crypt.

THE BARBICAN Culture vultures and architecture freaks will be in their element at the Barbican Centre. Officially opened in 1982, this £150 million Arts and Conference complex boasts a concert hall (home of the London Symphony Orchestra), a theatre (London base for the Royal Shakespeare Company), three cinemas, an art gallery geared to visiting exhibitions, a library, two exhibition halls and a massive conference area. Next door to the Centre is the Guildhall School of Music and Drama. Watch the press for details of special events at the Centre.

WESTMINSTER ABBEY in Parliament Square. Beautiful building founded in 1042 and serving as a burial ground for some of England's greatest. Poetry fans should look over Poets' Corner.

SPEAKERS' CORNER at Hyde Park, Marble Arch. Free. Any fine Sunday from around 2 p.m. Great place to let off steam, meet people, hear some really crazy people sounding off and (occasionally) to hear some clever speeches. Heckling is the order of the day.

BRITISH MUSEUM in Great Russell Street. A complete display of just about anything you're interested in. This must be the most complete summing up of the human race in existence.

VICTORIA AND ALBERT MUSEUM in South Kensington. A complex of museums. Art, architecture, furniture, clothes. If it's not at the British Museum it'll be here. If it isn't at either, it probably doesn't exist. Closed Fridays.

MUSEUM OF LONDON at London Wall, EC2, tells the story of London from prehistoric times until today. Closed Mondays.

NATIONAL GALLERY in Trafalgar Square. Great collection. Just about everyone is represented. Fantastic collection of Rembrandt.

TATE GALLERY on Millbank. Modern stuff, mostly. Superb collection of Turners and Blakes. Good retrospective exhibitions every now and again (which usually cost, but which are worth it).

CHURCHILL'S CABINET ROOMS under Horse Guards. Great visit for modern history freaks. See the underground 'bunker' from which Churchill directed the Second World War. Everything is exactly as it was when he left it in 1945. The map room, the cabinet room, his bedroom, etc.

MADAME TUSSAUD'S in Marylebone Road. Costs to get in. Huge display of waxwork figures, historical and contemporary, goodies and baddies. Some of the politicians seem more business-like in wax than they act in real life. Downstairs is the Chamber of Horrors. The waxworks were started when Madame Tussaud arrived in London in 1802 with models of the heads of guillotined victims of the French Revolution.

LONDON PLANETARIUM next door to Tussaud's in Marylebone Road. Admission charge. If you're an Arthur C. Clarke fan, it's great stuff. Also LASERIUM – rock and pop.

HOUSES OF PARLIAMENT by Westminster Bridge. The public is permitted to sit in on debates at the House of Commons. If you are doubtful about the efficiency of the English political system, you should try to listen to at least one debate. Queue at St Stephen's Entrance.

THE CENTRAL CRIMINAL COURT (known as the Old Bailey) in Newgate Street, on the site of the famous Old Newgate Prison. Free entry to the public galleries to hear court in session. Best to arrive around 10 a.m. No cameras. No children.

LONDON STOCK EXCHANGE in Old Broad Street. Visitors' gallery open weekdays from around 10 a.m. Free. Watch the immaculate men throw their money around. (Make sure your jeans are pressed.)

COVENT GARDEN, the site of the vegetable and flower market which served central London's needs from the seventeenth century until the 1970s, is now an uppercrust shopping area (with prices to match) housed within the original, restored halls. But, you don't have to spend money. Wander around and absorb the atmosphere. See the London Transport Museum, lodged within the old Flower Market (fee); St Paul's church in the Piazza, designed by Inigo Jones, completed in 1633, and featured in *My Fair Lady*; the craft stalls in the North Hall; and, best of all, the truly amazing London buskers (musicians, singers, magicians, acrobats, comedians, escape artists) who offer you entertainment every day (but particularly on Sunday mornings) for whatever small coin you care to throw their way.

BUCKINGHAM PALACE The Mall. Not open to the public. Official London home of Her Majesty the Queen. (She has several other homes, as well.) See the Changing of the Guard at 11.30 a.m. (Alternate days in winter.)

FREE BAND CONCERTS at Victoria Embankment Gardens, St James's Park and Regent's Park. Around 12.30 in summer. They've never heard of an electric guitar, but they try hard. For full details of a variety of free or nearly free outdoor entertainment, including summer Shakespeare productions in Regent's Park, ring the London Tourist Board (tel: 730 3488).

TRAFALGAR SQUARE Good place to rest your aching feet. Usually plenty of people around in like circumstances wanting to exchange information. Opposite the square is ST MARTIN IN THE FIELDS, a church. In the crypt, some nights, a charity organization gives free soup to those who need it. If you're really stropped for a meal, they'd probably help out in return for half an hour's work. But avoid troubling them if possible. Their time is taken up with alco's and mainliners.

MARKETS: PORTOBELLO ROAD (go to Notting Hill Gate and ask from there). Antiques one end, then fruit and vegetables beyond that. Most people stop there. Keep walking. The junk section beyond is where you find the bargains. Good place to pick up secondhand clothes and shoes if you need them. Don't take the first price. Never buy in a shop, even in the 'gear' shops. It's cheaper on the street. Best day, Saturday, or Friday morning if you just want to check the junk section. PETTICOAT LANE, Middlesex Street, E1: huge outdoor market every Sunday morning. OK and worth seeing but packed with tourists. For a better market continue up Bishopsgate to Brick Lane. Nearby are endless streets and alleys packed with junk of every description.

Sundays only. Closes at 1 p.m. Up in this area you'll be pleased to know you're in Jack the Ripper land. Check London Tourist Board for free guides to London's markets.

SOHO is, more or less, the area bounded by Charing Cross Road, Oxford Street, Wardour Street and Shaftesbury Avenue. It's London's square mile of sin and great to wander through. Fun parlours, strip joints, blue movies, porn shops, prostitutes ('Slinky black model. First floor'). 'Chinatown'.

THEATRES Sitting in the gods (the gallery) is usually the cheapest way to view London theatre, though some theatres have standing room for students. The National, the Aldwych and the Royal Court are three which consistently present good plays with good actors. At the Theatre Ticket Booth in Leicester Square you can buy 'leftover' theatre tickets at half price (plus a small service charge) *on the day of the performance*. The Booth is open from Monday through Saturday from 12 noon to 2 p.m. for matinée performances and from 2.30 p.m. until 6.30 p.m. for evening performances. Check *Time Out* for details of lunchtime and fringe theatre.

PUBS Plenty worth visiting, especially in the evening (5.30 p.m.–11.00 p.m. Mondays to Saturdays, 7.00 p.m.–10.30 p.m. Sundays). Try the *City Barge* at 27 Strand-on-the-Green, Chiswick, W4. *King's Head* at 48 Gerrard Street, W1. *Prospect of Whitby* at Wapping Steps, E1. *Sun in Splendour* at the top of Portobello Road, W11. *The Hansom Cab* at 84 Earls Court Road, W8, and *The Swan* at Lancaster Gate, W2. *Dirty Dick's* near Petticoat Lane, on the corner of Middlesex Street and Bishopsgate. *The Ship* in Wardour Street, W1. *George Inn* at 77 Borough High Street, SE1 (near London Bridge). Absolute musts are *Ye Olde Cheshire Cheese* and *Ye Olde Cock Tavern*, both in Fleet Street.

CINEMAS Unlimited choice of programme. Particularly try the *Paris Pullman* in Drayton Gardens, SW7. Best for double bills and limited distribution movies are *Phoenix* at East Finchley and the *Screen on Islington Green* (at guess where). West End prices are out of this world, £2·75–£3·50 for a decent seat. But most shows go out of the West End and into the suburbs within a month or so of release. Cheaper on Mondays.

RIVER TRIP A nice way of moving through London is by river launch. For instance, if you're in the centre of town and want to go to the Tower of London you can pick up a boat from Westminster Pier and get off at Tower Hill. Costs around £2·50, but it's more interesting than going by bus.

LONDON ZOO A great collection and well worth the visit – if you can afford it. One interesting feature is the Moonlight Hall where night and day are reversed so that you can see nocturnal animals and birds alert and awake in the middle of the day. For an extra charge you can see the excellent London Zoo Aquarium complete with man-eating sharks, stingrays and what-have-yous. At Regent's Park, NW1.

Meetings, discussions, ins and outs of what's happening, etc.
Several publications tell you all you need to know. The best single magazine for a complete rundown of everything happening in London in just about every field of interest is *Time Out*. Art, music, cinema (including every film on in London that week), demonstrations – you name it, *Time Out* has got it. Indispensable, especially if you're only in town a short time.

Other publications which really give value for money are Nicholson's *Students' London, Alternative London* and *Visitors London Guide Book. Students' London* includes city maps, Underground maps, bus routes, cheap eating, cheap sleeping, info on studying in London and lots more. *Alternative London,* edited by Georganne Downes, is far and away the best book ever written on how to live in London. Downes examines every aspect of living in the big city, starting with getting somewhere to live and giving hints on how to furnish it cheaply, then moving on through food cults, London markets, the mystical scene, sex, drugs, and on and on for a couple of hundred pages. If you can't cut your living costs by a third after studying this book (and this one!) you can count yourself stupid.

Project London was a dropout booklet distributed free in 1969. It was banned because of some of the frankly silly and dangerous crap it contained. It remains, though, one of the most fascinating documents ever written on how to survive in a big city for practically nothing. Richard Neville's book, *Playpower* (Paladin), reprints a lot of the booklet.

Robinson and Watkins Bookshop at 19 Cecil Court (off Charing Cross Road) for an amazing collection of tomes on mysticism and the occult.

Free newspapers: just pick them up out of the rubbish bins at any Underground station or in the central city streets. Latest editions. Wide range available.

Problems

If you strike hard times in London there are several organizations which will help you out. Two of the best are BIT who have vast amounts of information on the alternative society and RELEASE who are backed up by lawyers and doctors and who specialize in civil rights, what to do when you're busted for drugs, etc. Refer to BIT for general information, RELEASE for the heavy stuff. Don't bother either of them without good reason – they're busy. They both give information and help free and don't ask for money, but if you could spare something after they've helped you it would help them. Check any of the fringe publications for phone numbers and addresses.

Transport in London

There are two ways of moving around London by public transport. Bus or Underground. Prices depend on how far you want to go, of course, but an average trip on the Underground will cost about 50p. If you expect to be in town for only a short time and want to see as much as possible check with the London Tourist Board or at London Transport inquiry desks in main stations for details of special tickets. (For example, Travelcards at about £5 per week, allow you to travel on both bus and underground.)

Bicycles can be hired for around £14 per week (with about a £10 returnable deposit) from Kensington Student Centre, Kensington Church Street, London W8 (tel: 937 6089), and at a higher rate from Savile's, 99 Battersea Rise, London SW11 (tel: 228 4279) and Bell Street Bikes, 73 Bell Street, London NW1 (tel: 724 0456).

Student discounts

There is a tremendous amount to be gained from student discounts all over Great Britain and Ireland. Museums, galleries, concerts, cinemas, restaurants, bars, dry cleaning, cameras, tape recorders, typewriters, watches and clothing are just some of the places and items you can enter at a reduced rate, or buy at a discount, if you belong to the magic club. For details:

NATIONAL UNION OF STUDENTS, 302 Pentonville Road, N1 (tel: 278 3291).

Addresses

Main post office (for poste restante) at King Edward Street, London EC1.

American Express at 6 Haymarket, London SW1 (tel: 930 4411).

London Student Travel Bureau at 52 Grosvenor Gardens, London SW1W OAG (tel: 730 8111).

British Tourist Authority at 64 St James's Street, Piccadilly, London SW1 (tel: 499 9325).

London Tourist Board Information Centres at 26 Grosvenor Gardens, London SW1 (tel: 730 0791); Victoria Station Forecourt; Selfridges store (in Oxford Street), ground floor; Harrods store (Knightsbridge), fourth floor; at Heathrow Airport; and, in summer, at the Tower of London.

US Embassy at 24 Grosvenor Square, London W1 (tel: 499 9000).

Hitchers' Tips and Comments...

Here's some tips I'd like to pass on to fellow hitchers. For sleeping rough in London, a good place (if you can put up with drunks) is on the embankment near Westminster Bridge. The police move you on about 6 a.m., but it's still OK. Also, in the same area there are plenty of cheap cafés where you can eat well. Wimpy's ask a service charge on all meals, so if you don't have much bread, miss them. For other cheap meals try cafés around London docks. A tip for really cheap eating — mix Oxo cubes with hot water. *E. J. Major, Gunhild Close, London*

Sleeping rough in London: in Hyde Park you usually get moved on by police who sometimes have dogs. But you get away with it some nights. Don't go deep into the park because of muggers. Stay opposite the Hilton where it's lighter.

Check *Exchange and Mart* (in England) under 'travel' for things like ultra-cheap coach trips. Sometimes cheaper than hitching. *Dennis Chubb, Bletchley, England*

British pub meals are value for money but the rolls and sandwiches are not. Better to go to Woolworths or Littlewoods cafés.

Heading north from London up the M1 most hitchers take the tube to Hendon Central, but there are often 40 or more hitchers at this point. Alternative route: get tube to Watford Junction then take A412 and A405 to M1. *Dave Martill, Leicester, England*

For those in London wanting to hitch west along the Oxford–Cheltenham route, take the Underground to Hanger Lane. I find this better than at other places (White City, for example). Hold up a sign. You often get lifts from truck drivers going the whole way. *Patrick Hine, Oxford, England*

It's possible to hitch across the English Channel. Trucks crossing by ferry are allowed to carry a free passenger. Approach truck drivers before they buy their ticket and maybe they'll take you aboard. *Peter Brennan, Australia*

For rough sleeping in London, try the steps of St Peter's Church near Victoria Station. Usually lots of other people there. *Liss Arntsen, Bodo, Norway*

In the UK night-hitching is generally slow except on the A1 which has lit roundabouts every few miles and is truly hitchable 24 hours a day. *Doug Bissell, 'The Clydeside Rebel', Glasgow, Scotland*

Don't go on ferry to Orkney Islands. Ask fishermen for a lift, or offer them a small sum to take you aboard as a passenger. *Patrick Fitzgerald, South Lopham, England*

The best place to sleep rough in London must be Hampstead Heath. Besides the beautiful scenic view over the city, there are bathing ponds where you can take a morning dip. *Pete the Freak, London*

To get out of London to the west, catch a tube to Gunnersbury, turn left outside station and hitch from South Circular/North Circular/M4 junction with sign. I usually wait 15–30 minutes for lifts straight to Wales. *Evan M. Jones, Cardiff, Wales*

Don't sleep in Kensington Palace Gardens, London. Royalty, including the Prince of Wales, live in the palace and the police don't like dossers. The copper who kicked me out at 4 a.m. at least told me where Hyde Park is (next door). *Alan Barlow, Cheadle, UK*

Wales

population	2,700,000
size	8000 square miles
capital	Cardiff, population 260,000
government	Principality
religion	Protestant
language	Welsh and English
currency	Same as England

Best way into Wales is across the tremendous **Severn Bridge** just outside Bristol. If you continue on to **Monmouth** and then turn west along the A40 to **Abergavenny** where you meet up with the A465, you can travel through some of the strangest country in the British Isles. Luxurious green valleys, scarred by black cuts of coal mines – villages which from the distance seem to be gentle and fairytale-like turn out to be places of cold brick coated with the black dust of the mines.

Cardiff, down on the coast, is the capital of the country. Sights to see include the National Museum of Wales, the Welsh Folk Museum (this is at St Fagan's, four miles out of town) where typically Welsh buildings have been reconstructed to give the visitor an idea of the rural architecture of the country, and Cardiff Castle. Cardiff Castle is just one of more than 150 in Wales. The Welsh Tourist Office claim that their country has more castles per square mile than any other country in Europe.

Dylan Thomas fans will want to drop in on the village of

Laugharne which is on a side road off the A49 just outside
Carmarthen. The poet lived a good deal of his life in the village
and is buried there.

St David's, on the A487, has the dubious distinction of being the
smallest city in the British Isles. Its population of 1650 supports a
cathedral and the ruins of a bishop's palace.

On the river **Teifi**, which reaches the sea at **Cardigan**, you might
be lucky enough to spot a fisherman in a coracle. These
wicker-basket boats are the earliest form of water transport known
to man except for the log.

Heading north along the coast you reach **Aberystwyth**, an
important university town, while farther north again is **Harlech**
with its famous castle. North again, takes you to another castle
town, this time **Caernarvon**, traditional site of the investiture of
the Prince of Wales. It happened to Prince Charles in the summer
of 1969 with due pomp and ceremony. Certain strata of the Welsh
population – those interested in breaking ties with England – were
not impressed. Hitchers wanting more information on that subject
can probably find it amongst the students at Aberystwyth.

Just outside **Bangor**, which has a Museum of Welsh Antiquities,
is a village with only one claim to fame. It's called:
Llanfairpwllgwyngyllgogerychwyrndrobwllllantysiliogogogoch.
The main street isn't as long as the name. For wanderers new to
Wales, the word is a fair introduction to the Welsh language.

Heading back towards England along the A55, there's at least
one more worthwhile stop and that's at **Conway** which is a pleasant
enough town with yet another famous castle. The A5 passes
through beautiful Snowdonia National Park.

Scotland

population	5,200,000
size	30,414 square miles
capital	Edinburgh, population 453,000
government	Constitutional monarchy
religion	Church of Scotland
language	English; Gaelic is spoken in the Western Isles
currency	Same currency as England, although the three Scottish banks also issue their own banknotes. Both

English and Scottish notes are accepted throughout Scotland

Scotland is best approached by the A68 where the border is crossed at **Carter Bar** (1300 feet up). The southern upland towns of **Jedburgh**, **Melrose**, **Kelso** (all with ruined abbeys), **Hawick**, **Selkirk** and **Galashiels** (home of Sir Walter Scott) are well worth seeing.

Alternatively, if you are coming from Newcastle, take the A1 along the coast, but this is generally slower for hitching although picturesque.

You will probably be heading for **Edinburgh**, well worth a few days' stay as one of the most beautiful cities in Europe. The best time to visit is late August when the famous Festival is in full swing and the city is literally bursting with life. Accommodation can be a problem then, although there are plenty of parks in the city centre where sleeping rough should be possible (but don't try Calton Hill or Princes Street Gardens as you are liable to get hassled).

North of Edinburgh, after crossing the big Forth Road Bridge, you can join up with the M90 to Perth then the A85 which will take you through to **Dundee**. The city is nothing spectacular, but nearby, at a place called **Glamis**, is one of the better castles in Scotland.

Scotland is a place where you can enjoy the countryside – particularly the famous Highlands. In these heather-covered hills you will recognize the colours of the traditional tartans and you will notice a sense of spaciousness which you can't find elsewhere in the British Isles. Scotland is half the size of England, but with only one-tenth the population.

To get the full flavour of this Highland Scotland, probably the best route you can take is north from Dundee up through **Spittal of Glenshee** and **Devil's Elbow** to **Braemar**, which is the big centre for the Royal Highland Gathering, with caber-tossing and hammer-throwing. This takes place on the first Saturday in September each year. Just a little farther on is **Balmoral Castle**, still used by the British Royal Family for summer holidays. The Dee River, which runs through the Royal Estate, is well stocked with trout if you care to indulge in a little high-class poaching. Follow the river down to the sea and you come to **Aberdeen**, the self-proclaimed oil capital of Europe. Accommodation is expensive as a result, so try and stay out of town, but it is worth a visit nonetheless. Despite the oil wealth, the city has escaped too much development and thanks to the granite buildings looks remarkably clean.

Farther north at **Huntly** you can join up with the A96 which curves around the coast towards **Inverness**, a pleasant town with a cathedral and a museum containing relics of the Jacobites. It's known as the Highland Capital and sits at the northern end of **Loch Ness**, home of the monster which *everyone* in Scotland has seen except the scientists. Just outside Inverness is **Culloden**, site of the famous battle of 1746 when Bonnie Prince Charlie's Jacobites were defeated by the Hanoverians. You can visit a small museum housed in a contemporary farm dwelling, and see the burial mounds of the various clans. If you make it on a drizzly day (you probably will), you'll get a real feeling of how the moor must have been on the day of the battle.

From Inverness, if time is short, the A9 south has recently been upgraded and is excellent for hitching. It takes you through the **Spey Valley** and the famous resort of **Aviemore**, then farther south **Pitlochry** and **Perth**.

But if you have the time, go north again and you're heading for **John o' Groats**, the northern counterpart of England's Land's End. The towns of **Wick** and **Thurso** are interesting and quite different from towns in the south.

Orkneys and **Shetland** From Scrabster by Thurso you can catch the ferry to **Stromness** and the Orkney Isles, rugged, wild and beautiful, with no trees. The islands abound with prehistoric and Viking ruins, the most notable being the preserved Neolithic village at **Skara Brae**.

To get to the Shetland Isles, Britain's northernmost land, you have to take the ferry from Aberdeen, a longish trip. But it is worth it when you get there – buy some of their unique knitwear!

If you take the western route back south, you'll be travelling through some of the loneliest country outside northern Scandinavia. It's the real moor country with peat bogs and little else. I remember passing through one 'town' which consisted of a signpost, one house, one hotel, and then another signpost. How the two establishments supported each other is a difficult question to answer. The whole area is beautiful if you enjoy a little loneliness. Be warned that the hitching can get really bad between **Tongue** and **Ullapool**.

South of Ullapool and you're in the land of mountains and lochs

– the best part of the Western Highlands. See the tropical gardens (yes, tropical!) at **Inverewe** and then continue through **Gairloch** and alongside **Loch Maree**, perhaps the loveliest of all the lochs. **Skye** and **Hebrides** At **Kyle of Lochalsh** or **Mallaig** you can catch the ferry to Skye, the most beautiful of all the Scottish isles. The farther from the mainland you go, the more remote and beautiful the island becomes. If you feel really adventurous, cross over to the Outer Hebrides, wild, wild islands facing the Atlantic. The Scottish isles are strictly, almost fiercely, religious, so nothing at all moves on a Sunday – and I mean nothing. No trains, buses or cars, and even walking is frowned upon, so do all your travelling by Saturday. Back on the mainland, the road south continues through uninterrupted and outstanding scenery until you come to **Fort William** which is on Loch Linnhe and backed by the 4406-foot Ben Nevis Mountain. Twenty miles farther south again and you're at **Glencoe**, scene of the massacre of 1692.

Down the A82 and A84, through a whole lot of nice country and you arrive in **Stirling**, historically one of the most important cities in Scotland. Have a look at Stirling Castle, ex-home of the Royal Mint, and a great visit. A couple of miles north are the ruins of **Cambuskenneth Abbey**, while south is **Bannockburn** where Robert the Bruce defeated King Edward in 1314.

The next city you come to is **Glasgow** which is worth a day to look over the Art Gallery, Museum of Transport, and the thirteenth-century cathedral. Also have a look at Provand's Lordship, the oldest house in the city, dating from 1471. With two universities (Watt, of steam-engine fame, attended Glasgow University) the city is a good place to meet people.

South of Glasgow on the A77, is **Ayr**, and a couple of miles outside is **Alloway**, birthplace of Scotland's favourite poet, Robbie Burns. The cottage in which he was born in 1759 is now a completely restored monument. Inside you can see original manuscripts, letters, and objects associated with Burns.

Stranraer is where you can jump a ferry for Northern Ireland (see **Northern Ireland**). East along the A75 and you come to **Castle Douglas** with the huge Threave Castle nearby. Then you come to **Dumfries** where Burns died in 1796 and is buried. Then, just before you cross back into England, you come to **Gretna Green**, once famous around the world as the place where young people ran off to get married.

★**Highland Games** Main places for Highland Games are Fort William, Dunoon, Crieff, Glenfinnan, Edinburgh, Aboyne and Braemar, although almost every town in the Highlands will have its own games meeting. Generally they are held in July, August and September and feature the famous caber toss as well as traditional dancing and music. Ask the Scottish Tourist Board for dates.

★**Edinburgh Festival** The famous International Festival of Music and Drama is held every year in the second half of August and the first week of September.

Edinburgh: where to sleep

A bed in Edinburgh costs from around £2·60 at the youth hostels (£3 in July/August) to about £7 at a boarding house or in a cheap hotel. Breakfast is normally included. Accommodation is often difficult to find in August, so try to book well in advance.

Youth Hostels, 7 Bruntsfield Crescent, Edinburgh 10 (tel: 447 2994), and 18 Eglinton Crescent, Edinburgh 12 (tel: 337 1120).

YMCA, 14 South St Andrew Street (tel: 556 4304). Men and women.

YWCA, 4 Randolph Place (tel: 225 1875). Women only. Also at 2 Randolph Crescent (tel: 226 3842).

Pollock Halls, 18 Holyrood Park Road (tel: 667 1971). Student residence with 1500 beds; open to non-students July–September.

Also:

Carlyle Hall, East Suffolk Road. Student residence with 265 beds, open to non-students July–September.

Edinburgh is full of guest houses and bed-and-breakfasts. The best places to try are Mayfield Road (A7 road to south) and Gilmore Place (south-west of city centre).

For help in finding a cheap place try the Edinburgh Tourist Information and Accommodation Service at 5 Waverley Bridge (tel: 225 8821). For sleeping rough, take a bus out to Holyrood Park.

Edinburgh: where to eat

Two pounds should handle any hunger problems. And remember, as in London, if you're ever really broke, you can survive very well (survive, though scarcely thrive) on fish 'n' chips.

The YWCA and YMCA both serve well-priced meals. (Addresses in **Where to sleep**.) If you like to make lunch your main meal of the day you can have good feeds at any number of pubs and small restaurants for around £2. Try:

Milnes Bar at 35 Hanover Street.

Students' Refectory at 9 Chambers Street. Open July through October. Dinner served (very cheap) 5–7 p.m.

Wayfarer Café at Clerk Street. Good cheap food.

Bombay Tandoori Restaurant at 14a Nicolson Street, 10 per cent student reduction.

Lothian Restaurant at 16 Drummond Street. Cheap curry meals.

Edinburgh: what to see and do

THE CASTLE The huge military complex which dominates Edinburgh. Entrance charge. Good place for overall view of what is a beautiful city.

JOHN KNOX'S HOUSE at the foot of High Street. Entrance charge. Closed on Sundays.

NATIONAL GALLERY OF SCOTLAND on the Mound. No entrance fee. Some good stuff.

THE OLD TOWN This is the area between the castle rock and Holyrood House. It's the old quarter of Edinburgh which settled itself around the protective castle. Holyrood House was the home of several Scottish sovereigns, including Mary Queen of Scots. You can still see the room where Rizzio, her Italian secretary (and possibly, lover) was murdered in front of her eyes in 1566.

DEACON BRODIE'S TAVERN at the corner of Bank and High streets is a little touristy, but you can meet some good types there. Deacon Brodie was the evil man who inspired R. L. Stevenson to write *Dr Jekyll and Mr Hyde*. Prices OK.

THE TRAVERSE THEATRE CLUB is a sort of pub-cum-theatre-cum-art-gallery. Membership fee. Worth visiting to meet people and for general good talk.

BOBBY McGHEE at 92 Rose Street, North Lane. Live music. Nice people.

MUSEUM OF CHILDHOOD at 38 High Street. Four floors devoted to all the quaint paraphernalia of childhood. Strangely evocative. Worth a visit if you're in the right mood. Entrance fee.

ALTERNATIVE EDINBURGH If you're going to be in town for an extended stay you'll get some good tips on breadline living if you buy *Alternative Edinburgh* published by the University Student Publications Board, 1 Buccleuch Place, Edinburgh. It has chapters on eating, sleeping, seeing Edinburgh for nothing, etc.

Transport in Edinburgh
The bus service is the main means of public transport. It will take you everywhere.

Addresses

Main post office (for poste restante) at corner of Waterloo Place and North Bridge.

American Express at 139 Princes Street (tel: 225 7881).

Edinburgh University Students' Association at Bristo Square (tel: 667 0214).

Scottish Tourist Board at 23 Ravelston Terrace, Edinburgh 4 (tel: 332 2433). Postal and phone inquiries only.

City of Edinburgh Tourist Information Centre at Waverley Bridge, by the station (tel: 226 6591 for info; 225 8821 for accommodation).

US Consulate at 3 Regent Terrace (tel: 556 8315).

Hitchers' Tips and Comments . . .

When hitching in Scotland, before leaving the country make sure you trade all your Scottish pounds for English pounds.

Lots of people in England – especially in the south – won't
touch them, and on the Continent they don't want to know. I
only had twenty Scottish pounds left once in Germany, and I
starved for two days before I found a bank that would change
them. *Alan, Brockville, Canada*

*You can have similar troubles, particularly in small banks,
with Gibraltar pounds, Maltese pounds, Australian dollars,
most Middle Eastern, North African and all Communist
currencies. K.W.*

A visit to Skye is a good way to close the Knoydart gap on the
west coast. Sail from Mallaig to Armadale in south-west Skye,
proceed to Kyleakin and cross by ferry to mainland Kyle of
Lochalsh. *Moyna Gardner, Glasgow, Scotland*

Northern Ireland

population	1,500,000
size	5452 square miles
capital	Belfast, population 425,000
government	Constitutional monarchy
religion	Protestant and Roman Catholic
language	English
currency	Same as England

Crossing to Northern Ireland is done cheapest by jumping the
ferry in **Stranraer** (Scotland) and crossing to **Larne** which is just a
few miles north of Belfast. Other routes are from Liverpool
(England) to Belfast; and Cairnryan (Scotland) to Belfast.
   In the six counties of Northern Ireland (known also as Ulster)
the main stopping points are the capital, Belfast, the Giant's
Causeway and the ancient city of Londonderry.
   Belfast is a city of markets. Smithfield is the big one. It's open
every weekday and sells whatever you want to buy. Chichester
Street, May Street and Oxford Street are three others, but they
mostly sell food. Friday is the day at May Street and Chichester
Street when they hold the junk market, somewhat reminiscent of
London's Portobello Road, but not as touristy.
   Buildings worth looking over include City Hall and Queens
University. The Museum and Art Gallery are OK to wander

through, but a better display is at the Ulster Folk Museum which gives you a good idea of what Irish life was like in centuries past. It's located eight miles from Belfast on the A2 Belfast–Bangor road and is built along the same lines as the big open-air museum at Skansen in Sweden. (See **Scandinavia, Finland and Iceland**.) While you're out that way you can see **Stormont**, until 1972 the seat of the Irish government.

Carrickfergus, on the coast between Belfast and Larne, is a lobster-fishing port and the site of a big Norman castle. Gory story attached to the castle tells that during a siege, which came as the result of a war with Scotland, the garrison was so badly starved that they ate thirty Scottish prisoners. These days Carrickfergusians prefer seafood.

You reach the **Giant's Causeway** via the A2, following it up through Larne and **Ballycastle**. The causeway is one of *the* natural wonders of the world. It's a weird formation of basalt rock which was caused by volcanic action millions of years ago. At least that's how scientists tell it. The legendary explanation of the creation of the causeway makes more sense. It tells that a gigantic Irishman, Finn MacCool, heard of a Scottish giant Finn Gall and decided to fight him to find out who was the better man. So he built the causeway and walked over to Scotland. He found Gall's house and entered. He found Mrs Gall sewing and saw a huge body sleeping on a bed. He asked if it was her husband and she said her husband was out and that the sleeping figure was her two-year-old son – at which MacCool lost his cool and hurtled back to Ireland scared out of his wits at the thought of how big Finn Gall must be. They say he ripped up the causeway as he returned so that Gall couldn't come over and get him. And that explains why there's so little of it left.

Londonderry, forty-odd miles farther on from the causeway, is the second city of Northern Ireland and the one most laden with history. It was founded with the building of an abbey in AD 540 and has been a magnet for strife ever since. Before the year 1200 it had been attacked by Danes and Normans and burned seven times. In 1556 it was the headquarters of a rebellion and destroyed by a huge explosion from the city ammunition magazines. In 1608 it was burned again. And then in 1689 a terrible siege which lasted 105 days resulted in the death of 7000 defenders. The city walls, which saw much of this, date from the 1600s and (incredibly!) are preserved intact. At St Columb's Cathedral you can see relics of the great siege, and the modern Guild Hall contains other objects related to the city's past.

Those are the three main places to visit in Northern Ireland, but almost anywhere you go you run into pockets of Irish history, mostly so old or so bloody that now there is scarely anything left to see.

Warning! Travelling in this country could be dangerous if you loudmouth your political views. If you remember you are a visitor, you should be OK.

Hitchers' Tips and Comments...

Travelling in the North isn't that much more dangerous than elsewhere in Europe so long as you don't express strong views on the situation. Admittedly, a backpack can cause a hassle. Try to unload it somewhere before going into Belfast centre. You get searched going through security barriers surrounding the centre and also going into most stores. Also, I wouldn't recommend sleeping out in Ulster but, if you must, avoid the cities, towns and sensitive border areas. *Steve Ireland, Belfast, N. Ireland*

Ninety per cent of Ulster is very safe and normal – and beautiful. Also, Ulster people are far more interested in you as a traveller than are their southern counterparts. Before setting out, read the papers and listen to the news. Find out the current trouble spots and avoid them. *Helen Snively, Dublin, Ireland*

If you're in Newcastle, try the 'Beverly' bed and breakfast at 72 Tollymore Road (tel: 03967 22018). I thought it was a fantastic deal. *Bodgie, Melbourne, Australia*

Ireland (Eire)

population	3,443,405
size	27,137 square miles
capital	Dublin, population 525,882

government	Parliamentary democracy
religion	Predominantly Roman Catholic
language	English and Irish
currency	*Irish pound* One *IR£* equals 100 *pence*. Coins of ½, 1, 2, 5, 10 and 50p. Notes of IR£1, 5, 10, 20, 50, 100

For me, the Republic of Ireland is more interesting than the North. The people are more relaxed and perhaps that is why the countryside seems more beautiful. And there's much more to see. To get to the South, you can cross over from the North with scarcely any formalities. Or, if you're crossing over from England, the ferry routes are as follows: Liverpool (England) to Dublin, Holyhead (Wales) to Dun Laoghaire, Fishguard (Wales) to Rosslare, Holyhead (Wales) to Dublin, Pembroke (Wales) to Rosslare.

The Irish have a saying, 'Everyone is an Irishman and those that ain't are wishin' that they were.' If you check down the list of the top twenty names in Ireland (see page 125), you'll see how many of us *do* have Irish blood in the family. This strange fact derives from the exodus of the Irish from their country to escape the great famine of the early 1800s and the desolation which followed it. In less than eighty years the population dropped from eight to four million, and many of those four million expatriates went to America and the British colonies and took with them not only their family names but also the names of their towns which have become household words in the English language. Limerick, Killarney, Tipperary, Blarney, Galway, Cork – and plenty of others.

Tiny **Kilkenny** (population 9500) is known as the capital of medieval Ireland. See the beautiful thirteenth-century castle with its fine collection of manuscripts. The old castle stables house the Kilkenny Design Workshops which aren't open to the public, but there is a permanent exhibition and shop where you can see the best Ireland has to offer in textiles, silver, ceramics and glass. St Canice's Cathedral and the Dominican church also date from the thirteenth century. Towards the end of August, Kilkenny stages an Arts Week featuring concerts, lunchtime recitals, poetry readings and exhibitions. Well worth a visit if you are in the area and so inclined.

The **Dunmore Cave**, seven miles from Kilkenny on the Castlecomer road, is a fascinating example of a natural cavern formed in limestone. In AD 928, 1000 people who had hidden in the cave were slaughtered by the Vikings. The cave is fitted with special lighting and viewing galleries.

Cashel, between Kilkenny and Tipperary, is, after **Tara**, which is six miles south of Navan in County Meath, the most important historical site in Southern Ireland. Tara, in ancient times, was the capital of Ireland and the seat of the Irish kings. However, little remains to be seen today and it's scarcely worth the visit unless you're an archaeology or history crank. At Cashel, though, there is plenty to see. It's a town of 2500 people dominated by the dramatic Rock of Cashel, a 200-foot-high outcrop of limestone crowned by ruins. The town was the seat of the Munster kings from AD 370 to AD 1101 and also a place where St Patrick preached. It's said that it was in Cashel that he used the shamrock as an illustration of the doctrine of the Trinity, thus establishing for ever the national symbol of Ireland. On the rock you can see a round tower dating from the twelfth century, the cathedral, the hall of the Vicars Choral, and King Cormac's Chapel. (A story tells that the first cathedral on the site was burned down in 1495 by the Earl of Kildare. The earl later apologized and explained to Henry VII that he'd done so because he'd thought the archbishop was inside.)

Cork is the third city of Ireland and perhaps one of her prettiest. Best things to see are the streets around the quays (it's a riverside city), and Christ the King Church, an outstanding piece of modern architecture designed by an American, Barry Byrne of Chicago. The School of Art contains good examples of modern Irish painting. If you're musically minded, 20p allows you to play a tune on the historic bells of Shandon Steeple in St Anne's Church.

Five miles out of Cork is **Blarney**, a tiny village of less than 1200 people. The town boasts a fine old castle, and on the outside wall of the highest tower is the world-famous Blarney Stone. £1·20 buys you the privilege of performing a contortionist act to kiss the stone and, the deed being done, you are blessed for ever with 'the gift of the gab'.

Wandering up through Killarney, by **Dingle Bay** to **Tralee** you reach the village of **Adare** (eleven miles south of Limerick). The exact origins of Adare are unknown but it has survived, at least, since the reign of Henry II, when it was occupied by the Anglo-Normans. Even so, its population is still only 550. The point about Adare is that it's a perfect place to rest up a day or two, providing you like peace and quiet. Many travellers claim the

village is Ireland's prettiest. Sights to see in and around Adare
include the ruins of the Trinitarian Abbey and the Augustinian
Priory; the Franciscan Friary and Desmond Castle which dates
from the thirteenth century. If you can hustle up some tackle, try
the first-rate brown trout fishing on the Maigue River.

The city of **Limerick** is more famous for the making of fine lace
than the invention of dirty verse. See King John's Castle (one of
the castle's five towers is used twice weekly during the summer
months as the setting for evenings of Irish entertainment) and St
John's Cathedral. The 280-foot spire is the highest in Ireland. In
the old city Exchange (only the front wall remains) there was a
pedestal known as the 'Nail' where merchants paid their debts –
from which came the expression 'paying on the nail'. The nail in
question can be seen at the Limerick Museum.

Galway, a city of 37,835, sitting on the famous bay of the same
name, is a pleasant place with a long history. The Church of St
Nicholas dating from 1320 is said to have been visited by
Columbus on his way out to the Americas. Lynch's castle dates
from the same year and was the mansion of a city judge, part of
whose story is told in a skull and crossbone memorial erected in
the Old Jail: 'This memorial of the stern and unbending justice of
the chief magistrate of this City, James Lynch Fitzstephen, elected
mayor AD 1493, who condemned and executed his own guilty son,
Walter, on this spot.'

Galway, once described as the most Irish of all Irish cities, is a
good place to catch Gaelic sports. The Pearse Stadium is where
you can see Hurling or Gaelic Football. Feis Ceol an Iarthair – a
festival of Irish music, dance and drama with competitions for
various age groups – is held annually in late October/November.
And if you're in town between June and October, don't miss the
salmon at Salmon Weir Bridge, over the river Corrib. Near
Galway there is **Gort** where you can visit the house of Lady
Gregory who was a great friend of W. B. Yeats, Shaw, Synge and
O'Casey. There is still a beech tree in the grounds into which they
all carved their initials.

From Galway you can hop a ferry or boat to the lovely **Aran
Islands**, some of the most isolated in the world, and home of the
famous Aran sweaters. These beautiful islands are where John
Millington Synge went when he wanted to find his Irish 'roots',
which provided the inspiration for his magnificent play, *Playboy of
the Western World*.

From Galway head north through beautiful **Connemara** – even the name sounds beautiful – to Ireland's wild and wonderful west, **County Mayo**. Mayo is the largest of Ireland's counties and the least populated. You can wander for hours without seeing another human being. The town of **Westport** is a great place to use as a base. From here you can reach lovely **Achill Island** off the west coast where the mighty Atlantic breaks on the shore. The locals will tell you that the next parish west is New York.

From Westport head north to the village of **Killala**, where the French invasion force that landed during the Napoleonic Wars inspired Thomas Flanaghan's bestseller, *The Year of the French*.

North again takes you through **Ballina** and the Ox Mountains to **Sligo** – Yeats country. Ireland's greatest poet spent much of his life here and he is buried in **Drumcliff** churchyard under his beloved **Ben Bulben** mountain. The area offers miles of lovely scenery: try **Rosses Point** and **Mullaghmore** on Donegal Bay as well as the lovely green **Dartry Mountains**.

North yet again and you reach **Donegal** with its marvellous **Blue Stack** mountains and rugged scenery. The coastline around **Dungloe** and **Ardara** is particularly spectacular.

Don't ignore Ireland's Midlands. The lakes and the rolling green fields are as peaceful as you'll find anywhere. Try following the banks of the **River Shannon** (at over 300 miles the longest in these islands) along the N4 and N6 through **Athlone**. Boat hitching is possible. Visit the Shannon loughs like **Lough Ree** or **Lough Derg**.

★**Horse-drawn caravan travelling** Hitchers with a little spare time might be interested in this idea which has become popular – hiring a four-berth caravan with horse and covering a leisurely 10 miles a day. Cost ranges from £100–£300 a week – which split four ways isn't too bad. As you can do your own cooking and sleep by a campfire or in the caravan, it works out around the same as hitching and sleeping in hostels. Five people in the caravan works out a fraction cheaper per head. With food and sightseeing you could expect to pay out £60–£70 per person, per week. Four addresses to contact concerning the hire of caravans are:

Blarney Romany Caravans, Blarney, Co. Cork (tel: (021) 85700).

Ocean Breeze Horse Caravans, Harbour View, Kilbrittain, Co. Cork (tel: (023) 49731/49626).

Slattery's Horse-drawn Caravans, Slattery's Travel Agency, Tralee, Co. Kerry (tel: (066) 21722).

Dieter Clissmann Horse-drawn Caravans, Carrigmore, Wicklow (tel: (0404) 8188).

★**Trace your ancestors** If you think your family is Irish and you want to trace some relatives or find out more about your ancestors, then your visit to Ireland is the ideal time to do it. The Irish Tourist Board will send you a free pamphlet on the subject if you write to them but, in the meantime, here are some basic facts you should attempt to find out before you leave home: (*a*) the full name of your emigrant ancestor; (*b*) any background information as to his trade or social standing; (*c*) his religion; (*d*) the name of the county and town from which he came. With that information you have a good chance of finding out something about your family.

Just in case you're wondering if you *do* have Irish ancestors, here are the top twenty surnames in Ireland listed in order of frequency of occurrence:

Murphy	O'Brien	Reilly	Kennedy
Kelly	Byrne	Doyle	Lynch
Sullivan	Ryan	McCarthy	Murray
Walsh	Connor	Gallagher	Quinn
Smith	O'Neill	Doherty	Stewart

Dublin: where to sleep

Hostels and student residences are cheapest, of course. Hotels and guest houses usually cost from £8 upwards, sometimes including breakfast. Below is a list of hostel accommodation. Halls of residence are more expensive than hostels but accommodation is good. Double rooms about £10, including breakfast.

Youth Hostel at 39 Mountjoy Square, Dublin 1 (tel: 74 57 34). Open from 1 April to 30 September.

Youth Hostel at 78 Morehampton Road, Donnybrook, Dublin 4 (tel: 68 03 25). Open all year.

YWCA at Radcliff Hall, St John's Road, Sandymount, Dublin 4. Open all year (tel: 69 45 21).

These are some bed and breakfast places where the all-in price starts around £7:

Mrs A. Haire at 73 Dollymount Park, Clontarf, Dublin 3 (tel: 33 36 95).

Mrs M. Dunwoody, Eldar at 19 Copeland Avenue, Clontarf, Dublin 3 (tel: 33 90 91).

Mrs B. Creagh, St Aidan's at 150 Clonliffe Road, Clontarf, Dublin 3 (tel: 37 67 50).

Mrs J. Murnane at 56 Castle Avenue, Clontarf, Dublin 3 (tel: 33 64 02).

Mrs E. Byrne-Pool, Sea Front at 278 Clontarf Road, Dublin 3 (tel: 33 61 18).

Mrs M. McDonnell, Donnybrook, 3 Sandford Ave (off Marlboro' Road), Dublin 4 (tel: 97 16 39).

Mrs D. Abbott-Murphy, Sandymount, 14 Sandymount Castle Park (off Gilford Road), Dublin 4 (tel: 69 84 13).

Mrs P. McColgan, 40 Belgrave Square, Rathmines, Dublin 6 (tel: 97 56 19).

For full information on all accommodation see the people at the Irish Student Travel Service, 7 Anglesea Street, Dublin 2 (tel: 77 81 17), or contact Dublin Tourism at 14 Upper O'Connell Street, Dublin 1 (tel: 74 77 33).

For sleeping out try around Phoenix Park and the racecourse. Fair amount of police around, as the park is also the residence of the President of Ireland. But it spreads over 1700 acres, so you should find a spot OK.

Dublin: where to eat

You can make a good meal in Dublin town for around the £3·00 mark – and remember that like the British, the Irish have a big thing about fish 'n' chips. You can gorge yourself stupid on them for about £1·50.

University Restaurant at Earlsfort Terrace. Great lunches and very cheap. Closed August.

The Buttery Snack area at Trinity College. A student haunt. Cheap.

Stag's Head at 1 Dame Court. Lunch is served between 12 and 2. It's big, it's hot, and it's about £2. Good place for main meal of the day.

Bewleys Cafés Ltd at 10–12 Westmorland Street, 78–79 Grafton Street and 12–13 Sth Great Georges Street.

Casper and Giumbinis, Wicklow Street. **Murphy Doodles,** 18 Suffolk Street. **Murphs** at 99 Lower Baggot Street and 21 Bachelor's Walk.

The Coffee Inn at 6 South Anne Street.

Many hotels in Ireland and the British Isles offer counter-lunches and dinners. Pub lunches usually cost from about £1·75 and are filling enough to count as the main meal of the day.

Dublin: what to see and do

DUBLIN CASTLE in Castle Street. Thirteenth century. Hangout of the English until they were removed (ask in any pub for details of the removal). Entrance charge to see the *State Apartments,* but the *Heraldic Museum* is free. *City Hall* adjoins the castle.

THE GENERAL POST OFFICE in O'Connell Street was the headquarters of the Irish Volunteers during the insurrection of 1916. It was destroyed during the fighting but is now rebuilt.

THE CUSTOM HOUSE at Custom House Quay is the city's finest piece of architecture. Destroyed during the War of Independence, but restored to its former Georgian elegance.

GUINNESS BREWERY at St James Gate is the home of the famous 'drop'. You're welcome to visit between 10 a.m. and 3 p.m. Monday to Friday to see a film of its operation – and sample the product. See the Brewery Museum.

THE NATIONAL MUSEUM at Kildare Street. Fine collection of Irish antiquities. Closed Mondays.

THE HUGH LANE MUNICIPAL GALLERY OF MODERN ART at Parnell Square. Nice collection of modern Irish works. Admission free.

NATIONAL GALLERY at Merrion Square West. Collection of old masters. Admission free.

TRINITY COLLEGE LIBRARY at Trinity College Green contains over two and a half million volumes, plus manuscripts. Don't miss *The Book of Kells*, considered one of the world's most beautiful illuminated manuscripts. No charge.

THE JOYCEAN MUSEUM at Martello Tower houses manuscripts, photographs, etc., relating to Ireland's greatest writer. Take a number 8 bus from O'Connell Bridge and get off at Sandycove. Costs about 60p each way, 40p admission charge, less with a student card.

ST MICHAN'S CHURCH in Church Street offers a somewhat unique sight. In the vaults are bodies which have lain for centuries without decay. You can see these and, if you want, shake hands with a gentleman known as the 'crusader'. It will cost you 80p for the privilege. (Vaults closed on Sundays.)

ST PATRICK'S CATHEDRAL in St Patrick's Street. Fine old building dating back to the twelfth century. Jonathan Swift (*Gulliver's Travels*) was Dean of St Patrick's from 1713 to 1745. Fans can see his tomb.

You can spend a very pleasant day wandering in PHOENIX PARK. (Plus, as I've said in **Where to sleep**, you can find some good places to kip down.) You can watch horse-racing at the racecourse for free if you can find a way in, for over £2 if you're rich enough to pay. (Admission charge is halved for holders of student cards.) You can visit the zoo, one of the oldest in Europe. With a bit of luck you might find some Gaelic football. With extra luck you'll find plenty of the opposite sex wandering around. Especially Saturday afternoons and Sundays.

MOORE STREET MARKET Best place in Dublin to get an idea of what the Irish are really like. Great stuff and free. Saturday morning is best.

KILMAINHAM JAIL If you're interested in modern Irish history take buses 21, 23, 78 or 79 out to Kilmainham on a Sunday afternoon or between 10 a.m.–12 noon and 2.30 p.m.–4 p.m. on Wednesdays. You get a guided tour through the cradle of the modern Irish revolutionary spirit. It was here that those who signed the proclamation of the Easter Week Rising of 1916 were executed. The last political prisoner to be released from the jail (in 1924) was Eamon de Valera, the late President of Ireland.

DAVY BYRNE'S PUB at 21 Duke Street was one of James Joyce's haunts. Now a good place to meet young Dubliners.

THE BRAZEN HEAD, oldest pub in Dublin. Close to Christchurch Cathedral. Traditional folk groups meet regularly.

MULLIGAN'S in Poolbeg Street is a good rough pub in the Irish tradition. O'DONOGHUE's at 15 Merrion Row is a place where would-be-if-they-could-be folk groups meet to try themselves on the customers.

THE BAGGOT INN at Baggot Street features live entertainment every night (reasonable entrance charge) and LINCOLN'S INN at 18 Lincoln Place is where the Trinity College mob drink and talk.

Transport in Dublin

Bus fares are cheap, so don't be afraid to use the excellent system. There's a ticket called the Youth and Educational Travel Concession ticket which allows unlimited travel on all Dublin buses and suburban trains between Balbriggan and Greystones from April to September. It is one of the best deals in Europe, but technically you're supposed to be engaged on an educational or cultural project. (Hitch-hiking is highly educational and an excellent way of getting yer culture. After all, you're writing a book, aren't you?) Apply to the Youth and Educational Executive (at the Dublin Tourism office), 14 Upper O'Connell Street, Dublin 1. If you're feeling energetic, try renting a bike. Rental charges are around £3·50 per day and £21·50 per week.

Student discounts

Reductions to some cinemas and theatres; discounts on certain items at some of the department stores, and on tickets between Dublin and London. For information contact:

IRISH STUDENT TRAVEL SERVICE, 7 Anglesea Street, Dublin (tel: 77 81 17).

Addresses

Main post office (for poste restante) at O'Connell Street, Dublin.

American Express at 116 Grafton Street, Dublin (tel: 77 28 74).

Irish Student Travel Service at 7 Anglesea Street, Dublin (tel: 77 81 17).

Tourist Information Office at 14 Upper O'Connell Street, Dublin (tel: 74 77 33).

British Embassy at 33 Merrion Road, Dublin 4 (tel: 69 52 11).

US Embassy at 42 Elgin Road, Ballsbridge, Dublin (tel: 68 87 77).

Hitchers' Tips and Comments . . .

Your suggestion for sleeping rough in Dublin's Phoenix Park is not to be recommended. If the police don't throw you out, the army will. *D. G. Mulvey, Dublin, Ireland*

Re sleeping rough in Dublin's Phoenix Park. If the police don't get you, gangs might. You're safer dossing out in the countryside. Take a city bus to the end of the line and walk a bit (try No. 44B, 65, 31 or 60). *Helen Snively, Dublin, Ireland*

For dossing out around small Irish villages try the local primary schools (called 'national schools'). You can always spot them by the 'children crossing' signs. There's usually somewhere flat to pitch a tent, running water on an outdoor tap, often toilet facilities and always a schoolyard shelter to get you through a wet night. On weekday mornings get out well before nine o'clock. *Aidan Murray, Athlore, England*

To avoid paying on the ferry from Dublin to Holyhead (Wales), hitch a ride from outside the harbour. Drivers shipping their cars pay the price for the car and two passengers, so you can confirm a free passage across with the driver. *K. M. Fitchet, Johannesburg, South Africa*

7 Europe

Europe can never bore you. It stretches 2400 miles north to south, 3000 miles east to west and contains some 35 different states. Its highest elevation, Mount Elbrus in the Soviet Union, rises 18,481 feet, its lowest, the Caspian Sea, also in the Soviet Union, plunges 92 feet below sea-level. Its highest recorded temperature was at Sevilla in Spain with 124 degrees Fahrenheit and its lowest was −61 degrees at Ust-Tsilma in Russia.

But the people are the thing. With its 650,000,000 citizens stacked in 150 to the square mile, it is the most densely populated continent on the planet. You may never manage to remember which city the Forum is in or the gallery in which you saw the 'Mona Lisa', but you will certainly remember the city in which someone did you a good turn.

You meet hitchers on the road when you're heading, for instance, towards Austria and you ask if they've come from there. They tell you, sure. You say, what's it like? And they tell you that they met this guy in a bar and he bought them a drink and then went 40 miles out of his way to get them on to the road they wanted. So you ask what Vienna is like and they tell you there was this young kid in the marketplace who stole apples for them and that a cop came and chased the kid off and then pinched an apple for himself and started talking about his son who was hitching down in Africa.

You ask good travellers about a country and they never wax romantic about green fields or snow-capped mountains. They tell you about people. And everyone has a country in Europe they like best because of how the people were with them and everyone has a country they like least because they couldn't understand the people. There are 4,063,000 square miles filled with people.

What you will want to do in Europe depends on who you are. If history is your line, you can pursue history until it runs out your ears. If you're an artist, you can visit so many of the world's great galleries that you'll go cross-eyed. If you're a person with an ordinary job and a few months off to wander the hundreds of thousands of miles of European roads, then that's OK, too, because you can dip and choose as the mood takes you, without feeling the pressure of having to visit that city or see such a gallery.

If you can wander in Europe with just the vaguest idea of your route and enough money in your pocket and enough time up your sleeve to go as the road takes you, then you're lucky.

And there's nothing more to say, because Europe will say it all itself. Enjoy.

France

population	53,000,000
size	212,821 square miles
capital	Paris, population 10,825,000
government	Republic
religion	Predominantly Catholic
language	French
currency	*Franc* One *franc* equals 100 *centimes*. Coins of 1, 5, 10, 20, 50 *centimes*, and 1, 5, 10 *francs*. Notes of 10, 50, 100, 500 *francs*

From England, about the cheapest way into France (or on to the Continent) is by the hovercraft service which runs between Ramsgate and Calais and Dover and Boulogne. Full-time students who are under 26 years of age and who have a student card can claim a substantial discount. Other main routes are Folkestone–Boulogne, Dover–Calais, Southampton–Cherbourg, Newhaven–Dieppe, Southampton–Le Havre. Dover boats also go to Zeebrugge and Ostend in Belgium. Check out the price of day returns; on certain routes they are cheaper than a single – cheaper still if you manage to sell the return half when you reach your destination port.

St Malo, an old walled seaport badly bombed in the latter days of the war, but beautifully restored, and **Dinan,** inland on the river Rance, a citadel town with a medieval castle, are both beautiful, impressive, and well worth seeing. In Brittany, of the many colourful seaports, **Concarneau** and **Lézardrieux** are perhaps the most outstanding, while **Carnac** is a must for prehistory buffs. Its 300 menhirs and dolmens (that's standing stones for the uninitiated), spread over 4 kilometres and aligned for sunrise at solstices and equinox, date from Neolithic times and offer an even greater spectacle than Stonehenge.

If you're heading straight for **Paris**, you might want to stop in at **Rouen**, the capital of Normandy. An old, old city, it retains an ancient look with timber-framed houses (actually only eighteenth century) and huge Gothic structures dating from the twelfth to the sixteenth centuries. The Fine Arts Museum contains a fine collection of work from the French schools, including a good display of Impressionists. Buildings worth looking at include the gigantic Notre-Dame Cathedral and the Church of Saint Ouen. See also the Great Clock on Rue du Gros-Horloge. Its workings date from 1389. The Place du Vieux-Marché is the public square in which Joan of Arc was burned at the stake on 30 May 1431.

Around Paris, there are at least three places worth a visit. **Chartres** is the home of the 700-year-old Cathedral of Notre-Dame (they're all called that) which Rodin the sculptor described as the 'Acropolis of Christendom'. The 371-foot-high structure can be seen from Montmartre, in Paris, on a clear day. And that's 90 kilometres away. The church took 200 years to build and its 137 stained-glass windows cover an area of 25,000 square feet. See also the house known as 'Picasiette' which is decorated with pieces of broken china set into cement. The work, which took 36 years and 29,000 hours, is a mosaic of Chartres itself.

Fontainebleau, 60 kilometres south of Paris, is the site of the palace of the French kings. Begun in the twelfth century it was continually added to. You can go through various royal apartments, including Marie Antoinette's.

Versailles is only 20 kilometres out of the capital. On this trip you can see the palace of Louis XIV (the famous Sun King) and La Malmaison, home of Napoleon and Josephine.

Back in Normandy again, **Bayeux** is an old Norman town with yet another cathedral of Notre-Dame (it means 'Our Lady'). See the famed Bayeux tapestry, 225 feet long, dating from the eleventh century and depicting the Norman conquest of England.

Near Bayeux, on the coast, is the site of the 1944 D-Day landings. You can visit the beaches – **Utah, Omaha, Gold, Juno** and **Sword**. Plenty of things to see connected with the battle, including a museum of the invasion at the tiny village of **Arromanches**.

Mont St Michel, like the Alhambra in Granada, is claimed to be

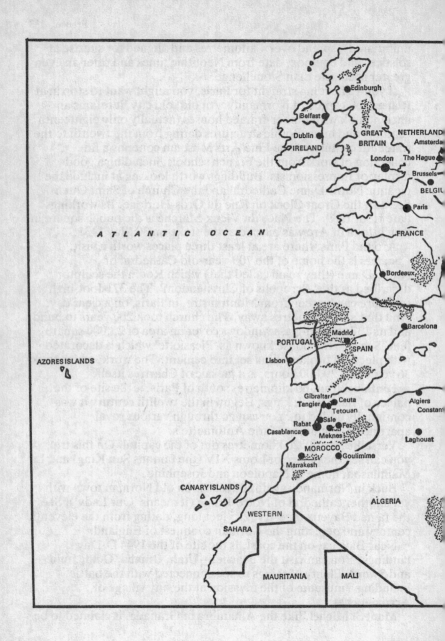

the eighth wonder of the world. Built on an island linked to the mainland by a road, the twelfth-century fortified town topped by its huge monastery looks quite unreal. And in springtime the *Grande Marée*, the big tide, comes rolling in from the English Channel at better than 16 kilometres an hour, covering the road and completely surrounding the rock with water.

Pushing down to Tours, you go through **Le Mans**, scene of the big international car-racing events. **Tours**, a medium-sized city of around 100,000, is an old commercial centre and of no great interest. But from there, if you're interested, you can head into the château country of the Loire Valley. There are more than 120 of the old fortress homes in the valley, the most spectacular of them being at **Amboise** (catch the *son et lumière* if you have the time and money), **Chenonceaux, Azay-le-Rideau, Ussé** and **Cheverny**.

Orléans, farther up the Loire, is where Joan of Arc got her act together and, as well as the many statues of her in the city, the cathedral has a series of stained-glass windows depicting her life. Orléans' location makes it an ideal centre to head off in any one of several directions and, being a university town, the hitching is usually good.

Hitching eastward through Auxerre and **Avallon**, a small medieval town with ramparts overlooking the Cousin valley, you enter Burgundy. **Dijon**, ancient capital of the Dukes of Burgundy, has plenty to offer. The ducal palace houses the Museum of Fine Arts, which is reckoned to have one of France's finest collections. The city is renowned as a gastronomic centre and a walk through streets crammed with *pâtisseries* and bistros does wonders for the appetite. If you work up a thirst too, don't despair. Burgundy is paradise for wine fans, especially since many famous vineyards (Gevrey-Chambertin, Nuits-St-Georges, and Volnay) offer *dégustations* – free tastings. Connoisseurs sip, swill and spit out the wine, but there is nothing wrong in simply drinking it.

Beaune, on the road to Lyons, has two unusual museums in its medieval centre. The fifteenth-century hospital (still in use, with nurses in medieval uniform) houses a museum of medical instruments while, just along the road, the wine museum traces the history of wine making. The enormous wooden wine presses have to be seen to be believed.

Lyons, with more than half a million people, is the gateway city to the south. Founded in 43 BC it has a lot to offer. To start with there are twenty-two museums. Try the Museum of Fine Arts for

Gauguin's 'Who are we? Whence do we come? Whither are we going?' – just a sample of what you can find there. The Museum of the History of Lyons is a fascinating visual presentation of what happens to a city during twenty centuries. The Museum of the French Resistance speaks for itself. On the Hill of Fourvière, which was the city centre in Roman times, you can see a Roman theatre and the remains of a temple. The main theatre seated 10,000 people. The Gothic church of St Jean is surrounded by some of Lyons' oldest streets. Fourteenth- and fifteenth-century houses are still standing.

South of Lyons and a few kilometres west of the Rhône Valley is **Le Puy**. This weird city is a place of strange, steep, narrow streets and is surrounded by volcanic pinnacles. The Chapel of St Michel d'Aiguille sits on top of a 250-foot volcanic needle. The cathedral of Notre-Dame de Puy has a façade of multi-coloured lava. Homely lady hitchers may be interested to know that Le Puy is world famous for its lace and that its Crozatier Museum contains a selection of same.

South of Le Puy, where the N86 joins with the N113 is **Nîmes**, the oldest Roman city in France. Roman ruins everywhere, including the huge Nîmes arena. The hitching can be pretty tough in this congested area, particularly in summer, though students heading for the university city of **Montpellier** help out a lot. Montpellier is a young people's town, with plenty going on. Try to take in the enormous Saturday morning flea market, where you're likely to meet kindred spirits. Browse for bargains or, if short of cash, find a space, sit down, and sell something – anything – it's that kind of place.

Inland from Montpellier you travel through **Hérault**, the largest wine-producing area in the world. You see hectare after hectare of vineyards stretched out on every side.

There are at least two cities in this province worth visiting: **Albi** because of its Lautrec Museum which contains the largest collection of Lautrecs in the world – some 500 paintings and sketches, right from the first the artist ever made – and, south of Albi, **Carcassonne**, one of Europe's most memorable landmarks. The old medieval **Cité** remains intact and completely walled. From the distance it looks like some gigantic 20th Century Fox movie lot. Within the walls you get a complete picture of what life was like eight or nine centuries ago. The road south of Carcassonne leads to **Andorra** (see **Luxembourg and the Small Countries**).

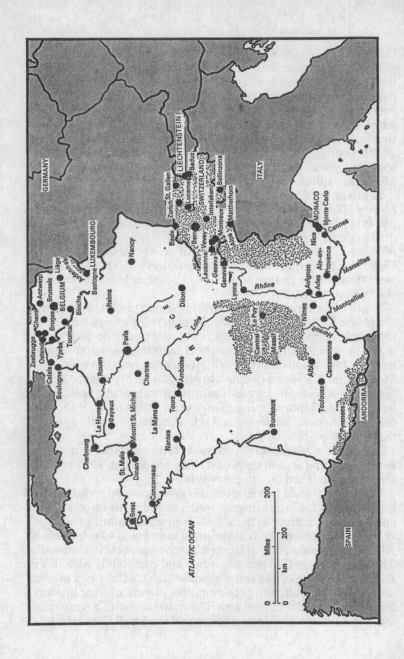

Over the other side of the Rhône you have **Avignon**, the papal seat from 1309 to 1403. See the Palace of the Popes and dozens of other monuments from that period. **Arles**, south of Avignon, is where Van Gogh lived and worked. **Aix-en-Provence**, where Cézanne worked, was founded by the Romans in 123 BC as a thermal resort.

South of Arles lies the **Camargue**, a vast marshy area famed for its white horses, black fighting bulls, and pink flamingos. **Aigues-Mortes**, a thirteenth-century crusader city, rises spectacularly from the marshes. Its walls, nearly two kilometres long, still intact and boasting twenty towers, give a great view of the flatlands. The white pyramids you see in the distance are stockpiles from the local saltmines. Nearby **Stes-Maries-de-la-Mer** is the gypsy equivalent of Mecca. Every May they come from all over the world to pay homage to Sarah, their patron. Don't miss this incredible spectacle if you are in the area at the right time.

Marseilles, the big port of southern France, is the country's oldest city, dating from 600 BC when it was founded by the Phoenicians. Much of the old city was destroyed in the Second World War, but there are still plenty of good areas to wander in. Around the Vieux-Port are some of Europe's grottiest and most interesting streets. Out in the bay stands the **Château d'If** from where Alexandre Dumas' fictional Count of Monte Cristo made his dramatic escape. If you want to visit the château (good trip), disregard the prices on the launch operators' placards and bargain like hell. A group of people should be able to cut the price per head nearly by half.

East of Marseilles is the expensive area of the French Riviera. It may qualify as the toughest hitching route in Europe, so be prepared for short hops and long pauses. If you're heading for **Nice**, largest town on the Riviera, the autoroute may not be as pretty as the Corniche but, if time is short, it should get you there a hell of a lot quicker.

Nice's Promenade des Anglais, running along the seafront, is the stuff of travel agency posters. Soak up the atmosphere with a summer's evening stroll and, if you're flush, risk the experience of a sidewalk apéritif, then just sit back and watch the world go by. Early risers can visit the flower market which is a riot of colour and perfume. Before heading off to explore the rest of the Côte d'Azur, stock up with supplies at one of the city's hypermarkets. The food prices in small shops are considerably higher.

Cannes, which hosts the International Film Festival each May, gives you the chance to rub shoulders with the glitterati. If you need reminding that this is a rich man's town, take an envious glance at the luxury yachts crammed into the harbour. Bus-boats make frequent trips out to the **Iles des Lerins**, a group of wooded islands which give scope for a bit of camping sauvage. Visit the castle on Ile Ste Marguerite, where the 'Man in the Iron Mask' was imprisoned.

If you fancy sunbathing with the beautiful people at **Antibes, St Raphael** or **St Tropez**, dress may be optional but, unless you are on a public beach, you'll be charged a hefty sum for the privilege. Prices in these chic resorts are horrendous, so buskers and sketch artists might like to try and recoup their loss by trying their luck with the jet set, the yacht set and the army of would-be's if they could-be's. St Tropez, originally made famous by artists, should prove the most fruitful.

Less exclusive (i.e., cheaper) resorts, with better beaches, can be found farther west at **Cavalaire** or **Le Lavandou**. Lavandou, named after the lavender that grows in the surrounding hills, still retains the atmosphere of the fishing village it once was. Here, as in the rest of France, campers should seek out the municipal camping, which is cheaper than most of the commercial counterparts.

For a change of scenery, an interesting trip is up to the **Canon du Verdon**, north from Nice. Billed as Europe's answer to the Grand Canyon, it's great back-packing country and makes a change from the overcrowded coast. (Male hitchers with female companions, beware. The route through the hills takes you into **Grasse**, the perfume-making town, where you'll be invited to tour the factories, sniff the products – and buy!)

The miles of sandy beaches, stretching from the Camargue to the Spanish border, make this the poor man's Riviera. Wind-surfing is the big sport here and the annual championships are a colourful spectacle at **Sète**, France's second largest port on the Mediterranean. Sète, which is situated on a strip of land between the sea and the vast lagoon of the Etang de Thau, and with canals connecting the two, is sometimes called the Venice of France. The town has scores of seafood restaurants and stalls. Try oysters fresh from the enormous beds in the Etang.

Béziers, which in August emulates Pamplona with a running of the bulls through the main thoroughfare, is a good stopover. Its campsite, on the banks of the river Orb, beneath the aqueduct of the Canal du Midi, and with a view of the cathedral, is a great place for meeting fellow travellers.

Southwards is the road to Spain, with the La Junquera road carrying more traffic than the Port Bou road, though the latter is prettier, taking you down the Costa Brava.

★**Rent-a-Ride** Ever get that never-gonna-get-a-ride feeling? Well snap out of it. Your French hosts have the problem licked! You get on the phone, tell them where you're going and they get you in touch with a driver who is going your way.

Remember that hitch-hiking is forbidden on motorways (autoroutes) but not on slip-roads or at 'péages' (where motorists pay their tolls). Several French organizations will put drivers and passengers in touch with each other; so contact the representatives of the 'Fédération Nationale des Associations d'Autostop organisé' at the following addresses:

Allostop-Provoya at 84 Passage Brady, 75010 Paris (tel: 246 00 66). Open from 9 a.m. to 8 p.m.

Allostop at 5 rue Duffour-Dubergier, 33000 Bordeaux (tel: (56) 81 24 59). Open from 3 p.m. to 7 p.m. from Monday to Friday.

Also, but not belonging to this association:

Dauphiné Information Jeunesse at Jardin de Ville, 38000 Grenoble (tel: (76) 87 79 04).

'You will be asked to pay an annual subscription and share petrol expenses. Or if you catch French radio and mainly RTL between 9 p.m. and 12 p.m. every day except Sunday, Max Meynier will put you in touch with really "sympas" lorry drivers with whom you can travel. His telephone number in Paris is 720 22 11 and his broadcast, *Les Routiers sont sympas.*'

★**Corsica** You can reach Corsica by ferry from Nice, Marseilles or Toulon in France, or from Genoa, Livorno and Piombino in Italy.

The island is one of the Mediterranean's largest, over 150 kilometres long and 75 wide. And with a high average temperature throughout the year (57·4°F average through January and February) it's as good a place as any to hole up for a few days during the winter. But be warned, it's expensive. Keep in the backstreets for eating and sleeping or you're going to get hit with jet-set prices.

If you like mountain scenery you'll be in your element, because this is a truly spectacular landscape (Mount Cinto, for instance, reaches nearly 9000 feet!). Top towns are **Ajaccio, Bastia** and **Bonifacio. Ajaccio**, the capital, was the hometown of Corsica's most illustrious citizen: Napoleon. Visit the Maison Bonaparte, his birthplace and old family home which is now a museum. More Napoleon stuff to be seen in the Palias Fesch museum and in the Musée Napoléonien at the Town Hall. Wander around the old fishing harbour. Usually plenty of people around the cafés facing the harbour, but watch the prices. You can get stung if you aren't careful. **Bastia**'s main attraction, in my opinion, is the beautiful old town. Great if you're a back-alley man. See also the museum, once the palace of the governors of Genoa, and the port with its superluxury ocean cruisers. (Some of them may need crew, so keep your eyes open if you're looking for a job.) The old fortified town of **Bonifacio** simply must be seen to be believed. Plenty of people claim it as the prettiest of all Mediterranean ports. 'Strangest' might be a better adjective. Have a look, anyway, and decide for yourself. History and art nuts should take the chance to drop in on the Bronze Age fort at **Cucuruzzu**. It's one of the best preserved in Europe. Also see the magnificent medieval frescoes at **Sermano di Bozio** which is in the centre of the island, near the ancient capital, **Corte**.

Camping out is permitted just about anywhere on the island, and with the high cost of hotel rooms you might as well get used to the idea, but check if it's national property 'forêt domaniale'! You can camp wild or pitch a tent at an organized site at Ota, Ajaccio, Corte, Calvi or Uccaini.

★Just been dropped off on the outskirts on the *wrong* side of a big town? Keep a lookout for the big hypermarkets (Mammouth, Euro-Marché, etc.). Cheaper shopping brings people in by car from all over, so station yourself at the exit with a sign; could save a long walk.

★If you find yourself bored with the road, you could give the canals and rivers a try. There is lots of traffic and, sometimes, boat owners are glad of extra hands for the locks. You won't travel fast but there are some great rides to be had. Most of the boats are pleasure craft, but there is commercial traffic, too, including barges carrying as much as a quarter of a million litres of wine.

★After Spain's liberalization of drug laws, French customs are taking increased interest in young people passing in from Spain.

★The French government says it will no longer allow in British visitors without passports, so Brits should make sure their passports are in order.

Paris: where to sleep

French youth hostels cost around 40 francs (except in Paris where they are more expensive) and cheap hotel singles about 70 francs. If you're in a group of two or three, you can take double or triple rooms and cut hotel costs to around 60 francs a person. With French hotels, more than any others in Europe, *always* ask, after you've been quoted a price, if they don't have something a little cheaper. Top-floor rooms in cheap Parisian hotels which don't have lifts are quite often two or three francs cheaper – but naturally the proprietors try to get rid of their expensive rooms first.

★The following list of student accommodation has been supplied by the Centre d'Information et de Documentation Jeunesse (CIDJ). You can contact them at 101 Quai Bronly, 75740 Paris 15e (tel: 566 4020).

1er arrondissement
Centre International de la Jeunesse at 20 rue J.J. Rousseau (tel: 236 8818).

4e arrondissement
Hôtel des Jeunes 'Le Fauconnier' at 11 rue du Fauconnier (tel: 274 2345).
Hôtel des Jeunes Maubuisson at 12 rue des Barres (tel: 277 8780).

5e arrondissement
Foyer International des Etudiantes at 93 Boulevard St Germain (tel: 033 4963). For girls only. Open July, August, September only.

6e arrondissement
Association des Etudiants Protestants de Paris at 46 rue de Vaugirard (tel: 354 3149).

9e arrondissement
Union Chrétienne des Jeunes Gens (YMCA) at 14 rue de Trévise (tel: 770 9094). Half-board compulsory.

11e arrondissement
Maison Internationale des Jeunes at 4 rue Titon (tel: 371 9921).

12e arrondissement
Centre International de Séjour de Paris at 6 avenue Maurice Ravel (tel: 343 1901). Half-board compulsory. Ask for dormitory.

13e arrondissement
Maison des Clubs UNESCO at 43 rue de la Glacière (tel: 336 0063). For ages 16 to 25 only. July and August.

14e arrondissement
Foyer International d'Accueil de Paris at 30 rue Cabanis (tel: 589 8915). Half-board compulsory.

20e arrondissement
M.J.C. Théâtre des deux Portes at 46 rue Louis Lumière (tel: 797 2451).
Paris Youth Hostel at 8 Boulevard Jules Ferry (tel: 357 55 60).
Butte Rouge Youth Hostel at 444 Avenue de la Division Leclerc, Châtenay-Malabry (tel: 1/632 1743).

Following is a list of hotels which are among the cheapest you will find in the centre of Paris:

Hôtel du Gros Caillou at 6 rue du Gros Caillou (tel: 551 24 56). Métro to Ecole Militaire.

Hôtel de la Tour Eiffel at 17 rue de l'Exposition (tel: 705 50 31). Métro to Ecole Militaire.

Hôtel du Bon Marché at 22 rue Saint Placide (tel: 548 10 67). Métro to Saint Placide.

Hôtel Joigny at 8 rue Saint-Charles (tel: 579 3335). Métro to Bir Hakeim.

For further information concerning student accommodation talk to the people at Accueil des Jeunes en France, 12 rue des Barres, Paris 4e (tel: 272 7209); and at Gare du Nord.

To sleep rough try along the banks of the Seine beneath the Louvre. There are usually some people sleeping there. (But see

Marcel Thomas' letter at the end of the chapter.) Other best bets are the cemeteries, with the one at Montparnasse being handy to the centre. Cops don't seem to worry rough-sleepers in Paris as long as they're quiet, though I imagine their mood varies with the political climate.

Another tip for sleeping: word has it that many of the churches in Paris are left open at night and that the priests don't mind if someone takes a pew.

To repeat: most rock bottom hotels come out at around 70 francs a single, but if you gang up with one or two others to take a double or triple, the per-person price drops a little.

Paris: where to eat

It's hard to find a decent meal in Paris for under 30 francs. For a filling, cheap restaurant meal expect to pay 30–35 francs, unless you are a student who can take advantage of student facilities, or a youth hosteller. For the average hitcher in Paris on a tight budget, someone who wants to stay on for a few days, it's necessary to buy food from shops and make picnic meals. But that's no hardship. A loaf of French bread, a slab of cheese and pâté, a piece of fruit and a bottle of wine will come out around 20 francs, and you can sit yourself down by the Seine or in the Luxembourg Gardens and it's nice enough. Invest another few francs and eat your food with a cup of coffee at a sidewalk café and it's the nicest way of eating a meal in all of Europe.

Student eating There are plenty of restaurants in Paris where students can get full meals for about 25 francs. For a complete list of addresses and for further information contact the Organisation pour le Tourisme Universitaire at 137 Boulevard St Michel. Métro to Port Royal, or telephone 329 12 88. Here are some samples from the full list:

Le Mabillon at 3 rue Mabillon. Métro to Mabillon.

Le Bullier at 39 Avenue Georges Bernanos. Métro to Port Royal.

Le Centre Albert Châtelet at10 rue Jean Calvin. Métro to Censier Daubenton.

Le Mazet at 5 rue Mazet. Métro to Odéon.

Le Censier at 3 rue Censier. Métro to Censier Daubenton.

Le Grand Palais at Cours la Reine. Métro to Champs-Elysées-Clemenceau.

The above are all classified as university restaurants. They are open 11.30 a.m.–2 p.m. and 6.30 p.m.–8 p.m.

Le Restaurant Chartière, rue de la Faubourg, Montmartre.

Latin Cluny Self-Service Cafeteria at 98 Boulevard St Germain.

Restaurant Jean at 132 Boulevard St Germain.

La Source at 35 Boulevard St Michel.

Cafeterias Tuesdays to Saturdays only. *Galeries Lafayette* and *Au Printemps*, both on Boulevard Haussmann, which is just at the back of the Opéra (Métro to Opéra). Good meals for about 25 francs if you stand up. More to sit.

Just about all of the little streets on the left side (with your back to the river) of Place St Michel – like rue de la Harpe, or rue St Severin – have cheap eating places. Head for the restaurants with the longest queues outside because those are the ones with the best meals for your money. A lot of students eat in this area and there are usually plenty of people hanging around the fountain in Place St Michel, so you'll have no trouble getting directions to the current best place.

Here are some samples where you should be able to make a decent meal around the 40-franc mark:

In rue de la Huchette: **Ristorante Pizza Pino** (number 8).

In rue Xavier Privas: **Restaurant au Bon Couscous** (number 7), **Privas** (number 9), **Restaurant Long Van** (number 20), **Restaurant Le Latin** (number 22), **India Restaurant** (number 11–bis).

In rue St Severin: **Restaurant le Vieux Paris** (number 9).

In rue de la Harpe: **Les Balkans** (number 3), **Restaurant Chinois Nan-wa** (number 12), **Grand Mandarin** (number 37).

Also at the corner of rue de la Harpe and St Severin, there's a great take-away sandwich bar called **Pâtisserie du Sud Tunisien**.

Next best eating area, though not so colourful, nor with such a young crowd, is in the Marais on the Right Bank – the section bounded by rue de Rivoli, rue de Temple and the Boulevard Beaumarchais.

Paris: what to see and do

JEU DE PAUME at the Jardin de Tuileries. Admission charge, but half price Sundays. World's greatest collection of Impressionist paintings.

LOUVRE in rue de Rivoli. Admission charge except Sundays when it's free. Great collection of paintings and sculptures. Closed Tuesdays.

RODIN MUSEUM, rue de Varenne 77. Entrance charge, but half price Sundays. Rodin is considered by many to have been the greatest sculptor since Michelangelo. Closed Tuesdays.

EIFFEL TOWER in Champ de Mars. There are three platforms on the 1033-foot-high tower, and it costs to go to each of them. By the time you reach the top you're in for more than 15 francs but you have a great view of Paris.

GEORGES POMPIDOU NATIONAL CENTRE OF ART AND CULTURE stands on the Plateau Beaubourg, bounded by rue Rambuteau and rue de Renard. Nearest Métro: Rambuteau. Open daily except Tuesday. The centre is the result of an attempt to bring together all forms of cultural expression. Thus, under one roof, you can visit the National Museum of Modern Art, featuring work by dozens of top painters including Matisse, Miró, Picasso and Chagall; the Public Information Library with one million books, films, records, slides, etc; the Institute for Research and Coordination in Acoustics and Music; the Centre of Industrial Creation; the Children's Workshop; the Cinémathèque, which tells the entire story of motion pictures, etc. In addition, anything up to forty exhibitions and demonstrations are held each year in this fantastic building which to some is a gem of modern architecture and to others a sewer on stilts. A day pass costs around 15 francs. Entry free if you're under 18. Don't miss the happenings in the plaza in front. On the right day it's the best entertainment in Paris, and all free. Great place to meet people.

FREE VIEW OF PARIS from Sacré Coeur which surmounts the Butte Montmartre. (When this church was built, the architects found that the soil of the Butte was incapable of supporting the weight of the building so they had to push the foundations right through the hill. Consequently, Parisians say that if the hill were removed the church would be left standing.) In summer, young Parisians often meet on the steps of the Basilica.

MUSÉE DE CLUNY 6 place Paul-Painlevé. Nearest Métro: St Michel. Admission charge. Open daily except Tuesdays. A collection of some 25,000 works of art including paintings, sculptures, carvings, metal work, fabrics and tapestries, ancient furniture, porcelain and glass, all housed in one of the city's most beautiful old buildings.

LUXEMBOURG GARDENS Métro to Gare du Luxembourg. Gardens (free) in which is contained the huge Luxembourg Palace which was built between 1615 and 1620 for the mother of Louis XIII. The palace was used as the headquarters of the Luftwaffe during the Second World War German occupation of Paris. Usually plenty of people wandering about the gardens if you're looking for company.

SEWERS Enter from the south end of the Pont d'Alma on the Quai Bronly, near Place de la Résistance. About a twenty-minute barge trip through the sewers from the Place de la Concorde to Madeleine. Check with people for ever-changing time schedules unless you're in town between May and June when trips usually take place at 2, 3, 4 and 5 p.m.

PLACE PIGALLE This was once the centre of Bohemian Paris (now MONTPARNASSE is more the place), but these days Pigalle and Boulevard de Clichy are neon-lit tourist traps, full of clubs like the famous *Moulin Rouge* (you can see the show for about 50 francs if you sit at the bar and hold your drink tight), third-rate strip-joints full of drooping boobies, half-baked sex shops and handbag-swinging prostitutes who case you with a smiling eye. (The pros, by the way, aren't always what they seem. Paris fuzz did a big round-up recently and found that a large percentage of the ladies were, in fact, gentlemen.) But it's a great free show and if you're lucky you'll be able to watch some expert fleecers in action against the slow-witted tourist cult.

NOTRE-DAME CATHEDRAL One of the classic sights of Paris. Worth looking through. Also try to make it up the tower for a good view. Entrance charge for the tower, but half price on Sundays. Closed Tuesdays.

VICTOR HUGO'S HOUSE is in the beautiful Place des Vosges which is buried in the Marais area. (Just a few minutes' walk from Place de la Bastille.) Fans of the old gent – and quite a gent at that – will enjoy the pilgrimage. Those not interested in literature will probably enjoy the square anyway. It's like stepping back a couple of centuries.

NAPOLEON'S TOMB at the Hôtel des Invalides. Take the Métro to Ecole Militaire. You'll see the granite sarcophagus in the crypt. Inside are six coffins, one within the other. In the last is the Emperor. See the room which contains his personal relics, including his death mask, his hat and his sword. Don't miss the nearby *Army Museum* (at the *Hôtel des Invalides*) which has one of the world's best collections of swords, bows, guns, cannon and other would-be problem solvers.

MONTMARTRE CEMETERY Enter from Avenue Rachel. Free. Interesting trip through a very strange scene. Some graves are crowned by monuments as big as houses which must have cost tens of thousands of francs to build. Quite unlike English or American style cemeteries. Zola is buried there, as are Stendhal, Berlioz, Offenbach, Delibes, and the son of Alexandre Dumas. The MONTPARNASSE CEMETERY is another free, weird trip. Enter on the rue Froidevaux. Famous people buried there include Saint-Saëns, de Maupassant and Baudelaire. A third is PÈRE LACHAISE CEMETERY, entrance on Boulevard Menilmontant, where you can see the graves of Rossini, Balzac, Oscar Wilde, and rock star Jim Morrison.

MARKETS Free. There are several worth a visit. The BIRD MARKET at Place Louis-Lépine, open Sundays 9 a.m. to 7 p.m. The DOG MARKET at 106 rue Brancion, open Sundays 1 p.m. to 4 p.m. The CLOTHES MARKET at Carreau du Temple, open all week, except Mondays, from 8 a.m. to 7.30 p.m. and on Sundays 8 a.m. to 1 p.m. The FLOWER MARKET at the east side of Madeleine, open every day except Mondays, from 9 a.m. to 7.30 p.m. The FLEA MARKET, the biggest in the world with open stalls and shops, at Porte de Clignancourt, open all day Saturdays, Sundays and Mondays. The STAMP MARKET at Avenue Gabriel and Avenue Marigny, open Thursdays, Saturdays, Sundays 8 a.m. to 7 p.m. HORSE, DONKEY AND MULE MARKET at 106 rue Brancion, open Mondays, Wednesdays, Fridays 9 a.m. to 12 midday.

THE CATACOMBS at Place Denfert-Rochereau. Small charge. 16 October to 30 June, first and third Saturdays at 2 p.m. 1 July to 15 October, every Saturday at 2 p.m. Originally the catacombs may have been a Roman quarry. Back in the 1780s, the city authorities were clearing an ancient cemetery and moved the bones into the catacombs. Some workmen took it into their heads to do a little interior decorating with the skulls – and you can still see the result of their efforts. The catacombs were also used as Resistance headquarters during the war.

PLACE ST MICHEL One of the best places to meet students is at the Place St Michel in front of the fountain showing St Michel with the Devil.

LES CAVES The famous Parisian institutions where you fight the haze of cigarette smoke and drown in the music are expensive. Entrance to most is in the vicinity of 25 francs, the price usually including one drink and you don't have to buy another. If you do they cost 10–15 francs each. But you meet some great people, hear some nice music, and have a real chance of latching on to someone of the opposite sex. If you can afford it, try:

CAVEAU DE LA HUCHETTE at rue de la Huchette. Métro: St Michel.

LE CHAT QUI PÊCHE at 4 rue de la Huchette. Métro: St Michel.

TROIS MAILLETS at 56 rue Galande. Métro: St Michel.

LE RIVER BOAT at 67 rue St André des Arts. Métro: St Germain des Prés.

Transport in Paris
With many of the major sights within half an hour of each other, Paris is a good walking city. Just as well, because the Métro (the underground railway) and the bus system are expensive. If you're going to be in town any length of time buy a *carnet*. (Make sure you get second class.) Bus prices are about the same as the Métro. Rich hitchers can buy a special four-day tourist ticket which gives unlimited travel on the Métro, plus on city and suburban buses. It's not a bad deal when you consider you can go as far afield as Versailles! Richer hitchers expecting to be in town for a week can buy a seven-day ticket. If you have that sort of money present yourself and your passport at any RATP office. (There's one at Place de la Madeleine and another at 53 Quai des Grands Augustins.) Bicycle rental is very expensive. Around 40 francs for the first day, about 25 francs each subsequent day. *Plus* you need an enormous deposit.

Student discounts
Reductions to all state museums and galleries, to certain other museums and galleries, plus to some theatres, cinemas and clubs. Check with: l'OTU, 137 Boulevard St Michel, Paris 5e (tel: 329 12 88).

Addresses

Main post office (for poste restante) at 52 rue du Louvre, Paris.

American Express at 11 rue Scribe, Paris 9e (tel: 073 42 90).

Organisation pour le Tourisme Universitaire (l'OTU) at 137 Boulevard St Michel, Paris 5e (tel: 329 12 88).

Office de Tourisme de Paris at 127 Champs-Elysées, 75008 Paris (tel: 720 04 96).

US Embassy at 2 Avenue Gabriel, Paris (tel: 296 12 02).

British Embassy at 35 rue du Faubourg Saint-Honoré, Paris 8e (tel: 723 61 72).

Hitchers' Tips and Comments...

I found the *Hitcher's Guide* fascinating. I can't wait for my next trip! I was disappointed that you left out the French Alps. I stayed in Grenoble for three weeks and I assure you it's worth visiting.

Some things in the area worth seeing are Collégiale St André, heavily war-damaged thirteenth-century church, one of the oldest in the area; Olympic Stade de Glace, ice arena where figure-skating competition was held (also Tremplin de Saut, the Olympic ski-jump near the village of St Nizier, fantastic views from there of the Alps and Grenoble); ruins of the Bastille and Grenoble's Téléphérique, you can spend hours exploring the ruins of the ancient prison, tunnels and city walls; Château de Vizille, south of Grenoble. Has nice formal gardens and a beautiful trout-filled lake (no fishing). Charles de Gaulle slept there. *David McDermot, University of Pittsburgh, USA*

Best time to get from Paris to the South in one hop is to be there on the day the big vacation starts (in August) and everybody leaves for their holidays. Autoroute 1 is the main line of escape. Take a bus to the main feeder just near Orly Airport. Watch that you get the dates right. There seems to be a sort of vacuum period of bad hitching for a week after the big exodus. *Clive Gill, Birchington, England*

Greetings from the Fastest Thumb in the West! In Paris don't sleep on the Ile de la Cité. You'll get ripped off. Try the woods called Bois de Boulogne where there are wooden shelters to keep the rain off. Take Métro 2 to Porte Dauphine. *Bernd Vahle (Phallus), Bochum, Germany*

Camp in Paris – at the pleasant site in the Bois de Boulogne. Don't walk from the Métro station (5km), get a suburban train from St Lazare station in central Paris to Suresnes, walk down the hill, over Pont de Suresnes and the camp site is on your left – about ten minutes' walk from the station. Suresnes station also has trains to Versailles. *Simon Calder, Coventry, England*

With reference to your comments on grape picking where you say 'most of the work is of very temporary nature and badly paid' I would like to recount our experience in Beaujolais (north-west of Lyons). We worked on two farms for a total of 14 days and were paid 820 francs each. We were woken at 6.30 a.m. for breakfast; tea or coffee and bread and jam. Work started between 7.30 a.m. and 8.00 a.m. and we worked until 12 noon. Sometimes there was a break in the morning of 15 minutes for bread, cheese, chocolate and a drink. Wine, water and squash were available for the asking. Lunch was a massive affair eaten in traditional French fashion with each course being eaten separately. Wine flowed like a river. Work started at 1.30 p.m. and finished between 6 and 7.30 p.m. Dinner was excellent – plenty to eat and drink. Some might regard the sleeping and toilet facilities as being rough. You slept at the farms in a bed or on the floor – most places have hot water and showers. The working day is 10 hours, rarely more. The pay was 58 francs per day. If it rained you didn't work and you didn't get paid but you got your bed and food. We must add that the work is hard and dirty – particularly when it's wet.

All in all it was a thoroughly enjoyable experience – you eat and drink well, can meet some pleasant and interesting people and you can save money because you have no expenses. On some farms (the ones we worked on) cigarettes were on the house. We would recommend the grape harvest (*Vendange*). Beware of organizations like the one we contacted which gave us a vineyard address and a starting date. They charged £11 each and told us they'd send us the information via a poste restante address. After much phoning and hassling we got an address but not a starting date which was important because the harvest was a month early this year.

We think that the best thing to do would be to visit an area in early September, get yourself fixed up with a farmer and drift off until the *Vendange* starts. Sometimes you can work on afterwards. Two people we know have got jobs for three months and one year – the exception rather than the rule. *Gail Pemberton and David Griffith, Lyons, France*

I've run this letter for several editions. The info is still correct. Only the wages have changed. If you're lucky enough to get a job you can earn up to 18 francs per hour. K.W.

Anywhere in France if you order a coffee, make sure it's a *petit* otherwise they serve you a super de luxe version at a price to match.

In Paris for crashing rough your book suggests the banks of the Seine near the Louvre – forget it! I slept there with a fellow English guy and several others and we were wiped out at 5 in the morning by a bunch of very professional heavies. They woke us up but we couldn't stand up. I was rolled for about £60 cash, stripped of valuables, watch, ring, etc. Even lost me Levis and travelling the Métro in underwear isn't funny! Everyone lost something so I suggest that spot gets black-listed in the next edition. *Marcel Thomas, Horndean, England*

On Paris you failed to mention a mass of cheap hotels directly outside of the Port de Vincennes subway stop. *Lynne Hoffman and Judith Zorfas, Canada and USA*

Just south of Paris, not too far from Porte d'Orléans, is the Rungis, an enormous fresh food market. Lorries leave from there for all over Europe. *Chris Moore, Bedford, England*

If drinking wine in a bar or restaurant, emphasize *vin ordinaire*. I got ripped off for some expensive wine, and you're obliged to pay. *John Heywood, Devon, England*

There was hardly a town in France that I passed through that didn't have an approved campsite. These can work out quite cheap although not as cheap as out on the road. They have several advantages; they are safe as there is always somebody about to watch your stuff; they have hot showers; and there is usually a supermarket nearby where you can get decent grub for a decent price. *Paul Lawrence, Belfast, Northern Ireland*

Underneath the Louvre and Eiffel Tower Gardens always rest your head on your kit and tie your pack to your sleeping-bag. *Nicholas M. Steven, Sherborne, England*

Boulogne to Paris is a really bad hitch. We managed it in 7 hours, but heard lots of tales of people taking one to three days! *Bill and Diana Martindale, No Fixed Abode, England*

If you're stuck for a cheap hotel in Paris, try the backstreets around Pont Neuf. You should find a good deal and it's a convenient base, being near the Louvre and Notre-Dame.

Watch Paris street urchins. These kids approach you in the street holding a newspaper in one hand. While talking to you, the concealed hand is going through your pockets. The kids are very young but, boy, are they professional!

When leaving Paris, if you're aiming for Belgium or Holland, catch the Métro to Porte de la Chapelle. Usually lots of other hitchers waiting, so you have to do something to stand out from the crowd. *Mike Plummer, Seaview, Isle of Wight*

For cheap digs in France, try the Foyers des Jeunes Travailleurs. There's one in most reasonable-sized towns. Also, because of the high tolls on most autoroutes in France (and Italy and Spain), many drivers prefer to use the national routes (A-class roads) for journeys less than about 200 kilometres. Because of this, hitching may often be faster on these roads than on the autoroutes. *Chris May, Sheffield, England*

To all hitchers! The autoroute entrance at Perpignan, which leads south to Barcelona, is hitcher's hell. I waited hours there, exposed to a vicious Pyrenean wind. I met many others who'd had the same trouble at the same spot. And you should've seen the exasperated scrawlings on the roadside barrier! Try not to get dumped there! *Patrick Hine, Oxford, England*

Montpellier is a lousy hitch out on the N113. Too many hitchers. Walk a couple of kilometres to the Péage and try your luck there.

Also, I find that the Calais to Paris N1 route is overhitched. Try the N43 instead. I never saw anyone else on it. *Mike Waldie, Shenfield, England*

A warning to back-packers travelling on the Paris métro. If it's crowded and you're forced to stand, take off your rucksack and put it in front of you where you can keep your eyes on it. Otherwise you're an easy mark for the pickpocket gangs who travel the Paris lines. *Daz Hodson, North Hykeham, UK*

Lyons is another hitch-hiker's hell on earth. Unless you really want to see it, try not to get dumped there. Even for a single girl it means hours of walking and waiting before you get a lift out. *Sandra Anderson, Ballater, Scotland*

Fontainebleau and Versailles are good visits any time except July and August when you can queue up to three hours to get in! In Paris, visit La Défense, Paris' contribution to futuristic architecture. Truly fantastic to see skyscrapers painted to resemble clouds and trees. *Claire Bettington and Susan Cooper, Ledbury, UK*

Don't camp on forested hillsides in Corsica during summer. Devastating forest fires are common on this island. *I.B., Hemel Hempstead, UK*

Anyone heading south from Strasbourg towards Lyons should ignore the autoroute and stay on the national highway. The hitching is good and the route provides some of the best scenery in all of France. *John Otis, Mankato, Minnesota, USA*

For cheap sleeping in Paris, go into a métro station at around 1 a.m. and wait for the attendants to lock up. They will almost always leave you alone, and you have a warm, dry kip until 5 a.m. when they open again. The only trouble is that you're locked in, so make sure that any other people trying the same thing are harmless. The town drop-outs use the métro as hotels.

In the south of France sleep on the town beaches with all the other bodies. No one bothers a group of 20 or 30 people except the police. They tend to come along around dawn and throw water at you. Forget the rail stations in the south unless you want bruised ribs. *John Pilkington, Bristol, UK*

When crossing into France from Spain try to get a lift that will take you beyond Bayonne (right in the south) because the area crawls with fellow hitchers. When we passed through Bayonne on the road to Bordeaux we counted about 20 hitchers who looked like they'd been there all day. Depressing sight. *Jon More O'Farrall, Trinity, Jersey, Channel Islands*

If an articulated truck picks you up on the way to the Channel ports, the driver can take you across for nothing in the 'free seat'. The 'free seat' is covered by what is sometimes known as a 'mate's ticket'. *Paul, London, UK*

If you are visiting St Malo, head south 10 kilometres to the Rance Barrage, the first electric station powered by the tides. You can go inside for a multi-lingual audio-visual display and see the giant turbines. Worth the visit. *Mike Fullen and Jeff Hoyle, UK*

Hitchers who miss the last ferry out of Calais can doss in a couple of Second World War bunkers nearby. Expect to be woken early by bait-diggers parking their mopeds in the bunkers. *Steve Richards, Warrington, UK*

If you care about your life don't sleep in Marseilles parks. Gangs rob rucksacks from hitchers and inter-railers. I've seen it happen. *Jens Reckman, Askim, Sweden*

A great place to sleep is under the pillars of the Eiffel Tower. Great shelter and fairly clean. Usually some company, too – and these days, man, you need safety in numbers. You can stay until about 9 o'clock when the tourists start arriving. No hassle from the cops, either. Boulevard de Clichy great place for meeting people during the daytime. If you're in need of a few francs, take your talents along to the Georges Pompidou

Centre – you might meet with a fellow traveller and be able to put an act together. *Paul Hinckley, Birmingham, UK*

To get out of Paris to Lille, the best place to hitch from is Porte de la Chapelle. *Stephan Herfurtner, Kaarst, West Germany*

Sleeping rough in Marseilles: try the public Jardin Emile Leclaux near the Vieux Port. Go down the grass slope off the path and conceal yourself behind trees. *Duncan Smith, Bournemouth, UK*

Patrick Hine's comments about the motorway junction at Perpignan also apply to those who want to go north. I was stuck there for a whole day in a wind so strong I had to sit down and thumb. However, the first car that came by the next day gave me a lift, but that's hitching for you. *Alan Barlow, Cheadle, UK*

If crossing the Channel from Dover, Folkestone, etc., keep your eyes open for special 'cheapy' returns. These can be half the normal single fare. *Hinsh, Glasgow*

Forget sleeping rough in the Bois de Boulogne. Quite a few people, including some locals, tell us that it's frequented by some very nasty male transvestite prostitutes and is therefore patrolled by rough gendarmes. *Simon Wadsworth, Shipley, West Yorkshire, England*

Monte Carlo – walk through the tunnel, keep to the lower road, walk past the sandy beach to the next stony beach and you reach the only place to sleep rough. You often find 50 people on this beach. *Mari Doyle, Godalming, Surrey, UK*

You always give the city of Nîmes a mention. As your readers are sure to be wearers of denim, would they not like to know that that is where it first came from – de Nîmes? *Moyna Gardner, Glasgow, Scotland*

In Paris, for those who sleep rough, Jardin des Plantes is a good place – especially around August when it is full of other people roughing it. Police check the place around 7 a.m. *Nige and Paul, Bath, Avon, England*

The cops in Paris won't hassle you unless you hassle them. Always carry your passport with you and try to have at least

10 francs on you or you could be pulled in for vagrancy. They have a right to hold you for 48 hours without charges (garde à vue). With the recent political riots, it pays to steer well clear of demonstrations in Paris and other university cities such as Montpellier. The CRS (riot police) are a very unfriendly lot. You don't ask them for the time! *Paul Hinckley, Birmingham, England*

Don't use the toilets just inside the entrance at Mont St Michel – free ones higher up. Don't even buy a postcard near the entrance – everything gets cheaper the closer you get to the top. And don't eat in the restaurants there – small portions and expensive. *Peter Nelson, Planet Earth*

Here's a tip for a rainy day in Paris: If you want to see the latest pop music videos for free, just go into any O'KITCH burger place and sit down. They're all over the place – I know of two in the St Michel area and one on the Champs Elysées. If you happen to be hungry and into junk food, then they also have very reasonable prices and the usual wide choice.

I hitched in France with a Canadian flag on my pack. The French seem to prefer the Canadians to us Brits because of the common language.

You seem to overestimate the cost of public transport in Paris. On the métro you can go anywhere for only 4F, cheaper if you buy a *carnet. Paul Hinckley, Birmingham, UK*

Belgium

population	9,800,000
size	12,000 square miles
capital	Brussels, population 1,200,000
government	Constitutional monarchy
religion	Mostly Roman Catholic
language	French, Flemish, and some German; English widely spoken
currency	*Belgian franc* One *franc* equals 100 *centimes*. Coins of 50 *centimes* and of 1, 5, 10, 20 *francs*. Notes of 50, 100, 500, 1000, 5000 *francs*

Entry into Belgium from England is by ferry from Dover,

Felixstowe, Folkestone or Hull to either Zeebrugge or Ostend. A jetfoil service (fast but expensive) also runs between Dover and Ostend.

Principal cities after Brussels are **Liège, Bruges, Ghent** and **Antwerp**.

Ostend is one of the country's largest seaside resorts and even though it has 186 hotels and caters to the very solid tourist types it's a rather likeable place – one day at a time. The port is nice and there are a few things to see, but don't stop there if you're pushed for time.

Bruges, just a dozen or so kilometres inland from the sea, is one of the big art centres of Belgium and one of the most unspoiled medieval cities in Europe. The most important commercial city in Europe during the thirteenth and fourteenth centuries, it is now one of the most popular for tourists. See the old market square and the 275-foot-high belfry with its treasure-room and 11,400 lb Triumph Bell. See the Basilica of the Holy Blood where they keep what is believed to be a drop of Christ's blood – and if you're in town on Ascension Day (Ascension Day is a moveable feast held in May) catch the famous Procession of the Holy Blood. To see paintings by Brueghel the Younger, Van Eyck and Bosch, drop into the Groeninge Museum. If you have a student card and feel like visiting each of the sixteen museums and galleries in Bruges, you can buy a special discount card from tourist offices or museums.

If you are interested in exploring the infamous Flanders Fields of the First World War visit **Ieper** (or Ypres). The town stands in the middle of the old battlefields 50 kilometres south of Bruges.

Ghent, 30 kilometres down either the E5 or the N10 from Bruges, is known as the City of Flowers, and every fifth year (1985–1990) hosts the Ghent *Floralies*, a huge international flower show. The other four years you can visit St Bavo's Cathedral, the Castle of the Counts (see the horrifying collection of torture instruments), the Castle of Gerard the Devil (not as good as the Castle of the Counts, but it has a better name) and see the Ghent Museum of Fine Arts for a fantastic collection of Flemish paintings. Have a look, also, at Mad Meg, a fifteenth-century cannon, 17 feet long, and weighing 16 tons, which used to spit out stone balls weighing 750 lb.

Antwerp, the world's leading diamond centre, is not a madly exciting city to my mind, but if you're going that way, drop in and see Rubens' house where the famous artist lived and worked. The Museum Mayer Van Den Bergh has a good collection, including 'Dulle Griet' by the mystical Mr Brueghel. Seagoing types might be interested in the National Maritime Museum and, talking of the sea, it's interesting to note that even though Antwerp is 75 kilometres from the ocean it's the world's fourth largest port. It has 45 kilometres of docks along the banks of the Scheldt River (which drains into the sea) and those docks see 50,000 barges and 10,000 oceangoing ships tie up each year. Try the barges for possible river rides. It's done quite often by hitchers who drop the hard word into the right soft ear. The port also boasts a wild nightlife.

Halfway between Antwerp and Brussels on the E10 is **Breendonk** where the Belgians have kept intact a Nazi concentration camp. Nasty to look at and a sledgehammer reminder of what 'people' are capable of doing.

Binche, between Mons and Charleroi, is the scene of one of the wildest carnivals in Europe, culminating on Shrove Tuesday – Pancake Day. Great show if you can make it; fancy dress (Peruvian), flour bombs, more booze than you've seen in your life and lots of single ladies and gentlemen guarantee that it's a swinging show. You'll probably need a full day to rest after it, so budget accordingly.

Tournai, 80 kilometres from Brussels on the N8, is a town of 35,000 which dates from AD 275 and mainly for those interested in history and architecture. For instance, its five-steepled Romanesque church is considered one of the finest in the world, while the belfry is the oldest in the country. Of particular interest are the ancient houses which dot the city.

Bastogne, on the N4 near the Luxembourg border, is a tourist centre for the Ardennes area. It's famous as the town where, during the Battle of the Bulge, when the Germans had the American forces surrounded and sent a man under truce to ask them to surrender, the American commander answered 'Nuts', thus leaving the German translator with an untranslatable word.

Waterloo, just north of Brussels, is the battlesite where Napoleon met his you-know-what. In the town's main street you can visit Wellington's headquarters and a museum, while on the battlefield itself you can see Napoleon's headquarters and other museums and memorials.

Liège is yet another of Belgium's important art cities, and if you visit don't miss the sixteenth-century Palace of the Prince Bishops, the Museum of Fine Arts or the Museum of Walloon Life which concentrates on life in Liège during past centuries.

Hitch-hiking is OK in Belgium, though the big main highway through from Ostend to Brussels – the E5 – can sometimes prove to be a trap. However, with any luck you'll meet someone on the ferry who is taking a car over and you'll be right on your way. Be warned that the Belgians are amongst the fastest and worst drivers in the world.

Brussels: where to sleep

Expect to pay 200 francs even for hostels and as much as 450 francs for a cheap room. Make sure VAT and 10 per cent service fee are included.

CHAB at 6 rue Traversière (tel: 219 47 50).

Hôtel de Jeunes-Saint Gilles at 14 rue des Etudiants (tel: 539 07 25).

YMCA at 31 rue Duquesmoy (tel: 513 47 55). Men only.

YWCA at 43 rue St Bernard (tel: 538 09 84). Women only.

International Youth Home at 21 rue du Congrès (tel: 218 48 53). Take student card.

Centre International des Etudiants at 26 rue de Parme (tel: 537 89 61). Ask for dormitory.

Cité Universitaire at 22 avenue Paul Héger (tel: 647 10 56). Open 1 August to 15 September.

'Sleepwell' Sleep-in, 27 rue de la Blanchisserie (near Pl. Rogier) (tel: 218 13 13).

Hôel des Touristes at 11 rue du Marché (tel: 217 64 37).

Hôtel Osborne at 67 rue Bosquet (tel: 537 92 51).

Ballon Nord at 24 rue de Brabant (tel: 217 54 87).

Résidence Botanique at 171 rue Royale (tel: 217 82 20).

Hôtel Ruche Bourse at 1 rue Grétry (tel: 218 58 87).

Hôtel Sabot d'Or at 5 Boulevard d'Anvers (tel: 217 48 69).

Hôtel Du Merlo at 2 avenue Fonsny (tel: 538 15 69).

Hôtel Sainte-Anne at 1a Boulevard Jardin Botanique (tel: 218 35 19).

Hôtel Alfa at 144 rue Defacqz (tel: 537 04 19).

Résidence Berckmans at 12 rue Berckmans.

For help finding hotels contact the Brussels Information Office at rue Marché aux Herbes. For help in locating student accommodation try the **MUBEF** at 61 rue Belliard.

For sleeping rough there's Parc de Brussels, the Botanic Gardens or the Parc Josaphat. But be warned – the word is that Belgian police are coming down hard these days.

Brussels: where to eat

As in most of Europe a good filling meal will cost 175–250 francs in a cheap restaurant or perhaps less if you use student facilities or chain cafeterias.

Cité Universitaire at 22 avenue Paul Héger.

YWCA at 43 rue St Bernard. Dinner served between 7 and 8 p.m. Women only.

YMCA at 31 rue Duquesmoy. Dinner between 7 and 8 p.m. Men only.

Sarma (department store) at 17 rue Neuve. Closes 6 p.m.

Au Bon Marché (department store) at Place Rogier. Closes 8 p.m.

Chez Georges at 24 rue des Chapeliers.

Restaurant Hubert at 33 rue du Progrès.

Brussels: what to see and do

THE GRAND' PLACE This is the heart of Brussels and has been since medieval times. Originally it was a marketplace and is still used as such in the mornings. Sunday morning is the scene of a bird market. The *Hôtel de Ville* (Town Hall) is one of the oldest and most beautiful of the buildings on the square. A few francs gets you in for a tour. Directly opposite the Hôtel de Ville is the *Maison du Roi*, a restored sixteenth-century building housing the Municipal Museum.

FLEA MARKET at Place du Jeu de Balle. Every day from 9 a.m. to 1 p.m. Best days Saturdays and Sundays.

THE OLD MARKET at Place du Grand Sablon. Mostly antiques (swords, furniture, rare books, etc.). All day Saturday and also Sunday morning.

MANNEKEN-PIS in rue du Chêne, near the Grand' Place. A small statue of a small boy taking a small leak. Not really worth seeing, but like the Mermaid in Copenhagen, you gotta go and have a look.

MUSÉE D'ART ANCIEN at 3 rue de la Régence. Free on Wednesday, Saturday and Sunday afternoons. Tremendous collection of Flemish art. This is where you can get a head full of Bosch and Brueghel.

THE BRUEGHEL MUSEUM at 132 rue Haute. Strictly for serious Brueghel fans, but for them it's going to be a real trip.

NEW POL'S JAZZ PLACE at 23A rue de Stassart. Live jazz, silent movies, friendly people. Closed Sundays and Mondays.

CLUBS Try along Avenue de la Toison d'Or (between Chaussée d'Ixelles and Porte Louise) for fairly cheap prices and a fairly good chance for some action.

MUSÉE DU CINÉMA at 9 rue Baron Horta in the Palais des Beaux-Arts. This is a museum of the cinema which also shows several classic movies in the original language each night. You might catch an old one you've been hunting for. There are 12,000 titles in the archives (tel: 513 41 55).

YOUTH INFORMATION CENTRES You can find information and advisory centres throughout the country. They will help you locate beds and meals at reasonable prices, and introduce you to youth associations, societies and clubs. The following are all in Brussels:

Infor-Jeunes, 27 rue Marché aux Herbes (tel: 512 32 74).
J-Center, 27 rue de la Blanchisserie (tel: 218 13 13). They have another office at the Brussels South Station (Gare du Midi). Open 6–9 p.m.

SOS Jeunes, open day and night (tel: 736 36 36). (For addresses of youth information centres elsewhere in Belgium, ask the tourist office for a free copy of their budget holidays brochure.)

Transport in Brussels

Bus and tram tickets are expensive enough, but if you're in town a few days prices will really add up. So try investing in a six-journey card or a weekly ticket (Monday to Friday). Each offers big discounts; buy them at stations.

Student discounts

Special reductions to most museums, galleries, theatres and cinemas throughout the country. Information from:

MUBEF, 61 rue Belliard, Brussels 4 (tel: 513 07 12).

Addresses

Main post office (for poste restante) at rue des Halles, Brussels.

American Express at 22–24 Place Charles Rogier, Brussels (tel: 219 01 90).

Tourisme des Etudiants et de la Jeunesse (MUBEF) at 61 rue Belliard, Brussels 4 (tel: 513 07 12).

Brussels Information Centre at 61 rue Marché aux Herbes, Brussels (tel: 513 89 40).

Belgian National Tourist Office at 61 rue Marché aux Herbes, Brussels (tel: 513 90 90).

US Embassy at 27 Boulevard du Régent, Brussels (tel: 513 38 30).

British Embassy at 28 rue Joseph II, Brussels (tel: 219 11 65).

Hitchers' Tips and Comments . . .

Brussels. Cafés really expensive. Stick to picnic meals. Good place to rest is railway station lounge – soft leather couches.
Malcolm Frankland, Glaslum, England

If you need a clean-up in Brussels, go to the services under the main station. You get a good, hot shower there for a reasonable price. *Patrick Hine, Oxford, England*

In Belgium and France us females can get hit up to 30p a time for using public toilets. Take advantage of cafés and hostels. *Avril Horton, Leeds, UK*

To get out of Brussels, go to the central tram station and take the tram to Diamant. From Diamant it's only 200 yards to the motorway slip road which takes you south. *Doug Bissell, 'The Clydeside Rebel', Glasgow, Scotland*

The Snuffel Sleep-in in Bruges is a cheap place to stay. *Craig Seaton, Worksop, Notts, England*

In Brussels, while sleeping in a small park in the city centre, we were 'accosted' by the police about 8 a.m. All they did was check our passports and send us on our way. Cooperate and smile and you'll be all right. *Nige and Paul, Bath, Avon, England*

The Netherlands

population	14,300,000
size	15,892 square miles
capital	Amsterdam, population 710,000
government	Constitutional monarchy
religion	Protestant and Roman Catholic
language	Dutch; a lot of English spoken, especially in the cities
currency	*Guilder* One *guilder* equals 100 *cents*. Coins of 5, 10, 25 *cents*, and of 1 and 2½ *guilders*. Notes of 5, 10, 25, 50, 100, 1000 *guilders*

After Amsterdam, the most important cities to see are Rotterdam and The Hague.

Rotterdam, with 600,000 inhabitants, is the largest port in Europe and the second largest in the world. Its 47 kilometres of dockside are worth going down to see. Waalhaven Dock is the largest artificial harbour in the world. For a great view over the port, climb to the 383-foot-high lookout on the 600-foot Euromast (if you can afford the heavy entrance charge) – but avoid the restaurant, it's expensive. The Boymans-van Beuningen Museum claims to be the richest in Holland after the Rijksmuseum in Amsterdam. If it's half as good it's doing well. For a look at a building of a different sort, try the largest one in Western Europe. The Groothandelsgebouw, or wholesaler's building, is 220 metres long, 84 wide and 43 high. In it are 300 offices, a restaurant, meeting-halls, a post office, bowling alleys plus lots more, including a staff of 5000. Another interesting feature is its 1½ kilometres of road – inside! – leading to various indoor parking facilities. Americans might be interested in seeing Delfshaven, embarkation point of the Pilgrim Fathers in 1620.

The Hague, just a few short kilometres up the E10 from Rotterdam, has a lot more to offer. This city of 500,000 is the seat of Holland's government and the home of the Peace Palace, the International Justice Court. See the Municipal Museum with its fine line-up of modern art, including the world's largest collection of Mondrians. Philatelists should try the Dutch Postal Museum. To see one of the most unusual (and largest) paintings in the world, drop in on the Mesdag Panorama, while for a somewhat ghoulish hour go to the Prisoner's Gate to see the collection of torture instruments.

Don't miss the miniature town of Madurodam. It's built over an area of four acres, complete with three kilometres of railway track, houses, castles, churches, and even an airport, all constructed perfectly to a 1/25th scale. Open April to September.

Near The Hague is the seaside resort of **Scheveningen**. The long, long beach is the ideal place to sleep while you're visiting The Hague and a marvellous place – on sunny days – to make contact with sunbathers of the opposite sex. The pier is a sideshow-type place jutting 1200 feet out into the sea and makes for pleasant evening walking. The fishing harbour is a riot of smells just about any morning.

North of The Hague and a few kilometres from Amsterdam is **Haarlem**, where you can see the Frans Hals Museum and the Great Church of St Bavo which houses one of the largest organs in the world.

North again and you come to **Alkmaar** where the big sight on Friday mornings from April to September is the cheese market which has been held there for centuries.

Utrecht, south of Amsterdam, with a population of nearly half a million, is dotted with ancient houses and canals. Its cathedral, the Dom, built between 1254 and 1517, has a steeple 360 feet tall, the highest in the country, and it's a great place from which to get an overall view of the city. Try, also, to see the Viking ship in the Municipal Museum. Music buffs might want to try the 'From Musical Box to Barrel Organ' exhibition at the National Museum.

For Van Gogh fans there are two special treats in Holland. The first, of course, is at the Van Gogh Museum in Amsterdam. The second is at **Otterlo National Park**, a few kilometres north-west of **Arnhem**, where there is another large and excellent collection of the man's work housed in the Kröller-Müller Museum.

Maastrict, right down in southern Holland in the enclave which juts in between Germany and Belgium, is an industrial city which is worth visiting for two reasons. First, because as a result of its geographical position, it uses three languages and has a strange mixture of Dutch, Belgian and German customs; and second, because just outside town is the St Pietersberg with its 300 kilometres of man-made tunnels bored into a 110-metre-high limestone hill. Thousands of people have visited them over the centuries and carved their names in the soft walls, including Napoleon, Voltaire and Sir Walter Scott.

★**Hitching** Hitching in Holland is generally good – you can cross the entire country in a couple of hours – but remember that if you want to travel fast you must keep to the big highways. Holland is one of the most densely populated areas in the world and it's very easy to get trapped on a village to village, town to town tour if you stay on the small roads. (Not that there's anything wrong with that if you have the time to spare!) The same rules apply on the highways as on the German autobahns – no hitching! You must grab your ride on the exit or entrance roads. Cops in white Porsches are around to make sure you do just that.

★**Tulips and windmills** There used to be 9000 working windmills in Holland. Now, unless you know where to look, you can travel through the entire country without seeing one. The place to go is **Kinderdijk**, a few kilometres east of Rotterdam, where the largest concentration of those still remaining can be found. (During July and August the nineteen mills operate on Saturdays.) The tulips can be seen at their best around mid-April to early May – acres of them. Best areas are between **Leiden** and **Haarlem**. If you

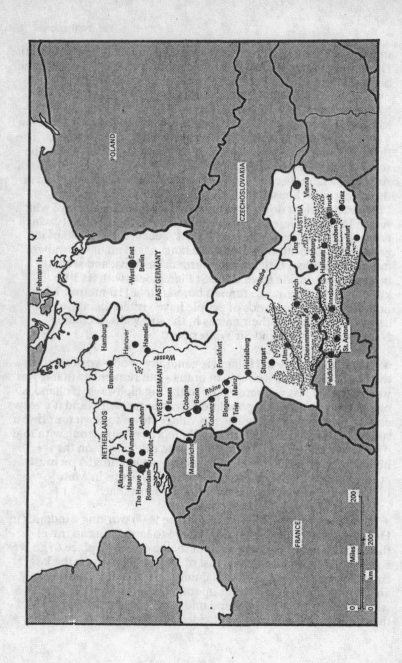

specifically want to see them you should avoid the big roads and plot a route which will take you through the small villages west of the N99.

★**Hitching barges** This is becoming a more and more popular method of offbeat travel – but you must have plenty of time if you want to do a complete trip. Rotterdam is the place to start and from there you can go right through the Rhine into Switzerland. Just ask a barge captain – some will tell you to go to hell, but plenty won't. Most charge for food, some don't. If, because of the time factor, you decide you can only afford one day aboard, you'll have much less trouble finding a boat.

Warning! Two readers have written in warning about the drug scene in Holland. The gist of it is this . . . people are lulled into a false sense of confidence because everyone in Amsterdam seems so free and easy. When they try their same tricks in the provincial towns they get busted so fast their heads spin. Take care!

Amsterdam: where to sleep

Sleeping prices are high in Amsterdam – even the youth hostel costs 18 guilders – but the blow is softened a bit when you discover that the price always includes a breakfast guaranteed to set you on your feet for the day. Most of these breakfasts are large enough so that you can take a portion away with you and use it as a lunchtime snack. Generally, expect to pay between 35 and 70 guilders for bed and breakfast in an hotel.

Youth Hostel Stadsdoelen at Kloveniersburgwal 97 (tel: 24 68 32).

Youth Hostel Vondelpark, Zandpad 5 (tel: 83 17 44).

Fat City at Oude Zijds Voorburgwal 157 (tel: 020–226 705).

Hotel Adolesce at Nieuwe Keizersgracht 26 (tel: 26 39 59). Ask for dormitory.

Bob's Youth Hostel at Nieuwe Zijds Voorburgwal 92 (tel: 23 00 63).

Hans Brinker Hotel at Kerkstraat 136 (tel: 22 06 87). This one is very good, but also pretty expensive.

Hotel Cok at Koningslaan 1 (tel: 64 61 11).

Hotel Groenendael, Nieuwendijk 15 (tel: 24 48 22). Ask for dormitory.

The Shelter (Christian), Barndesteeg 21–25 (tel: 25 32 30). No breakfast. Ask for dormitory.

Adam & Eva at Sarphatistraat 105 (tel: 24 62 06). Ask for dormitory.

Hotel de Beurs, Beursstraat 7 (tel: 22 07 41).

Eben Haëzer (Christian) at Bloemstraat 179 (tel: 24 47 17). Ask for dormitory.

Magic Inn at Nieuwe Zijds Voorburgwal 27 (tel: 24 96 06). Ask for dormitory.

H88 at Herengracht 88 (tel: 24 44 46). Closed in winter. Ask for dormitory.

Hotel Clemens, Raadhuisstraat 39II (tel: 24 60 89).

Kabul Student Hotel at Warmoesstraat 38–42 (tel: 23 71 58). Ask for dormitory.

Hotel Brian at Singel 69 (tel: 24 46 61).

Hotel Anja at Single 97 (tel: 24 16 17).

Studenten Hotel at Keizersgracht 15 (tel: 25 13 64).

Hotel Ronnie at Raadhuisstraat 41B (tel: 24 28 21).

Hotel Schirmann at Prins Hendrikkade 23 (tel: 24 19 42).

Hotel Schröder at Haalemmerdijk 48B (tel: 266 272).

Hotel de Westertoren at Raadhuisstraat 35B (tel: 24 46 39).

Hotel Galerij, Raadhuisstraat 43 (tel: 24 88 51).

Hotel van Onna at Bloemgracht 102 (tel: 26 58 01).

Hotel Grégoire at Nic Maesstraat 77B (tel: 72 95 67).

It's worth remembering that student hostels in Holland are generally open to anyone, with or without student credentials, as long as they look *something* like a student.

Also, if you're travelling with someone, double rooms work out cheaper per person than singles.

For help with all accommodation problems, contact the VVV Tourist Information Office at Stationsplein 10 which is open every day in summer until 11 p.m. They operate a Sleep-In at Mauritskade 28, near Metro Station Weesperplein (tel: 94 74 44) – a huge dormitory of 800 beds. Cost is around 12 guilders. You bring your own sleeping-bag. Check VVV for current addresses and price.

Also ask them for *Use-it*, a free newspaper published annually, featuring money-saving advice on accommodation and restaurants for travelling youth (that's you!). A *Use-it* weekly is published throughout the summer months, telling you what's on that week.

Sleeping rough should be no problem. Julianapark, Vondelpark and Beatrixpark are your best bets, but be warned that sleeping in public parks is illegal. There are youth camping grounds at: **Zeeburg**, IJdijk (A'dam-Oost) (tel: 94 66 88). **Vliegenbos**, Meeuwenlaan 138 (A'dam-Noord) (tel: 36 88 55). (Both cost around 7 guilders.)

Amsterdam: where to eat

Beds are expensive in Amsterdam and so is food. Expect to pay as much as 15–18 guilders for the main meal of the day. If you're eating breakfast away from your hotel, try a slice of *ontbijtkoek*. If you have a sweet tooth, try the deep-fried *poffertjes*.

Student Mensa at Damstraat 3 (behind monument in Dam Square).

The Chinese and Indonesian Restaurants in the Binnen Bantammerstraat near Central Station. Good filling meals. The lunchtime specials are the best deals.

Van Dobben at Korte Reguliersdwarsstraat 5–9. Sandwich shop. Cheap.

Moeders Pot at Vinkenstraat 119.

Kow Loon at Single 498. Very cheap Oriental-type food.

Oldewelt at Nieuwendijk 100. Cheap Dutch food.

Hema Department Store Cafeteria at Nieuwendijk 174.

Blauwe Hollander at Leidse Kruisstraat 28.

VGK Restaurant at Spuistraat 4. Open Monday to Friday and closes 7 p.m.

Ta Dung at Bethaniendwarsstraat 10. Chinese and dirt cheap.

Restaurant Leto – Plate service at Haarlemmerdijk 114.

Quick Snackbar at the corner of Martelaarsgracht and Nieuwendijk 50. An automat place where you can fill yourself for 10 guilders.

H88 at Herengracht 88. Cheap.

Coffee Haesje Claes at Nieuwe Zijds Voorburgwal 320.

Indonesian Restaurant Sukasari at Damstraat 26.

Buddha's Belly at Rozenstraat 145. Indian food.

De Lantaarn at 2e Const. Huygenstraat 64.

Kosmos at Prins Hendrikkade 142. Macrobiotic food at reasonable prices.

Amsterdam: what to see and do

THE STEDELIJK MUSEUM in Paulus Potterstraat is probably the greatest museum of modern art in Europe. The collections are superbly displayed and unbelievably good. De Kooning, Mondrian, Miró, Degas, Cézanne, Chagall, Picasso . . . you name it. Admission charge. Closed on Mondays.

VAN GOGH MUSEUM on Museumplein. Entrance in Paulus Potterstraat. A mind-bender! Don't miss it! Closed Mondays.

THE RIJKSMUSEUM is just a couple of hundred yards from the Stedelijk. Admission charge. The museum houses a superb classical collection. Particularly strong on Rembrandt (they have his 'Night Watch'). Also Vermeer, Goya, Tintoretto, Hals, Rubens, Jan Steen, etc.

THE WATERFRONT AREA Free and fascinating. Set in amongst the streets and alleys of the Zeedijk/Nieuwmarkt area is Europe's vastest collection of bars, dives, queer-shops, clubs, cafés, and brothels. Also, be warned that the Zeedijk plays host to some of

Europe's nastiest drug-pushers. No point in describing it all – just get down and have a look round about 11 at night. (Lone lady hitchers should find company before setting out to see the area at night.)

MOVIES Shown in original language. Plenty of first-run American and English shows. Prices lower than in most capital cities.

REMBRANDT'S HOUSE at Jodenbreestraat 4. Admission charge. Rembrandt lived here for twenty years. It contains a large collection of his etchings and drawings.

THE HOUSE OF ANNE FRANK at 263–265 Prinsengracht. Admission charge. This is where Anne Frank, the young Jewish girl who wrote the famous *Diary*, lived with her family in total isolation and secrecy for two years during the German occupation of the city. In 1944 the family was betrayed, the Gestapo arrested them and they were sent to a concentration camp where Anne died. The secret apartment has been preserved in its entirety. A permanent exhibition on contemporary anti-semitism is displayed in the building.

FREE BEER! FREE FOOD! The Heineken brewery at Van der Helststraat 30 give guided tours of their establishment at 9 a.m. and 11 a.m., Monday to Friday. At the end of the tour there's free beer, free cheese and sometimes free cigarettes. I hear, though, that in summer the breweries are asking a small fee which is donated to UNICEF.

CANAL TRIPS cost money but are a fine way of seeing Amsterdam if it's your first day there (and if you can put up with the same jokes being cracked by the same hostess in four different languages!). Trips last about an hour. You'll see the boats and advertisements near the Central Station.

FLEA MARKET at Waterlooplein. Every morning except Sundays. Good for secondhand clothes.

MUSEUM AMSTELKRING at Oude Zijds Voorburgwal 40 is more popularly known as 'Our Lord in the Attic'. This strange church is completely camouflaged and hidden within the top floors of several old canal houses. It was built during the Reformation when the Roman Catholics were having trouble with the authorities.

WORLD'S NARROWEST HOUSE Said the coachman to his boss, 'Sir, if only I had a house as wide as your front door.' Said the boss,

'You shall.' The result is at Singel 7 – the house of Mr Tripp's coachman.

Transport in Amsterdam

Cheapest way to travel around is by trams, buses and metro.

For bicycle rental try Koenders, Stationsplein Oostzijde 1012AB (tel: 24 83 91).

Student discounts

Reductions to some theatres, cinemas, galleries, museums, restaurants and nightclubs. For information, contact: NBBS STUDENT CENTRE, Dam 17, Amsterdam (tel: 23 76 86).

Addresses

Main post office (for poste restante) at NZ Voorburgwal 182, Amsterdam.

American Express at Damrak 55, Amsterdam (tel: 262 042).

NBBS (Netherlands Bureau for Foreign Student Relations) at Dam 17, Amsterdam (tel: 23 76 86).

NBBS at Rapenburg 8, Leiden (tel: 071 145044).

Amsterdam Tourist Office (VVV) at Stationsplein 10, and Leidseplein 15, Amsterdam (tel: 26 64 44).

US Consulate at Museumplein 19, Amsterdam (tel: 79 03 21).

British Consulate-General, Koningslaan 44, Amsterdam (tel: 76 43 43).

Hitchers' Tips and Comments ...

You never mention Groningen; it's known as 'The Amsterdam of the North' and well worth the trip. Start hitching from the entrance to the E35 motorway outside Diemen (south-east of Amsterdam). There is a gas station there. *Mike Plummer, Seaview, Isle of Wight*

For those hitching from Amsterdam south to Germany, towards Cologne; it's much faster to go via Eindhoven, not via Arnhem. *Patrick Hine, Oxford, England*

Interesting and cheap hunting ground for rooms in Amsterdam is around the station and post office. An alternative to hotels and hostels is the fluctuating population of houseboats offering accommodation. *Alan Thatcher, New Zealand*

Please tell your readers that they should leave their valuables in a safe locker or hand them in at reception when staying at hostels. More and more travellers are the victims of robbery and pickpockets. Too many people lose their money, and their holiday pleasure, because they keep everything on them even when they don't need it. Lady hitchers should be particularly careful if walking around with any sort of handbag. They're an easy target for snatchers. *Hostel Warden, Jeugdherberg 'Stadsdoelen', Amsterdam, Holland*

When crashing in Amsterdam, beware the higher than usual percentage of creeps and nasties – most of whom have been on one trip too many. For safety, get locked in a park. I succeeded in Wertheim Park. It's not so far out as your other suggestions, either. Just make sure the railings aren't too high to clamber over next morning and that no addicts or psychos are locked in with you. *Philip Attwool, Orpington, UK*

Many truckers going to and from Holland and Germany cross the border at Venlo. Try hitching with Venlo sign for good lift. *Evan M. Jones, Cardiff, Wales*

I discovered special places in Amsterdam called 'Liftplaats'. To head south, east, or north-east out of Amsterdam, take tram 12 to Amstel Station. There is a Liftplaats area nearby. Such areas are set aside especially for hitchers! However, just because they are set aside for the likes of us doesn't mean they are the best places. Heading to West Germany, I waited five hours and eventually got a ride to Apeldoorn.

Groningen is nice to visit but terrible to leave. There is a horrendously complex ring road system, signs pointing in every (wrong) direction. To head into West Germany, don't go to the Liftplaats area (left out of station, underneath the

flyover), it's in the wrong direction. Take the bus or train to
Hoogezand. From then on, it's plain sailing into Germany.
Mark Naisbitt, Darlington, Durham, UK

West Germany

population	62,000,000
size	(excluding West Berlin) 95,742 square miles
capital	Bonn, population 300,000
government	Federal republic
religion	All denominations
language	German; some French and English understood
currency	*Deutschmark* One *Mark* equals 100 *Pfennige*. Coins of 1, 2, 5, 10, 50 *Pfennige* and of 1, 2, 5 *Marks*. Notes of 5, 10, 20, 50, 100, 500, 1000 *Marks*

There's a lot to see in Germany, but I'll start by mentioning
something which you *can't* see unless you're in Europe in 1990 or
2000. This is the famous Passion Play which is held in the village of
Oberammergau every ten years. The play, which is performed by
the villagers and which attracts crowds from all over the world,
was first staged in 1634 after the village prayed that the Black
Death which was ravaging Europe at that time should spare the
tiny town. It did. From then on the play was performed every
decade until 1934 when Hitler stopped it. It resumed in 1950 and
the most recent performance was in 1980.

Ulm, which is about 100 kilometres north-west of Oberammergau,
is a city of 100,000, large enough to be interesting but small
enough to walk in. It's fairly representative of what you'll find in
Germany. Clean, spacious, and dotted with ancient landmarks
(many rebuilt since the devastation of Second World War
bombing). The city, birthplace of Albert Einstein, houses a
fourteenth-century Gothic cathedral with the highest stone church
spire in the world – 528 feet.

To the west of Ulm is the beautiful **Black Forest** area – ideal for
slow village to village wandering.

Heidelberg is the favourite German city of thousands of tourists.
Celebrated in songs and plays it still seems to cling longingly to the
memories of its past. It's the home of Germany's oldest and most
famous university, founded in 1386. Visit the Red Ox, an old

student inn, which was the scene of many a duelling challenge. You might also go and see the thirteenth-century castle which houses the Apothecary Museum and the famed Heidelberg Tun, a gigantic wine barrel which hold 221,726 litres – or about 50,000 gallons.

Continuing down the Rhine you reach **Frankfurt** where you can see Goethe's House and Museum and the Stadel Art Institute which displays a good collection of European paintings.

Bingen am Rhein, just west of **Mainz** (which holds a wine festival in August and September) is a wine town crowned by Klopp Castle. Climb up there for great views over the Rhine Valley.

Koblenz, at the head of the twisting, turning vineyard-lined Mosel Valley, is a city of 100,000 and another wine centre. Its big landmark is the Ehrenbreitstein Fortress. If you have time, try to catch a river barge from Koblenz which will take you down along the Mosel to **Trier** (just near the border with Luxembourg) which is the oldest town in Germany and one of the oldest in Europe. Lots of Roman ruins to see. Whether you hitch a barge or a car, the Mosel trip is worthwhile. (Also possible to find grape-picking work in this area around September.)

North-west of Koblenz is **Bonn**, capital of the Federal Republic, birthplace of Beethoven (see his house and the museum), and home of Poppelsdorf Castle. A few kilometres farther on is **Cologne** (or Köln) which was founded by the Romans in 32 BC and badly battered by the Allies in the last war. See the famous cathedral (if you can stand the sight of yet another) which dates from 1248 and is one of the largest Gothic buildings in the world.

North of Cologne is the huge industrial complex centred on **Essen**. A nightmare of converging autobahns and twisting ring-roads, for me it's one of the ugliest areas in Europe. Getting in and out of the various towns and cities without spending money is virtually impossible. It's a hitch-hiker's hell on earth.

Hamelin, way away from all that and just south of **Hanover**, is a pleasant town of 60,000 which contains some of the best examples of timber-façaded houses in Germany. It was, also, the home of the legendary Pied Piper who is supposed to have led invading rats away from the town to the sound of his pipes and then, when he wasn't rewarded by the townspeople, to have caused the children to follow him in the same way. In the summer there is a Pied Piper procession through the streets every Sunday at noon.

Bremen, 63 kilometres inland on the Weser River, is the oldest seaport in Germany. The old part of the city is great for wandering. In the eleventh-century St Peter's Cathedral you can see 500-year-old mummies preserved in a lead-lined vault.

North of Bremen is **Hamburg** (population 2,000,000), which was terribly damaged in the Second World War. Her citizens have completed an amazing job of rebuilding. There are half a dozen museums worth looking through – especially the Kunst und Gewerbe which features arts and crafts dating back to the Middle Ages. But outdoing all the galleries and museums in the visitor stakes is the district of St Pauli where 300,000 souls per month go to enjoy themselves in the most up-to-date red-light district in the world. As *Time* magazine described it, you can 'swing into an underground garage, park, choose a Fräulein at a discreet *Kontakthof* (contact court), then take an elevator to one of two six-storey, modern sexscrapers named Eros Centre and Palais d'Amour'. Poorer types still go to streets like Herbertstrasse, just off the Reeperbahn, where sex is dished up like ham and eggs but at a slightly higher price.

Whichever road you take north of Hamburg leads you into Denmark. For ferry prices from **Fehmarn Island** (Puttgarten), see **Scandinavia, Finland and Iceland**.

★**Happenings** Germany is filled with festivals and concerts. The famed *Munich Oktoberfest* is mentioned below. Some others to look out for are: the *Great Marksmanship Contest* at Hanover in July; the *International Fair* at Frankfurt, March and September; the *Pied Piper of Hamelin Festival* at Hamelin, June to August; the *Christmas Fair* at Nuremberg in December; the *Killing of the Dragon* at Furth-im-Wald in August; the *Bach Week* at Ansbach in July and the *European Weeks* at Passau in June and July.

★**Auer Dult** This is a fantastic flea market of both junk and antiques which is held only three times a year in Munich's Mariahilfsplatz. Approximate times are April/May, July/August and mid-October. If you're looking for an unusual souvenir from your European trip, this'll be the place to find it. Check with German tourist office in any major city for exact dates from year to year.

★**Oktoberfest** The world-famous Munich beer festival draws thousands from all over the world – including Australians who have earned themselves a bad name in Munich ever since the year

a gang of them got stoned on the suds and hijacked a streetcar.
These festivities last 16 days and end on the first Sunday in
October. Precise details from any German tourist office.

★**Buy a ride!** Feeling lazy? Want a break from hitching? From
Munich you can buy a ride in a private car to a score of
destinations through Mitfahrzentrale, Lämmerstrasse 4, 8 Munich
2 (tel: 594561/63 or 592510). People driving between, say, Munich
and Essen, inform the company when they are going, saying they
want to take a passenger to share petrol costs. The company finds
the passenger and takes a commission. Typical prices:
Munich–Barcelona, 110 marks; Munich–Berlin, 60 marks;
Munich–Paris, 70 marks; Munich–Zurich, 40 marks. You can even
buy insurance and pay a booking fee! It mightn't be hitching, but
it's a good idea. Also try the bulletin board at the 'Studenthaus',
Leopoldstrasse 15.

★**Hitching** Important! You can only hitch on entry and exit roads
to autobahns. On entry roads, you are not supposed to stand
beyond the blue sign showing the white auto.

Munich: where to sleep

Outside of youth hostels, which in Germany cost around 15 marks,
there are not many cheap beds. Even student accommodation
costs about 13 marks. In cheap hotels be prepared to pay around
35 marks.

Youth camp at Kapuzinerhölzl (tel: 14 14 300). Tram No. 21 from
Main Railway Station (North) to Botanischergarten. About 6
marks a night. Open July and August.

YH Jugendherberge at Wendl-Dietrich Strasse 20 (tel: 13 11 56).
Closed from 2 January to 1 February.

YH Jugendgästehaus Thalkirchen, at Miesingstrasse 4 (tel: 72 36
550/72 36 560).

YH Jugendherberge Burg Schwaneck, Burgweg 4–6, Pullach
(about 12 kilometres from the centre of Munich) (tel: 7 93 06 43).

Haus International (Jugendhotel) at Elisabethstrasse 87 (tel: 18 50
81/82/83). Ask to share in five-bedded rooms.

YMCA-CVJM-Gästehaus at Landwehrstrasse 13 (tel: 55 59 41).

Übernachtungsheim at Goethestrasse 9 (tel: 55 58 91). Girls only.

St Paul's Kolleg at Paul-Heyse Strasse 18 (tel: 53 17 21). Ask for dormitory. Men only.

Kolping-Haus at Adolf Kolping Strasse (tel: 59 38 59).

For help in finding student accommodation contact the MUNICH STUDENT TRAVEL SERVICE at Luisenstrasse 43, 8 Munich 2 (tel: 52 30 00), or try JUGEND INFORMATIONSZENTRUM at Paul-Heyse Strasse 22, 8 Munich 2 (tel: 53 16 55). For help in finding hotels contact the *Verkehrsamt* at the main railway station. For sleeping out try the parks on the banks of the Isar River, or the huge park up behind the Haus der Kunst. (Hitcher Hugh Dunne reports: *Think twice about sleeping out there. Police with dogs search the place each night. You might get by if you stay north of the ringroad, but it's a hell of a walk, and you're better off on the banks of the Isar.*)

Remember that as in most of the big European cities you can drop your per-person bed costs considerably by taking a double or triple room in company with others.

Munich: where to eat

It's no problem to feed yourself for around 12 marks in Munich and the following list names some places where you can do just that:

Mensa Universität at Leopoldstrasse 15. Student card required.

Mensa Technische Universität at Arcisstrasse 17. Student card required.

Donisl Pschorr-Gaststätte at Weinstrasse 1 (Marienplatz).

Cornelius Schuler Buffeteria at Bayerstrasse 13.

Herties Department Store (cafeteria) at Bahnhofsplatz.

Kaufhof Department Store (cafeteria) at Karlsplatz.

Wienerwalds (chain group). There are 48 of them in Munich.

Good meals – carefully chosen – will cost you around 12 marks. Try:

Leopoldstrasse 44   Herzogstrasse 25
Frauenstrasse 4   Lindwurmstrasse 48

Nordsee Restaurant at Shutzenstrasse, near Herties Department
Store.

Ratskeller at Marienplatz 8.

Munich: what to see and do

DEUTSCHES MUSEUM One of Europe's great museums and the
largest science and technical museum in the world. Plenty of
buttons to push and a bonanza for anyone who can recognize a
wheel when they see one. Admission charge. Half price with
student card. On the Isarinsel.

ALTE PINAKOTHEK at Barerstrasse 27. Featuring paintings of the
fourteenth to eighteenth centuries, including some great ones.
Huge collection of Rubens and works by Velázquez, El Greco,
Leonardo, etc. Entrance charge, but free on Sundays.

HAUS DER KUNST at Prinzregentenstrasse 1. Fine collection of
French Impressionists. Admission charge, but free on Sundays.

NEUE PINAKOTHEK at Barerstrasse 29. Collection of nineteenth-
century paintings.

SCHLOSS NYMPHENBURG Take tram 21 from Dachauerstrasse. This
place was built between 1664 and 1823 as the Bavarian kings'
summer residence. A huge and remarkable complex in the
baroque-rococo style sitting in 500 acres of sculptured gardens.
Tough entrance fee which is halved if you carry a student card.
(The place was used as a setting in *Last Year in Marienbad*.)

DACHAU CONCENTRATION CAMP Take the S-Bahn to the town of
Dachau, then the Dachau–Ost bus to the camp. The place was
once one of the best organized slaughter yards in the Third Reich.
It implants in your mind once and for all that those figures in
history books were people.

THE GLOCKENSPIEL The performing clock on the tower of the town
hall. Animated figures do the usual stuff at 11 a.m. each day.

BEER HALLS With southern Germany's 1600 breweries producing
about a quarter of the world's beer supply you have to enter into

the spirit of the thing – and you do that in the beer halls. Entrance is free, except to certain sections where there is entertainment, and a half-litre stein costs about 4 marks. Try the *Hofbräuhaus* at Platzl 9 and the *Platzl* across the street. Two others worth a look-in are the *Löwenbräukeller* at Stiglmaierplatz and the *Mathäser Bier Stadt* at Bayerstrasse 5 which claims it can seat no less than 5500 beer-swilling customers.

DRUGSTORE at Wedekindplatz. Music and lots more.

Transport in Munich
The Munich transport system includes trams, buses, underground trains (*U-Bahn*) and suburban electric trains (*S-Bahn*). Tickets are expensive. Cost depends on length of journey. A 24-hour ticket allowing you to use all four systems in the city area costs around 12 marks.

Student discounts
Reduced tickets to theatres, cinemas. Reduced tickets or free entry to State-run galleries and museums. Cheaper entrance to fairs and exhibitions. For information contact:

MUNICH STUDENT TRAVEL SERVICE,
Luisenstrasse 43, 8 Munich 2 (tel: 52 30 00).

Crossing East Germany to West Berlin
The best hitching route into West Berlin is along the big Hanover–Berlin autobahn which crosses the east–west border at Helmstedt. This is the fastest route to Berlin from the industrial complex of Dortmund, Essen and Düsseldorf and the track most businessmen from those areas follow. But whichever road you take through East Germany, the following information is pertinent.

Foreigners are not permitted to hitch-hike on East German roads. Because of this you have to stop a car in West Germany which will take you right through to Berlin. This is one time when a placard stating your destination will come in handy. Petrol stations near border-crossing points are a good place to grab rides, but wherever you set yourself up remember that the West Germans do not permit hitch-hikers to stand on the side of the autobahn and the roads are continually patrolled. You can only hitch at the entrance – or *Einfahrt* – of an autobahn.

The following information comes from a pamphlet issued by the West Berlin Tourist Information Office.

REQUIREMENTS

1 German and foreign nationals: passport. A transit visa is issued at the checkpoints.

2 When driving by car: car registration papers, green international insurance card and initial plaque indicating nationality.

3 Make sure your car has enough petrol for driving through before entering the German Democratic Republic.

CURRENCY

The amount of West German marks and foreign currency allowed is unlimited. It is forbidden to take East German marks either into or out of East Germany.

CHECKPOINTS BETWEEN WEST GERMANY AND EAST GERMANY

Trains

Büchen–Schwanheide
Helmstedt–Marienborn
Bebra–Gerstungen
Ludwigsstadt–Probstzella
Hof–Gutenfürst

Cars

Gudow–Zarrentin
Helmstedt–Marienborn
Rudolphstein–Hirschberg
Herleshausen–Wartha

As a rule foreigners must also pay for a liability insurance in addition to fee for visas.

Berlin: where to sleep

The price structure is roughly the same as for Munich.

Youth Hostels at Berlin 19, Bayernallee 36 (Charlottenburg) (tel: 305 30 55). Berlin 28, Hermsdorfer Damm 48 (Hermsdorf) (tel: 404 16 10). Advance bookings to: Landesverband Berlin, Bayernallee 35 (Charlottenburg), 1000 Berlin 19 (tel: 305 30 55).

Jugendgästehaus at Berlin 30, Kluckstrasse 3 (Tiergarten) (tel: 261 10 97), and at Berlin 38, Kronprinzessinenweg 27 (Wannsee) (tel: 803 20 34). Advance bookings as above.

Gästehaus Elton at Pariserstrasse 9 (tel: 883 61 55).

Pension Carmer at Carmerstrasse 2 (tel: 317 060).

Hotel Pension Hanseat at Kurfürstendamm 35 (tel: 881 4746).

Bahnhof Mission at Bahnhof Zoo (in the central railway station). Cheapest place in town outside the youth hostels and it's more central.

YMCA at Einemstrasse 10 (tel: 261 37 91). Groups only.

Pension Atlas at Uhlandstrasse 171, Berlin 31 (tel: 883 79 19).

Centrum Pension at Kantstrasse 31, Berlin 12 (tel: 31 61 53).

For help with student accommodation, talk to the student travel organization Artu Berliner Gesellschaft für Studenten und Jugendaustausch mbH at Berlin 12, Hardenbergstrasse 9 (tel: 310 771).

The *Verkehrsamt* people at Europa Center will sort out hotel problems for you and charge 2 marks – unless they help you into hostel or student accommodation in which case it's free.

For sleeping out in Berlin it's best to move half an hour out of the city – there are a hell of a lot of police and uniforms around. Try anywhere round the Wannsee or the Grünewald – though these places are going to cost you about DM2·50 to reach on public transport. If you want to sleep out in the city, you should check with locals.

Two camping grounds are **Kohlhasenbruck** at Neue Kreisstrasse (tel: 805 17 37) and **Kladow** at Krampnitzer Weg 111–117 (tel: 365 27 97). The first is open only from April to September, the second all the year. Both are cheap and both have good facilities.

Berlin: where to eat

Same price structure as Munich.

Studentenhotel Berlin at Meiningerstrasse 10. Dinner served from 5 until 8 p.m. Only for groups of at least 10 people.

Kadewe Department Store at Wittenbergplatz.

Wienerwalds (chain group). Some of the more than a dozen
addresses are:
Kantstrasse 35   Tauentzienstrasse 16
Schloßstrasse 1   Kurfürstendamm 90

Burger King at Kurfürstendamm 224.

Sandy Snackbar at Kurfürstendamm 20.

TU Mensa at Hardenbergstrasse. Open 11–2.

Schipkapass at Hohenzollerndamm 185. Bohemian specialities.
Good quality at reasonable prices.

Shanghai (Chinese restaurant) at Bleibtreustrasse 31.

Bilka Department Store at Joachimstalerstrasse 5. The cheap,
fixed menu meal is only served until 6 p.m.

Athena Grill at Kurfürstendamm 156. A large Greek restaurant –
good value for money.

Hardtke's at Meinekestrasse 27 A and B does a good and
reasonably cheap three-course meal from about 1 o'clock until 3.

Sausage stands You can find them all around town – indeed, all
around Germany. A couple of big sausages with bread for about 3
marks apiece fills you up well if you're short of money.

Berlin: what to see and do

KAISER WILHELM GEDÄCHTNISKIRCHE in the Kurfürstendamm. A
new and very beautiful church standing beside the war-gutted shell
of the old. The West Berliners call the ruin the 'Hollow Tooth'.

CHECKPOINT CHARLEY at Friedrichstrasse brings back memories of
the Cold War when it was a real freeze. Near Charley is the
MUSEUM OF THE WALL which offers vivid testimony of escapes and
shooting incidents around the Wall.

DAHLEM MUSEUM at Arnimallee 23–27. This is one of Europe's
greatest galleries and if you like paintings, don't miss it. All classic
stuff, nothing after about 1800. Rembrandt, Brueghel, Dürer, El
Greco, Goya. And it's all for free. Closed Mondays.

BERLIN ZOO beside Tiergarten. Europe's largest zoo, with more than ten thousand animals, including – in the excellent aquarium – Europe's largest collection of crocodiles. Student card gets you in cheaper.

CHARLOTTENBURG PALACE at Luisenplatz. A day's outing in itself if you're an art-lover. The seventeenth-century palace is the home of half a dozen galleries and museums, including the Department of Egyptian Antiquities, opposite the palace, where you can see the famous 3300-year-old bust of Queen Nefertiti. The museums are all free but it costs to go into the palace and the mausoleum. The museum is closed on Fridays and the palace is closed on Mondays.

BRANDENBURG GATE which separates the East and West zones of the city.

THE REICHSTAG BUILDING, near the Brandenburg Gate, once housed Germany's Parliament. Its burning in 1933 was used by Hitler as an excuse to purge his opponents. The reconstructed building houses a photographic exhibit of German history from 1800 to the present.

NIGHTLIFE Try the *Big Eden* at Kurfürstendamm 202. It costs you about 7 marks to enter, which includes the first drink, and all drinks after the first are 7 marks. It's a big, big disco which can hold 2000 people – many of whom are looking for partners. Last I heard was that unescorted girls could enter free. Try also the *Big Apple* at Bundesallee 13 (disco, not too expensive).

Transport in Berlin
The subway is the cheapest way around. There are two systems – the U-Bahn and the S-Bahn both run by the West Berliners. Both lines operate in both the West and the East.

Best deal in town, though, is the 33-mark Touristenkarte which gives you unlimited travel on all buses, the U-Bahn and S-Bahn subway lines within the city for four days or 17 marks for two days. Buy it at the Berlin Public Transport Office at Potsdamerstrasse 188, or at the Zoo Station at Hardenbergplatz.

Student discounts
For details of what's available contact:
ARTU BERLINER GESELLSCHAFT FÜR STUDENTEN UND

JUGENDAUSTAUSCH mbH, West Berlin 12, Hardenbergstrasse 9
(tel: 310 771).

How to get to East Berlin
At the time of writing, crossing into East Berlin for a day's
sightseeing is no problem. Easiest way to do it is to present
yourself with your passport to Checkpoint Charley on
Friedrichstrasse.

There is some red tape to go through, but nothing that should
take more than twenty or thirty minutes. Anyone who is worried
about going into the Eastern sector (perhaps someone whose
family came from there recently) can cover themselves by
registering with the West Berlin authorities at the checkpoint and
stating what time they expect to be back. If they have not returned
soon after that time, something is done about it.

People going in in cars must have the vehicle's registration
papers, green-card insurance, international car identification letter
and, for the sake of economy, enough petrol to see them through
the day.

Everyone who enters the Eastern sector on foot or in a private
vehicle is obliged to buy 25 East German marks and pay DM5 for
the visa. These 25 marks cannot be changed back into D-marks. If
you don't spend it you'll have to donate it to an East German
charity. Unspent money which is changed in excess of 25 marks
may be changed back into other currencies.

Foreigners must leave East Berlin by midnight by the same
checkpoint by which they entered.

(One hint I can give anyone who is going over to the East for a
one-day trip is to carry as little stuff as possible. I went through on
the Underground to the Friedrichstrasse station with a
shoulder-bag stuffed with my usual assortment of notebooks, city
maps and tourist information. The customs guy (complete with
pistol and looking like something out of a spy movie) spent ten
minutes going through every piece of paper I was carrying and
then spent a further five minutes carefully leafing through the last
edition of this book which was covered in notes for new info. The
whole long process was punctuated by him asking questions in
German – which I don't understand – and me muttering away in
English – which he didn't understand. But he smiled when he'd
finished.)

Warning! Rules and regulations regarding crossing from West Germany to East Germany and from West Berlin to East Berlin are liable to change at any time. Best to check with tourist offices before you start the trip.

East Berlin

There are three major information offices in East Berlin where you can get city maps and sightseeing data. They are located at the Berolina Hotel in Karl-Marx-Allee, next to the S-Bahnhof at Alexanderplatz, and at Friedrichstrasse 162.

Sights to see include the complex of galleries and museums on Museum Island; the Museum of German History on Unter den Linden (a museum which displays its goods with a political bias – very interesting); the Memorial to the Victims of Fascism and Militarism, also on Unter den Linden; and, perhaps as the biggest sight, the streets and department stores of the city itself.

To meet up with East German students, drop into the Humboldt University on Unter den Linden and find your way to the canteen around lunchtime. You'll get a cheap meal and some interesting conversation.

If you've come in by Underground to Friedrichstrasse, you can get a quite good and cheap enough meal in the station restaurant. It's a good way of blowing any East German marks you have left before leaving. (You can buy your homeward-bound ticket with West German marks.)

Addresses

Main post office (for poste restante) at Munich, Postamt 32, Bahnhofplatz 1.

Main post office (for poste restante) at Berlin 12, Postamt Berlin, Bahnhof Zoo.

American Express at Munich, Promenadeplatz 3 (tel: 22 81 66).

American Express at Berlin, Kurfürstendamm 11 (tel: 882 75 75).

Munich Student Travel Service at Munich 2, Luisenstrasse 43 (tel: 52 30 00).

Artu Berliner Gesellschaft für Studenten und Jugendaustausch mbH at Berlin 12, Hardenbergstrasse 9 (tel: 310 771).

German Student Travel Service at Hamburg 13, Schluterstrasse 18 (tel: 45 44 09).

Tourist Information Office at Munich, Rindermarkt 5 (tel: 23911).

Tourist Information Office at West Berlin, Europa Center (tel: (030) 262 60 31).

British Consulate-General at Munich, Amalienstrasse 62 (tel: 39 40 15).

British Consulate at West Berlin, Uhlandstrasse 7 (tel: 30 95 293).

American Consulate at Munich, Koeniginstrasse 5 (tel: 23 011).

American Consulate at Berlin, Clayallee 170 (tel: 83 24 087).

Hitchers' Tips and Comments...

Crossing to East Berlin: in your bit on this subject you don't mention that receipts must be obtained for all money spent in East Berlin. The officials don't tell you either, until you're coming back. *D. F. Dickson, London N4*

If you sleep rough on the banks of the river Neckar in central Heidelberg watch out for the rats – they're like cats! *Jonah, Neath, South Wales*

The student Mensas of most German university cities have noticeboards offering rides to almost anywhere. You get in contact with the person offering the lift and make a deal about sharing petrol expenses. *Glyn George, Merseyside, UK*

Best hitching point into West Berlin seems to be the Allied checkpoint at Helmstedt.

Some West Berlin banks will give you 4 East German marks for 1 German mark. Only problem is, it's illegal to take East German marks into the DDR. If you take the risk and get through you can have a really cheap time. *Jeff Hoyle and Mike Fullen, Bury, UK*

Here's a letter to me from the Berlin Tourist Office: 'Since it is strictly forbidden to import or export any eastern *currency we think it irresponsible in regard to security of your readers to publish this advice in your guide book. This serious offence is highly prosecuted by East German authorities. Even small amounts lead to long interrogations and of course to the loss of the money. Smuggling of larger amounts is being punished by jail sentences. Searches, also bodily, are very frequent. Many times persons that had these experiences came crying to the Tourist Information Office afterwards. Moreover, there is almost no possibility to spend this illegal money in addition to the minimum exchange of DM 25.'*

You have the information. The choice is yours. Personally, I wouldn't do it. K.W.

Hitching out of Munich to Salzburg can be difficult, because traffic is usually heavy and fast-moving at the point where it enters the autobahn. If you're getting desperate, try this: get the S-bahn to Starnberg and hitch down to Garmisch-Partenkirchen; from there you should easily get a lift to Innsbruck and on to Salzburg.

In large German towns you can sometimes get a free bed in an immigrant workers' hostel (if you don't mind being up and away at 5 a.m. the next morning). To pull this off you need to find a sympathetic immigrant worker, but this isn't too difficult. Many hang around railway stations and places like Munich's Marienplatz or outside the cathedral in Cologne. They're looking for someone to talk to as they have nothing to do with their time. *Hugh Dunne, Dublin, Ireland*

If you're heading into Scandinavia load up on food in German supermarkets. It's much cheaper! *Andrew Price, Torquay, UK*

The only hitching place out of West Berlin is the Allied Checkpoint at Nikolassee, and hitching from there is good. When a car stops by a line of hitchers the nearest guy shouts the driver's destination down the line and the driver takes the people for whom his destination is most useful. *Mike Fullen and Jeff Hoyle, UK*

The Glockenspiel in Munich only does its stuff at 11 a.m. with an extra show at 5 p.m. during the summer. *A. R. Brzozowski, Kettering, Northants, England*

For going to East Berlin, you need at least 42 DM. If you want a bath, get one at Berlin main station. *Peter Walsh, Truro, Cornwall, UK*

Nuremberg – well worth a mention: ancient walls, castle, excellent dungeons with torture instruments beneath town hall. The town has real character. Much more than just the place where Hitler held his rallies.

Löwenbräu brewery in Munich. Another free tour. Free Bavarian breakfast of bread and sausages and lots of free beer to follow. *Simon and Geoff, Sheffield, England*

In Germany we met an absolute legend, Dieter Wesch, the self-styled 'King of Hitchers', who spends his Sundays patrolling the Autobahn between Stuttgart and Karlsruhe, giving lifts to hitchers stranded at petrol stations. You each have to sign his guest-book in the car (he is now on his thirteenth book!) and are given a number – we were 5461 and 5462. *Pete Fraser, Maggie Wilcock, Harlow, Essex, England*

En route to West Berlin, from Munich, East German officials said our Inter Rail Cards were no good. Because we were travelling through East Germany we had to pay an extra 53 Marks each (about £12–£15). Two of us had to pay another ten Marks because our passports were not valid (visitors' passports). *Philip Annand, Aberdeen, Scotland*

Luxembourg and the Small Countries

There exist in Europe a number of independent or semi-independent territories which are complete anachronisms. They are mini-countries which have little business existing in this hurlyburly century, but somehow they survive. Most of them have fewer citizens than the Ford Motor Company has workers. The territories are Luxembourg, Monaco, Andorra, Gibraltar, San Marino, Liechtenstein and Malta.

Luxembourg with its 999 square miles of territory and population of 357,000 is the largest of these. Its modern history as a Grand Duchy began in AD 963 when a nobleman took over the ruins of a Roman fort which sat on a huge rock over the Alzette River, and built it into a castle. By the thirteenth century the country was one of the strongest in Europe and embraced an area 500 times the size it is today. Then the empire fell and its power diminished. Because of its central location it became an axiom that whoever controlled Luxembourg controlled the Continent. As no power could tolerate another having this advantage, an agreement was made at the London Congress of 1867 which guaranteed the independence of the country and demanded that the fortress be made inoperative.

In the city of Luxembourg, with its population of 90,000, the things to see include the remains of the fortifications (the castle is known as the 'Hollow Tooth') and some of the 21 kilometres of underground passages cut into solid rock. The fortifications, the city's eighty bridges and its cathedral, are all illuminated during the summer.

In Luxembourg cigarettes are about the cheapest in Europe outside of Spain. Good place to stock up in, especially if you're heading up north into expensive Scandinavia. Luxembourg currency (francs) has the same value as Belgian money.

The 188 square miles of **Andorra** sit high in the Pyrenees between France and Spain. Her 27,000 citizens speak Catalán, French and Spanish and trade in Spanish pesetas and French francs.

Legend says the country was founded by Charlemagne in AD 784. The present co-principality dates from 1278 and is under the joint suzerainty of the President of France and the Bishop of Urgel in Spain. A feudal toll is still paid each year, one year to the French, the next to the Spanish. In 1968 the Bishop of Urgel received 900 pesetas in cash, plus 6 hams, 12 chickens and 24 cheeses.

After tourism, which brings in plenty of cash owing to the practically duty-free state of its shops, tobacco is one of the big businesses. Cigarettes are about the same price as in Spain. Liquor is cheaper. Petrol, if you're driving a van, is cheaper than in either France or Spain – so fill up.

In this weird little place which boasts that it is the smallest country in the world and which is locked in by 8000-foot snow-capped peaks, they have reached one state of affairs towards which you can only wish other countries would strive. The 1969 defence budget was £2 ($3·12). This gross expenditure bought bullets for the police force's pistol practice and shotgun shells for the mountain gamewardens.

Hitch-hiking both in and out of the place can be hard. It's all up and down or curves and the roads are narrow. Unless you want a long, long walk, pick yourself a nice position and stay there with your thumb propped in the air.

★**Shopping** Prices are good on things like cameras, film, radios, cassettes, tapes, etc. But on decent-size purchases (say, over £15) you can still get 10–20 per cent off by asking. The bigger the purchase the more chance of the discount, so it's worth shopping with friends and getting all the things you want on the counter at the one time so you've got better bargaining power.

Monaco with its 25,000 inhabitants stacked into an area of 368 acres on France's Côte d'Azur is a principality governed by Prince Rainier, the gentleman who was married to the late American screen actress Grace Kelly.

The Principality has been independent since 1415 and has been ruled by the Grimaldi family (of which the current prince is a member) since 1297. Many efforts have been made to destroy its independence, the most recent being in 1963 when De Gaulle blockaded the state in an effort to make it fall in line, economically, with the rest of France. Prince Rainier held out until a 90-page document was signed by both parties guaranteeing, in part, that Monaco's citizens would continue to enjoy their tax-free status.

The State makes a good half of its income from tourism. Way over a million tourists visit each year, most to soak up the sun and sample the delights of the rich Mediterranean lifestyle. Some go to play at the famous casino, all hoping that they'll be the second person to break the fabulous bank of Monte Carlo. If you want to play the wheels, good luck to you, but it's strictly for hitchers expecting an inheritance!

For such a small place (small, but it has the greatest population density in the world) there is plenty to see. Not to be missed is the fantastic Oceanographic Museum. If you expect to be hitting the area around May, check with a tourist office for the exact dates of the *Grand Prix de Monaco*, one of the most exciting races in the car-sport world. Other sights include the quite good collection of paintings in the National Museum of Fine Arts and the Prince's Palace.

Note that the hitching is slow all along this area during summer.

Gibraltar perches right on the end of the Iberian Peninsula and, at the time of writing, is the subject of negotiations between the English and the Spanish. The border is now open, but only for residents of the Rock and Spanish passport-holders. The rest of us can still only reach Gib by air or sea. This means that to get there by sea you have to travel to Tangier in Morocco and then from Tangier to Gib, and then, when you want to leave, you reverse the whole thing. Many dollars and many kilometres later you come to journey's end; a journey which used to cost nothing as you walked across the Spanish–Gibraltar land frontier.

Gib has an area of 2¼ square miles and a population of 25,000. The huge Rock is 1396 feet high and you can walk up or, if you're feeling rich, take the cable-car. Whichever way, go. On a clear day, the view from the top goes clear across to the Atlas mountains in Morocco. Halfway up is where you can see the famous Barbary apes who are said to have arrived in Gibraltar by way of a secret tunnel from Africa. The superstition is that if the apes ever leave Gib, then British rule will come to an end. The British, with typical thoroughness, have the apes on garrison strength and feed them daily rations. Be warned that the beasts bite. I know. I've been bitten. The population of Gibraltar is a weird mixture of Genoese, Maltese, Spanish, British and Arab. The people's temperament seems to be somewhere between that of a Spaniard and an Englishman. Everyone is bilingual in Spanish and English and can change languages without batting an eyelid.

The name Gibraltar comes from the Arabic *Gibel Tarik*, or Tarik's Hill. Tarik was Tarik-ibn-Zeyad the Moor who started the invasion of Spain near Gibraltar in AD 711. Today there are several Moorish ruins to be seen, including the castle, the wall and the baths. Other sights include St Michael's Cave in which occasionally there are held rock (so to speak) concerts, the Gibraltar Museum, and the Trafalgar Cemetery in which sailors killed at the Battle of Trafalgar are buried.

For cheap eating try Smoky Joe's just off Main Street. It's an English truckie-style café. For cheap sleeping go to TOC 'H' at the opposite end of Main Street.

Warning! Being partly tax-free, prices in Gib can be amongst the lowest in Europe for luxury items like cameras and tape recorders. But after the Spanish–Gib border was closed tourism dropped badly and many shopkeepers have raised their prices. I've seen cameras in Main Street shop windows marked at higher prices than in the centre of London. Prices can also vary as much as 20 per cent between different shops. Make sure you're getting value before you put your money on the counter – and bargain hard.

San Marino, completely surrounded by Italy, is the oldest state in the world, dating from the fourth century. Its official title is the Most Serene Republic of San Marino. With a population of some 20,000 and an area of 24 square miles, its big industries revolve around tourism and postage stamps. Tourism brings in 1,000,000 visitors each year. The big sight is the city of San Marino itself, which sits 2200 feet above and just inland from the Adriatic Sea. Have a look at the Rocca Fortress and the Palazzo Valloni.

Liechtenstein, sitting between Switzerland and Austria, covers an area of 62 square miles and has a population of 24,000. It's just big (or small) enough to provide a pleasant day's walk so that you can at least say you've been through a country on foot.

The state was founded in 1719 and gained independence in 1806 after a spell as part of the Holy Roman Empire.

Vaduz, the capital, is a huge metropolis of 4400 souls, including a prince who lives in a castle on a hill above the town. The town itself is very much tourist-oriented. It has to be because Liechtenstein is much too pleasant a place to worry much about industrialization. Postage stamps, however, are big in this tiny land and any wandering philatelists should have a look at the excellent Philately Museum in the capital. Also check over the local art gallery which has better stuff in it than you might imagine.

The Republic of Malta lies in the heart of the Mediterranean, 95 kilometres south of Sicily and 340 kilometres north of Libya. The archipelago consists of three main islands, Malta, Gozo and tiny Comino, which total only 122 square miles and support a population of 330,000 which speaks Malti (one of Europe's smallest languages, a unique mix of Arabic, Italian and French), and English. The use of English as a second language by about 75 per cent of Maltese gives hitchers immediate access to the Mediterranean culture of these islands.

Best visits reflect the complex and often bloody history which is the heritage of the tiny Roman Catholic Republic. On Malta itself, the two essential cities to roam around are the capital, Valletta, and the ex-capital, Mdina.

Valletta's origins lie in the defeat of the Knights of St John on Rhodes by Suleiman the Magnificent in the sixteenth century. As a result, the Knights based themselves in Malta in 1530, and after driving off the Turks during the Great Siege of 1565, Grand Master Jean Parisot de la Valette raised money to build the fortified mini-city of Valletta. Now you can walk the walls of Valletta for an overall impression of towers, forts and bastions. Visit the old Auberges, the inns once used to accommodate the Knights; many, like the Auberge de Provence which now houses the National Museum of Archaeology, are used as public buildings. See St John's Co-Cathedral, and don't miss the Grand Master's Palace which includes a fascinating armoury of medieval weapons. If you have spare cash – the cost is a matter of intricate negotiation – take a ride in a *dghajsa* (a water taxi which you can hire at Customs House wharf) and see the incredible Grand Harbour, with Valletta on one side and the 'three cities' of **Vittoriosa, Senglea** and **Cospicua** on the other. The Grand Harbour was the main target of German bombs during the second Great Siege, the 1939–45 war, when Malta was awarded the George Cross for its heroism. Nearby **Sliema** abounds in reasonably priced cafés and offers some nightlife. (Movies are shown in English!)

Ten kilometres from Valletta stands **Mdina**, known as The Silent City. Don't miss it. It's tiny and unpretentious, but for my money one of Europe's most exquisite architectural gems. Wander the quiet, narrow streets, visit museums, churches and the Cathedral, burn up some film on the view from Bastion Square across to **Mosta**, dominated by St Mary's church with its 122-foot-diameter dome – amongst the world's largest. At neighbouring **Rabat** visit St Paul's Grotto where the saint traditionally stayed after his shipwreck on the island, and don't miss the impressive Christian catacombs. (You'll have to stash your pack somewhere because of the narrow passages.)

Elsewhere on Malta, places with flavour include the mysterious Hypogeum cave temple cut into the rock 40 feet underground at **Paola** (an absolute must for archaeology freaks and dreamy romantics); the temple ruins at **Tarxien**, just a few hundred yards from the Hypogeum; and **Hagar Qim**, a stone circle reminiscent of Stonehenge, which sits on a cliff top with views to uninhabited

Filfla Island. If you make it to Hagar Qim, on the way home you can join a boat ride to visit the **Blue Grotto**. Do it on a sunny day and before 11 a.m. That's when the sun enters the cave and the water is most luminous.

Comino is inhabited only a by a few locals and guests at the island's one hotel, and not worth a visit unless you want to play Robinson Crusoe.

Gozo is reached by ferry from Valletta or from **Cirkewwa**, the port north of **Mellieha** (which boasts Malta's best beach). In contrast to Malta's barren landscape, Gozo is refreshingly green. The capital is **Victoria**, though many people still call it by its old name of **Rabat**. It stands in the centre of the island just a short distance from where the ferry berths at **Mgarr**. Best visit in Victoria involves a climb up the hill to the Citadel. It's worth the short walk. Elsewhere on the island, visit the **Ggantija Temples** dating from around 3000 BC; the **Ramla Bay** beach with its cave which legend claims is where Ulysses stayed with Calypso; the tiny fishing hamlet of **Xlendi**, now popular with tourists; and the 'inland sea' at **Dwejra**.

Buses are dirt cheap on the islands, so don't hesitate to use them when heading to out-of-the-way spots. Neither Gozo nor Malta have camping grounds, but on Gozo, particularly, you'll find some marvellous out-of-the-way beaches if you feel like roughing it for a few days.

Hitchers' Tips and Comments . . .

To get out of Andorra into Spain, the best bet is to take the St Julia bus to the end of the line, then walk to the petrol station just past town. It has a big parking lot and average waiting time for a ride out is about ten minutes. *David Fremon, Palatine, USA*

Andorran banks offer better exchange rates on pesetas and francs than French or Spanish banks. Also, a special note for van-travellers. When heading from Andorra into France watch out for customs spot checks anywhere between the Andorran border and Aix-le-Thermes. *T.B., Chelmsford, UK*

Cheapest way I found to Malta was to take the ferry from Syracuse (Sicily). You can buy duty-free aboard. I found hitching on the island easy. Most cars that had any room stopped. I travelled with three other hitchers and the *four* of us got around without problems. Buses are very cheap and it's advisable to take one in the built-up areas around Valletta. If you keep away from hotels, discos and other tourist traps, prices are amongst the lowest in Europe. The Maltese are extremely generous and friendly. *Clive Buckman, Trowbridge, UK*

You can use Belgian money in Luxembourg, but many places in Belgium won't take Luxembourg francs. *Jon Glanville and Martin Elston, Bristol, UK*

Switzerland

population	6,300,000
size	15,941 square miles
capital	Berne, population 141, 300
government	Federal republic
religion	Roman Catholic and Protestant
language	French, German, Italian, and the little-used Romansch are the national languages; some English spoken in cities
currency	*Swiss franc* One *franc* equals 100 *centimes* (French) or *Rappen* (German). Coins of 5, 10, 20 *centimes* or *Rappen* and ½, 1, 2, 5 *francs*. Notes of 10, 20, 50, 100, 500, 1000 *francs*

Berne is the capital of Switzerland, but Zurich is the largest city and perhaps the best to wander in for a few days. After those two, the towns to visit are Geneva, Lausanne, Lucerne, Basel, and St Gallen. In the south are the big mountains which are famous the world over – Monte Rosa at 15,023 feet, Dom at 14,920 feet, Matterhorn at 14,780 feet. And there are the high alpine passes – Umbrail at 8218 feet and Bernina at 7643 feet – and the long, long mountain tunnels – Simplon (rail), stretching 20 kilometres and St Gotthard (road), 15 kilometres.

The mountains are beautiful, but when you're up that high it can be very cold so keep an eye on the weather. A good route if you're

chasing snow and glaciers, is to head out from Lausanne to
Interlaken (an out-and-out tourist town, but in a beautiful
situation) and take, in turn, highways 11 and 2 down to **Bellinzona**
near the Italian border. This route takes you through some
spectacular scenery which is a good cross-section of the mountain
country. You cross the Susten Pass at the 7299-foot level, catch a
glacier just near there, and then climb to the St Gotthard Pass at
nearly 7000 feet (as long as you can get a ride over the pass, rather
than through the tunnel). On the other side of the St Gotthard
Pass in **Ticino** everything is different: the climate, vegetation,
colour of the landscape, and the language (Italian). It's an
exhilarating trip, especially if you can do it on a blue-sky day. (It
usually rains!)

 Geneva, which is where most hitchers enter Switzerland after a
French tour, is a good introduction to the country – and a hint of
what to expect pricewise. It is slick, one hundred per cent modern,
and beautiful the way a jetplane is. It's no place for us cheapskate
hitchers. The youth hostels are usually full during the summer, so
if you're thinking of staying it's worth booking in advance. Sights
to see include the *Jet d'eau* on the lake (not in winter), a fantastic
spout which hurls water 400 feet into the air; the Palais des
Nations, the United Nations European home; and the Museum of
Art and History which contains a beautiful display of Impressionist
and post-Impressionist work. Music buffs may like to visit the
Museum of Old Musical Instruments. Philosophers shouldn't miss
the Rousseau Museum.

 The *Youth Hostel* is on rue des Plantaporrets (tel: 29 06 19) but
is closed from mid-December until late February. If you don't
have your hostel card it'll cost you nearly double. The
YMCA-YWCA is at 9 Avenue Sainte-Clotilde (tel: 28 11 33). Ask
for the dormitory and if you can do without sheets you'll save a
couple of francs. *Centre Masaryk* at 11 Avenue de la Paix (tel: 33
07 72) is cheap enough, but make sure you don't get the
breakfast-included price. The *Salvation Army* has an hotel *for men*
at 1 rue Baudit (tel: 33 77 04) and an hotel *for women* at 14 rue de
l'Industrie (tel: 33 64 38). There's cheap eating at the
YMCA-YWCA and at the *University Mensa* at 2 Avenue du Mail,
Cité Universitaire at 20 Avenue de Miremont, the *International
Student Club* at 6 rue de Saussure and at *Résidence Internationale*
at 63 rue des Paquis.

 Lausanne, just a hop, step and jump from Geneva along the fast autoroute, is a city of 128,800. Like Geneva, it sits on Lake Léman. But for me it offers more charm than many other Swiss cities because it is not a big international or business centre. The cathedral is worth a visit, as is the old Episcopal Palace of the Bishops of Lausanne.

Just outside of town is the village of **Vevey**, a pretty lakeside spot which has seen more than its share of famous people. Courbet, Byron, Hugo, and Rousseau all made visits or lived there at one time or another. A few kilometres farther on is **Montreux**, famous for its international music festivals, the Festival of Jazz, beginning on the second Friday of July, and the Festival of Classical Music held each September. Nicknamed the 'Swiss Riviera', Montreux and its surrounds have been on and off with the international set for a century – and that, along with the casino in town, should give you an inkling of the sort of money that's floating around. But outside of town, the Castle of Chillon is worth a visit.

After Montreux you have a choice of travelling north to Berne, or south to **Valais** (Wallis in German). Valais is the valley of the upper Rhône with numerous side valleys worth exploring. **Sion**, the capital, has two castles. **Zermatt** is an out-and-out tourist resort at the foot of the Matterhorn. You can't hitch the last few kilometres but must take a train or walk from **Täsch**, as no cars are allowed above here. Valais is a good centre for anyone who wants to try some mountain walking. See **Derborence**, a lovely lake surrounded by mountains, try hitching from **Pont-de-la-Morge**, just out of Sion or walk a few hours up from **Ardon**. There are numerous other possibilities; just go exploring. You can even walk over **Col de Balme** into France. At the top of Valais is the **Rhône Glacier**, and from there you can connect up with the mountain trip from **Interlaken**.

Berne, the capital of Switzerland, is a small city of 154,000 people, but it has enough to keep you amused for a day. The clock tower is the principal attraction, one of those jobs which put on a complete stage-show each hour. Don't miss the bear pit for a show of a different type (real bears). You get a good view over the attractive Old Town from the tower of the cathedral or from the public park called the Rose Garden. In here you may also find a place to lay your head (and if you can't, try down by the river). On the edge of Berne is a hill known as the Gurten. You reach the top on foot or by rack-railway. Walk along the top and, on a clear day, you'll be rewarded by views of the Bernese Oberland.

From Berne you can head south to Interlaken (Highway 6), then on to Lucerne or the mountain trip previously mentioned. From Berne, Lucerne is more easily accessible by thumb via the motorway (highways 1 and 2), but the scenery is not so good.

Lucerne, on Highway 10 from Berne, is small (62,400) and perhaps the prettiest of all Swiss cities. It is the site of another international music festival, in late August, and also of the Great Lakeside Evening Festival, in late June. Two things to see, if the subjects interest you, are the Swiss Transport Museum, which features wheeled monstrosities from all ages, and Tribschen, a house where Wagner lived and worked. Glacier Garden is a favourite with the tourists but, without a doubt, the nicest thing to do in Lucerne is wander around the old section near the strange Chapel Bridge.

Basel, north of Berne and north-west of Lucerne, is Switzerland's second largest city. Situated exactly on the junction of France, Germany and Switzerland, you have a nice choice of direction after you've seen the sights. The ancient cathedral, surrounded by medieval houses and standing beside a beautiful square, is nice to wander around. If you look closely at the outside of the cathedral you'll see where it was reinforced after it (and the rest of Basel) was largely destroyed by an earthquake in the fourteenth century. The strange animals on the outside at the river end of the building are supposed to be elephants, but the sculptor had never seen an elephant! Basel is famous for its innumerable museums. The Art Museum (Kunstmuseum) holds one of the world's outstanding collections on Holbein as well as a superb display of modern works. The Basler Papiermühle is a paper and printing museum where you can even have a go at making your own paper. The Zoo is considered one of the world's best. Sitting, as it does, on the Rhine, the city is also the home of the Swiss navy – not a joke after all – the navy consisting of river transport vessels. Late February or early March is the time of the four-day Basel carnival, known as the *Fasnacht*. Basel can be rather difficult to hitch out of if you're heading towards Zurich, Lucerne or Berne. Best bet is to try from Grosspeterstrasse.

St Gallen, in the north-eastern corner of the country, is about the same size as Lucerne. It's a pretty town, but its sights are of a specialist nature. It is built around a huge baroque cathedral which contains the famous Abbey Library, a collection of 2000 ancient manuscripts and nearly 2000 more very old printed books.

Hitching in Switzerland is no great problem although you might find it slow in the backwood areas. Major cities are well linked by fast highways, and the student population is flush enough to own its own transport – and they seem to be helpful in offering rides. In some countries it won't break the bank if you get stuck and have to catch a bus or train. In Switzerland it *will*.

Remember that many of the high passes are closed during the winter months. If travelling between October and May, be sure to check ahead of yourself. Good maps like Michelin tell which passes you can expect to be closed, and the Swiss National Tourist Office in London hands out a leaflet called *Switzerland by Car* which offers complete information on alpine passes.

Warning! The Swiss hit hard on drug users. In their eyes there is no difference between hard and soft drugs. Offenders face a maximum of 20 years in prison and/or an SFr 1 million fine. Nevertheless, if you need help with a drug problem (support that is, not supply), talk to the people at *Drop-In* at Dufourstrasse 131, Zurich (tel: 55 53 11), open 8 a.m. to 8 p.m.

★**Buying money** You can find good rates of exchange in Switzerland on most soft currencies, e.g., Turkish lira, Moroccan dirhams. Sometimes you can buy up to 20 per cent cheaper so it's a good investment if you expect to be spending time in the 'soft' currency countries. But remember that most of those places have a limit on the amount of money you are permitted to carry across their borders . . . in fact, most of them practically force you to break the law.

Zurich: where to sleep

Try to keep out of hotels in Zurich or, for that matter, anywhere in Switzerland. They are fantastic places, clean, comfortable, with all mod-cons, but at an average 45–60 francs a night for a single, they're budget-wreckers. Unless you're fairly well heeled you should try to sleep rough or at least stick to hostels or other special facilities. And even then, student hostels can cost you as much as 24 francs. Most of the ones listed below are bargains by Swiss standards, but try to ring before you go to the place you choose. Because of the high prices of normal hotels the budget places are often booked up.

Youth Hostel at Mutschellenstrasse 114 (tel: 482 35 44). Ask for dormitory, because there are also double rooms (at double the price per person).

Limmathaus Tourist Hotel at Limmatstrasse 118 (tel: 42 52 40). Ask for dormitory. Open May–September.

Studentinnenhaus at Freudenbergstrasse 16 (tel: 252 75 00). Open end of July through September only. For women only. Cheaper with student card.

Foyer Hottingen at Hottingerstrasse 31 (tel: 47 93 15). Girls or married couples only. You must be in by midnight.

YMCA at Sihlstrasse 33 (tel: 221 36 73). Men only.

YWCA (Marthahaus) at Zähringerstrasse 36 (tel: 251 45 50). Men and women.

Hotel Italia at Zeughausstrasse 61 (tel: 241 43 39).

Hotel Rothaus at Langstrasse 121 (tel: 241 24 51).

Hotel Splendid at Rosengasse 5 (tel: 252 58 50).

Hotel Limmathof at Limmatquai 142 (tel: 47 42 00).

Hotel Rothus at Marktgasse 17 (tel: 252 15 30).

Justinusheim at Freudenbergstrasse 146 (tel: 361 38 06).

At the Tourist Office, Bahnhofplatz 15 (at the main station), you can get a free Hotel Guide, which includes maps and prices, and sort out any hotel problems. The same office can also give you information on locations and costs of half a dozen camping grounds in the area – which, in summer, can help you save a packet. **Campingplatz** at Seebucht, Seestrasse 557 (tel: 482 16 12), reached by taking Bus 61 or 65 from Bürkliplatz to Grenzsteig, is open May to September and costs around SFr 4 per person, SFr 2 per tent. Showers extra. Believe me, it's as good a deal as you'll find in the city.

For roughing it, you might find a spot by the Zurich-See at Seefeld Quai. Otherwise, best bet is out around the Dolder sports park.

Zurich: where to eat

Twelve francs should handle things and for that you can get some
good food. As in most cities, it's wise to keep an eye open for the
chain restaurants and cafeterias. In Zurich, best bets are: **Migros**,
Silberkugel, and especially the **Stadtküche Zurich** (or Zurich's
People's Kitchen). These, for anyone on a limited budget, are
perfect but they open between 11.30 a.m. and 12.30 p.m. only!
There are thirteen of them and the addresses are:

Selnaustrasse 46,	Luggwegstrasse 27,
Untergraben 4,	Sihlquai 332,
Schipfe 16,	Zentralstrasse 34,
Nordstrasse 101,	Dufourstrasse 146,
Neunbrunnenstrasse 4,	Hofwiesenstrasse 9,
Dorflindenstrasse 4,	Kernstrasse 11.
Bederstrasse 130,	

Other places to consider are:

Mensa-Polyterrasse at Leonhardstrasse 34. Cheap meals but you
may need your international student ID.

Rheinfelder Bierhaus at Marktgasse 19. Cheap luncheon plates.

Culmann at Culmannstrasse 1. This one is a student haunt.

Catalana at Glockengasse 8. Spanish restaurant.

Kantorei at Spiegelgasse 33. Popular with student types.

Select Café at Limmatquai 16.

Weisser Wind at Oberdorfstrasse 20.

University Restaurant at Künstlergasse 10.

Cafeteria of the Institute of Dentistry (Zahnärztliches Institut) at
Plattenstrasse 11. Closed mid-July to mid-August.

Another excellent chain where you can eat for 10 or 12 francs if you
choose carefully is run by the Zurich Women's Association. They are:

Karl der Grosse at Kirchgasse 14.

Rütli at Zähringerstrasse 43.

Seidenhof at Sihlstrasse 7–9.

Olivenbaum at Stadelhoferstrasse 10.

The Tourist Office has a leaflet on the cheaper restaurants in Zurich called 'Preiswerte Verpflegungsmöglichkeiten', which gives opening hours and an idea of prices.

Zurich: what to see and do

SWISS NATIONAL MUSEUM on Museumstrasse, near main station. No entrance fee. Good rundown on the history of Switzerland.

RIETBERG MUSEUM in the Rieterpark. Free on Wednesday nights and Sundays. One of Europe's great collections of non-European art.

KUNSTHAUS on Heimplatz. Includes good collection of Swiss art. Entrance charge but Wednesdays and Sunday afternoons free.

GROSSMÜNSTER CATHEDRAL near City Hall. The largest Romanesque church in Switzerland, built between 1100 and 1300. In the ninth century Charlemagne founded a church on the same spot.

OEPFELCHAMMER at Rindermarkt 12 is one of the city's oldest beerhalls. Prices are OK (though avoid the expensive restaurant next door). Good place to meet people. For jazz, *Casa Bar* at Münstergasse 30 is fine (no cover charge but the drinks are expensive), while for dancing try *Club Zabriskie-Point* at Leonhardstrasse 19 or *Hazyland* in the Kongresshaus. If you want to meet up with local students go to the *International Student Club* at Augustinerhof 1, but you'll have to show a student ID card to get in.

CINEMA Anything made in English will probably be shown in English – with up to three (German, French, Italian) subtitles on the screen. For programme info from cinemas, theatres and concert halls ask for the Zurich Weekly Bulletin, available free at the Tourist Office (Bahnhofplatz 15). Each cinema has complete listings for Zurich posted outside.

FLEA MARKET Held every Saturday between 8 a.m. and 4 p.m. on Bahnhofstrasse towards the lake. There's also a CURIOSITY MARKET held Thursdays between 9 a.m. and 9 p.m. in the Rosenhof, the small square between Limmatquai and Niederdorf.

Transport in Zurich

You must have a ticket before you board trams or buses. There are vending machines for these at all stops. At the major stops you can also buy 12-ride tickets and day tickets. Trips cost between 1 and 2 francs depending on distance. Best way, for a day of sightseeing, is to buy the special day ticket for 4 francs which allows you unlimited travel right through until midnight.

Student discounts

Discounts for some concerts, cinemas and theatres. Reduced admission to galleries and museums. Discounts in many large stores. For information, contact:

SWISS STUDENT TRAVEL OFFICE, Leonhardstrasse 10, 8026 Zurich (tel: 242 30 00). SSR publish a handy book, complete with colour maps, called *Switzerland the Cheap Way*. The latest edition is a bit dated (1978) but if you remember to double the prices it's still very useful and, what's more, they seem to be giving them away now.

Addresses

Post office (for poste restante) at Sihlpost, Kasernenstrasse 95–99, Zurich.

American Express at Bahnhofstrasse 20, 8022 Zurich (tel: 211 83 70).

Schweizerischer Studentenreisedienst at Leonhardstrasse 10, 8026 Zurich (tel: 242 30 00). Closed Monday mornings.

Tourist Office at Bahnhofplatz 15, Zurich (tel: 211 40 00).

US Consulate at Zollikerstrasse 141, Zurich (tel: 55 25 66).

British Consulate at Bellerivestrasse 5, Zurich (tel 47 15 20).

Hitchers' Tips and Comments ...

Basel. Signposting for getting out of the city is terrible. I walked in a complete circle, wasting two hours. When you reach the Football Stadium, keep right ahead for Lucerne road – don't turn left! *Malcolm Frankland, Glaslum, England*

If you're down on your luck hitching and have to take buses, don't try to jump fares, particularly in Switzerland. Inspectors are numerous and come down heavily. On-the-spot fines. *Graham Curry, Retford, England*

Hitchers and van vagabonds leaving Switzerland should beware of Swiss customs. They seem to be taking a lot of time searching packs and vans. Seems to take longer getting out of the country than getting in. *John Purnell, Birmingham, England*

To hitch from Basel to Berne, Lucerne or Zurich, you have to hitch on the slip-road in town. Don't try it on the main highway. It's hopeless. Traffic speed is fast and there's nowhere cars can pull over.

In university cities (like Berne) the student halls are normally empty during vacation and sometimes the caretaker allows you in.

To hitch from Lausanne to Geneva, start in town. The lake route is very, very slow and hitching is forbidden on the motorway, and the law is strictly enforced. *Jez, Hemel Hempstead, England*

Warning! Our Swiss friends tell us they are clamping down on tents in parks, etc., especially in the Italian part, with fines of up to 200 Swiss francs. *Simon Wadsworth, Shipley, West Yorkshire, UK*

Austria

population	7,500,000
size	32,374 square miles
capital	Vienna, population 1,700,000
government	Federal republic
religion	Roman Catholic
language	German; some English and Italian spoken
currency	*Schilling* One *Schilling* equals 100 *Groschen*. Coins of 2, 5, 10, 50 *Groschen*; and of 1, 5, 10, 50 *Schillings*. Notes of 20, 50, 100, 500, 1000 *Schillings*

A pleasant morning's walk through Liechtenstein (see **The Small Countries**) and then a quick hitch and you're in **Feldkirch**. That's as nice a way as any of entering Austria. Feldkirch is an old-world kind of town. Her 17,000 inhabitants move slowly and don't seem to give a damn about anything. See the tenth-century Schattenburg Castle. There is a wine festival in the second week of July.

A few kilometres north is **Dornbirn**. On the edge of town you get good alpine views from the top of the Karren Gondola. If you continue up the road from the base of this, you come to the **Rappenlochschlucht** and the **Alplochschlucht**, two narrow gorges which walkers will enjoy.

A little farther north is **Bregenz** on the shores of Lake Constance (the Bodensee). Have a look at the Vorarlberger Museum, which gives a good idea of the history of Vorarlberg Province, and wander through the Altstadt, the old section.

The Innsbruck road takes you through some really great country (*Sound of Music* all the way). If you manage a ride over the 5000-foot Arlberg Pass, instead of through the expensive tunnel, you'll pass through **St Anton**, a famed ski-resort with Europe's oldest ski-school.

Innsbruck is 700 years old and, many say, Austria's most beautiful city, though in my opinion Salzburg could lay a pretty solid claim to that title. Innsbruck was Winter Olympics city in 1964 and 1976. Those interested in snow sports might like to see the Olympic speed skating oval, the Bergisel Olympic ski-jump, and the Olympic bobsleigh and toboggan runs in **Igls**. Anyone heading down into Italy from Innsbruck will go over the famous Europe Bridge, the highest in Europe, 897 yards long and standing 624 feet above the river bed. In the city itself see the Imperial Palace, the Museum of Tyrolese Art, and the Alpine Museum at Emperor Maximilian's Arsenal.

The fastest way to **Salzburg** (population 120,000) is along the E17 which cuts briefly across Germany at **Bad Reichenhall** (a town with a local reputation for its healing mineral springs and a good base for hiking in the Alps). Sitting beautifully on a plain and backed with huge mountains, Salzburg's focal point is the twelfth-century Hohensalzburg Castle. The Franziskanerkirche Cathedral is worth a look, as is the superbly presented Carolino Augusteum Museum. Mozart fans will know that the musician was born in Salzburg and will want to see his house and museum. They should note that the city holds a Mozart Week each January (exact dates may vary from year to year) which features the Vienna Philharmonic Orchestra. Then, of course, there's the fantastic Salzburg Music Festival which is held every July and August. Thirty or forty kilometres north of Salzburg is the quite pleasant frontier town of **Braunau** – Adolf Hitler's birthplace.

Hallstatt is a tiny village of about 2000 people a few kilometres off the Salzburg–Graz highway. Most of the village lies perched along the lake, with the road running behind it through tunnels in the cliff. Apart from being the ideal place to get a whiff of rural Austria it offers the added attractions of the Hallstatt Museum which features prehistoric objects found in various tombs, and the Dachstein Caves which you reach by cable railway. It's a great area for hiking. If you've had some experience you can climb up to the Hallstatt Glacier. It's quite a long way, so it's best to stay in Simony-Hütte for the night – bedding and food are provided. Hallstatt is in the Salzkammergut, and athletic hitchers will find dozens of lakes to swim in and mountains to climb.

The road now takes you through the lushness of Styria, over the 2500-foot Schober Pass, through the towns of **Leoben** and **Bruck** (and precious few others) until you arrive in **Graz** which, with 250,000 people, is Austria's second largest city. Things to see include the fantastic Arsenal with the world's largest collection of medieval armour (30,000 pieces in all), the ornate mausoleum of Emperor Ferdinand II, the castles which you reach by cablecar, and several important galleries and museums.

Two main roads run south of Graz. The 67 leads you into Yugoslavia (only 40 kilometres away) and the 70 goes to **Klagenfurt**, with side roads into Yugoslavia. The 70 then becomes the 100 and joins up with **Lienz**, a small Tyrol city crowned by a castle and as typical as they come. Here's the ideal place for any hitcher who has enough spare cash to take a few days off for some skiing. Thirty kilometres south of Lienz and you're in Italy.

The romantically minded could enter Austria from Germany at **Passau** and follow the Danube right down to Vienna. First stop would be the **Abbey of St Florian**. Lots to see, including a magnificent library of books and manuscripts. Music fans will want to visit the church. Anton Bruckner, who was born near St Florian, is buried in the crypt beneath the organ. Farther along the route – just to put a dent in your romanticism – drop in to **Mauthausen** and visit the Nazi concentration camp. About 200,000 people died here, many from exhaustion after being forced to struggle up the infamous Stairway of Death carrying as much as one hundred pounds of stone from the quarry below. Imagine walking up a couple of times with your pack! A more pleasant stop is **Melk**, perhaps the most beautiful area in the entire Danube valley; the river meanders between vine-covered hillsides. Take time off to visit **Stift Melk**, the Benedictine Abbey, once a castle and handed over to the monastic order in 1106. Medieval **Dürnstein** is the site of the castle where Richard the Lionheart was held prisoner for ransom on his return from the Third Crusade in 1192. Blondel the Minstrel sang beneath these very walls!

Hitching tends to be rather erratic compared to Switzerland. There's no problem on routes such as Salzburg to Vienna but in some parts of the country it can be quite slow. For example, if you head north of **Linz** to Czechoslovakia, you might as well resign yourself to catching a train, or catching a bus from **Freistadt** (a lovely old walled town) to the border, no matter what your map says about this being an 'E' route.

Vienna: where to sleep

Prices fairly high. Student and hostel accommodation ranges from 70–200 schillings per bed. Hotels? Count on paying 150–300 per head.

Don Bosco Turmherbege at Lechnerstrasse 12 (tel: 73 14 94). Men only.

Kolpinghaus Meidling at Bendlgasse 10–12 (tel: 83 54 87). Men only.

Jugendgästehaus Schloss Potzleinsdorf at Geymullergasse 1 (tel: 47 13 12). Open March through October. Long way out.

Jugendgästehaus Hütteldorf at Schlossberggasse 8 (tel: 82 15 01). Long way out.

Katholisches Studentinnenheim at Servitengasse 3 (tel: 34 34 09). Open from 1 July to 20 October. Students only. Women only.

Studentenheim des Asylvereines der Wiener Universität (Vienna University Student Home) at Porzellangasse 30 (tel: 34 72 83). Open 10 July to 25 September. Students only.

Hotel Adlerhof at Hafnersteig 7 (tel: 63 29 61).

Studentenheim Rudolfinum at Mayerhofgasse 3 (tel: 65 44 51). Students only. Men only.

Pension Vandasek at Wickenburgasse 23.

For help with student accommodation talk with the people at Austrian Student Travel Office at Reichsratstrasse 13 (tel: 42 15 61), who operate a student accommodation service.

For sleeping out try the golf-links on Hauptallee and the Prater Park, or Donaupark on the east side of the canal.

Vienna's camping grounds are all a fair way out but they'll save you money on accommodation. Two of them, Wien-West I and Wien-West II, are close to each other in Hüttelbergstrasse. Take the U4 underground westwards to the end of the line (Hütteldorf), then change to bus 52B. Camping I is open mid-May to mid-September; camping II from April to October.

Vienna: where to eat

Count on paying 70–100 schillings in a cheap restaurant. But if you're a student, try the first two listings below and you'll eat dinner for around 50 schillings.

Mensa der Osterreichischen Hochschülerschaft at Führichgasse 10. Students only. Dinner served from 6 to 10 p.m. Open during student holiday periods only.

Mensa des Hauptausschusses at Universitätsstrasse 7. Students only. Open all year except Easter and Christmas. Dinner served from 6 to 10 p.m.

Leopold Kainz at Wiedner Gürtel 16.

WOK's are chain restaurants. There are more than a dozen of them in Vienna. Try:

Schonbrunnerstrasse 45,   Liechtensteinstrasse 4,
Mariahilferstrasse 85,   Schottengasse 1.

Cooking School Just down from the WOK on Schottengasse. Only open for lunch (12 until 2) and Monday through Friday. Cheap and good.

OK Restaurant at Kärntnerstrasse 61. Very cheap.

Residenz Café at the Opera end of Mariahilferstrasse, where the shops end. Also try eating at any of the wine houses and cellars. Prices will usually be a bit more than 80 schillings, but the food is great. Don't forget to buy Vienna pastry from the *Konditoreien*. Cheap enough and great breakfast food, especially if you have a sweet tooth. Only rich hitchers will be able to buy anything there, but the rest of you bums can torture yourselves for free by taking a look at the marzipan displays in the window of Demel at Kohlmarkt 14.

Vienna: what to see and do

SCHLOSS SCHONBRUNN is a huge baroque palace containing more than 1400 rooms. It was the modest summer residence of the Hapsburgs from 1695. Costs about 40 schillings for a guided tour in English, but less if you're a student.

KUNSTHISTORISCHES MUSEUM at the Ring. Fine collection of masters. Works by Rembrandt, Brueghel, Vermeer, Velázquez, etc. Closed Mondays. Admission fee, but free for students.

HOFBURG was the official residence of the Hapsburgs. Lots to do. You can visit the imperial rooms where Emperor Franz Josef lived, or the *Schatzkammer* which contains the royal treasures, including the insignia of the Holy Roman Empire and the sword of Charlemagne. Then there's the famous Spanish Riding School (check with tourist office for performance times, closed July and August) and the *Schweizer Kapelle* where the Vienna Boys Choir perform each Sunday except in summer. It'd take you days (and some expense) to get through the place if you wanted to see everything.

ST STEPHAN'S GOTHIC CATHEDRAL at Stephansplatz. Climb the tower for a tremendous view over the city and head down into the crypt and have a look at some skulls. Admission charge for both tower and crypt. Organ concerts.

MUSICIANS MUSEUMS are essential visits for music lovers. The Beethoven Museum at Moelkerbastei; the Haydn Museum at Haydngasse 19; the Mozart Museum at Domgasse 5 (in the Figarohaus); the Schubert Museum at Nussdorferstrasse 54.

SIGMUND FREUD MUSEUM at Berggasse 19. Freud, the man who invented psychoanalysis, lived in this house for 47 years until the annexation of Austria by the Nazis in 1938 forced him to leave the country. (He died in London the following year.) If you don't get offered one, ask for the guide to the museum in English. Admission cheaper with student card. If you find the opening hours too short, you can return without paying again if you keep your ticket.

KELLERS AND HEURIGE are wine cellars and wine gardens and were once – not so much now – an integral part of the life of the Viennese. But still good fun. Costs depend on how thirsty you are. One good Keller, though rather hot in summer, is Esterhazykeller at Haarhof. The Heurige are out in the north-western suburbs – try to avoid the touristy ones, especially the Grinzing area.

PRATER is an amusement park featuring the world's largest ferris wheel. No entrance charge to the grounds. Sometimes a good place to meet the opposite sex.

THEATRE for those who want a taste of the Vienna of old. Try the *Theater an der Wien* at Linke Wienzeile 6 for operettas (standing room is cheapest).

BURG KREUZENSTEIN is a moated medieval castle thirty minutes from the centre of Vienna. Take a train from Landstrasse.

Transport in Vienna
Single ticket on the street-cars costs a high 15 schillings but you can get about 30 per cent discount by buying five tickets at a time at **Tabak Trafic**. There's also a 3-day ticket (valid for 72 hours, not 3 calendar days) available for 66 schillings.

Student discounts
Free entrance to public museums and reductions to theatres and cinemas. For information:

AUSTRIAN STUDENT TRAVEL OFFICE at Reichsratstrasse 13, Vienna (tel: 42 15 61).

Addresses

Main post office (for poste restante) at Fleischmarkt 19, Vienna.

American Express at Kärntnerstrasse 21, Vienna (tel: 52 05 44).

Austrian Student Travel Office at Reichsratstrasse 13, Vienna (tel: 42 15 61).

Student Travel Service at Hildmannplatz 1a, Salzburg (tel: 84 069).

Student Travel Service at Erlerstrasse 19–25, Innsbruck (tel: 28 997).

Vienna City Tourist Office in the underground passage by the Opera (Opernpassage) (tel: 43 16 08).

US Embassy at Boltzmanngasse 16, Vienna (tel: 31 55 11).

British Embassy at Reisnerstrasse 40, Vienna (tel: 73 15 75).

Info centres at Damböckgasse 1 (tel: 57 95 21); Rötzergasse 29 (tel: 46 86 69); and Pragerstrasse 20 (tel: 30 33 89).

Hitchers' Tips and Comments...

Innsbruck. Don't try to walk out to the east. You face a ten-kilometre walk! Good place to sleep is under the Brenner Autobahn above the Olympic Stadium – good view of city lights. Keep out of pastry shops – too expensive. Don't try sleeping in the centre of Salzburg. Police are on the look out. Try out in the forest. It's only a couple of kilometres' walk. Hope this helps fellow travellers. *Malcolm Frankland, Glaslum, England*

In Austria and Switzerland, good places for a night's kip are in the little huts you see in fields or on mountains. They're usually open and keep you 100 per cent dry when it rains. *True Brit, Chelmsford, England*
    Ask permission if the place is obviously on someone's land, and – thinking of hitchers who'll pass that way in the future – leave things exactly as you find them. K.W.

Visit Vienna flea-market on Saturdays between 8 a.m. and 6 p.m. Come early for bargains and haggle like mad. Avoid vendors with tables. They have a one-year concession and out-of-your-mind prices.

Worth hitching down to Baden (about 26 kilometres south-west of Vienna). It's a beautiful spa town dating from Roman times. Lots of sulphur springs and baths. Also, a large 'cure' park which features free classical music concerts in summer. Baden is expensive, but you can save if you shop at *Eisenberger's Supermarket*. I found food cheaper there than in Vienna. *Tobias Williams, Vienna, Austria*

In Salzburg we couldn't afford an hotel and crashed in the entrance hall of the railway station. There were dozens of other hitchers there, too, and the police didn't worry anyone. *A. Brown-Grant, Oxford, England*

In Vienna, the Prater Park is a bit of a walk out of town, so if you're tired and want to crash right away try the small parks near the Rathaus (town hall). *Philip Attwool, Orpington, UK*

In Innsbruck, try dossing out at the deserted green hut near the Olympic ski-jump. It's well hidden, waterproof and has an inside lock. We stayed two nights and had no bother. *Gregor Murphy, Paisley, Scotland*

Italy

population	55,000,000
size	116,372 square miles
capital	Rome, population 4,000,000
government	Republic
religion	Roman Catholic
language	Italian
currency	*Lira* Coins of 10, 20, 50, 100, 500, 1000 *lire*. Notes of 500, 1000, 2000, 5000, 10,000, 20,000, 50,000 and 100,000 *lire*

The four most common entry routes into Italy are (1) along the French Riviera to **Genova** (Genoa, birthplace of Columbus), with its fantastic harbour area, (2) in over the French Alps to **Torino** (Turin) where you can catch the important Egyptian Museum and Museum of Ancient Art, (3) from Switzerland through the Swiss-Italian town of Lugano to **Milano** (Milan), or (4) through the Mont Blanc Tunnel.

Winter travellers coming in on the Turin route should note that the Col du Mt Cenis on the French side of the border may be impassable between December and May. Most of the passes in Switzerland (No. 3 route or any near it), like Simplon, Lukmanier or Splugen may be closed during the same months.

Summertime travellers should remember that the Riviera route is blanketed with family holiday cars from June through August and that the hitching can sometimes be very, very slow.

Milan is not my favourite city. With a population of more than one and a half million it's big, dusty, noisy, and industrial, but there are many things to see, notably the church of Santa Maria delle Grazie which houses Leonardo da Vinci's famous 'Last Supper'. The Gothic Duomo cathedral stands 357 feet high and has (if you're interested in such facts) 4400 statues serving as decoration. A trip to the roof gives you a fantastic view over the city and allows you to wax poetic to gargoyles if you feel so inclined. La Scala is the big stop for opera lovers. It's a superb theatre and features the best singers in the world. Cheapest way to view a show is to buy standing room.

Museum fans will have a ball in Milan. Right near La Scala is the Museo Teatrale which relates the history of the 150-year-old theatre, while the National Museum of Science and Technology (free on Sundays and Thursday mornings) has a Leonardo Gallery in which you can see models of da Vinci's fascinating inventions. Then there's the Pinacoteca di Brera (free on Sundays) which Milan claims as the second gallery in Italy after Florence's Uffizi. Finally, drop in on the thirteenth-century Castello Sforzesco, and the strange, ornate cemetery known as Cimitero Monumentale.

Halfway between Milan and Venice (Venezia) is **Verona**, used by Shakespeare as the backdrop to *Romeo and Juliet*. See a well-preserved Roman amphitheatre, Italy's largest outside Rome. Don't miss the fruit market at the Piazza delle Erbe, nor the Old Castle or the church of St Zeno Major. But most of all, enjoy the centre of the old town with its jigsaw of squares, alleys and stairways: a photographer's delight.

Venice may be the world's weirdest city. Built on a lagoon 4 kilometres from the mainland (but with a road connection) it spreads over 118 tiny islands. It is criss-crossed by more than 160 canals and, as no cars are allowed into the city, you either walk from place to place or jump a *vaporetto*, a canal boat. Take a tip that Lines 1 and 3 might be slower than Lines 2 and 4, but they are cheaper. Also remember that though *vaporetti* are fun and certainly not to be missed for at least one ride, they aren't essential; the city is small enough to walk in comfortably.

Venice vies with Florence as the most expensive city in Italy. To keep the budget intact, consider eating and sleeping in neighbouring **Mestre**, particularly around the station area. From Mestre you can bus or train into Venice each day. Don't do what one ambitious hitcher did and take coffee at Florian's or one of the other posh sidewalk cafés on St Mark's Square. His extravagance cost him about half his food budget for the day.

Big sights in Venice, apart from the city itself, include the Cathedral of San Marco (climb into the galleries for a close look at the incredible mosaic ceiling) and the neighbouring Palace of the Doges; the Gallery of Modern Art (great collection, free on Sundays) and the Guggenheim Collection (outstanding collection of twentieth-century paintings). For a look at Venetian glass-blowers in action jump *vaporetto* No. 5 at Fondamente Nuova, which will take you to the island of **Murano**. Another interesting island trip (leaving from the same place) is to **Torcello** with its old, old churches. If you want to find yourself a little company, try the Lido beach. To get there you take another boat ride. Once on the beach you must make sure you avoid paying several thousand lire for a dressing room. Lonely souls can also search for mates (only in summer) at the nearby tourist resort of **Lido de Jesolo**, reached by boat or bus. Your friend found, tempt the romantic in yourself by walking together on the Rialto Bridge around ten or eleven in the evening and listening to the music coming from the gondolas. The people *in* the gondolas are paying a small fortune for the privilege (like enough to keep you on the road for two or three days!).

Heading back across the country, you pass through **Ferrara** with its marvellous moated Castello Estense and its twelfth-century cathedral, and then through gracious **Bologna**, perhaps the best place in the country to try some good Italian home cooking. See the Fountain of Neptune and climb the 320-foot Asinelli Tower for a great view over this ancient town.

Next big stop (there are plenty of nice villages in between) is **Firenze** (Florence). Considered *the* great art city of the Western world, it's a natural target for thousands of students from all over the globe. Consequently, you have an excellent chance of finding someone who'd just love to accompany you on a tour. Good

meeting places are all around the central Piazza della Signoria and the Uffizi.

All museums and galleries in Florence are free on certain days which seem to change constantly (check tourist office), otherwise they will set you back a hefty entrance fee (less on student cards, of course). With something like 50 places to visit in the city, you have to choose carefully what you want to see. The Piazza della Signoria with the Loggia della Signoria and the copy of Michelangelo's 'David' standing in front of the Palazzo Vecchio are absolute musts and, in my opinion, should be visited at least twice, once in the day, once at night. Most people consider the Uffizi Galleries and the Pitti Palace indispensable. What else? Try the Baptistry opposite the Duomo cathedral with its unparalleled 'Door of Paradise' by Ghiberti, or the Piazzale Michelangelo (bus 13) where you can see yet another copy of 'David' and look out over Florence and the Arno Valley. Visit Santa Croce, badly damaged during the 1966 floods, but now restored. If you're particularly interested in Michelangelo, see the Casa Buonarroti, bought by the artist for his family, and stuffed with paintings and letters relating to the man himself. Drop in on the Medici Chapel where you can see Michelangelo's work adorning the tombs of the famous family. Try – well, work it out for yourself – free literature from the tourist office at Via dei Tornabuoni 15. There is so much to see and you will be surrounded by the masterpieces of so many famous artists that you may end up wondering if perfection isn't a trifle claustrophobic.

For a pleasant break, visit **The Paperback Exchange** at Via Fiesolana 31, just a five-minute walk from the Galleria dell' Accademia which exhibits the original 'David'. The Paperback Exchange offers 10 per cent discount off cash sales on secondhand books to hitchers who show this guide.

Pisa stands just an hour or two west of Florence. Here you can see the famous Leaning Tower. Ask for Il Campanile. It was begun in 1173 and leans 14 feet out of plumb owing to land or foundation subsidence after construction. Galileo used this very tower when making experiments before formulating his laws of gravity and when studying the acceleration of falling objects. In the same square (Piazza del Duomo) see the twelfth-century cathedral and the dome-shaped Baptistry, built between the twelfth and fourteenth centuries. On the side of the square opposite the kilometre-long line of souvenir stalls (can you live without a Leaning Tower of Pisa lamp base?) is the Cemetery (Campo Santo) with 600 tombstones and a chapel with fifteenth-century Old Testament frescoes. The dirt of the Campo Santo is said to be mixed with earth from the Hill of Calvary brought from Jerusalem by crusaders.

Heading south, make for Siena via **Volterra** (cathedral, palaces, first-century Roman ruins, etc.) and then try and get to **San Gimignano**, a fourteenth-century hill-top town famed for its 14 soaring stone towers – all that are left of 72 which once dominated the skyline. San Gimignano seems scarcely changed since the day it was built. A stroll through the streets – particularly just after sunrise – truly evokes a sense of the past.

Siena, about 30 kilometres south-east, is the most important town in Tuscany after Florence. Once again, there are galleries and churches enough to keep you busy. But, with a population of only 55,000, this beautiful medieval city is small enough to wander in at leisure. Maybe a nice resting place before hitting the bustle of Rome. If you're in the area in July or August, try to catch the Palio, a wild horse race around the Piazza del Campo with riders wearing medieval costume. (Exact dates from tourist office, and be warned that there's not a bed to be had during the festival.) Climb the Campanile (*without* your pack!) for tremendous views across the rooftops and the green, rolling Tuscan countryside.

You're probably getting the idea by now that you'll never see all of Italy, or even most of Italy, in one trip but, if you've still got the strength and the time try continuing south-east through **Perugia** (yep, great square, great palaces, great galleries, great cathedral) and on to **Assisi**, home of St Francis, mystic and poet (he is said to have written the first poems in the Italian language). The value of the visit is in the sheer beauty of the town. Long, narrow streets, ancient houses and a lifestyle apparently undistorted by the excesses of the twentieth century make it worth the detour. And, for such a small place (population about 25,000), there's plenty to see. The local tourist office can supply a free brochure devoted to Assisi and nearby villages.

After Rome, the next big 'must' is the Bay of Naples. **Napoli**, a city of one and a quarter million, has for centuries been subjected to earthquakes and volcanic eruptions, but the place just keeps on going. It is a marvellous town in which to wander – it's so Italian that it's nearly a cliché. The two big things to see are the Castel

Nuovo, dating from 1282, and the National Museum with its collection of ancient sculpture and important finds from Pompeii.

Pompeii is the greatest standing remnant of the Roman world. Once an important city of 20,000 people, it was completely buried by an eruption of Mount Vesuvius in AD 79. The memory of the place died in the succeeding centuries until the name became a mere legend. Then, late last century, it was rediscovered, and for decades the work of digging it out of millions of tons of dirt has continued. Now you can wander for hours in a complete Roman city – and it's weird. In some streets you see ruts in the cobbles from chariot wheels. In doorways you see grooves scraped into floors by the doors which once opened across them. And you can see the stone-entombed bodies of some of the citizens. (If you're not heading as far south as Pompeii and still want to see the ruins of a Roman town, try **Ostia Antica**, 22 kilometres south-west of Rome. Founded in the fourth century BC, Ostia Antica served as Rome's trading port with her colonies and at its zenith was the home of 100,000 citizens.)

Herculaneum, close to Pompeii, is another city which was buried in the same eruption. Not as fascinating as Pompeii, but OK.

The villain of the piece, Mount Vesuvius, is a volcano 3984 feet high, and it's still active. You can walk up to the top, if you're feeling fit, or take the expensive chair-lift if you're not, and then descend into the actual crater amongst the fumes drifting out from crevices. Interesting stuff.

Also in the Bay of Naples area is the famous resort town of **Sorrento** (beautiful and expensive) and the fabulous island of **Capri**, once the favourite haunt of old Emperor Tiberius (you can see the ruins of his palace). Don't miss the Blue Grotto if you can afford the dollars that the excursion will cost you. To get to Capri, the cheapest way is to take a steamer from Naples. It's a 1½-hour trip each way and makes for a fascinating day. If you want to hitch out to Sorrento (difficult because it's a built-up area), you can buy a return fare to Capri from there, but you get a much better look at the bay by leaving from Naples.

The island of **Ischia** is a rich man's place, but apart from private yachts and bikini'd kittens, it's laden with plenty of sights to see. Take a return trip by steamer from Naples.

South of Naples and you're into Calabria which, though progressing fast, still tends to prefer a lifestyle unchanged for centuries. See, too, the Greek temples at **Paestum.**

You can cross into **Sicily** from **Reggio Calabria** to **Messina** quite cheaply. Once there, forget the Mafia. Just remember that Sicily (pop. 5,000,000) is the largest island in the Mediterranean (10,000 square miles) and home of some of its richest archaeological finds.

Capital and chief port **Palermo** (pop. 700,000) is an Arab-Norman-influenced city of baroque squares, running fountains and Florentine statues. Plus odd gentlemen wearing pink ties who try to sell you contraband watches which may not even work. See the twelfth-century Palace of the Normans with its marble-floored Palatine Chapel and dazzling mosaics.

At **Segesta**, 56 kilometres west of Palermo, a desolately beautiful but unfinished Doric temple dates back to the fifth century BC. Farther south, at **Agrigento's** Valley of the Temples, a clutch of imposing temples overlooks a labyrinthine on-site museum containing a superb collection of Greek art.

Syracuse (pop. 100,000), 128 kilometres south of Messina, was the birthplace of Archimedes, who discovered the theory of water displacement whilst taking a bath. Once Syracuse was the most important city in the Western world after Athens. Half a million people lived there. Today it's a stylish town, with baroque palaces, beautiful piazzas, and a seventh-century cathedral. The massive archaeological zone includes a Roman colosseum, well-preserved Greek theatre and interesting caves and catacombs.

Don't miss **Etna**, at 10,725 feet the highest volcano in Europe. You reach it by bus, funicular and foot from **Catania**, Sicily's second largest city, on the east coast. The walk from the funicular terminal to the summit takes one hour. (If you're lucky enough to see Etna erupt when you hit town, keep your distance. When she blew in the summer of 1979 several tourists who disobeyed police orders and were too close won free cremations.)

Warning! The Italians are tough on drugs and the word is out that they're using the old hippie-type spy gimmick. So choose your friends carefully. If you're copped out and you're lucky, you'll only get three years.

★**Hitching in Italy** Generally OK. There are a tremendous amount of *autostradas*, but I find I've always had more luck on the smaller roads. You're allowed to hitch on the *autostradas*, but the rules are the same as anywhere else in Europe. Namely, you can only pick up rides on entrance roads; hitching on the actual *autostrada* is a no-no and will result in you being turfed back to where you belong by the scores of patrolling *polizia*.

★**Crossing to Sardinia** From Genoa to Olbia will cost around 25,000 lire, one way. From Naples to Cagliari, the same but cheaper if you sit up in a chair all night. From Civitavecchia (north of Rome) to Olbia will cost about 15,000 lire one way.

Rome: where to sleep

In Rome expect to pay between 5000 and 7000 lire for student accommodation. Hotels and *pensiones* – cheap ones – will take as much as 10,000 lire from you unless you find a real bargain. Doubles and triples, of course, give you a good saving per head. Make sure you don't land in a place which insists that you pay full pension (bed and all meals) – they may offer a good deal, but it won't be as much fun as eating out. Incidentally, when you're arranging for your room or buying a meal you'll find that speaking Spanish (if you've got some) will solve most problems (unless you can speak Italian, in which case you can solve *all* the problems).

Del Foro Italico Youth Hostel at Viale delle Olimpiadi 61, Flaminio, Rome (tel: 396 47 09). Fair way out of town.

Hotel Vanni at Via Treviso 31 (tel: 85 93 54). Fifth floor.

NBBS Hotel at Via dei Bichi 17, Forte Aurelio (tel: 622 41 98). Open 16 June to 15 October. Fair way out of town.

Casa dello Studente, Città Universitaria at Via Cesare de Lollis 24 (tel: 49 02 43). Ask for dormitory. Open 21 June to 20 September.

Pensione Cristallo at Via Montebello 114 (tel: 47 98 10).

Pensione Melinelli at Via Montebello 114 (tel: 47 03 27).

Casa Gizzi at Via Codorna 29 (tel: 48 19 77).

Albergo del Popolo at Via Apulia 41 (tel: 49 05 58). Women admitted from 1 July to 30 September only. Otherwise men only.

Dino at Via Cernaia 47 (tel: 475 90 93).

Protezione della Giovane at Via Urbana 158. Hostel run by nuns. Women only. Non-religious.

For cheap *pensiones* head for Via Principe Amedeo which is bang in the middle of town and two blocks to your left as you stand at the front of and with your back to the Terminal Station (in Piazza dei Cinquecento). The Via Palestro, a couple of blocks to the right of the station, is another good area. For help in finding accommodation go to the EPT information office in the Terminal Station.

For sleeping rough, head into the gardens of the Villa Borghese, *but only if there's four or five of you*! Gangs hang around waiting to rob loners. Second choice is the park at Colle Oppio, near the Colosseum. Third choice, the slopes leading up to and also around Piazza Garibaldi (behind and above the Trastevere) but, again, *only in groups* and, even then, don't let anyone see you bedding down. (When sleeping rough never let anyone see you bedding down *anywhere*!)

Warning! See hitch-hiker's letter in **How to survive** chapter (page 74).

Rome: where to eat

Expect to pay around 9000 lire for a filling meal. To cut costs, remember that in Italy, as in Spain, Greece and France, bar-owners usually don't object if you bring in a pile of food you've bought elsewhere to make a meal – as long as you buy a drink or two in the process. In the Colosseum/Colle Oppio area there are plenty of cheap food shops where you can buy in small quantities. The *Rosticcerie* and *Tavole Calde* are eating places which feature cheap, quick meals ideal for travellers low on lire.

In most Roman bars, sitting down for a coffee or drink costs double. Note that more and more Italian restaurants are charging extra for *servizio* (service) or *coperto* (cover charge) or both. These additions can bump your bill 20 per cent above the food price! Look for places that offer a tourist menu (usually three courses) with service and cover charge included. Even then, drink may not be included and this can add substantially to costs. Try and hold off and have a drink later, preferably from your own pack bottle.

Da Peppino at Via Castelfidardo 35 (couple of blocks to the right of the Terminal Station) is one of the cheapest places in town – but it's closed on Fridays. All around that area to the right of the station is dead cheap.

Mario's at Via del Moro 53. Just over the river near Ponte Sisto. Cheap!

La Fieramosca, Piazza de Mercanti, Trastevere. Excellent, but for splurgers only!

Imperiale at Via Flaminia 11.

Falconi's at Piazza dei Cinquecento 47, in front of the station.

Rome: what to see and do

THE ROMAN FORUM AND THE PALATINE Open every day except Tuesday. Entrance charge, but half price on Sundays. Ticket gives entrance to both sites. The *Forum* was the heart of the Roman Empire, the place from which all roads started and the market and meeting place of Rome's citizens. It is said that the site was first built upon, in wood, as far back as the sixth century BC. The *Palatine* is a low hill between the Forum and the Tiber and was the first of Rome's seven hills to be inhabited. At night (check the tourist office for times) a *son et lumière* display is held in the Forum. It costs a lot to enter, but from the back of the Capitoline Hill (or Campidoglio), once the sacred hill of Rome, you can watch the display (even if you can't hear it all) for nothing. Also, on Campidoglio is the *Capitoline Museum* (entrance charge) which contains a fine antique collection, much of it related to Imperial Rome. In the summer try visiting the Forum late in the afternoon – say 6 p.m. It's cooler, there are fewer people and it's much more evocative. If you can't afford the stiff entrance fee, you can see the Forum and Palatine (and the Colosseum and Circus Maximus) by taking a long walk. Start at the Campidoglio, make your way down the Via dei Fori Imperiali, along St Gregorio, up Via dei Cerchi and complete the circuit by wandering up Via di San Teodoro. It won't be any fun at all if you're carrying your pack.

COLOSSEUM The Colosseum was built between AD 70 and AD 80. The big inauguration show lasted 100 days during which 5000 wild animals were slaughtered. Not too long after, the Romans graduated to watching people being killed. The Colosseum could hold 50,000 spectators. It is undergoing long-term restoration and is sometimes closed.

THE PANTHEON at Piazza della Rotonda is the best preserved of all Rome's ancient buildings. It was built in AD 27 and then, after being burned down, rebuilt by Hadrian in the second century AD. Various Italian kings, as well as the painter Raphael, are buried in the building.

THE VATICAN CITY The Vatican became an independent state led by the Pope as the result of a treaty signed on 11 February 1929 between the Papacy and the Italian State. The city covers an area of 109 acres and has a population of 1000. It has its own newspaper (*Osservatore Romano*), its own postal service, radio station, railway station, court of law, and its own diplomatic representatives. It imports food and exports a nebulous hope which affects the lives of millions around the world. It is an indispensable stop on a Roman tour. Principal sights in the city are the fabulous *St Peter's Basilica*, the *Sistine Chapel*, the *Vatican Museum* and the *Raphael Rooms*. (About 30 per cent discount off entrance charge to holders of student cards.) Tickets for papal audiences can be picked up at several points around Rome and in the Vatican – check at the tourist office about this. If you just want a quick look at the Pope, at noon most Sundays he gives a sermon from the balcony overlooking St Peter's Square. In St Peter's, walk up the centre aisle and see marked on the floor the comparative sizes of other cathedrals around the world. If you can afford it, take the lift to the roof for a great view across the square. From there it costs nothing to enter the gallery and look down over 100 feet into the cathedral. Then climb up and around inside the dome (packs definitely don't fit!) to the very top for a stunning view over all of Rome. Back in the church again, don't miss Michelangelo's 'Pietà' (first chapel to the right of the main doors), now unfortunately protected by a glass wall after some nutter tried to smash it several years ago.

CHURCHES St Peter's is the main church to see, but others, all of artistic or historical interest, include *Santa Maria degli Angeli, St Peter in Vincoli* (which houses Michelangelo's 'Moses'), and *Santa Maria Maggiore*.

CATACOMBS Bus number 118 from the Colosseum takes you out along the Old Appian Way and passes the *Catacombs of St Sebastian* and the *Catacombs of St Callistus*. Both are worth seeing. The Catacombs of St Callistus are considered the most important in Rome. Entrance charge to both.

MUSEUMS AND GALLERIES Amongst the many to be seen are the *Galleria Borghese, The Lateran Museum, The National Museum of Rome, The National Gallery of Modern Art* and *The National Gallery of Antique Art.* If you only have time for one museum, then the *Vatican Museum* is considered amongst the most important.

THE TREVI FOUNTAIN at Via del Muratte. This is the place where, if you're romantically inclined, you toss a coin into the water and make a wish that you will soon return to Rome. If you're a hitch-hiker, you'll notice that a lot of young Italians have figured out how to get the coins back on dry land without getting their feet wet. They use magnets on a fishing line, hurl them into the water and slowly drag them back along the bottom. Guys using bigger and better magnets – I saw one a foot long and about an inch wide – bring in as many as five coins at a time. The fishing takes place just after dark and about an hour after it starts there aren't many coins left – so if you want to try it get there at the right time. (Beware of two things: the locals who don't like foreign competition, and the police who think it's all illegal.) Incidentally, I haven't seen fountain-dragging done anywhere else in Europe. Perhaps it hasn't caught on. It might be a good way of picking up pocket money. If you don't want to make money, go to the Trevi after dark during summer anyway. It's a great meeting place.

THE SPANISH STEPS These 137 steps lead off the Piazza di Spagna up to the church of *Trinità dei Monti.* Nearby is *Keats' House,* where the poet died in 1821. The Piazza, and the steps, which in the eighteenth and nineteenth centuries were the centre of the English colony in Rome, are now the meeting place of American travellers visiting American Express for their mail. Good place to meet people and dig out information. Keep away from cafés in this square (or any other important square in Italy). A simple cappuccino can cost you four times what it costs standing up in a backstreet bar. While in the area, check out 'The Economy Book Centre'. It's down the first passage on your left with your back to the steps at Piazza di Spagna 29. They stock new and used titles and offer 10 per cent discount on cash sales of secondhand books to hitchers who show this guide. You can trade in or get cash for your paperback books.

FLEA MARKET One of the better markets in Europe. It's at the Porta Portese and held every Sunday morning. There's a smaller market at Piazza della Fontanella Borghese held every afternoon (except Sundays) from 3 p.m. Mostly antique and imitation. Not as good as Porta Portese. Both are notorious for pickpockets and pack-slashers.

MOVIES Several cinemas around town show original version films. For information, buy the daily paper or a copy of the English-language publication *This Week in Rome*.

CONCERTS Check with tourist office for dates of concerts held outdoors in the Basilica of Maxeusis. Great setting with the cheapest seats around 1000 lire.

Transport in Rome
Trolleycar and underground tickets all cost around 250 lire. A flat rate of 250 lire operates for the bus system in Rome.

Student discounts
Reductions in some museums and art galleries, some theatres and cinemas, to some *son et lumière* spectacles, and for goods purchased in some department stores. For information:

MINISTRY OF PUBLIC INSTRUCTION, Viale Trastevere 76A, Rome.

Addresses

Main post office (for poste restante) at Piazza S. Silvestro, Rome.

American Express at Piazza di Spagna 38, Rome (tel: 68 87 51).

State Tourist Office in Terminal Station.

Relazione Universitaria at Via Palestro 11, Rome (tel: 47 55 265) (for student travel).

Ministry of Public Instruction at Viale Trastevere 76A, Rome. For matters relating to students.

US Embassy at Via Vittorio Veneto 119, Rome (tel: 46 74).

British Embassy at XX Settembre 80, Rome (tel: 475 54 41).

Hitchers' Tips and Comments...

Travellers catching Italy to Greece ferries should remember to save some lire to pay port tax. I didn't, and had to accept a lousy rate of exchange on a travellers' cheque in the port office in order to pay the tax. *Tini Williams, Chilwell, England*

If you're crossing to Sicily, take the ferry from Villa San Giovanni, which is much cheaper than the one from Reggio Calabria. *Hugh Dunne, Dublin, Ireland*

If you're sleeping out in Rome, be careful of the gardens outside the Terminal Station — lots of rip-offs happening. Also, in Italian trains, careful of police in civilian clothing looking for dope. Keep on truckin'. *Paul Rouse, Sion Mills, N. Ireland*

In Italy, soft drinks with restaurant meals cost the earth. Eat dry, then buy a drink elsewhere. *Avril Horton, Leeds, UK*

I followed suggestions in the *Hitcher's Guide* and slept in the grounds of the Villa Borghese in Rome. But I disregarded the warnings in the *How to Survive* chapter and was robbed of money, passport and camera. Please advise readers *not to crash out alone in Italian parks!* Sensible people were sleeping out at the Termini railway station, *in groups! Philip Attwool, Orpington, UK*

People wearing shorts and/or with bare shoulders are not allowed into St Peter's, Rome and many other Italian churches. *David McGonigal, Leeds, UK*

Here I sit locked in a hotel room in Fabriano, Italy, pretending to be brave while the porter keeps calling through the door. I was going to see more of Italy, but this is the last straw. I have only spent two days in Rome, two in Pompeii and now one here and it's been a continuous hassle. I am not particularly pretty, am short and round, and am sick of being pawed. Other girls I've spoken with have had the same problem. Spain was as you warned us, but there, at least, the men weren't persistent and neither did they manhandle. *Please* warn girls about Italy! It must be the deadliest place ever. I'm well able to look after myself, but this is getting me down. I'm shooting through. I'm heading to Austria. If I survive one more day of Italy to get there, I can survive anything! *Jane, New Zealand*

In Rome beware of the old gypsy trick of holding a tray of trinkets up to your chest. While they're trying to convince you to buy, their kids are going through your pockets, and you'll never even know! *Frank Bauroth, University of Dallas, USA*

Beware of the little gypsy kids on buses in Rome — pickpockets extraordinaire. Rucksacks with back and side pockets are very accessible — keep your backs to the wall.

When sleeping rough, use your spare laces to tie yourself or your sleeping-bag to your rucksack and other possessions. Easily cut or untied but, at least, it's another insurance policy. *Simon and Geoff, Sheffield, England*

Where to crash in Venice. First hitch as far as Mestre, which is where the road to Venice begins. Find the railway station. Cross the lines using the bridge. As you cross, you can see the flyover beneath you. Just crash out under the flyover. In the morning dump your gear at the railway station, and get a day return to Venice. Then, when you leave, the toll stations for the autostradas going west are only about a four-kilometre walk.

Why no mention of the most famous balcony in history? Just off the market square in Verona is Juliet's house with the balcony where she heard Romeo do his thing. *A. R. Brzozowski, Kettering, Northants, England*

Italian theft is getting silly. You can be approached by someone asking the time who then snatches your necklace, bag, watch, etc., even if you are wearing it. One bloke had his sleeping bag cut open, his trouser pocket cut open and his wallet stolen while he was asleep.

If hitching from Bari (southern Italy) further south, get bus 12 from the central station to the Mobil service station. *Simon Wadsworth, Shipley, West Yorkshire, England*

In Rome try Pension Esedre, Pension Eureka and Pension Terminus, all in the same building at 47 Piazza della Repubblica. *C. Hopper, Brighton, Sussex, England*

For camping near Venice take vaporetto No. 14 from St Mark's to Punta Sabbioni. Once there, turn right and after a 5-minute walk you arrive at the campsite.

Also, in Venice, a 24-hour go-anywhere vaporetti ticket is a sound deal. *Creb and Wez, Birmingham, England*

For a safe, convenient outdoor spot to crash in Florence, try the Palazzo dello Congresso's Park right beside the station. Its grounds are surrounded with an iron fence and they lock the gates about 10 p.m. You can easily climb the smaller cement fence portion if you have to. Once in there, you're safe from the thugs and loonies that everyone else is complaining about. *Mark Quail, St George, Canada*

Spain

population	37,500,000
size	194,883 square miles
capital	Madrid, population 3,147,000
government	Constitutional monarchy
religion	Roman Catholic
language	Spanish is the official language but Catalán is spoken in the north-east, Basque in the Basque provinces on the northern coast, and Gallego in Galicia
currency	*Peseta* Coins of 1, 5, 10, 25, 50 and 100 *pesetas*. Notes of 100, 200, 500, 1000, 2000, 5000, 10,000 *pesetas*

Unless you have unlimited time, travelling in Spain presents one big problem – where to go! The cities in Spain which have become household words outdo those of any other country. Madrid, Barcelona, Pamplona, Segovia, Toledo, Sevilla, Granada, Salamanca, Málaga, Valencia,Alicante, Cartagena, Córdoba, Zaragoza, Bilbao, San Sebastián, Tarragona, Gerona. All names with which the mind has some vague association.

But after Madrid, if you only have time to see five cities, they should probably be Sevilla, Granada, Barcelona, Toledo and Málaga. They are my personal choices and I'm a little one-sided when it comes to Spain. I particularly prefer the southern region of Andalucia, the land of tiny white mountain villages, old and smelly bars and cafés, cheap wine, bullfights, and a to-hell-with-it philosophy which leaves plenty of scope for tomorrow to look after itself. Sevilla, Granada and Málaga are all part of the south.

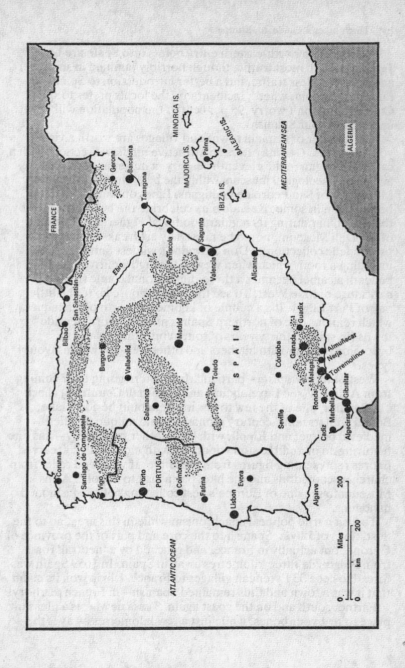

The two main north-eastern entry points into Spain are **La Junquera** (with most traffic, though horribly jammed in summer) and **Port Bou** (less traffic, but a better introduction to Spain – or rather, Catalonia, where, incidentally, the locals prefer to speak Catalán; but don't worry, 95 per cent of the population will understand your Spanish).

Any number of Catalán towns and villages are worth a visit if you have time. **Gerona** offers an attractive medieval section, with a cathedral begun in the eleventh century, a museum of city history and an archaeological museum within the beautiful twelfth-century Monastery of San Pedro de Galligans. Lines on walls with dates beside them in some riverside bars celebrate the height reached by the river Oñar during its regular floodings! **Figueras** is the home of the Dali Museum, not to be missed by art freaks – a truly psychedelic collection of Don Salvador's wildest fantasies, including a room which when viewed through a mirror hung beneath a camel becomes a three-dimensional comic strip caricature of Mae West. To see the artist's house go to the little bay of **Port Lligat**. It's a couple of kilometres north of **Cadaqués**, which remains one of northern Spain's most beautiful seaside towns (in spite of thirty years of tourist infiltration) and is becoming popular with hitchers and other well-known unsavoury types.

West of the *autopista* – particularly if you're going to or coming from Andorra (see **Luxembourg and the Small Countries**) check out **Bañolas**, one of the few towns in Spain built beside a lake; **Besalú** with its tenth-century monastery and unique fortified medieval bridge; and **Ripoll**, with yet another monastery – this one featuring an incredible stone doorway with more than 200 carved figures representing figures from the Bible. If you need relief from churches, cathedrals and the like, pay a visit to Ripoll's Arms Museum to see one of Europe's best collections of old-fashioned handguns.

To visit a true political anachronism while in this area, go to the 'lost' town of **Llivia**, Spanish to the core and part of the province of Gerona, but actually in France, and reached by a 'neutral' road from **Puigcerda** three kilometres away in Spain. In 1659 Spain was forced to cede 33 Pyrenean villages to France. Llivia won its claim that it was a town and thus remained Spanish – in French territory!

Farther south and on the coast again, **Tossa de Mar** is a pleasant place to rest your bones, while just a few kilometres away is the

place Spaniards call 'The Tourist Factory', **Llorret de Mar**. Lloret
in high summer is not exactly a poet's heaven on earth, but here
you could find company or a little work in one of the scores of
foreign-run bars. (Be warned that in Spain it's illegal to work
without a work permit – so watchit!)

Barcelona is Spain's second city, but vies with Madrid in its
claim to be the most dynamic. It is the largest seaport in the
Mediterranean and that, along with a population of two and a half
million, contributes to its reputation of being the liveliest city in
the country. The port is a good place to start wandering. Stroll
down the Ramblas to the 190-foot-high Columbus monument. The
25-foot-high statue of the explorer is heroically pointing to the
Americas – unfortunately he is pointing the wrong way. Moored
close by is a replica of Columbus' ship *Santa Maria*, a full-sized,
completely fitted reconstruction from the original plans. To see an
even more dramatic piece of reconstruction work, visit the
Maritime Museum (diagonally across the square from the *Santa
Maria*) which houses a meticulously built copy of an oared galley,
the *Real*, flagship of the Christians in the 1571 Battle of Lepanto.
Back on the portside again, rich hitchers can lighten their bulging
wallets by buying a ticket on the cablecar which will take them
across the port or up to Montjuich mountain. Views across the city
during the ride are truly stupendous. Destitute travellers can
forget the cablecar and take Bus 57 from the railway station up to
Montjuich. Visit the castle which houses a military museum, and
check out what is claimed to be the world's largest amusement
park. The mountain also offers good views over Barcelona. While
up there see the **Pueblo Español** – the Spanish Village – built in the
1920s and containing examples of every type of regional
architecture in the country. Back in the city, wander through the
famous Barrio Gótico (check the Cathedral and the Plaza del
Rey), and if you're into art see the Picasso Museum with many
works from the artist's blue period, and the Museum of Modern
Art which has more works by Picasso and some by Dali. Don't
miss Gaudí's still unfinished La Sagrada Familia church (you'll
love it or hate it, but you've got to see it!) and the apartment
buildings he designed on the Paseo de Gracia. To meet people try
the Plaza Real off the Ramblas where you should also find cheap
pensiones, and for more cheap food and accommodation try
Barceloneta, the fisherman's and workingman's suburb.

Just off Highway N11, 40 kilometres north-west of Barcelona, is

the famous old monastery of **Montserrat**. This eleventh-century
Benedictine building sits in a tremendous mountain location and,
if you feel like fighting it out with the 500,000 tourists who visit
each year, it's worth going up.

The coast road is the quickest way down south and goes through
some good places. **Tarragona** is one of them. It's small enough
(45,000 people) to wander around easily and it's one mass of
monuments and ruins. It's one of the oldest cities in Spain and St
Paul is said to have visited it during its Roman period and
converted the locals to Christianity. A few kilometres away are the
seaside resorts of **Salou** and **Cambrils**.

Heading farther south, towns worth seeing include **Peñíscola**, a
small place of only 3000 but perhaps one of the most beautiful
villages in Spain which sits dramatically on a promontory jutting
into the sea. **Sagunto**, 22 kilometres south of Castellón, is a
fortified town and historically one of the most interesting on the
coast. Greeks, Romans, Carthaginians and Moors all paid
business calls. **Valencia** and **Alicante** are both cities which could
take a couple of days of anyone's time (and between the two is
Benidorm, one of Spain's biggest resort towns), but if you have to
keep moving then Granada is next stop. On the way, you will pass
through **Guadix** and see the weird troglodyte dwellings.

Granada is where the Alhambra is, but it is more than that. It's
the sort of city which is good to return to or to tell yourself you will
return to one day. It dates back to at least the fifth century BC and
its crumbling age is one of its fascinations. Old streets twist and
turn, weeds grow from the roofs, and it is commonplace rather
than unusual to look through a door or an archway to find a
courtyard left over from Moorish days. It was the Moors who built
the Alhambra and to look over this reconstructed Arabian relic
takes at least half a day, even for a swift visit. If you plan to visit
the neighbouring Generalife – the summer palace – the whole tour
will take most of a day. Tickets cost about 250 pesetas, but student
cards will get you in for half price. Historians should visit the
Royal Chapel behind the sixteenth-century cathedral, where they
can see the tombs of Ferdinand and Isabel, the Catholic monarchs
who drove the Moors from the country and created a united Spain.
See also Sacromonte (go at night), one of the world's best-
organized tourist traps, where gypsies operate flamenco dives
from the depths of all-mod-con cave-houses. If you want to sample
what they're offering, be prepared to pay too much.

Málaga is the next stop if you decide to have a look at the Costa del Sol. Whichever route you choose to get down to the coast can be a rough one so don't move too far after you've found a prime hitching spot. The road is either bend-ridden or has bad edges – which doesn't encourage motorists to stop. Villages worth looking at if you're travelling along the N340 include **Almuñecar** and **Nerja**. Nerja is the site of a recently discovered cave which has traces of human habitation dating back 20,000 years, and a 195-foot stalactite, the world's largest.

In Málaga there is not much in the way of specific sights to see, apart from the beautiful old Arab fortifications, but the whole city is a trip in itself. There are literally hundreds of bars, for instance, in which you can go berserk trying to taste the dozens of famous sweet wines which Málaga province produces. At about 40 pesetas a glass it's a pleasant way to kill yourself.

Fourteen kilometres west of Málaga is the much-written-about tourist resort of **Torremolinos**. Twenty years ago it was a not-very-attractive fishing village. Now it's a not-very-attractive city of skyscrapers packed with package tourists. For the hitcher its main advantage is that all year round there are people in town looking for partners. Best place to start the hunt is down on the Carihuela beach. Plenty of bars there with like-minded souls. Also great fish restaurants. Best place to eat in the centre of Torremolinos is the *Lanjarón Restaurant* in the old section called Calvario. They also have cheap rooms.

Another good thing about it is the *Torremolinos Secondhand Book Market* where you can pick up something to read real cheap. It's upstairs at 26 Calle San Miguel (the main shopping street). They have a free notice board where people advertise for rides to Morocco, cheap airfares back to London, things to buy and sell, etc. They offer a 10 per cent cash discount on secondhand books to any hitch-hiker who flashes his copy of the *Hitcher's Guide*.

From Torremolinos, the N340 continues straight down to **Algeciras** for ferry connections with Morocco (see **Morocco and North Africa**) and from Morocco to Gibraltar (see **The Small Countries**). If time is available, a detour to **Ronda**, 50 kilometres into the Sierra de Ronda along the C339 is a nice trip. The city perches on the edge of a 600-foot-high cliff.

Sevilla can be reached by continuing along the N340 past **Cádiz** and then going north via **Jerez de la Frontera**, the sherry-producing area where there's plenty of free wine-tasting, or by

going north-west from Málaga and meeting up with the N334 at
Antequera. Sevilla with its population of half a million is the fourth
city of Spain and so old that legend tells it was founded by
Hercules. Like many other southern Spanish cities, it reached its
zenith during the long Arab occupation and today one of the best
things to see is the 320-foot-high Giralda Tower and the beautiful
cathedral alongside. In the cathedral is a tomb said to contain the
remains of Christopher Columbus. But the really big thing to see
in Sevilla, apart from the city's own lifestyle, is the three-day-long
feria, or fair, which is held each year around April when the entire
population goes mad with bullfights, flamenco, and all things
Spanish. The *feria* is heavily attended by tourists, but the
Sevillanos tend to disregard them and keep to the business in
hand. Check local or international Spanish tourist offices for exact
dates of the fair and also of the *Semana Santa*, or Holy Week
Fiesta, which precedes it. The processions are considered the best
in the country.

If you have gone as far as Sevilla, you might as well continue to
Córdoba, just 140 kilometres away. The old section of Córdoba is
more than worth the effort. Particularly, see the tenth-century
Mezquita, the largest mosque in the world after the one in Mecca.
It covers 22,000 square metres and contains 850 columns, and a
complete Roman Catholic church. See also the superb
Archaeological Museum and check the display of Spanish
handcrafts at the government-run shop Artespaña, which is
housed in a magnificent fifteenth-century inn not too far from the
mosque.

Toledo, 70 kilometres south of Madrid, is said by the Spaniards
to be the city which most perfectly includes all the most important
elements of Spanish history. It is an historical and architectural
monument to all that Spain has been, and in 1937 the entire city
was declared a national monument. Toledo was the home of El
Greco and a house said to have belonged to the artist has been
refurnished to imitate the style of his period. A gallery next door
contains many important works. Around the corner from the
house is the tiny church of Santo Tomé which contains what many
experts consider his best painting, 'The Burial of the Count of
Orgaz'. Other points of interest include the Gothic cathedral
which is claimed as the best in Spain, and the huge Alcázar, scene
of a tremendous siege during the civil war.

South of Toledo is **La Mancha**, Don Quixote country, and fans of the sprightly gentleman can pick up a free pamphlet from tourist offices describing a trip through villages associated with his adventures. Best place to see those famous windmills is at **Consuegra**.

From Sevilla, the E52 leads into Portugal for those heading for Lisbon, and the N630 leads north, joining with the E3 for those travelling to France. (The cheap living ends at the border! Load up with cigarettes and wine before crossing into France!) The four major cities on this route are all worth time if you can spare it: **Salamanca**, **Valladolid**, **Burgos** (home of the legendary El Cid) and **San Sebastián**. For me, Salamanca is the pick of the bunch. Start at the superb Plaza Mayor, one of Europe's most beautiful squares, then wander through the nearby university area (the university was founded in the thirteenth century). See the House of Shells and choose between the Old (twelfth-century) and New (sixteenth-century) cathedrals.

North of Portugal is the region of Galicia, a beautiful and rewarding part of the world, but completely impossible in the summer when every coastal road is clogged and every seaside campground overflowing. Unfortunately, most of the rest of the year it rains in Galicia. However, once in the region, make your way around the truly spectacular *rías*, or fjords, and try and visit **Santiago de Compostela**, a city of 90,000, third city in Christendom after Jerusalem and Rome, and named after Spain's patron saint, San Yago, or St James (whose remains are said to be in a silver urn in the crypt beneath the cathedral). Because of James during the Middle Ages the city became the destination of hundreds of thousands of pilgrims a year. Visit the cathedral and take a long look at the Obradoiro façade, and the Door of Glory. With luck you will see modern-day pilgrims doing what pilgrims have done for centuries – pushing their fingers into the notches of 'The Tree of Life' and praying for protection. On either side of the cathedral are the plazas de España and de la Quintana, both beautiful and both good meeting places.

★**Bullfights** Tickets are expensive. Generally, a seat in the shade (*sombra*) will cost between 750 and 1500 pesetas. Seats in the sun (*sol*) are cheaper, while standing room is cheapest of all. But as the fight takes about two hours it's worth investing in sitting space.

★**Fiestas** There's nothing quite like a Spanish fiesta, and you should try to visit one if you're anywhere near it. Here's a list of some of the more important fiestas, including the months they are usually held. You'll have to check with the Spanish Tourist Office to get exact dates, as they change from year to year. *Cabalgata de Reyes*, the Fiesta of the Kings, is a parade held in most Spanish cities on the Eve of Epiphany in January. *Moros y Cristianos*, mock battles between Moors and Christians, are especially popular in the Levante area. Some of the best known are at Bocairente (province of Valencia), in February; Alcoy (Alicante), in April; Villajoyosa (Alicante), in July; Villena (Alicante), in September. *Fallas de Valencia* is one of the most spectacular shows in Spain. Don't miss it if you're a firework freak. Huge firework-filled statues are burned in the streets. Held in Valencia on Saint Joseph's night in March. Alicante has a similar show on Saint John's Eve. *Semana Santa*, Holy Week, features vast Easter parades; best places to see them are Sevilla, Málaga, Valladolid, Granada. Also, during Holy Week, Passion Plays are held in various towns. Most outstanding in Esperraguera (Barcelona), Ulldecona (Tarragona), Moncada (Valencia). The Passion Plays are relics from the medieval theatre, as are certain other plays held during the year in Spain, namely the *Misterio de Elche* in Elche (Alicante) in August, and the *Misterio de San Quillén y San Felicia* in Obanos (Navarra) in August. *Ferias:* all cities have their *ferias* (or fairs). Amongst the best: Sevilla's Spring Fair, in April, and Madrid's San Isidro in May. *Feria del Caballo*, the Horse Fair, is held in Jerez de la Frontera in May. *Corpus Cristi* in June, especially in Granada, Sevilla and Toledo. In Sitges (Barcelona), the roads are paved with magnificent flower carpets. *Romería del Rocío* in Almonte (Huelva) in June: the most famous *romería* in Spain. But you need about a week spare and a horse to join in properly. *San Fermín*, in Pamplona, in July: the famed running of the bulls. (Be warned: statistics show that more foreigners than Spaniards get gored!) The *International Festival of Music and Dance*, at Granada in July, is held in the fabulous Alhambra. You have to book well in advance. *Human Castles:* you have to see it to believe it. People on top of each other, up to nine high; popular in the north. Try Vilafranca del Penedés (Barcelona) in August. *Batalla de las Flores* in Laredo (Santander) in August: parade during which those taking part and the spectators pelt each other with flowers. *Fiesta de la Vendimia:* the grape-harvest fair in Jerez de la Frontera in September.

★**Wine** Many, many villages in Spain make a small supply of local wine. So when roaming through the back areas, drop into local bars and ask for *vino del terreno* (the wine of the land). Some of it is remarkably good. It's usually cheap.

★**Cigarettes** They come as cheap as 20 pesetas for 20 and you can buy a first-class cigarette for 50 pesetas a pack. English or American-style filter-tips cost about 80 pesetas. Imported cigarettes over 120 pesetas. Worth stocking up to carry you through more expensive countries.

★**Piropos** If you're a lady hitcher, don't be surprised if a Spaniard suddenly walks up and starts whispering passionate sounding phrases to you. Keep your nose in the air and keep walking. It's purely the Latin manifestation of hairy-chestedness, like a harmless wolf-whistle in London or New York. The *piropo*, or compliment, is usually of a very personal nature and if you don't speak Spanish you're going to miss out on some wildly endearing pieces of Don Juanism, like: 'If only I was worthy to be the father of your children,' or 'Your body is a flower to be plucked by the grateful.'

★**Drugs** Don't be tempted to bring drugs into Spain from Morocco via Algeciras (or anywhere else). The Algerciras customs post uses specially trained dogs to sniff out the goodies. Even if you arrive in Algeciras from Ceuta, or in Málaga from Melilla, you may still be searched by mainland customs. Ceuta and Melilla are Spanish territories on the Moroccan coastline, but people entering the mainland from these cities are subject to a second customs hassle.

Crossing to the Canary Islands The seven main islands of the **Canaries** lie about 1500 kilometres from Spain's southern tip and just off the Saharan coast. (The nearest, Lanzarote, is only 112 kilometres from Africa.) They're blessed with year-round springtime temperatures and thus are popular with hitchers heading south to escape the annual northern freeze. There's no way of hitching there, unless you catch a yacht from Gibraltar or one of the harbours on the Costa del Sol (try Puerto José Banús just west of Marbella and the Estepona harbour), but regular ferry services run from Cádiz.

Here's a rundown on the islands, starting with the biggest:

Tenerife (area: 790 square miles, pop. 500,000)
Chief town **Santa Cruz de Tenerife** (pop. 180,000) is one of the
world's busiest shipping ports, but a surprisingly quiet and
pleasant town to walk through. Apart from the relaxed colonial
atmosphere it has nothing special to offer, but check out the
archaeological museum if you want a little local history.

Puerto de la Cruz, 35 kilometres west across the island, is where
the action is. A former fishing village turned high-rise resort, it's
filled with bazaars, hotels, bars, restaurants and discos; yet the old
centre still retains genuine charm. Plenty of chances to meet the
opposite sex. **Warning!** Meals and rooms are expensive here. This
is Charterflightsville and priced accordingly. (Avoid the Tenerife
wine, too. It's more expensive than mainland plonk and tastes
worse.)

The **Botanical Gardens** just outside Puerto de la Cruz are worth
a look. Founded in 1788, they are famed for a collection of trees
brought from all over the world. Don't miss the monkeys.

La Orotava, 6 kilometres inland, is a typical Canary town.
Houses with traditional wooden balconies overlook the
banana-filled valley below. Farther inland, after crossing giant
pine woods, you reach the foothills of **Mount Teide**. Standing at
12,000 feet, it's the highest mountain in Spain – mainland or
islands. A cablecar takes you to the peak. The views are worth the
price of the ticket. (You can see several islands on a clear day.)

West of Puerto de la Cruz, the town of **Icod de los Vinos** boasts
the world's oldest dragon tree. This monstrous sixty-foot-high
shrub is said to be 3000 years old, but is almost certainly not.

Two of Tenerife's best beaches are at **Los Cristianos** fishing
village tourist resort and **Playa de las Americas**, a custom-built
seaside package holiday town. To reach them, hitch down the 64-
kilometre coastal highway from Santa Cruz. The inland route is
more interesting but can be tough going.

Gran Canaria (area: 600 square miles, pop. 550,000)
Capital **Las Palmas de Gran Canaria** (pop. 275,000) is a raucous,
bustling wide-open port, full of duty-free shops (most things are
cheaper in England and America: watch out for tricks like
seemingly cheap cameras which are mounted with third-rate,
unheard-of lenses), bars, restaurants and dives. You name it, you
can usually get it. La Vegueta is the town's old quarter. Amongst
its historical buildings is the Casa de Colón (Columbus' house,

where the famous explorer lived during a stay on the island). Now it's a fine arts museum and home of the island's historical archives. Nearby, the Canary Museum has nine galleries devoted to the culture of the Guanches, Gran Canaria's original inhabitants. The Canary Village, in the beautiful Ciudad Jardín (Garden City), has a museum of local paintings, traditional Canary architecture and a folklore show. Worth a visit if you don't mind tripping over a few tourists. For cheap restaurants and rooms in Las Palmas, nose around behind the old fishing port and 'Muelle de la Luz' (literally, Jetty of Light). Swimmers should head for the long, wide sandy beach of Las Canteras, shielded by an offshore reef. It's right in the town.

Caldera de Bandama is the island's biggest extinct volcano. It's about one kilometre across and tomatoes grow like weeds on the fertile valley floor. From the lookout point on top you can see Las Palmas in the distance.

Teror, the island's prettiest village, is peaceful in spite of its name. It's full of medieval houses lined with delicately carved wooden balconies. In September it celebrates Gran Canaria's greatest religious festival, when each village on the island brings a float to participate in a massive procession. It's all in honour of the patron saint, Our Lady of the Pines. Teror's fifteenth-century church stands on the spot where she is supposed to have appeared.

Lanzarote (area: 310 square miles, pop. 45,000)
Here is a desolated volcanic landscape of craters, caverns and weird lava formations. The island's last eruption occurred in 1736.

Capital **Arrecife** (pop. 20,000) is a simple port with little going for it, but you can find cheap restaurants and pensions. Watch out when the wind blows the wrong way from the fish-canning factory.

You can find not-so-cheap accommodation in nearby **Puerto del Carmen**, a fishing village whose good beaches have turned it into the island's main tourist area.

Playa Blanca, down south, is an unspoilt little port with beach tavernas and a couple of bars. On clear days you can see both Fuerteventura Island and the African coast 112 kilometres away. Quiet, white-sanded beaches offer ideal free accommodation.

For the full tourist bit in Lanzarote, ride a camel over orange-black dunes near the **Fire Mountain** and feel the heat coming out of live volcanoes. If you walk or hitch into Fire Mountain, don't wander too far off the road into the lava fields.

Seemingly sturdy lava rocks chip when stood upon and the surface of the rocks is incredibly abrasive. A fall could do you real damage.

Up north try not to miss **Jameos del Agua**. It's a massive cave, complete with tiny lake, formed from a volcanic bubble. On Saturday night it doubles as a nightclub with a folklore show one end and a disco the other.

Interesting villages inland are **Haria**, with its palm oasis, and **Yaiza**, which must be the most immaculate 'pueblo' in Spain. Try the local green-white Malvasia wine – 15 per cent proof and truly volcanic.

Fuerteventura (area: 780 square miles, pop. 20,000)
This looks like a giant chunk of the Sahara which landed in the sea. Tourism is well rooted now, but you can still get away from it all. Head for the marvellous sandy beaches that seem to cover half the island. The island's first capital, **Betancuria** (pop. 950), is a simple village that has seen few changes since Jean Bethancourt, a Norman adventurer, founded it in the fifteenth century. The present capital is **Puerta del Rosario**, which has little to offer. But you might find some action at nearby **Playa Blanca** with its excellent beach. **Corralejo**, in the north, is the main tourist resort. Hitchers carrying masks and snorkels should set out for **Isla de los Lobos** (Wolf Island) three kilometres offshore from Corralejo. You'll find the best underwater fishing in all the Canary Islands.

La Palma (area: 280 square miles, pop. 100,000)
This lush, pear-shaped island is famous for its cultivated craters. Capital **Santa Cruz de la Palma** (pop. 20,000) is quiet and quaint with several pensions and a seafront promenade lined with neat old houses.

La Cumbrecita, in the centre of La Palma, is one of the world's biggest craters. It's 25 kilometres across, 28 kilometres around, and over 7000 feet deep. The valley floor is planted with subtropical vegetables and citrus fruits. Visit **Fuencaliente**, scene of the 1971 San Antonio volcanic eruption.

Best swimming and best chance of finding company is at **Tayacorte** on the west coast.

Gomera (area: 146 square miles, pop. 25,000)
On this rugged island of fertile valleys and mountains, locals communicate with each other by a remarkable whistling language

known as *silbo*. Capital **San Sebastián de la Gomera** (pop. 7500) has a few pensions and not much else. But this town was Columbus' last stop before heading into the unknown Atlantic in search of the new world and San Sebastián offers several memorials to his visit. Wandering through the few island villages is relaxing and rewarding (hitching can be slow!). Gomera has no airport and few tourists, except those coming across with you on the Tenerife ferry (from Los Cristianos).

Hierro (area: 107 square miles, pop. 7500)
This wild island counts over a thousand volcanic mountains. It's the most westerly of the Canary Islands. Capital **Valverde** (pop. 5000) is 2000 feet above the tiny port of **La Estaca** where boats arrive from Tenerife. Few tourists visit the island; out here you really can find a spot to get away from it all. Hierro was once considered by geographers as the 'official' end of the world.

Crossing to the Balearic Islands Ferries from Valencia, Alicante or Barcelona to Palma. Don't believe all that newspaper claptrap about the **Balearics** being spoilt. Of course, they're popular. You only have to read travel brochures to see that. But there's a lot more to them than that clichéd world of concrete and fish 'n' chip signs harped on by journalists who seldom stagger beyond their hotel bar.

The archipelago includes four islands which lie halfway between the Spanish Mediterranean coast and Algeria. Boats from Barcelona, Valencia and Alicante visit them all, except Formentera which you reach from Ibiza:

Mallorca (area: 1405 square miles, pop. 450,000)
Capital **Palma de Mallorca** (pop. 250,000) crams in nightclubs, sophisticated shops, a big yacht harbour and fishing port, and an old Gothic quarter. A great city for walking. Don't miss the Gothic cathedral, begun in 1230 and finished over 300 years later. Four Majorcan kings are buried here, and the treasury, with its gold plate and jewelled candelabras, is worth visiting. In nearby Terreno suburb see the well-preserved Moorish Castle of Bellver and the Pueblo Español not far away (same as Barcelona's, only smaller). Plaza Gomila, below, is the Pigalle-like nightclub area. Good spot for meeting up with the opposite sex, though expensive. Rooms in many of the *fondas* behind Pio XII Square at the top of the Borne (Palma's central boulevard) are cheap. For

eating out try the cheap but simple restaurants at the far end of the gaudy Apuntadores alleyway off the Borne.

Take the little train from the station in the Plaza España across the mountains to the French-looking **Soller**. It's easier than hitching, and cheap. Notable hill villages nearby are **Deya**, for thirty years home of English author Robert Graves, and claimed by many to be the prettiest village in Spain; and **Valldemossa**, where Chopin passed a lousy winter with George Sand in the Carthusian Monastery. A mass of island caves (Drach, Arta, Campanet, Genova) are worth viewing. The best is **Drach**. But be warned: in summer up to 1000 visitors at a time are stumbling through. Good unspoilt beaches are **Alcudia** and **Cala Ratjada** in the north.

Menorca (area: 250 square miles, pop. 45,000)
Nicknamed the 'blue and white island', the most northerly Balearic island sports neat white villages and blue-watered coves. It also has green fields with cows, wet, windy winters and a few Georgian-fronted houses to remind you the British occupied it for fifty years.

Capital **Mahon** (pop. 20,000) is a sleepy, rather staid town huddled around the longest inlet in the Mediterranean. They say that 200 years ago Nelson dallied here with Lady Hamilton in Villa San Antonio (just across the inlet from the town), thereby scandalizing the local populace. By day Mahon is pleasant enough, but at night it's a crock. So after sundown try one of the lively open-air bars in the neighbouring harbour town of **Villa Carlos**. Someone's usually playing a guitar. Soloists are welcome – in any language. **Cala Fonts** at Villa Carlos is tempting, particularly at night. Enjoy a drink on the waterfront there but not a meal, unless you're well heeled. You pay for the view!

Ciudadela, at the other end of the island, is a quiet Moorish town that suddenly goes crazy during the wild San Juan horse-riding *feria* on 24 June.

For archaeological buffs, the island is dotted with *taulas* and *talayots*, huge Stonehenge-type constructions that date back to the Bronze Age. They're the oldest traces of previous inhabitants to be found in any of the islands. There are a hundred different sites to visit. The most convenient is the *taula* at **Trebalugar**, just behind Villa Carlos. The beaches of **Arenal d'en Castell** (in the north) and **Santo Tomás** and **San Jaime** (in the south) provide some of the best swimming in the Balearics. Cross-country trekkers can find beaches which are empty even in the middle of summer (don't break your neck scambling down to them). Behind **Son Bou** beach are caves which were inhabited thousands of years ago.

Don't leave without trying the local gin, another legacy of the British. It's good value at 300 pesetas a bottle, and a dash of soda and lemon gives you the favourite Menorquin apéritif, *pallofe*.

Ibiza (area: 220 square miles, pop. 40,000)
Capital **Ibiza Town** (pop. 20,000) was once a haven for freaks. Now you mostly find put-ons who can safely play the Bohemian because they have big bank accounts to back their independence. Still, there are plenty of good types around and in the cobbled Dalt Vila (old quarter) above the town strange dives are full of local artists and eccentrics. At the top of the Dalt Vila see the fifteenth-century Gothic cathedral and fine views of the bay and town. The Archaeological Museum opposite the cathedral contains a unique collection of Punic relics excavated from Puig, the nearby Phoenician burial ground. You can find low-budget restaurants and pensions behind the waterfront. (And a joint called Johann Sebastian Bar.)

Santa Eulalia del Río, 12 kilometres up the coast, is a relaxed town, popular with artists and writers, but the area is fast sinking beneath hotels and apartments.

On the other side of the island, 16 kilometres from Ibiza Town, the one-time small fishing port of **San Antonio Abad** staggers under an avalanche of package tourists. But, amongst the sea of high-rises, you can still find cheap bars and eating-spots (mainly at the back of the town). If you avoid July and August, boat trips to the half-dozen beaches outside San Antonio Bay are pleasant and cheap.

Formentera (area: 45 square miles, pop. 3500)
This tiny sickle-shaped island has white beaches and a bleached port, **La Sabina**, that looks as if it's a leftover from the old Spanish Sahara.

Tiny capital **San Francisco Javier** (pop. 1000) is a dusty one-horse town with an eighteenth-century church which used to have cannon on the roof to repel pirates.

Es Pujols is the island's single diminutive resort. Its handful of apartments and restaurants are filled mainly by German tourists.

Just beyond it, the simple village of **San Fernando** provides the best-value meals and rooms on the island, and is a good place to meet fellow-travellers.

The island is lined with unspoilt beaches which provide ideal free accommodation in summer. **Playa Mitjorn**, in the south, is the longest.

Warning! Australians, New Zealanders and South Africans cannot enter Spain without a visa granted in a Spanish consulate outside Spain. *You cannot get the visa at the border or at a Spanish airport!* The visa is cheap, nearly always granted and can usually be obtained on the day of application. All non-EEC members should check with Spanish consulates before attempting to enter Spain, just in case the rules have changed even further.

Madrid: where to sleep

Spain is one of the few countries where you can relax and let your hair down moneywise. It's amongst the even fewer countries – Portugal, Greece, Turkey, Morocco – where you are advised to keep away from student accommodation because it is generally more expensive than what you can find around the streets. You should always stay in a *pensión* – never in anything calling itself an hotel – and in Madrid it is no great thing to find a *pensión* for 500 pesetas. This is a good average price. Try in the Plaza Mayor area, in the little streets off Calle de Toledo.

Madrid: where to eat

Eat where you like. Just avoid anything with chrome or plastic trimmings. In the warren of streets between Plaza Mayor and Puerta del Sol you can find little bars which will serve small omelets for 150 pesetas and a *caña* (draught beer) for 50 pesetas a glass. Choose your place well and you can treat yourself to a good meal, wine included, for 350 pesetas. Avoid the three-course tourist menus you will see advertised all over the place. Most of them offer a good deal but you can eat cheaper by just ordering yourself one big special course. Calle del Barco, which is off Avenida José Antonio, has half a dozen really cheap and good restaurants. Don't be frightened to drop in on some bars before you eat to have a few *vinos* and *tapas* (tiny appetizers) – they'll set you up well for your meal and usually won't cost you more than 50 or 60 pesetas a go. Spaniards, incidentally, don't eat their evening meal until 9 or 10 at night.

Madrid: what to see and do

THE PRADO One of the really great art galleries of the world. Unbelievable collection of Goya, just about everything that Velázquez ever put on canvas, rooms full of El Greco and four or five fantastic works by Bosch – and that's just part of it. Admission charge, except on Saturday afternoons when it's free.

EL RASTRO This is the flea market along Ribera de Curtidores. Open every morning, but at its best on Sundays. (It's too crowded to carry a pack comfortably.) Costs nothing and it's great fun. If you want to buy something, haggle like mad – but you'll be haggling against experts, because half of the stallholders are gypsies.

THE PLAZA MAYOR One of the most beautiful squares in Europe and a good place from which to start exploring the 'old' Madrid. Don't eat or drink in the plaza – too expensive. Move to the streets behind.

STAMP MARKET for philatelists who want to try to pick up a bargain, or people who want to watch some expert haggling. Plaza Mayor between 11 in the morning and 2 in the afternoon every Sunday.

BULLFIGHT TICKETS To buy a ticket (May is one of the most active months), and to get a glimpse of the Madrid Hemingway wrote about in *The Undefeated*, go to Calle Victoria – a small street on your right as you walk up Carrera de San Jerónimo which leads out of the Puerta del Sol. Streets in this area, like Calle Echegaray, have great bars.

BULLFIGHT MUSEUM at the Las Ventas bullring. This shows the history of bullfighting in paintings, engravings and models. Small admission fee. Open from 10.30 a.m. to 1 p.m. and from 3.30 to 6.30 p.m.

PALACIO REAL (Royal Palace) at Plaza de Oriente. A huge and richly decorated palace probably of interest to architectural fans. Stiff entrance fee.

Transport in Madrid
It's all cheap. The rock-bottom method of getting around is on the Metro. Anywhere to anywhere in the city will cost you about 35 pesetas. Next cheapest are the buses. If you're in a group, say four people, don't be scared of taxis. A long trip, 4 to 5 kilometres, will only cost you around 250 pesetas. Trouble is that the vehicles are driven by hell-drivers.

Student discounts
Theoretically, in Spain, you should get reduced admission to various places like the Prado and the Alhambra. Practice and theory in Spain, however, are two different things. If you have a student cart try your luck by flashing it everywhere. Details from: TIVE, José Ortega y Gasset 71, Madrid (tel: 401 95 01).

Addresses

Main post office (for poste restante) at Plaza de Cibeles, Madrid.

American Express at Plaza de las Cortes 2, Madrid (tel: 222 11 80).

TIVE at José Ortega y Gasset 71, Madrid (tel: 401 95 01).

Viajeseu at Avenida José Antonio 615, Barcelona 7 (tel: 231 34 62).

Tourist Information Office at Plaza Mayor 3, Madrid (tel: 266 48 74).

US Embassy at Serrano 75, Madrid (tel: 276 34 00).

British Embassy at Fernando el Santo 16, Madrid (tel: 419 02 00).

Hitchers' Tips and Comments ...

No problem dossing in Algeciras when you're waiting for the Ceuta or Tangier ferry. Police seem friendly enough. But if you're kipping in the seafront garden, beware the mad gardener who insists on hosing down the grass around 8 a.m.
Dave P., Leeds, England

For cheap accommodation in Barcelona, try Casa de Huéspedes Mari-Luz, Calle Palau 4 (tel: 317–3463). Walk down Ramblas, turn left on Calle Fernando, then right at Hotel Rialto. (You have to climb about 80 stairs.) Also try Pension Fernando, Calle Fernando 31 (tel: 301–7993) run by Mari-Luz's husband. For good cheap food try Casa José, Plaza San José Oriol 10, off the Ramblas. The paella is good value for money. *Steve, Heckmondwike, England*

At La Junquera, just across the Spanish border where the A17 and N11 intersect, there are usually about 50 trucks pulled over and waiting to clear customs. Ask around and you can often pick up a ride to major Spanish cities. *John Otis, Mankato, Minnesota, USA*

Hitchers sleeping out on beaches in Spanish tourist resorts should be warned that they're in danger of being mugged and/or robbed. I heard several nasty stories from Benidorm and Torremolinos. *Paul Johnson, Park Ridge, Illinois, USA*
 Try never to sleep rough alone. Try and get a group of four or five together. To protect yourselves from sneak-thieves who try and spirit away back-packs, tie all luggage together with rope, or belts. K.W.

Paper napkin dispensers in just about all Spanish bars supply unlimited quantities of (thin) toilet paper. *J. D. Boyle, Topeka, Kansas, USA*

Portugal

population	10,000,000
size	35,404 square miles
capital	Lisbon, population 1,500,000
government	Republic
religion	Roman Catholic
language	Portuguese
currency	*Escudo* One *escudo* equals 100 *centavos*. Coins of 50 *centavos*, and 1, 2½, 5, 10, 25 and 50 *escudos*. Notes of 20, 50, 100, 500, 1000, 5000 *escudos*

Oporto, Portugal's second city, with a population of 325,000, lies

just 150 kilometres across the Spanish border. If you have a nose
which enjoys tracking the smell of the grape, this could be your
idea of heaven because the city lends its name to port wine, and
the Douro River which it straddles is the waterway which carries
barge-loads of grapes down from the vineyards. Much of the final
product ends up stored in vats holding as much as 100,000 litres in
the wine *bodegas* near the bridges at Vila Nova de Gaia. Some
bodegas offer free tastings. If you're sober enough after finding the
ones that do, don't miss the cathedral and the cathedral square,
and visit the Soares dos Reis Museum in the eighteenth-century
Carrancas Palace, which features Portuguese painting.
(Interesting to note that in Roman times there were two towns,
Portus – the harbour – on the right bank, and Cale on the left
bank. The twin cities were known as Portucale – thus Portugal.)

If you're in a wandering mood head inland to the province of
Trás-os-Montes. **Bragança** is a good destination. The trip can be
slow and the landscape is not exactly lyrical, but I like the
austereness of it. It's a slice of the country the tourists usually miss.
In Bragança head for the old section, completely walled and
fortified. From the keep of the twelfth-century castle you enjoy a
great view over the town.

South-west towards Coimbra lies the **Buçaco Forest**, a 250-acre
national park containing over 700 varieties of trees and plants.
Several trails offer planned walks. One takes you by the Fonte Fria
– the Cold Fountain – a cascade tumbling down a 144-step
staircase. If you're interested in Portuguese history, check the
Military Museum which commemorates Wellington's victory over
the French in the Battle of Buçaco in 1810.

Coimbra (population 60,000) is the seat of an ancient university
founded in Lisbon in 1290 and transferred to the city in 1308. I
hitched in and out of town with students and found them open and
friendly. You'll notice that some male students wear torn black
cloaks. The rips commemorate successful amorous adventures!
Nearly all the main sights are in the photogenic old section, a
frustrating but beautiful maze of narrow alleys and time-worn
stairs. Visit the Old University, the cathedral and the Machado de
Castro Museum. About 15 kilometres south-west of Coimbra
stand the Roman ruins of **Conimbriga**, considered to be among the
most important in the entire Peninsula.

Farther south again and you come to the Monastery of **Batalha**
(the word means battle), built in the fourteenth and fifteenth

centuries to commemorate the Battle of Aljubarrota (1385) when an ill-equipped Portuguese army defeated a superior Spanish force. Henry the Navigator is buried in the Founder's Chapel, and the Unknown Soldiers are buried in the Chapterhouse. The multi-turreted building is among Portugal's most popular sights. Just a few kilometres down the road is **Alcobaça** where there's another monastery built to celebrate another battle. The complex, comprising the church, the exquisite Cloister of Silence and various peripheral buildings, makes it Portugal's biggest church. Check the eighteenth-century kitchens just off the cloister. Inland a few kilometres lies the sanctuary of **Fátima**, where in 1917 the Virgin Mary is said to have made a series of appearances to three shepherd children. If you are interested in religion, or in the phenomenon of crowd psychology, visit Fátima on the 13th of any month, when pilgrims flock there to worship. On 13 May, the anniversary of the first apparition, up to a million people congregate on the esplanade. Whatever your beliefs, it's really something to see. And so is the gross commercialism which has turned a sacred place into a gigantic supermarket full of tin and plastic religious trivia.

Continue inland to **Tomar**, wonderfully situated on the Nabaõ River and presided over by a twelfth-century Knights Templar castle. See the Convent of Christ with its famous Templars' Rotunda, modelled on Jerusalem's Holy Sepulchre. But if you want to enjoy a more down-to-earth experience, head in the other direction, to the coast, to the fishing town of **Nazaré**. This is undoubtedly the most photographed town in Portugal, and in summer is inundated by tourists. Some of the gnarled fishermen the tourists line up to photograph after paying their escudos aren't even fishermen, but old-timers who have realized that *looking* like a fisherman can be a profitable sideline. But Nazaré is still a real fishing village.

Try to visit it in winter when things are quieter. The famous Nazaré scene of fishing boats being hauled from the water and up the beach by oxen is rare now – tractors are much more efficient. Camera-toting hitchers should try for a shot from the Sitio quarter which perches on a 300-foot cliff north of town. If you fancy a spot of fishing yourself, head south again and make a detour over to **Peniche**, from where you can take a boat (in calm weather!) to **Berlenga Island**, about 10 kilometres offshore. The island offers superb line and underwater fishing (got your spear in your pack?).

Approaching Lisbon via the N8 you can choose between several visits on or near the Estoril coast. **Sintra**, a few kilometres inland, is a town of magnificent buildings, and the surest way to see one for free is to get picked up for vagrancy or some other dastardly deed because the town jail is in a castle. Sintra's fame as a summer resort began centuries ago when it was favoured by Portugal's kings as a retreat. See the Royal Palace, the whimsical Palácio da Pena and the dramatically situated but skeletal Moorish castle. If you're in Sintra on the second or fourth Sunday of the month, catch a bus to neighbouring **São Pedro de Sintra** for the town market. Stock up on genuine, old-fashioned, homemade bread and cheese and fresh country produce. Back on the coast, **Cascais** is pleasant for an overnight stay. Like Sintra, it owes its beginnings as a tourist destination to royalty who started using it as a summer resort in 1870. You won't find anything truly old in Cascais because it was wrecked in the earthquake of 1755, but you'll enjoy the beach and the bay which it shares with neighbouring **Estoril**. Visit the Castro Guimarães Museum where you can examine archaeological exhibits tracing the history of the area which was first settled by Palaeolithic man and then by Romans, Visigoths and Moors. Try to make it down to the **Boca do Inferno** (the Mouth of Hell), just two kilometres south of Cascais. The 'Mouth' is a geological freak which sucks in the sea and spits it out in huge spouts of spray along with a great booming accompaniment. Best on a day when the sea is really wild.

South-east of Lisbon the indispensable visit is to **Evora**, capital of the Upper Alentejo province. The town of 40,000 has been declared by the government to be a 'museum city'. It's a fair description of the place. Though its white walls and narrow streets give it a completely Moorish feeling, within an hour you can stroll by the second-century Roman Temple of Diana, a twelfth-century cathedral, the fifteenth-century Dos Lóis Monastery and a gruesome sixteenth-century chapel called the Casa dos Ossos (the House of Bones), which has 5000 skulls decorating the walls. If you feel like wandering off the beaten track, try a sidetrip towards the Spanish border to the ancient fortified town of **Monsaraz** which seems hardly to have changed for centuries. From Monsaraz it's easy enough to find your way into Spain via any one of several inland routes.

The usual coastal route into Spain is via the **Algarve**; **Sagres**, **Lagos**, **Albufeira** and **Faro** are the principal towns. All can be suffocatingly busy in summer, to the point where it is nearly impossible to move a car in the crowded streets, much less park it within a kilometre of where you want to go, so you can guess what the hitching is like! Winter is the time to visit. Cold wind can sweep in from the Atlantic, it may rain, but at least you will be able to see what you came to visit.

★**The Madeira and Azores islands** The volcanic, subtropical Madeira Archipelago, 850 kilometres from Lisbon in the Atlantic Ocean, comprises the island of **Madeira** itself, the island of **Porto Santo** and two uninhabited groups, the **Desertas** and the **Selvagens**. The Azores Archipelago comprises ten major islands totalling 902 square miles spread across 500 kilometres of the Atlantic, the nearest island lying 1100 kilometres from Portugal's Cape Roca. The Azores are divided into three main groups, the Eastern, Central and Northwestern. **São Miguel** in the eastern group is the largest island. The Madeira and Azores islands, which belong to Portugal, are most easily reached by plane or ship from Lisbon.

★**Bullfights** If you find the Spanish version of the bullfights bloody, you may prefer the Portuguese fights which come into the category of sport rather than ritual. The bull is never killed. All good, clean fun. Check at the tourist office for dates. Students can buy half-price tickets through SIAEIST, the student travel bureau.

★**Festas** Festivals and fairs in Portugal are great fun. You should check with Portuguese national tourist offices for exact dates, as they tend to change. Try some of the following: *Mardi Gras Carnivals* in Estoril-Cascais, Torres Vedras, Loulé and Ovar during the four days up to Shrove Tuesday. *Holy Week* – Easter religious processions in Braga. *Festivals of the Popular Saints*, Lisbon, in June. *Festival of St John* in Porto features funfair, fireworks, handicrafts, regional cooking; in June. *Festival of the Red Waistcoats* at Vila Franca de Xira (Lisbon) with bullfights, amusements; in July. *International Music Festival* in Sintra, during second fortnight in August. *Festa of Our Lady of Nazaré* in Nazaré in September with fair and bullfights.

Lisbon: where to sleep

Portugal is not as cheap as Spain, but it tries hard. All round I'd say things are about ten per cent more expensive. You can find a bed for 600 escudos, and I have heard of them as low as 500 escudos. The best place to search for a *pensão* is in the nest of streets on the hill leading up to the Castle of St George, but on the *west* side. The southern side, the real Alfama, caters to the tourist types, and prices are correspondingly higher. The next best place is on the west side of the Rossio, the big main square, or failing that, in the area called Bairro Alto which is to the west of Rua da Misericórdia. All of these places are right in the main commercial area of town. Make sure you hire a bed only, and don't get quoted a price which includes all meals.

Here is a list of some of the really cheap places.

Pensão Chave de Ouro at Rua de Alegria 19, lst floor (tel: 32 47 49).

Pensão Glória at Rua D. Duarte 2, 1st floor (tel: 86 36 30).

Pensão Imperial at Praça dos Restauradores 78, 4th floor (tel: 32 01 66).

Pensão Madeirense at Rua da Glória 22, 1st floor (tel: 32 58 59).

Pensão Luanda, Rua dos Anjos 77, 1st floor (tel: 5 04 70).

Pensão Pérola da Baixa at Rua da Glória 10, 2nd floor (tel: 36 28 75).

Pensão Santiago at Rua dos Douradores 222, 3rd floor (tel: 87 43 53).

Pensão Norte at Rua dos Douradores 159, 2nd floor (tel: 32 66 32).

Pensão-Restaurante Vinhais at Calçada do Garcia 6, 1st floor (tel: 86 29 47).

Lisbon: where to eat

Pick your place carefully and you have a feast for 250 escudos. Happy hunting grounds for cheap meals are in the Rua das Portas de Santo Antão (parallel to the Avenida da Liberdade), the Rua da Madalena and in many of the small streets leading off those two.

Lisbon: what to see and do

THE CASTLE OF ST GEORGE, begun by the Visigoths in the fifth century, offers you a stunning view over Lisbon, the harbour and Tejo River. Walk up through the Alfama or ride up on Bus 37 (from Praça do Rossio).

THE ALFAMA is the oldest section of Lisbon and for most visitors the essence of the city. A memorable and insoluble maze of narrow, winding streets, crumbling steps, multi-coloured house fronts; an amazing tangle of drying washing between the houses and a forest of TV aerials above them; street vendors, suspicious characters, and scruffy kids being chased by their mothers. A poor place, but a nice place.

THE CATHEDRAL was built in the twelfth century but remodelled after the earthquake of 1755. See the sacristy and the cloisters.

PRAÇA DO COMÉRCIO, the big square down by the waterfront, is the hub of the city, and a good place to run into fellow hitchers. Street vendors and fish sellers work there most mornings.

THE MONUMENT TO THE DISCOVERIES was built in 1960 to commemorate the 500th anniversary of the death of Henry the Navigator. It's shaped like a ship's prow and decorated with dozens of carved figures. Henry himself, model caravel in hand, stands on the very end of the bow staring out over the river.

THE BELÉM TOWER on the waterfront near the Coach Museum was built in the sixteenth century to guard the river approach to Lisbon. It was the first sight of home after long years at sea for generations of Portuguese explorers.

JERÓNIMOS MONASTERY and the Tower of Belém were two of the few important buildings to survive the 1755 earthquake which killed 40,000 citizens and left Lisbon in ruins. Built in the fifteenth and sixteenth centuries, it's considered a masterpiece of Manueline (after King Manuel I) art. Even if you're up-to-here with churches, take a look at the cloister. Worth the effort.

THE '25TH OF APRIL' BRIDGE is the longest suspension bridge in Europe. It's two kilometres across and the foundations go down 259 feet to bedrock beneath the river. Try to get a ride across. You'll be 230 feet above the water and looking down over the city. Nearest thing to an aerial view of Lisbon without being in an aeroplane.

STATUE OF CHRIST THE KING If you *do* get that ride across the bridge, watch for the 90-foot-high statue – reminiscent of the one in Rio de Janeiro – which dominates the other side of the river. Better still, take the lift to the balcony up top which gives a great view over river and city.

MUSEUMS Among the many: the Coach Museum in Belém, considered to hold the world's best collection of non-motorized vehicles; the National Museum of Archaeology and Ethnology beside the Jerónimos Monastery, which gives a comprehensive introduction to Portuguese history; the Gulbenkian Museum, Praça da Espanha, containing an amazing collection of just about everything from Egyptian antiquities to Rembrandts and Impressionists; the Museum of Folk Art in the Avenida Brasília, Belém, with the country's largest collection of traditional art.

NIGHTCLUBS Best districts for Portuguese-style nightclubs are the Alfama and Bairro Alto districts. It's there that you can find the *fado* singers. Well worth seeing, but it'll cost you at least 250–500 escudos for a drink even if you play it on the cheap.

MOVIES are nearly always shown in original language with Portuguese subtitles. Plenty of English-language shows around, most quite recent. Seats are reasonably priced even in the city centre.

THE FLEA MARKET at Campo Santa Clara on Calçada de São Vicente is in full swing Tuesdays and Saturdays.

Transport in Lisbon
The subway is the quickest method of getting around Lisbon and the cheapest. City buses are just as cheap, but slower. Taxis, as in Madrid, are among the cheapest in Europe. If you're in a group they're the ideal way of moving around.

Student discounts
For information contact:

SIAEIST – Turismo Universitário, Av. Rovisco Pais, Lisbon 1 (tel: 77 18 84).

Addresses

Main post office (for poste restante) at Praça dos Restauradores, Lisbon 2.

American Express at STAR, Avenida Sidónio Pais 4a, Lisbon (tel: 53 98 71).

SIAEIST – Turismo Universitário at Avenida Rovisco Pais, Lisbon 1 (tel: 77 18 84).

Tourist Office at Palácio Foz, Praça dos Restauradores, Lisbon 2 (tel: 36 25 31).

US Embassy at Avenida Duque de Loulé 39, Lisbon 1 (tel: 57 01 02).

British Embassy at Rua de São Domingos à Lapa 37, Lisbon 3 (tel: 66 11 91).

Hitchers' Tips and Comments...

For cheap eating in Lisbon, buy take away food at the Expresso Supermarket near the youth hostel. To crash out, take a train to Cascais, a really nice little place with lots of possibilities. Get off at Cais do Sódre station. For sightseeing, don't miss Sintra. Take the train from Rossio. *Luis Mourao, Lisbon, Portugal*

Unlike in Spain where the hitching is reasonable (away from the coastal areas), in Portugal it's really bad. The locals just aren't into it. Be prepared for long waits. But the country is marvellous. *Jon More O'Farrall, Trinity, Jersey, Channel Islands*

Greece

population	9,050,000
size	51,123 square miles
capital	Athens, population 3,500,000

government	Republic
religion	Greek Orthodox
language	Greek. Some French understood, English widely spoken
currency	*Drachma* Coins of ½, 1, 2, 5, 10, 20, 50 *drachmas*. Notes of 50, 100, 500, 1000 *drachmas*

If you enter Greece from Yugoslavia or Bulgaria, **Thessaloniki** will probably be your first stop. It is the country's second city (after Athens) and was founded in 315 BC on the site of an even older city – Thermai. As guardian of such a long history, you'd think the city would offer a rich selection of ruins to visit. Unfortunately, a devastating fire in 1917 burned out much of the city centre and, consequently, the choice is limited. But the old Turkish quarter in the upper part of the city survived and remains one of the most fascinating sections to wander through. To really appreciate the age of Thessaloniki you should visit the Archaeological Museum. Amongst its exhibits see the fantastic treasure of gold jewellery found in tombs as recently as the late 1970s. Also worth a visit: the city's ancient churches, particularly the fifth-century Basilica of St Demetrius and the third-century church of St George.

About 150 kilometres south-east of Thessaloniki, on the tip of the easternmost of the three peninsulas of Chalkidiki, is the strange place called **Mount Athos**. This is an autonomous region, in effect a state unto itself, and run by monks. There are twenty monasteries, many of them around 1000 years old. Known as the 'Holy Mountain', Mt Athos cannot be visited unless you arrange for your embassy or consulate to get authorization on your behalf from the Greek Ministry of Foreign Affairs or from the Ministry for Northern Greece. According to a law made in 1060 by a monk called Constantine the Gladiator which is still in force, no woman is permitted to approach the monasteries. And that goes for all female creatures – dogs and cats included.

At 150 kilometres north-west of Athens is **Delphi**, situated at 2000 feet on the slopes of Mount Parnassus. This is the place where the famous Oracle lived – he who was known as the 'Holy of Holies'. See the Temple of Apollo and plenty of other excavated ruins.

The plain of **Marathon** traditionally lies forty-two kilometres from the centre of Athens. It was here that the decisive battle of 490 BC took place between the Athenians and the Persians.

Outnumbered ten to one the Greeks nevertheless won and sent a messenger named Pheidippides to tell the people of Athens the news. The guy made it in record time, gave the message, and died on the spot. Exhausted. The Olympic Marathon honours the event. It's hardly worth hitching out to see the field – it's marked only by the grave of the Greeks who fell – but if you do, continue on an extra few kilometres to **Ramnous** where there are two temples, one of them to Nemesis, the goddess of divine vengeance. (She still wreaks it – the road to Ramnous is rotten.)

Seventy-two kilometres due south of Athens, on the tip of the peninsula and at **Sounion**, is the beautiful temple of Poseidon, one of the best sights in the country.

Corinth is one of a cluster of important sites on the Peloponnese Peninsula. Modern Corinth, a city of 16,000, is seven kilometres from the ancient city which was once the largest and most powerful in Greece. It was razed by the Romans in 146 BC, then again by the Goths, and then hit by an earthquake in AD 521. Understandably there are plenty of ruins to see.

Fifty kilometres on from Corinth are the ruins of **Mycenae**, a city inhabited as far back as 3000 BC. It was the German businessman/archaeologist Heinrich Schliemann – the man ridiculed by popular opinion when he set out to find Troy – who excavated here and found skeletons of men and women adorned with gold masks and crowns. Schliemann believed them to be the bodies of Agamemnon and his companions, though this has yet to be proven. You can see the treasure he unearthed in the Mycenaean Room of the Archaeological Museum in Athens. At the site itself, you can see the Gate of the Lions, the Treasure of Atreus and the Royal Tombs. All in all Mycenae counts as one of the most exciting archaeological spots in Greece.

Farther south again and you come to **Epidaurus**, which in ancient times was a famous health centre – perhaps the first ever – and which was visited by ailing people from all over the civilized world. The main sight is the old theatre, the most perfect in Greece, which can seat 16,000 people and is still used each year at the annual Epidaurus Festival (July–mid-August).

There's not much left of **Sparta**, the capital of Laconia, to tell you what the place once was. These days it's a deadly boring town of 11,000 with only a few identified ruins surviving from the days when it was the most powerful city in the world. (The Pass of Thermopylae where Leonidas and his handful of Spartans held the

Persians at bay in 480 BC is just a few kilometres south of **Lamia**.)
Seven kilometres west of Sparta, on one of the slopes of Mt
Taygettus is the ruined city of **Mistra**, which dates from AD 1249.
Even though by Greek standards the place is a 'modern' ruin, it's
worth looking over because it's a treasure house of Byzantine art.

Whatever you do, try not to leave the Peloponnese without
getting up to **Olympia**, site of the ancient Olympic games, first
held in 776 BC. (Not to be confused with Mt Olympus, south of
Thessaloniki, and home of the ancient Greek Gods.) The sacred
flame of the Olympics is still kindled at Olympia every four years
and carried by relays of runners to whichever city is staging the
spectacle. Plenty to see, including the museum and the stadium;
best of all, though, is the rare beauty of the setting.

Hitching in Greece, on the main highways, is about the same as
anywhere else, but if you get off the beaten track – easy to do in
Greece – it can be very slow. If you're stuck on the way to some
mountain village, don't hesitate to grab the local bus. It'll be cheap
enough.

★**Trips to Crete and the Islands** The main tip is to always go 'deck
class' which is the cheapest. The best place to find out about costs
(and also to check if your student card will get you a fare
reduction) is ISYTS at 11 Nikis Street, Athens. This is a student
outfit and not a regular travel bureau.

Crete (area: 3245 square miles, pop. 440,000)
Iraklion (pop. 80,000) is an untidy, bustling town founded by the
Saracens in AD 823. Visit the daily market to buy cheap food.
Low-budget pensions in town are near Daidolou Street. Don't
miss the Archaeological Museum, which covers Crete's 4000-year-
old Minoan civilization in fascinating detail. See the Venetian
fortress at the port.

Five kilometres inland is **Knossos**, the ancient Minoan capital
lovingly restored by British archaeologist, Sir Arthur Evans, in
1900. Among its best sights are the throne room (oldest in Europe)
and the well-preserved central court. See the wall paintings of
bull-vaulting.

Rethymnon, 72 kilometres west of Iraklion, has a Turkish-
Venetian waterfront, and a skyline of minarets and turrets
proclaiming the town's Ottoman past. Low-priced spots are on
Makedonia Street. If you're in town in July don't miss the wine
festival in the municipal park.

Chania, 72 kilometres farther west, has a crescent-shaped Venetian harbour promenade lined with taverns and open-air restaurants.

Inland, the rugged Sfakia mountains form a natural stronghold which centuries of Venetian, Turkish and German invaders failed to crack. You understand why when you tackle the arduous mountain paths leading to the Sfakians' hospitable but fiercely independent villages. Try *raki*, the local firewater. It'll blow your head off.

An energetic five-hour walk there (locals do it in three!) is along the 19 kilometre **Samaria Gorge**, largest in Europe. Cliffs rise as high as 2000 feet, while at its narrowest the gorge is only 16 feet across. In spring, streams run along the valley bottom. Starting point is the inland village of **Omalos**. At the end of the gorge you catch a boat round to the tiny fishing village of **Chora Sfakion**, where British troops made their final escape from the island in 1941. From here you can hitch or bus your way back to Chania.

Phaestos, on a hill overlooking the Messara plain 60 kilometres south of Iraklion, houses the well-kept ruins of Crete's second largest Minoan city. Worth the trip for the evocative location.

Aghios Nikolaos, 70 kilometres east of Iraklion, is the island's top resort, an Aegean St Tropez with expensive bars and a self-consciously attractive harbour setting. But a great place to meet people. Boats run from here in summer to the Cyclades islands and Rhodes.

Try not to miss the fertile inland **Lassithi** plain with its 10,000 windmills and **Cave of Dikte** where legend says Zeus was born.

The Greek Islands

Argo-Saronics The four main islands of this group run closely parallel to the Greek Peloponnese mainland as it descends south from the Saronic into the Argive Gulf. But hitching is difficult in the Peloponnese because of lack of cars, so only try it if you have plenty of time to spare. All (except Spetsai) are easy to reach from Piraeus if you can only spare a day for island tripping. You need two days to enjoy Spetsai at leisure, due to the travelling time involved.

Aegina (area: 35 square miles, pop. 12,000; 1½ hours from Piraeus) Capital **Aegina Town** has plenty of cheap waterfront rooms and restaurants. But be warned: at weekends the place is packed with day-trippers from Athens.

Aghia Marina, 15 kilometres across the island, is a popular beach resort stacked with tavernas. A short walk up through orchards of pistachio trees brings you to the impressive Doric temple of Aphaia, with its Parian marble sculptures and limestone columns, standing evocatively above the sea.

Poros (area: 25 square miles, pop. 5000; 2½ hours from Piraeus) The island capital of **Poros** is a tumbling white port with lively harbourside cafés facing the Peloponnese town of Galata only 400 yards away. Here the channel between island and Greek mainland is so narrow that it resembles a large river. The caique (boat) crossing only takes three minutes. Caiques also run regularly up the island coast to Monastiri, an eighteenth-century monastery.

Inland, among Poros' pinewoods, is the ruined Temple of Poseidon (the Greek god of the sea) where the Athenian orator Demosthenes poisoned himself.

Hydra (area: 21 square miles, pop. 4000; 3½ hours from Piraeus) **Hydra Town** boasts eighteenth-century Venetian houses (symbols of its seafaring past) and a waterfront array of fashionable boutiques and restaurants. Once a backwater for artists, it's now inundated by international trendsetters and hourly cruise ships. So avoid that incredibly expensive harbourside. Cheaper rooms and meals can be found at the back of the town.

Because of the island's barren and mountainous terrain local transport is still by donkey. (The island also has *one* taxi.) Hike up to the hilltop monastery of **Aghia Triada**. Its views over the Peloponnese mainland and sea are out of this world.

Spetsai (area: 10 square miles, pop. 5000; 5 hours from Piraeus) **Spetsai Town** is a stylish port popular with Athenians. The waterfront Dapia Square is a stage set of bars and open-air restaurants. Ask at Takis Tourist Office near the jetty for cheap rooms in town.

Spetsai's so small you can walk round the pine-wooded coastline in six hours. Take a caique (very cheap) to **Anarghiri**, the island's best beach. As few cars are allowed on the island, main transport is by horse and buggy. (**Warning!** They are expensive.) Spetsai was the setting for John Fowles' book *The Magus*, wherein he called the island Phraxos.

Sporades Our word 'sporadic' is taken from the Greek word used to describe these green isles which are strewn haphazardly offshore from Euboea, a large island attached by drawbridge to the eastern Greek mainland at Chalkis. Boats run to most of them from Kymi, Aghios Konstantinos and Volos. Here's some basic information about the three largest:

Skiathos (area: 25 square miles, pop. 4000)
Capital **Skiathos Town** is a white, red-roofed port surrounded by pines. It's a favourite with writers and artists. Inland, the ruins of **Castro** are worth a visit. **Koukounaries**, fringed by stone pine groves, is the pick of the island's fine beaches.

Skopelos (area: 35 square miles, pop. 5000)
Skopelos Town, the capital, has a rising amphitheatre of multi-coloured houses, and low-priced, waterfront pensions. Two clifftop churches guard the harbour entrance. Inland **Episkopi** boasts the medieval ruins of a bishop's palace. Several nearby seventh-century monasteries have been converted into hotels. Visit the southern village **Agnonda** for the island's best beach.

Skyros (area: 75 square miles, pop. 3000)
You'll find rooms to let in the white, flat-topped houses which climb the precipitous slopes behind the capital of **Skyros**. At the town's entrance stands a statue erected in the name of British poet Rupert Brooke, of a nude youth symbolizing 'immortal poetry'. Brooke died of fever on board a hospital ship in Tris Boukes, or Trebuki Bay, during the First World War and is buried in an olive grove near the fishing village of Linaria.

Skyros' barren and isolated villages are depositories of folk arts like woodwork, weaving and embroidery. The coast offers kilometres of unspoilt beaches and dozens of caves ideal for underwater exploration. (Got a mask and snorkel in your pack?)

Cyclades These barren islands surround the holy island of Delos in the centre of Homer's 'wine-dark' Aegean Sea. Altogether 211 islands (yes, 211!) form this group, though only 24 are inhabited.

Boats regularly make the five-hour run from Piraeus to Mykonos. Connections to other islands from here are frequent and cheap. (**Warning!** Avoid August for two reasons: the *meltemi* wind can give you a rough ride, and room prices on the islands rocket.)

Mykonos (area: 30 square miles, pop. 3863)
Capital **Mykonos Town** (pop. 5000) is picture-postcard Greece, all windmills and white cube houses set against the blue sea. The place brims with open-air cafés, crowded shopping stalls and lively tavernas, popular with tourists and locals alike. Seven of the island's 365 churches are situated in Paraportiani Square, and the little museum on the quay contains religiously significant tombs from Delos. Private houses and a youth hostel provide cheap lodgings, and outside of town there's a camping site. For good beaches try **Aghios Stephanos** and **Ornos**.

Visit **Delos** for the day. Four thousand years ago this was the religious centre of the Greek world. Now, the ten square miles of rock are inhabited only by a few goatherds and their animals. The archaeological site includes a museum, shrine and mosaic ruins. Most impressive remains include the Sanctuary of Apollo and the Terrace of Lions.

Santorin (area: 30 square miles, pop. 6400)
Santorin, previously called Thira, is the capital and her brilliant white houses stand on an ash-grey pumice cliff, the outer rim of a vast volcano which disappeared in a cataclysmic explosion 4000 years ago. You can walk up the 2km zigzag path to the town from the harbour, but it's easier to use the donkey transport or the recently installed funicular. Local houses have low-priced rooms to rent.

The island is dotted with small ruins: Minoan, Doric, Roman and Venetian. Best are the Minoan excavations near **Akrotiri** on the south coast. Inland, tomatoes and vines grow miraculously out of the multi-coloured rock landscape. Try the strong Santorin wine – famous since the Middle Ages.

Naxos (area: 180 square miles, pop. 15,000)
The largest Cyclades island lives from agriculture, not tourism, and is full of vineyards, lush valleys and citrus orchards.

Capital **Naxos Town** offers cheap rooms, tavernas and a beautiful old Venetian quarter called the Castro.

Across the island the unspoilt village of **Apollon** lies beside a near-deserted beach. If you want to see what real Greek island life is like, stay here in a private house. It's idyllic and easy on the pocket.

Ionian Islands
These six cypress-and-olive-green islands lie off the coast of
north-west Greece. Boats run regularly to Corfu, the most
important, from Brindisi in southern Italy and Igoumenitsa on the
Greek mainland.

Corfu (area: 225 square miles, pop. 100,000)
Capital **Corfu Town** beautifully blends its past cultures. French
colonnades overlook an English cricket pitch, and Venetian
backstreets merge with a market wafting smells of Oriental spices.
You'll find cheap pensions near the Old Harbour. Worth a look is
Mon Repos, the former Greek royal summer residence where
England's Prince Philip, Duke of Edinburgh, was born.

The fishing village of **Benitses**, 12 kilometres south, is popular
with both expatriate artists and tourists. Lively tavernas line the
waterfront, and in summer spontaneous street dancing often
brings traffic to a standstill. At nearby **Gastouri** see Kaiser
Wilhelm's monstrous Achilleion. Built in 1891 in mock-Florentine
style, it's a museum by day and a casino by night.

Paxos (area: 20 square miles, pop. 3000)
This is a mini-island of olive trees and coves and only three hours
by boat from Corfu Town. Prices in **Gaios** (pop. 600) have boomed
since the arrival of the yacht-set.

Cephalonia (area: 300 square miles, pop. 70,000)
The modern port of **Argostoli** was totally rebuilt after an
earthquake in 1953. Worth visiting on the island are the **Necropolis
of Mazaracata**, with its 83 Mycenaean tombs and the fishing village
of **Assos**. Inland are vast unspoilt pine forests, and mountains
rising to 5000 feet.

Zante (area: 180 square miles, pop. 45,000)
Zante Town, once known as the 'Flower of the Levant', now
nestles under a solitary ruined Venetian castle. The 1953
earthquake robbed the island of any architectural glory, but there
are beautiful Italianate gardens and vineyards to visit. **Porta Roma**
boasts one of the island's many fine beaches.

Levkas (area: 110 square miles, pop. 6000)
In August **Levkas Town** hosts an international folklore festival
which gobbles up every free bed on the island. But it's worth
visiting if you don't mind sleeping on the beach (which the tourist

office says is forbidden). See **Vliko**'s beautiful bay, and the Temple of Apollo in the south, where seventh-century-BC poetess Sappho jumped to her death from the cliffs.

Ithaca (area: 40 square miles, pop. 2500)
This is Homer's 'precipitous isle', home of Ulysses. Capital **Vathy** is a tiny modern port with an inlet and a beach. Above it stands the ruined medieval Parachorion. Mount Aetos' 2600-year-old Alaleomenae castle offers incredible views of the island.

Dodecanese Greece's most easterly islands, the Dodecanese, lie just a few kilometres off the Turkish mainland. The trans-Aegean boat trip from Piraeus to Rhodes takes 20 hours. Of the group's twelve islands, try these three:

Rhodes (area: 550 square miles, pop. 70,000)
Capital **Rhodes Town** (pop. 35,000) is an international tourist town of bars, hotels and restaurants. The busy harbour is guarded by two statues of deer which mark the spots once straddled by the 100-foot-high Colossus of Rhodes, one of the seven ancient wonders of the world, which was destroyed by earthquake in 227 BC. In the walled medieval quarter Turkish minarets and the Suleiman Mosque vie with the Christian-built Grand Masters' Palace and the Street of the Knights. Cheap rooms and restaurants are in Apellou Street. There's a youth hostel nearby.

Don't miss beautiful **Lindos**, 60 kilometres south, a white village of cobbled lanes overlooking a sandy bay. No cars are allowed here: only donkeys, which carry tourists up to the superb clifftop acropolis behind the village. Avoid summer if you want a room. They're all booked by travel agencies.

Also worth a look here are the third-century-BC ruins of ancient **Kamiros** on the west coast, and **Petaloudes**, where giant plane trees shade a gorge filled by millions of butterflies. Catch superb island views from **Mount Philerimos**, with its nearby Byzantine monastery.

Kos (area: 115 square miles, pop. 15,000)
Mosques remind you of the Turkish heritage lurking in the modern port capital of **Kos**. (Look for cheap pensions near the harbour.) Hippocrates, the famous physician, was born here; outside town see the ruins of the fourth-century-BC Asclepeion, sanctuary and site of his medical school.

Inland Kos is green farming country, full of citrus and vegetable orchards. The coast is lined with unspoilt sandy beaches, which solve accommodation problems.

Patmos (area: 15 square miles, pop. 3000)
Capital **Chora** rears above the harbour village of **Skala**. See the medieval, fortified monastery built as a memorial to St John the Divine, who is supposed to have written his Apocalypse in a grotto between Skala and Chora. The monastery perching above the town houses a library containing precious manuscripts and ecclesiastical relics. Well worth the climb if you're in the mood.

Caiques run along the wild barren coast to beautiful coves and beaches.

★**Language** Greek is not the sort of language you conquer overnight. For most of us it's not the sort of language which is conquered at all. But a few odd words can be picked up without too much trouble.
Try these:
yes – *neh*   no – *oh-yee*
please – *pah-rah-kah-lo*   thanks – *ef-ha-ree-stoh*
good day, good evening, goodnight and goodbye are all covered by – *yas-sou*

★**The evil eye** The Greeks are still a little superstitious. The Greek Orthodox Church has a special prayer to ward off the evil eye and many people, women especially, carry special little blue stones to help them in their fight against evil. Shy girls secretly pin the stones to their bras – though God knows which evil eye *they* are trying to divert. You can buy these stones very cheaply. Nice souvenir.

★**Important** Greek authorities will ban entry to the country to any traveller who has visited North Cyprus since 15 November 1983, and carries in his passport the stamp 'Turkish-Cypriot Federal State' or 'Republic of Northern Cyprus'.

Athens: where to sleep

Expect to pay between 250 and 400 drachmas, except in youth hostels which charge 200 drachmas. (It's much cheaper in the outer suburbs, but *all* the sights are in the centre which is where you've got to be.)

Youth hostel at 57 Odos Kypselis Street (tel: 8225 860).

Residence Pagration at 75 Damareos Street, Pagrati (tel: 751 95 30). Ask to sleep on the roof – it's even cheaper!

Hotel Carolina at 55 Kolokotroni Street (tel: 322 08 37). Ask for dormitory.

Cleo's Guest House at 18 Apollonos Street (tel: 323 56 40).

Hotel Orion at 105 E. Benaki Street (tel: 362 84 41). Open 1 January to 30 October. Ask for dormitory.

Guest House Giorgos at 18 Eolou Street (tel: 32 22 997).

Pension Olympia at 16 Karatza Street, Philopappou (near the Acropolis under Philopappou Hill) (tel: 92 37 650).

Lord Byron Youth Hostel at 20 Kallipoleos Street (tel: 76 64 889). Fair way out of town. Open 1 April to 30 September. Students only. Ask for dormitory.

YWCA (XEN) at 11 Amerikis Street (tel: 3624 294). Ask for dormitory. Women only, but the cafeteria is open to both sexes.

YMCA (XAN) at 28 Omirou Street (tel: 3626 970). Men only. Ask for dormitory.

Fantis House at 39 Nikis Street (tel: 23 25 92).

Joy's Hostel at 38 Farron (tel: 823 10 12).

Pension Kirki at 40 Kefallinias Street (tel: 823 57 33).

Piraeus Youth Hostel at 85 Kolokotroni Street (tel: 412 55 32).

For help with all student accommodation, drop into ISYTS at 11 Nikis Street. They know it all and probably won't insist that you be a student (as long as you look like one) before helping you.

If sleeping rough, check with the local kindred souls before bunking out. Athens is one place to keep right away from the cops. In fact, a note from the polite and very efficient Greek Tourist Office informs me that: 'Greece has a police force of a high standard. Camping . . . is not permitted other than on authorized camp sites. Drugs, nude bathing/sunbathing and other well-known infringements of the law are also not permitted.'

Athens: where to eat

Cheap eating in Athens presents no problem. 170–220 drachmas should see you through a fairly big meal. Stick to the tavernas rather than restaurants and keep away from where the tourists eat.

Which may leave the problem of figuring out a Greek menu, which is no easy task. The following are some standard dishes which are OK:

Dolmades is rice and minced meat wrapped in vine leaves. A traditional dish.

Souvlaki is a shishkebab – spiced meat and vegetables on a skewer. Buy them from street stalls for cheap eating.

Moussaka is a casserole of aubergines, meat and spices.

Kalamaraki is squid.

Retsina is a local wine which has a resin flavour.

Ouzo is a killer drink just right for setting you on your ear.

If you want to live it up with a big meal (got 350 drachmas?) try one of these two:

Costa Yannis at Zaimis Street (behind Polytechnic).

Fatsio at 5 Efroniou.

Athens: what to see and do

THE ACROPOLIS For many people this hill in Athens will be the climax of their European wanderings. It's beautiful. You can spend half a day up there without even knowing it. It costs about 50 drachmas, but half price with student card and free on Thursdays and Sundays. What to see? The *Parthenon*, first of all. Then the *Acropolis Museum*, the *Temple of Athena Nike*, the *Erechtheum*, the *Propylaea*, the *Theatre of Dionysus*, the *Theatre of Herod Atticus*, etc.

THE AGORA to the west of the Acropolis. This was the old city centre. Don't miss the museum.

TEMPLE OF OLYMPIAN ZEUS on Leoforos Amalias. Also, nearby, the *Arch of Hadrian*.

NATIONAL ARCHAEOLOGICAL MUSEUM in Pattission Street. Entrance charge but free on Thursdays and Sundays. Closed Mondays. Very important museum of Greek sculpture and objects discovered during digs all over Greece.

SON ET LUMIÈRE AT THE ACROPOLIS Costs about 100 drachmas. Tickets and information from 4 Stadiou Street.

MUSEUM OF POPULAR ART in Kydathineon Street. If you're into the handicrafts scene, drop in here for some ideas. Good collection of handicrafts from all over the country.

FLEA MARKET on Ifestou Street near Monastiraki Square. Best days, Saturday and Sunday. Good place to go to find items of equipment you want to replace. (Remember to bargain!) Also a big underground book market with secondhand books in most languages.

GREEK MUSIC AND BAR LIFE Go into the *boîtes* in the area known as Plaka which is just below the Acropolis. Try the following streets – Mnisikleous, Erechteous, and Tholou. This is where you can hear the *bouzouki* music and watch the *sirtaki* danced. And good luck to you: the *retsina* and *ouzo* will kill you!

MOVIES Most Athens cinemas show up-to-date films in original-language versions with Greek subtitles. Prices are OK.

Transport in Athens
At 15 drachmas a long ride, subway and buses are the best way to get around. If operating in a group, you can save money by taking a taxi. They're cheap.

Student discounts
Large reduction on entrance to museums, galleries and archaeological sites; also fare reductions on inter-island ferries. For information contact:

ISYTS, 11 Nikis Street (2nd floor), Athens 118 (tel: 322 12 67 and 323 37 67).

Addresses

Main post office (for poste restante) at 100 Eolou Street, Athens.

American Express at Constitution Square, Hermes Street, Athens (tel: 324 49 75).

ISYTS (for students) at 11 Nikis Street (2nd floor), Athens 118 (tel: 322 12 67 and 323 37 67).

National Tourist Information Office at 2 Amerikis Street, Athens (tel: 322 31 11/9) ands at Syntagma Square, Athens (tel: 322 25 45).

US Embassy at 91 Vasilissis Sophias Boulevard, Athens (tel: 71 29 51).

British Embassy at 1 Ploutarchou, Athens 139 (tel: 73 62 11).

Hitchers' Tips and Comments . . .

In Thessaloniki the gardens on the waterfront are good for kipping, but watch your gear. *M. Pickersgill, South Africa*

The rundown on Greece doesn't cover the route Thessaloniki–Istanbul. Hitchers hitting this trail should stop off at Kavala, it's a beautiful place, the sort worth a promise for a return trip one day.

Athens train station is OK to bed down for a night or two, cops wake you about 7 a.m., but no pressure to move on. Dunno what it's like from Piraeus to the Greek Islands but from Volos to the three eastern islands (Skopelos, Skiathos and Skyros) make sure you take the *same* boat back as you went on. The situation is that they promote one boat company out to the islands, and once there another company covers the advert boards for the run back. Those that aren't informed (and deciphering a Greek boat ticket is like deciphering a Greek anything else) get it all explained on the way back, stating that they've got to pay again, with no refund on the first ticket. I noticed a lot of travellers were getting caught out this way – me included! *Marcel Thomas, Horndean, England*

Loads of cheap places to eat and sleep in the Plaka district of Athens, at the base of the Acropolis. *Richard Walford, Reading, England*

Athens still no good for dossing out. Particularly, forget National Park. Some real nasties hanging around there.
  Lots of half-completed villas on Greek and Italian

coastlines. They provide ideal cover and ideal surroundings for a quiet night's kip. *Dave P., Leeds, England*

When kipping in half-finished houses or buildings, remember that many of the bigger projects have a nightwatchman who may have a dog, and that construction workers are on the job at seven or eight o'clock in the morning. So (unless you have permission to be where you are) that means no fires, and an early morning start. K.W.

Athens flea-market great for selling unwanted objects or clothing. *Patrick Hine, Oxford, England*

If you're camping out in Greece, consider buying the green mosquito coils which burn slowly during the night and suffocate the wretched creatures. *Michael Picker, Sheffield, England*

I hear the Greek police are clamping down on people sleeping on the beaches. *Ralph Hunt, Cheshunt, England*

I've heard that Greek authorities now demand an address in Greece before they'll let you in. The way around it is to get a hotel or campsite address out of a guide book and stick that down on the immigration form. Then forget all about it. *John Pilkington, Bristol, UK*

In Crete, don't try the Samaria Gorge walk during winter because some parts are flooded and impassable and *very* dangerous! El Greco freaks will want to visit the tiny village of Fodele (a couple of kilometres inland along the Iraklion to Rethymnon route), where the painter is said to have been born. Booze and cigarettes much cheaper at duty free counter of Iraklion airport. Great pleasure for me in Crete was absolute honesty of the Cretans. They might try and take you for a few extra drachmas when you're buying souvenirs (that's biz, after all), but you could leave your rucksack in the main street of a village and return two hours later and it'd still be there. (But that doesn't mean some *tourist* wouldn't rip it off!) *'Johnny the Wonk', Liverpool, UK*

Plaka area in Athens pretty touristy, but you can still find places which are cheap even by Greek standards. Nikis Street is a good bet for accommodation and also for travel bargains. Check the ISYTS, notice-boards in hostels and travel agencies for special offers. *Paul, London, UK*

Try Elena's Guest House at 14 Apollonos Street, Athens. Clean, cheap, and friendly management. *Sylvia Smitas, Mississauga, Canada*

Dossing in Athens really good. Try sleeping just outside the Agora (Plaka district: just follow the signs to the Acropolis). If you want total safety, climb the fence and sleep inside. *Tony Miller, Newcastle-upon-Tyne, England*

If your budget is tight, avoid Syntagma square in Athens. Drink prices can be double what you'll pay elsewhere. Also, girl hitchers should note that the square is happy hunting grounds of the *kamaki* (fishermen), the nickname for men out after tourist girls. *Claire Bettington and Susan Cooper, Ledbury, UK*

Dasia and Barbati beaches on the north of Corfu are ideal for sleeping out as they are right off the roadways and you don't get disturbed by anybody. *Janet Pawlter, Chelmsford, UK*

On the backroads of Greece, most of my rides came from tractors. Don't be proud! It's a great way of viewing the countryside, and you'll get there eventually. On Crete, a nice place to rest up is Matala. There are lots of caves in the surrounding hills where you can crash out free. But go over the hill to the south of the village because the caves by the village beach are periodically raided by the cops. *Alan Thatcher, New Zealand*

Cheap place to stay in Athens is: Hotel Larissiakon, corner of Philadelphia and Liosion Streets. *K. M. Fitchet, Johannesburg, South Africa*

I am the owner of a small student hostel in Athens at 20 Ioulianou Street (tel: 82 13 940). Five minutes' walk from the Central Railway Station with 27 rooms ranging from dormitories with 6–8 beds to doubles with bathrooms and showers. Open to travellers 24 hours a day. International staff speaking 10 different languages. *Antasios Spartalis*

Try to get a coach back to London from Athens, rather than from Istanbul, thus avoiding a change at Thessaloniki, where we had to wait three days for a bus. *Mark Shepherd, Bailrigg, Lancs, UK*

8 Scandinavia, Finland, and Iceland

For the hitcher from Australia or North America, the big
wastelands of Norway and Sweden will spur a memory of the
endless, brooding countryside typical of their homelands. Think of
Nevada or the Nullarbor and take away the heat but keep the
distance. The sort of distance where you can drive all night and by
dusk of the next day be only halfway to where you're heading. The
scenery is different, vastly so, but the distances hold the same
mood because Norway and Sweden are the big lands. Malmö to
Kiruna, for instance, is about 2000 kilometres.

The physical beauty of Norway, Sweden, and Finland is
legendary (Denmark is flat, not very interesting visually) and the
beauty of the female inhabitants of the four countries has entered
the spectrum of legend. It's all true. The fjords and mountains and
tundra plains are exciting. The women are unbelievable.

But apart from such physical aspects, Scandinavia is exciting
sociologically. It is in these countries that the finer ideas of
socialism have been put into practice. Poverty is practically
unknown, education is an experimental science, medicine is
available to all, prison reform is a reality, the arts are encouraged
by the governments, and the housing problem – in places like Oslo
– is treated as a problem. Taxation, of course, pays for all this and
it's high, but the money seems to be put to fair use.

Scandinavia seems to have reached the level of balanced
affluence craved by the rest of the world. Its citizens nevertheless
are the first to point out the many failings of their governments.
They gripe and groan until you nearly believe they are getting a
bad deal. Well, a bad deal is a relative thing, I suppose, and
perhaps the Scandinavians aren't getting all that they should. But
you only need to look around some place like Helsinki's Tapiola
Garden City or a couple of Denmark's experimental schools or
consider that neutral Sweden hasn't been involved in a war since
1814 to know that whatever the failings of the governments, their
achievements are not only many, but bright.

The common complaint you hear from students in Scandinavia is that for all their worldly goods and social benefits, the bulk of people are bored. This seems to be true. The Scandinavian middle classes are amongst the most affluent in the world, but also the most complacent.

It's an axiom of human existence that if you give a man something he has fought for most of his life the odds are he won't know what the hell to do with the *rest* of his life. He has nothing left to fight for. The problem is not what do you do with a car, a house, a washing machine, a television and a stereo, but what *else* do you do? Physical acquisitions solve physical problems and add a bonus of comfort and convenience. They offer freedom from drudgery – but freedom to do what? The answer should be that, after the body is cared for, man must attend his mind. But man doesn't. Man turns to television for six hours a night and indulges himself to the point of zombie-ism in what J. B. Priestley has termed the 'secondary gratifications'. Sadly, to most men, the primary gratifications, those that the mind can offer, are unreachable, for as surely as a man must learn to use his hands and be in the habit of using them, so he must also learn to use his mind and be in the habit of using that, too.

But this is not only Scandinavia's problem. It is becoming the major problem confronting the entire Western world. Perhaps Scandinavia may be the first to find the answer to it.

Sweden, any conversational bore will tell you, has the highest suicide rate in the world. Not true. For instance, in 1961, Sweden's suicide rate per 100,000 persons was 16·9. Austria's was 21·9, Czechoslovakia's was 20·6, West Germany's 18·7, Hungary's 25·4, Japan's 19·6 and Switzerland's 18·2. The rumour started, believe it or not, when, to quote from Erwin Stengel's book *Suicide and Attempted Suicide*, 'President Eisenhower singled out the Swedish suicide rate as a warning of what happened to a country with a leftish government. He must have been unacquainted with the even higher suicide rate of some other countries whose political complexion was more to his liking.'

Other 'facts' which really break Scandinavians up include the popular belief that Nordic ladies lay at the drop of an appropriate word. The rest of the world's attitude to Scandinavian sexual mores is really remarkable. Men's magazines from Tokyo to San Francisco tell you that people are practically fornicating in the

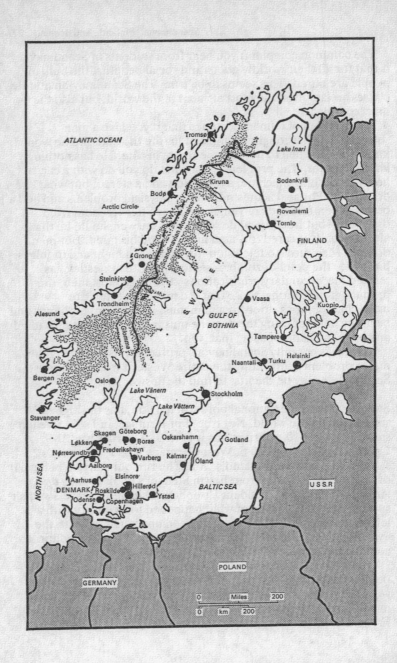

gutter and then throw it in your face that the whole thing has come about through enlightenment.

Well, even if the outlook is a sight more optimistic for the vagabond male than it is in, say, Spain, the emancipated northerners certainly don't throw themselves into the nearest set of hairy arms which comes their way. They're not *that* enlightened. They seem to be pretty honest about sex, but because they're honest doesn't mean they're easy. Scandinavian girls are just like any others – only they're more beautiful, which makes guys try harder – which naturally results in a higher rate of success. Which may have been what started the story.

Scandinavian humour is something that takes a little getting used to. It's just a trifle droll. A classic story from the seventies concerns the American hitcher with his national flag on his pack who had been walking along a back road in Denmark for hours without even sighting a car. Finally one came and he frantically gave it the old international. The young driver slowed down and rolled to a stop 200 yards beyond the American and then hung out the window and waved him forward. The Yank, dragging his heavy pack after him, ran stumbling down the side of the road. As he reached the car the driver yelled, *Get out of Vietnam, mother-fuckers!* and took off with a maniacal laugh in a stone-spitting churn of rubber.

A somewhat gentler story concerns my wife and me when we pitched our tent amongst some trees half a mile from the youth hostel on the outskirts of Helsingborg – we were nearly broke and couldn't afford the price of a bed. We thought we were in the wide open spaces, but morning dawned brightly with a knock on the door. I struggled out of my bag and untied the tent flap. A smiling policeman bid us good morning in perfect English and then bemusedly inquired if we would normally pitch a tent in, say, the middle of Hyde Park, London. I told him, normally not. He suggested we vacate the Helsingborg public park immediately.

All in all, the Scandinavians seem fairly easy to get along with. The older generations have that perpetual hint of suspicion on their faces that you find on the faces of older generations the world over when they're confronted by a beard and a dirty pair of boots, but they're OK and react well when you're in company with them. The Finns seem, if anything, more withdrawn than their Scandinavian neighbours. This might have something to do with their extremely complicated history. Forty-two lost wars with the Russians have left them with plenty to be moody about.

The students of Scandinavia are *really* the citizens of tomorrow – especially the travelling types. Danes, particularly, have filtered into every corner of Europe and North Africa. The Danish universities must have more members on the road, either hitching, or bounding around in Citroën 2CVs, than they have in their lecture halls. They're a great bunch.

Finally, with cigarettes in Scandinavia approaching the price of gold, make sure you take in enough to keep you going. If you're staying for a while it might be best to take rolling tobacco which can be picked up cheaply in Belgium or Luxembourg. If you do that, don't forget cigarette papers – they can cost a fortune in Norway!

Denmark

population	5,100,000
size	16,615 square miles
capital	Copenhagen, population 1,400,000
government	Constitutional monarchy
religion	The state religion is Lutheran
language	Danish: English and German widely understood and spoken
currency	*Krone* One *krone* equals 100 *oerer*. Coins of 5, 10, 25 *oerer*, and of 1, 5, 10 *kroner*. Notes of 20, 50, 100, 500, 1000 *kroner*

You can enter Denmark through Germany, by the E3 Flensbury–Kolding highway and then cross over to the main island of Sjælland by the Knudshoved–Halsskov ferry (approximate cost: 30 kroner), or by going up to Fehmarn Island in Germany and crossing on the Puttgarden–Rødbyhavn route (approximate cost: 55 kroner). Both ferries cross a minimum of twenty times daily in both directions.

Be warned that when you get off at Rødbyhavn there is no traffic except what comes off the ferry with you. If you miss a ride, you must wait an hour for the next ferry to dock. Often you *do* have to wait because the Rødbyhavn immigration officials are notoriously rough on hitchers. If you're loaded you're all right, if you're not you have to talk fast. They're extremely concerned about the amount of cash you have in the pocket. If you're expecting to pick up funds in Copenhagen, try to carry some documentary proof of the fact. Once I was going through with only £5 and had to strike up with nearly an hour-long Academy performance before I got the magic stamp.

Once through Danish customs and immigration you're right for the rest of Scandinavia. You're unlucky to get picked up at the Norwegian or Swedish points of entry – they're often not even manned – though you might have a performance with the Finns.

Hitching in Denmark, as with all of Scandinavia, seems OK. After two visits, I can't complain. One of the beauties of travelling in these countries is that you're very unlucky – except in Finland – if you don't get at least half your rides with people who speak English. Consequently you can pick up a lot of information in a very short time.

Principal cities after Copenhagen are Aarhus, Aalborg and Odense.

One of the things worth seeing at **Aarhus** is its 'Old Town' museum, which is a collection of some 60 houses dating as far back as 400 years and transplanted from all over Denmark into the one area. The city's Prehistoric Museum is the most recent resting place of the Grauballe man. He lay in a bog for 1600 years and remains in an excellent state of preservation.

Aalborg, the chief city of North Jutland, is a gourmet's paradise. This city of 155,000 boasts something like 170 restaurants. It's worth picking one for a splurge meal! For those interested in Vikings, the remains of a Viking village and a 682-grave cemetery can be seen at **Nørresundby** just outside Aalborg. The site of the village is known as **Lindholm Høje**. If you're American and passing through Aalborg on 4 July, head on out to Rebild National Park, 30 kilometres south of the city. Each year since 1912 they have held Independence Day celebrations there.

Although primarily visited by tourists to see the monuments and museum connected with Hans Christian Andersen (1805–75), **Odense** has plenty more to offer. It's one of the oldest towns in Denmark. St Canute's Cathedral – King Canute was killed in Odense 900 years ago – is one of the most important Gothic buildings in the country. The Funen Village, two kilometres from the centre of town, is a museum of peasant culture and an operating farm. At **Ladby**, 20 kilometres north-east of Odense, you can descend into an underground mound and see a tenth-century Viking ship. The 72-foot ship was the coffin of a Viking chief who was buried with his weapons and jewellery, four hunting-dogs, and eleven horses.

Hillerød, some 40 kilometres north of Copenhagen, is famous for its Frederiksborg Castle. Built originally between 1602–20 in Dutch Renaissance style, much of it was destroyed by fire in 1859. A fair lump of the money used for its restoration came from J. C. Jacobsen, the famous Carlsberg brewer.

Castle fiends will also want to see Kronborg Castle at **Helsingør**, 30 kilometres north-east of Hillerød. It is the setting of Shakespeare's *Hamlet*. Unfortunately, there is a confusion of dates. Hamlet was a twelfth-century gentleman and Kronborg is a sixteenth-century castle. Nevertheless, worth seeing, especially as the castle contains the Danish Museum of Trade and Shipping.

Ten kilometres west of **Roskilde**, at **Lejre**, is an Historical Archaeological Experimental Centre which is working on the reconstruction of an Iron Age village – not just the house, but the crafts and farming techniques as well.

Finally, for summer wanderers of both sexes who are yearning for the opposite sex, the beach resorts of North Jutland might provide the answer. Towns like **Skagen, Lønstrup** and **Løkken** (the largest resort) are where the summertime action is: but remember that they're tourist towns and expensive (though beach-sleeping is obviously in) and that they're inundated by suburbia on the loose.

Copenhagen: where to sleep

With hotels costing around 160 kroner for a single room, student accommodation is all that's left for the hitch-hiker. But even these can take a fee of up to 40 kroner, so you see that things can be pretty rough.

The following list of youth and student hostels starts with the least expensive and works up. The cheapest you can expect is around 35 kroner.

Bellahøj Vandrerhjem at Herbergvejen 8, DK-2700 Brønshøj (tel: 28 97 15). Closed 1 December to 2 January. Otherwise open all year. Youth Hostel membership card needed.

Amager Vandrerhjem at Sjællandsbroen 55, DK-2300 København

S (tel: 52 29 08 or 52 27 08). Closed 21 December to 1 February. Youth Hostel membership card needed.

Vesterbro Ungdomsgaard at Absalonsgade 8 (tel: 31 20 70). Open 5 May to 1 September.

Active University at Olfert Fischersgade 40. No Youth Hostel card needed.

One big disadvantage of student accommodation is that many places insist on a curfew (of course, they *might* let you stay out late to go to the movies if you ask *nicely*), but with the high prices in Scandinavia you have to put up with such institutional-type carryings-on or lump it. If you're in Copenhagen and considering lumping it, I wish you and your wallet the best of luck and suggest you find your way to the street called Istedgade. There are quite a few reasonably priced hotels there around the 120-kroner mark. If you're with someone and can make up a double or a triple, you'll probably save 5 or 6 kroner each. Here is one worth a try:

Hotel Absalon at Helgolandsgade 19 (tel: 24 22 11).

You'll find lots of friendly ladies around this area, but even the most uninspiring conversation starts at around 150 kroner.

Eslewhere try:

Saga at Colbjørnsensgade 20 (tel: 24 99 67).

Sankt Jørgen at 22 Julius Thomsensgade, DK-1974 København V (tel: 37 15 11).

West at 8 Dannebrogsgade/11 Westend, DK-1661 København V (tel: 24 27 61).

If you still can't find anything, and you're looking fairly clean, you can drop into the **Copenhagen Tourist Association** office at the Central Railway Station, Kiosk P, and they might be able to find you lodgings in a private house. But the association charges a 10-kroner fee per person for this service. The rate goes from 90–110 for a single and from 150–180 for a double room.

Failing all that, head out to Langelinie and sack out on the grass. Find a quiet spot and play it cool. Needless to say, sleeping in Langelinie is absolutely and completely forbidden.

For all sorts of info about Copenhagen contact **Use It,** at

Magstræde 14 (tel: (01) 15 65 18). Ask for the excellent *Playtime* magazine which is free, and contains a useful city map plus pages of facts about accommodation, food, entertainments, etc. in the capital. At the Use It office you can check the board for offers and messages, get free use of a locker (for a 10-kroner returnable deposit) and even arrange a ride. Use It also allows you to use their address as a poste restante address. Here it is again: USE IT, Magstræde 14, DK-1204 Copenhagen.

Copenhagen: where to eat

Eating out anywhere in Scandinavia can be an expensive proposition, but the list which follows will allow you to have a meal for around 35–50 kroner if you watch the menu carefully and eat a lot of *smørrebrød*, the tasty open-cut sandwiches. For breakfast, try Danish pastry at about 3 kroner apiece. For midday snacks you can't beat the *pølser*, Danish hotdogs sold at street-corner stands for 10 kroner each.

In fact, remember that *pølser* can save your life in Copenhagen. It's pretty hard to eat more than four of them which means that if you pick a cheap stand you can stuff yourself for 40 kroner. There is a student restaurant at 52 Købmagergade, Copenhagen K, open from 9 a.m. to 5 p.m. (closed in July). You must have a student card. Here is a list of reasonably priced restaurants:

Skipper Klement, Læderstræde 18.

Spisehuset, Magstræde 14.

Universitetskafeen, Fiolstræde 2.

Chinese Cafeteria, Dronningens Tværgade 30 and Nørrebrogade 51.

In high-priced Scandinavia remember that Chinese restaurants are amongst the best deals you can find – rice is cheap and fills you up quickly.

Vista Self-Service Restaurant upstairs at Vesterbrogade 40.

Cafe Sorgenfri at Brolæggerstræde 8.

Copenhagen: what to see and do

TIVOLI GARDENS The fun-park to end all fun-parks. Entrance fee around 16 kroner. Open from 1 May to 17 September. Plenty of opportunity to meet the opposite sex.

BREWERIES The two great Danish breweries, *Carlsberg* at Ny Carlsbergvej 140 and *Tuborg* at Strandvejen 54, offer a tour of their premises and plenty of free beer at the end of the walkabout. Visit *Carlsberg* at 9 a.m., 11 a.m. or 2.30 p.m. weekdays and *Tuborg* between 8.30 a.m. and 2.30 p.m. weekdays.

LIBERTY MUSEUM OF DENMARK (also called the Danish Resistance Museum) Fascinating collection of objects used by the Danes in their underground fight against the German occupation forces during the Second World War. On Esplanaden. No admission fee.

LANGELINIE A pleasant walk – if you like that sort of thing – along the favourite promenade in Copenhagen. High spot for those over forty is the famous *Little Mermaid* sitting on her rock. Those under forty – like Copenhagen students – have a bad habit of painting her a variety of colours and, once, even knocked her head off. But she's OK. Good sleeping-out area.

FIOLSTRÆDE This, apart from being a pleasant street, is where the university is. Good place to meet up with students or get information about whatever is worrying you.

THE GLYPTOTEKET MUSEUM This houses the national art collection. Free on Sundays and Wednesdays. Some good works by Degas, Renoir, Manet, and Cézanne, and also Rodin's 'The Citizens of Calais'. The museum was founded last century by Carl Jacobsen who also founded the Carlsberg breweries. At Dantes Plads.

THE ROUND TOWER at Købmagergade. Costs to get in but it gives you a good view of Copenhagen from the top. There are no steps, but a spiral ramp all the way up. Legend tells that Peter the Giant galloped up to the top on his horse followed by his queen in a carriage.

CIRCUS BENNEWEIS World-famous circus and well worth seeing. Bit of a hit to get in. Cheapest seat over 40-kroner. Open 1 April to end of October.

BAKKEN AMUSEMENT PARK Not as flamboyant as Tivoli, but free admission and plenty of chance to meet the opposite sex. Open April through August. Twenty-minute train ride from Central Station to Klampenborg Station, so probably cheaper to go to Tivoli anyway.

BELLEVUE A beach between Copenhagen and Helsingør. It's also known as *Fluepapiret* which means 'fly-paper', meaning it has a great attraction to bikini'd blondes which in turn means it's an attraction to bearded Danes. Draw your own conclusions – and the best of luck.

LOUISIANA This is Denmark's museum of contemporary art. It's on the coast at **Humlebæk**, about 40 kilometres out of Copenhagen and beyond Bellevue. Worth a trip for the art freaks and architecture students.

CINEMA Movies in Copenhagen are usually shown in the original language with Danish subtitles. All the latest American and British movies are showing. Prices reasonable. Much cheaper in the suburbs, of course.

NYHAVN This seamen's quarter is worth a couple of hours one night. Maybe they'll hit your pocket if you step inside for a drink (you can usually spot the clip-joints), but it's a trip just digging the characters – tourists included – in the streets.

Transport in Copenhagen
Best way of getting around Copenhagen is by bus or train. Tickets are interchangeable and can be used on as many buses and/or trains as you like within one hour. Cheapest way to buy rides in the central area is to invest in a 9-ride ticket for around 50 kroner. Single-ride tickets are more expensive. If you're broke and want to go somewhere, stand at the appropriate bus or train stop and watch people getting off. If they throw away their ticket, grab it. It may be valid for a few minutes more, in which case you can jump aboard for free. Conversely if you're finished with a ticket which has time left on it, pass it to any waiting types who look like they could use it.

  If you're staying in town for some time and are feeling energetic, a cheap way of getting around is by bicycle. About the cheapest place to rent from is *Københavns Cyklebørs* at the corner of Gothersgade and Nansengade, where the rate is 25 kroner a day. You have to leave a deposit of around 100 kroner.

Student discounts
Half price on admission to museums and art galleries for card holders.
Also possible to buy certain goods on discount. Check with:

DANISH INTERNATIONAL STUDENT COMMITTEE, Skindergade 28,
DK-1159 Copenhagen K (tel: 11 00 44).

Addresses

Main post office (for poste restante) at Vesterbro, Tietgensgade
35, DK-1704 Copenhagen.

American Express at Amagertorv 18, DK-1160 Copenhagen K
(tel: 12 23 01).

Danish International Student Committee at Skindergade 28,
DK-1159 Copenhagen K (tel: 11 00 44).

Scandinavian Student Travel Service at Islands Brygge 81,
DK-2300 Copenhagen S (tel: 54 45 35).

Danish Tourist Board at H. C. Andersens Boulevard 22A,
DK-1553 Copenhagen V (tel: 11 13 25).

US Embassy at Dag Hammarskjöldsallé 24, DK-2100 Copenhagen
Ø (tel: 42 31 44).

British Embassy at Kastelsvej 36–40, DK-2100 Copenhagen Ø
(tel: 26 46 00).

Hitchers' Tips and Comments...

Many apartment houses in Scandinavian countries have no
flats on the garret, or attic, floor. Stairs continue up under the
roof. Usually there's no door. Such places offer free, dry,
warm places to sleep. Great in winter weather. Some German
apartments are built the same. *Klaus Kruger, Germany*

Plain-clothes police search and frisk long-hairs on trains
heading into Denmark. *Duncan Smith, Bournemouth,
England*

Head for the YMCA in Helsingør. They do a fantastic
breakfast. *Craig Seaton, Worksop, Notts, UK*

Sweden

population	8,300,000
size	173,654 square miles
capital	Stockholm, population 1,402,000
government	Constitutional monarchy
religion	Lutheran
language	Swedish; English widely understood and spoken; some German and French
currency	*Krona* One *krona* equals 100 *öre*. Coins of 5, 10, 25, 50 *öre*, and 1, 5 *kronor*. Notes of 5, 10, 50, 100, 1000, 10,000 *kronor*

Presuming that you'll be crossing into Sweden from Denmark you have several ferry crossings to choose from. Among them:

1 Dragör to Limhamn, costing about 18 Swedish kronor.
2 Copenhagen to Malmö, by hydrofoil costing about 50 Swedish kronor.
3 Helsingør to Helsingborg, costing about 8 Swedish kronor.

If you're entering Sweden from Norway, the two fastest routes are the E18 if you're heading for Stockholm, or the E6 if you're going to Göteborg and the south for a crossing into Denmark.

Göteborg, along with Kiruna, Visby, Kalmar and Ystad (and Stockholm, of course) can give you a pretty fair picture of Sweden. But remember that Sweden is a summertime place if you want to do it on the cheap. With the high cost of hotels in Scandinavia, sleeping out when you're on the road is just about mandatory unless you're loaded, and you can't sleep out in the Scandinavian winter! The Swedish law, *Allemans Rätt*, or Everyman's Right, allows you to camp out anywhere for one night without the landowner's permission, except public parks (see introduction to this chapter) or in someone's front garden, as long as you don't cross ploughed fields, leave rubbish lying about, or light fires where they can be dangerous.

Göteborg is a city of 693,000. Things worth seeing include the Guldhedens Vattentorn, the 400-foot water tower, the Røhss Museum of Arts and Crafts which will give you a rundown on the best of Swedish design, the Maritime Museum, the Archaeological Museum (featuring finds back to 2000 BC), and the Military Museum in Kronan Fortress. The best museum in this city of museums, though, is the Göteborg Art Gallery which features dozens of good pictures by Pissarro, Rousseau, Matisse, Picasso, Van Gogh, and Braque. Also sculptures by such greats as Rodin and Moore, and a superb representative collection of Scandinavian painters. For stage buffs there is even a Theatre Museum – something you don't find in many cities.

At **Boras**, 70 kilometres east of Göteborg on Route 40, is the Freedom Zoo in Boras Park, something really worth seeing if you're one of those people who likes looking at animals but hates the conventional method of caging them. These beasts – elephants, giraffes, rhinos, and all the rest – roam in wide open spaces.

If you're heading south to Ystad, you might want to drop into **Varberg**, 80 kilometres from Göteborg, where, in the Varberg fortress you can see the remains of Bocksten Man, another gentleman, this time medieval, who was recently hauled from a bog. He was preserved so well that his clothing is claimed as the only complete set of medieval clothes in existence.

Ystad, right on the southern tip of Sweden, in the province of Skane, is interesting because of its Middle Ages aspect. Ancient winding streets, half-timbered houses, and old churches dot the town, while in the surrounding countryside you find castles, manor houses, and also a medieval monastery.

Visby, on the **Island of Gotland**, is another leftover from the old Sweden. Unfortunately, it costs a packet to get there. The trip from Oskarshamn or Vastervik (about four hours) costs better than 80 kronor each way. (Flash your student card for a reduction.) Known as the City of Ruins and Roses, Visby, population 16,000, was once an extremely important seaport, but after being captured in the 1300s it drifted out of history and towards oblivion. It remains today the only walled city in northern Europe. To see? Everything. Just walk around – the Maiden's Tower, where a girl was entombed alive for helping an enemy king, Gallow Hill, the ancient Powder Tower. Catch 22 . . . you'll get your money's worth if you've got some money.

Kalmar, 80 kilometres south of Oskarshamn and on the E66 east coast road up to Stockholm, is a worthwhile place. A city of 52,000, it is the sister city of Wilmington, Delaware. This international handshake salutes the first Swedish emigrants to America who came from Kalmar and went to Wilmington in the 1600s. The main sight is Kalmar Castle and its museum.

If you can't afford the Gotland Island trip, you may like to compensate with a trip to **Oland Island**, which is a fantastic area for amateur archaeologists interested in the Iron Age. A fair percentage of the Swedes in America, incidentally, must have Olander ancestors, because about twenty-five per cent of the island population emigrated. You cross the island via Europe's longest bridge – nearly six kilometres long.

Kalmar is in the middle of an area containing about 20 of Sweden's famed glass factories. For a free visit to the best-known glass factory in the world, visit **Orrefors**, which is easy to hitch to, being 45 kilometres west of Kalmar on Highway 31. The factory is open all year and conducted tours are available Monday to Friday from 8.00 a.m. to 3.00 p.m.

Kiruna, in northern Lapland, is the big trip. It is 1350 kilometres north of Stockholm and 150 kilometres into the Arctic Circle. From Stockholm you have a choice of routes: the east coast E4 up to Lulea and then a swing inland on Highway 97, connecting with the 98 outside Gällivare; or the E4 up to Sundsvall and a swing west along the E75 to Osterund, followed by a straight northern route to Kiruna along road numbers 88, 343, 97 and 98. If you're working against a time limit, then you're better off on the eastern sea-road to Lulea. The inland route takes you through a cross-section of Swedish geography – really great country – but the population is spread thin and so are the cars.

Although it hosts only 31,000 citizens, Kiruna is the world's largest city in area, containing within its distended limits, plains, lakes, Lapp camps, 30,000 reindeer, and two mountains of iron totalling some two billion tons of ore.

The town itself is not wildly interesting, but it's a good stopping place after a long haul from Stockholm, and it's the ideal place to watch the midnight sun between 31 May and 14 July. For those six weeks there is continual daylight and you can enjoy the unique experience of watching the sun beginning to rise again without first sliding below the horizon. Mosquitoes, incidentally, are really bad in mid-July.

★**Canoeing** If you're in the forest areas of Dalsland and Värmland (north of Göteborg), you might want to try a two- or three-day canoe trip. Check at lakeside towns. At **Dals Langed**, just off Highway 172, a canoe costs about 85 kronor a day. A rich hitcher's sport, but great fun!

★**Prospecting** For semi-precious crystals and stones and alluvial gold, the Kopparberg district of Orebro county is the place. (Orebro is 200 kilometres west of Stockholm.) Check for precise details from the tourist office in Stockholm or Orebro. I've never done it myself, but have heard of people making the odd pound. Don't count on it!

Stockholm: where to sleep

Sweden is as expensive as its Scandinavian neighbours. Single hotel rooms for 100 kronor are cheap. Once again it's the hostels and dormitories which save the day. The following list starts at the cheapest, which are still exorbitantly expensive, and works up . . . and up.

Af Chapman at Skeppsholmen (tel: 10 37 15). This is the famous floating youth hostel, the **Af Chapman** being an ex-Swedish navy training vessel. Open 1 March until 15 December.

Zinken, Pipmakergränd 2 (tel 68 57 86).

Columbus Hostel at Tjärhausgatan 11 (tel 44 17 17).

Anno 1647 at Mariagränd 3 (tel 44 04 80).

The **International Youth Centre**, sponsored by the Community of Stockholm, at Valhallavägen 142 (tel: 63 43 89) offers low-price beds during the summer period. Also cooking facilities, sports activities, showers, and even sewing machines for running repairs. Write to them for 1985–86 opening dates. Also try the *Hotellcentralen* at the central rail station. They probably won't be too interested in booking you into a dormitory, but they'll be polite enough to give you the information you need. If they do place you somewhere they'll charge you a booking fee of about 10 kronor for hotels and 5 kronor for youth hostels, so you'd better decide if you'll get your money's worth before you let them do the work.

Camping grounds are good in Stockholm. The **Sätra** grounds (tel: 97 70 71) are fairly close to town and can be reached by Number 15 underground train. All mod cons, clean, and reasonably priced at about 30 kronor per tent.

For sleeping rough, try around Kaknäs Tower (take Bus 69). Sleeping out should present no problems – as long as it's warm enough – because just about all of the many islands upon which Stockholm is built are bordered with trees and parks.

Stockholm: where to eat

Be warned . . . buy at the supermarket, eat at student restaurants, department-store cafeterias, or at self-service places. Most restaurants have a 'dish of the day' Mondays to Fridays lunchtime.

Look for the **DOMUS** and **TEMPO** department stores. Their cafeterias serve breakfast and lunch. You will get a lunch for about 30 kronor.

The **Restaurant** at the railway station offers an all-you-can-eat breakfast for about 20 kronor between 6.30 a.m. and 10 a.m. (Sundays from 8 a.m. to 11 a.m.) Fill up and palm a few morsels into the pocket. You should get enough to take you through most of the day if you're cool about it.

Stockholm: what to see and do

GRÖNA LUND'S TIVOLI on Djurgaarden. Entrance charge. Super amusement park, not as pretty as the Copenhagen Tivoli, but OK if you like that sort of thing. Mainly of interest because there are plenty of friendly people of the right age floating around and because on the grounds are two clubs. The *Dance In* is more expensive than the *Dance Out*, but there's a better class of people. All in all, not very exciting, but it might amuse a sad hour. Open April through September.

CLUBS Most clubs and discotheques require membership but try the *Glädjehuset,* Holländargatan 32, at the Student Union Building, or the *Big Brother,* at Grev Turegatan 11. Also try the pubs. They only serve beer, and close at midnight, but you can have some fun. *Mocambo* at Körsbärsvägen 2A is a student pub. The *Engelen* at Kornhamnstorg 59B is in the old town and OK.

THE WASA on Djurgaarden. This warship which sank moments after being launched in 1628, was rediscovered in 1956 and lifted from the seabed in 1961. The story of the recovery is told in a film shown at the museum. One of the best examples in the world of an ancient sailing vessel. Admission charge.

SKANSEN Also at Djurgaarden. Open all year round. An open-air museum with examples of farms, town sections, etc., from all over Sweden, and demonstrations of arts and crafts. Mostly eighteenth century. Entrance fee.

THE NATIONAL MUSEUM OF ART on Södra Blasieholmshamnen. Fairly good collection. Admission charge during week, but free on Tuesdays.

MUSEUM OF MODERN ART on Skeppsholmen. Reasonable collection of modern European masters and good collections of Swedish stuff. Closed Mondays. Entrance charge.

MILLESGARDEN on the island of Lidingö. Home and works of the famous sculptor Carl Milles. Closed during winter season. Admission charge.

SAUNA BATHS Saunas are usually fairly expensive. This one, *Vanadisbadet* at Vanadislunden, is cheap and good. Used to cost 5 kronor. Worth trying.

BLUE MOVIES If you want to see one – it'll cost you 20–25 kronor – go to the street called Klara Norra Kyrkog. There are quite a few porn shops and blue cinemas there. (Make sure you don't cop an American-made show. The product isn't up to standard.)

Transport in Stockholm
The best deal in town is the *turistkortet* (tourist card) which allows visitors to wander for three days on the buses and trains of Stockholm. At 55 kronor, the cost is high but it includes free entrance to Gröna Lund, Skansen, the TV tower and to almost all museums. Buy them at the Tourist Centre, the 'Pressbyra' kiosks, or at stations.

Addresses

Main post office(for poste restante) at Vasagatan 28–34, Stockholm.

American Express at Resespecialisterna, Sturegatan 8, Stockholm (tel: 22 88 60)

Sveriges Forenade Studentkarer (Student Travel Department) at Drottninggatan 89, Stockholm (tel: 34 01 80).

Tourist Centre in Sweden House at Kungsträdgärden, Stockholm.

US Embassy at Strandvägen 101, Stockholm (tel: 63 05 20).

British Embassy at Skarpögatan 6, Stockholm (tel: 67 01 40).

Hitchers' Tips and Comments...

The phenomenal cost of travelling in the Nordic countries is no secret. But, while in Stockholm, I discovered that by trying to pay for a ticket with a 100 kronor note, explaining in my best English that it was all I had, the result was a free ride every time. For two weeks I rode the Tunnelbana saving the price of a cup of coffee with every ride. *Bruce Alan Whitham, Newcastle, Canada*

In some large shops in Sweden the food halls (often in the basement) have free left luggage lockers. (You have to pay a deposit for the key.) Useful if you want to ditch your pack for a couple of hours. *Kevin Bilke, Southampton, UK*

To eat cheap in Sweden, note that most restaurants do a daily special Monday through Friday, usually served between 12 midday and 2 p.m. The special includes a main dish, often with as much side salad as you can eat, a glass of milk, beer or mineral water and sometimes coffee as well. The dish and price are advertised outside restaurants as Dagens Rätt (Today's Dish).

If you're a student, try the Student Reception Service in university towns. You'll get information about all sorts of things, plus the bars are much cheaper (though expensive by British standards). Sweden has universities in Lund, Linköping, Göteborg, Stockholm, Karlstad, Uppsala and Umea.

Finally, when getting off the ferry in Helsingborg, go to the main truck depot just 500 metres from the ferry station and try for a ride from the truck drivers. The depot is called *Asg-Centralen. Mats Rönne, London, UK*

If you're stuck in Stockholm without a ticket home, try busking on the main street. When the police ask what you're up to just say you're broke. I did and got a night in jail, food and a free flight back to London. *Paul Dowrick, Andover, England*

More often in these circumstances the local police pass you over to the British Consul who, if he loans you funds to get home, also arranges for your passport to be confiscated until the loan has been repaid. Avoid desperate moves – like the one suggested by Paul – except as an absolute last resort. K.W.

Stockholm: if you want to catch up on the news in Stockholm you can read all sorts of foreign newspapers for free in the library in the Culture House of Sergelstorg Square. *Alan Barlow, Cheadle, UK*

Norway

population	4,000,000
capital	Oslo, population 465,000
government	Constitutional monarchy
religion	Lutheran
language	Norwegian; English widely understood and spoken; some French and German
currency	*Krone* One *krone* equals 100 *øre*. Coins of 5, 10, 25, 50 *øre*, and 1, 5 *kroner*. Notes of 5, 10, 50, 100, 500, 1000 *kroner*

The cheapest way of reaching Norway is through Sweden (see Swedish section for ferry fares from Denmark) and then hitching along the E6 to the Norwegian-Swedish border. If you have more money and/or less time, two other ways of getting there are:

1 Copenhagen to Oslo ferry. Sixteen-hour journey, costing around 350 Danish kroner (one way).
2 Frederikshavn (Jutland) to Larvik ferry. Six-hour journey, costing about 200 Norwegian kroner (high season).

Top towns in Norway, after Oslo, are Bergen, Stavanger, and Trondheim. **Stavanger**, some 584 kilometres from Oslo, is Norway's fourth city and one of the best from the point of view of seeing what the old Norway was like. The wooden houses in Old Stavanger and the narrow, winding, cobbled streets are a sight for eyes glazed by the dazzle of metal and plastic. Two sights in one are the cathedral at the marketplace. The market swings every day, except Sunday, until 2 or 3 in the afternoon. The cathedral, a twelfth-century structure, is an outstanding example of Middle Ages architecture in Norway. For a cheap sightseeing trip, jump bus Number 8 at St Olavsgarden. It covers most parts of Stavanger. For a good look at the fjords, particularly if you're not heading up farther north, try the Stavanger to Sand ferry. It's a 3–4 hour trip which costs around 80 kroner, but you see some fantastic sights. Highly recommended. After heading out of Sand, and if you're going to Bergen, it's necessary to take another ferry, this time across the Hardanger Fjord. (Kinsarvik to Kvanndal is one way, costing 25 kroner and taking about an hour.) If in that area, see the huge Folgefonn Glacier and the Laatefoss Waterfall near **Odda**.

Don't miss **Bergen**'s colourful harbour. It's a pleasure just to walk in the area. Right on the waterfront is the Fish Market – a sight and a smell in itself – while on your right as you face the water is the beautiful street called Bryggen, a row of timbered houses built in 1702 to recreate a slice of medieval Bergen after a fire destroyed much of the city. Also on Bryggen is the Hanseatic Museum which is devoted to life as the German merchants who traded in Bergen centuries ago lived it. The Rasmus Meyer and the Stenerson collections are worth seeing because they contain many of Edvard Munch's works. For a display of a different sort, try the Fishery Museum, which gives a rundown on Norway's most famous industry. All are at the Permanenten on Olav Kyrresgate. For getting around the city, the Tourist Information Office, and most hotels, sell a special tourist ticket which allows unlimited bus and tramcar travel for forty-eight hours within the city limits. If you can afford it and want to see a great view over this Viking city with its seven hills, you should invest a few kroner and take the funicular up the 1050 feet of Mount Fløien. Along the waterfront you'll find dozens of fjord boat trips advertised and costing anywhere from 20 to 200 kroner. All are good because the scenery around Bergen is spectacular. It's just a matter of figuring if you want to pay out – and if so, how much. Not far from Bergen is **Troldhaugen** (Troll's Hill) which was the home of Edvard Grieg.

If you're heading farther north, **Alesund** is Norway's greatest fishing town and its large fleet, which operates from Baffin Bay, heads out after seals as well as smaller fry. There might be the possibility of odd jobs in Alesund.

Trondheim, Norway's second largest city and the principal city to the north, was founded nearly a thousand years ago. A pleasant place with an ancient cathedral and a very interesting Museum of Music History, it has been known as the Royal Town since the days when Norway's monarchs were crowned there. When the Norwegian Royal Family visit Trondheim these days they stay at Siftsgarden which is claimed to be the largest wooden building in Europe.

Near the city is the village of **Grong** which sits on the Namsen River, just one of Norway's 200 salmon-filled streams. Hitching fishermen may be interested in knowing that there are a quarter of a million lakes in Norway, most of which play host to trout. Fishing licences cost money but, if you can figure a way of rigging some light tackle, you should be able to haul a cheap meal out of most stretches of water in the backwoods without much trouble. (Fishing with a licence does not mean that fish bite better.)

Once above Trondheim, you're heading for the Arctic Circle. **Bodø** is the most popular place for viewing the midnight sun (5 June to 9 July and *no* sun from 19 December to 9 January) and there's plenty of traffic to that point. After Bodø the roads can be lonely and the people scarce. Most of the time you have no proof you're on a civilized planet. Once in Finnmark you're in an area bigger than Denmark but inhabited by only 78,000 people. It's wild and it's beautiful and it's lots of other appropriate clichés – but don't find yourself twenty kilometres from the nearest town at night at the wrong time of year. You might get a cold.

On the way up to the North Cape, **Tromsø** is worth stopping at if only to see its fabulous Arctic church. (The wreck of the German battleship, *Tirpitz*, which was bombed there by the RAF during the Second World War can no longer be seen.) The Tromsø Museum will give you an idea of how people – particularly the Lapps – have managed to live in the Arctic.

After **Steinkjer**, the road, National Highway 6, is mostly gravel, but as you get farther and farther north you'll notice more and more tourist facilities because the North Cape is slowly becoming the place to have been. Finally, when you reach **Honningsvaag** (ferry from Käfjord – 17 kroner), you've made the northernmost village in the world! Forty kilometres farther on is the barren North Cape – the end of Europe – a rocky plateau on a latitude of 70° 10′ 21″ N which rises 1000 feet straight out of the Arctic Ocean.

Oslo: where to sleep

Oslo doesn't come as expensive as Copenhagen or Stockholm, but it tries hard. One of the cheapest places around is the International Youth Hostel (Haraldsheim) which charges about 65 kroner for bed and breakfast! After that, expect to pay 65–75 kroner.

Haraldsheim Youth Hostel at Haraldsheim 4, Oslo 5 (tel: 21 83 59). Closed for Christmas and New Year. Must be a member of YHA.

Bjerke Youth Hostel at Bjerke Studentheim, Trondheimsveien 271, Oslo 5 (tel: 57 99 33). Open 20 June to 18 August. Overnight charge around 45 kroner.

Baptistsamufunnets Skoler at Drammensveien 406 (tel: 53 38 53). Open from 1 June to 3 August.

If you don't want student accommodation, you must be prepared to fork out – but there are a few reasonably priced places: for instance, **Seamen's Mission** or **Oslo Sjømannshjem**, Tollbugata 3. (Entrance is in Fred Olsens Gate near the railway station.) Men only (tel: 41 20 05). For 7 kroner the *Innkvartering* desk (the hotel-finding service) at East Station will help you locate a hotel room to suit your budget or get you into a room in a private house. If you're staying in Oslo for more than a few days – especially in summer when hotels are often full – the investment could well save you money.

If you want to sleep for nothing, you have several choices (providing it's summer). There's the 75-acre Frogner Park in western Oslo which should provide nesting holes for the sore of pocket without much trouble; there are several smaller parks, for instance on Akersbakken; there's the cemetery at Ullevalsveien (you have to get over the wall) and on the Bygdøy peninsula there are large parklands. (BUT I've had a letter from the Norwegian Tourist Office in London which passes on to me information given them by authorities in Oslo who seem to have read this book: 'We will not – repeat not – condone sleeping in the parks or have this even suggested. Loiterers will, in fact, be removed by the police.')

Oslo: where to eat

Norwegians have the habit of eating only two meals a day. A big breakfast and a big dinner – with maybe a snack somewhere along the line. As with most places in Scandinavia, expect to pay out between 40 and 60 kroner for a meal.

Aulakjelleren and **Frokostkjelleren** Student cafeterias in the university buildings at Karl Johansgate. Very cheap. They don't ask for student cards. You should fill up for 40 kroner.

Restaurant Frederikke at Universitetssentret in the suburb of Blindern (tel: 46 68 80). Open all year.

Stratos at Youngstorget 2.

Helserestauranten Bios at Kronprinsensgaten 5. Good prices and 20 per cent discount if you flash a student's ID card.

Wimpy Bars (same as in London!) Neutral food, cheap prices. Several around Oslo, including one at Akersgate 8 and another at Stortingsgaten 20.

Christiana Dampkjokken at Torggt. 8.

Expressen Cafeteria at Fred. Olsensgt. 11.

Frogner Baths Cafeteria at Middlethungst. 28.

Gamie Radhus Cafeteria at N. Slottsgt. 1.

Cristiana Glasmagasin, Stortorgt. 10.

Promenadi Kafeen, Øvre Slottsgt. 12.

Friskportrestauranten (vegetarian), Grensen 18.

Oslo: what to see and do

EDVARD MUNCH MUSEUM Admission free. At Tøyengate 53. Munch (1863–1944) is considered a leading European contemporary painter. The work is interesting, giving a clue to the psyche of the Northerner. The man had a phenomenal output, creating over 1000 paintings and 4000 drawings. The museum exhibits about 300 paintings, plus sketches and some sculpture.

THE VIGELAND SCULPTURES Admission free. At Frogner Park. Gustav Vigeland, another great Norwegian artist, was financed by the city of Oslo to create the 150 pieces of work on display in this park. The work took him thirty years.

NATIONAL THEATRE Behind the theatre used to be a good meeting place for kindred spirits.

AKERSHAUS CASTLE Small admission charge. Open April to October. Used to be the strongest castle in Scandinavia. Used as office space by the Germans during the war. See its Resistance and Defence museums in the castle grounds.

KON-TIKI MUSEUM Admission charge. In the Bygdøy area. This houses the balsa raft in which Thor Heyerdahl and his crew sailed 4300 miles across the Pacific in 1947. Apart from proving his theory that pre-Inca Indians might have travelled the same way to reach Polynesia, Heyerdahl made around a million pounds out of the adventure and had his book, *Kon-Tiki*, translated into more than eighty languages. Also see the reed boat *RA II* which Heyerdahl and his multinational crew sailed and drifted 3270 nautical miles across the Atlantic to Barbados in 1970.

THE VIKING SHIPS Admission charge. At Huk Aveny 35 in the Bygdøy area (within walking distance of the *Kon-Tiki*). You can see three Viking ships in fair state of preservation, along with a display of artifacts found with them. One ship is 1100 years old.

HOLMENKOLLEN SKI JUMP The oldest in the world and the site of Olympic competitions. Twenty minutes or so by train. A very interesting Ski Museum (for snow-sport fans) is situated inside the jump tower. Admission charge to the museum.

FRAM MUSEUM This museum, built in the style of an ancient Norwegian boat-house, exhibits the polar exploration ship *Fram*, used by several famous Norwegian explorers. Amundsen started his celebrated South Pole dash in the *Fram* in 1910. The museum is in Bygdøynes. You reach it by taking a ferry from Pier 3 or Bus 30 from the National Theatre.

NORWEGIAN FOLK MUSEUM at Museumsveien 10, Bygdøy. (Bus 30 or Pier 3.) Over 150 wooden buildings have been dismantled and shifted from their original sites and taken to Bygdøy where they have been re-erected to form a nearly complete collection of Norwegian rural architecture. All are complete with their original furnishings. All that – and more – is in the outdoor section of the museum. Indoors you'll find over 100,000 exhibits including playwright Henrik Ibsen's study and a section on the culture of Lapland.

TOWN HALL Town halls aren't usually recommended in this book. But have a look at this one! It's as much a gallery of contemporary Norwegian art as a red-tape machine.

CLUB 7 at Munkedamsveien 15. Plenty of action, lights, and sound, but not up to the standard of London or New York clubs. Entrance fee. Another OK place is *Amalienbar-Jazzhouse* at Eerbeidergaten 2. Folk-singing, jazz, student hangout.

Transport in Oslo
The tram and bus system in the city charges about 8 kroner a ride. It's cheaper to buy a *trikkekort* for about 45 kroner which gives you eleven rides on either tram or bus.

Student discounts
For details contact:

THE UNIVERSITIES TRAVEL BUREAU, Universitetssentret, Blindern, Oslo 3 (tel: 46 68 80).

Addresses

Main post office (for poste restante) at Dronningensgate 15, Oslo.

American Express at Karl Johansgate 33, Oslo (tel: 20 50 50).

Studentenes Reisekontor at Universitetssentret, Blindern, Oslo 3 (tel: 46 68 80).

Studentenes Reisekontor at Parkveien 1, Bergen (tel: 33 191).

Tourist Information Centre at Munkedamsveien 15, Oslo 2 (tel: 42 71 70).

US Embassy at Drammensveien 18, Oslo (tel: 56 68 80).

British Embassy at Thomas Heftyesgate 8, Oslo 2 (tel: 56 38 90).

Hitchers' Tips and Comments ...

If you're out of money in Oslo, don't sleep in the parks or at Bygdøy. Take the tram to Frognerseteren or a bus (No. 41) to

Sorkedalen and walk ten minutes into the woods. *Johs Anken, Oslo, Norway*

The carnivorous insect life in western and northern Scandinavia, Norway especially, can be terrifying from June to August. It makes you wonder what the beasts eat when fresh Englishman is unavailable. British repellents don't seem to work. Local ones are better. You can't emphasize this insect plague enough. I've known people made quite ill by mosquito and horsefly bites up there.

Also, if you're up in those parts in early summer when the sun shines strongly, but there's still plenty of snow about, *you must wear sunglasses*. The reflections are blinding, and dangerous to your eyes. *Adrian Park, Preston, England*

In Oslo they use the same ticket system as in Copenhagen. You can transfer to another bus or tram within the hour. *Alan Barlow, Cheadle, UK*

The E6 is now surfaced much further north, but beware – in places there's road, but no roadside! Watch it if you're stuck out there at night! *Aidan Murray, Athlore, England*

Nothing wrong with sleeping in Bygdøy, except for the wildlife. A fox stole one of my friend's training shoes and kept on coming back for the other one. Generally, I found Oslo easy to crash out in. *Philip Attwool, Orpington, UK*

In Oslo go to the top of the hill overlooking Oslo – up past the Olympic ski-slope. Spectacular view and free binoculars. When everyone's gone (about 9 p.m.), you can pitch your tent for free and camp. *A. P. Kik, Middlesbrough, Teesside, UK*

Norway's quarter of a million lakes aren't full of fish. As a matter of fact, 90 per cent of the lakes south of Dovre are empty of fish due to air pollution.

Cheap places to eat (good food and large helpings) in Oslo are the Spisestedet in the 'working commune' (an underground leftover from the hippy era) at Helmsgat 3.

Oslo's latest and most international disco is Studio 26, Universitetsgaten 4. *Joker, Baerum, Norway*

Finland

population	4,841,000
size	130,085 square miles
capital	Helsinki, population 500,000
government	Republic
religion	Evangelical Lutheran and Greek Orthodox
language	Finnish and Swedish are the official languages: some English spoken
currency	*Markka* One *markka* equals 100 *pennis*. Coins of 5, 10, 20, 50 *pennis*, and 1, 5 *markkas*. Notes of 5, 10, 50, 100, 500 *markkas*

Getting to Finland can be an expensive proposition. You have to spend a lot of days on the road and enter at the Swedish-Finnish border at Tornio on the E4 highway (fine if you're travelling south after the Kiruna trip) or pay a fair wallop on the ferry boats. Four of the ferry points are:

1 Stockholm to Helsinki, costing about 140–160 markkas and lasting around 14–16 hours. Daily.
2 Stockholm to Turku, costing about 80–100 markkas and lasting about 9½–11 hours. Daily.
3 Kapellskär to Naantali, costing about 70 markkas and lasting about 8 hours. Daily.
4 Umeå and Sundsvall to Vaasa (if you're a long way up north in Sweden), costing about 65–80 markkas and lasting about 4–8 hours.

Turku, a ferry port, is Finland's second city, with 165,000 people. It is the oldest city in the country and the former capital. (Åbo is its Swedish name, as Helsingfors is the Swedish name of Helsinki.) Resurrection Chapel is considered a masterpiece of modern Finnish architecture, while for something a little older, the cathedral and Turku Castle date from the twelfth century. Music fans will be interested in the Sibelius Museum, while sport nuts might want to see the Turku Sports Park running track, reputed to be the fastest in the world and on which Olympian Paavo Nurmi set many of his world records. Of more general interest is Scandinavia's biggest open-air marketplace at the old trade hall in the city.

Tampere, 180 kilometres north-west of Helsinki, is about the same size as Turku. It is known as the City of Sapphire Lakes.

Twenty-two lakes are within its city limits, as are the Tammerkoski Rapids. At Pyynikki, the National Park, is the famous summer theatre, which was the first in the world to operate with a revolving auditorium. Watching a production as you move around the stage is quite something. For details of plays check with the tourist office – but it's generally expensive – 15–25 markkas a ticket. The university, a nice piece of architecture, is the best place to meet up with people.

For those in Finland only briefly, Helsinki, Turku and Tampere are probably the best bets for a quick look around. For those with time and money and who are heading north into Lapland, **Kuopio** (population 75,000) is a good stopping place. This city, four hundred kilometres north of Helsinki, is one of the centres of lake shipping. (In Finland there are 60,000 lakes, comprising nine per cent of the country's total area and resulting in another 30 per cent being marshland.) The big thing at Kuopio is to climb the 700-foot Puijo Hill and the 225-foot tower on top of it for one of the best views of Scandinavia. From the top you can gaze over 18,000 square miles of the lake country! If you're in the Market Square, try the *kalakukkos*, hard-crusted fish pasties native to the province.

Vaasa, on the west coast, where many cross to from Umeå in Sweden, is a pleasant city of 55,000. There are actually two towns, Old Vaasa and New Vaasa. The Old was destroyed by fire in 1852 and is now a place of ruins and monuments. Worth visiting is the fishing village of **Björkö**, 10 kilometres north of Vaasa.

If you've crossed the Swedish-Finnish border up north, the first town you'll come to is **Tornio**. It's an island, accessible only by bridges and a good town to meet people. Population 22,000. Try to get out to the salmon weir at **Kiviranta**.

Just a few kilometres below the Arctic Circle and 850 kilometres from Helsinki is the capital of Finnish Lapland. **Rovaniemi** was completely destroyed during the Second World War but has been rebuilt and is now three times as large, with 30,000 inhabitants. There are only a few thousand Lapps left in Lapland, but many of them work around Rovaniemi. Here you can learn about Lapp handcrafts and their nomadic lifestyle. If you're up there before or after summer when the snow is down, try the Pohtimolampi Sports and Excursion Centre (28 kilometres out plus a 3-kilometre walk) where they run the only reindeer-driving school in the world. For the midnight sun you have to go farther north. Try **Sodankylä**.

Beyond Rovaniemi is a strange wilderness of frozen lakes, rivers, and tundra plains – and very few people.

★**Language** *Minä rakastan sinua! Ymmärrätko? Minä rakastan sinua!* It doesn't matter how sincere you are, you won't get away with it. It means, 'I love you! Do you understand? I love you!' Try English or French, or even Swahili. It's easier. The language is of Finno-Ugrian origins, related to Hungarian and Estonian. (Wouldn't hurt to try *kiitos*, meaning thank you.)

★**Pori Jazz Festival** Second week in July at Pori, a coastal town in West Finland. Finnish and international names. Details from: Pori Jazz Festival, Mikonkatu 30, 28100 Pori 10.

★**Turku Music Festival**, 10–17 August, includes a whole spectrum of music – classical through rock and jazz. For further info on this or any other festival, write to Finland Festivals, Aleksanterinkatu 19, PB56, 00100 Helsinki 10.

★**Reindeer Joring** Exclusively a Lapland winter sport. You get in a *pulkka* – a one-seated chariot fitted with skis – have a quiet word with your power source, which is a frisky reindeer, hang on tight and wish yourself *bon voyage*.

★**Trips to Russia** See **The Communist countries**.

Helsinki: where to sleep

Helsinki just doesn't have hitchers at heart. The average year-round temperature of 5° C/41° F (minus °C/below 20° F most of the winter, though it averages around 21° C/70° F in July) makes it hard to sleep out and hotel prices are astronomical, with low-priced singles around 100 markkas. However, there are a few hostels and dormitories which offer singles around 50–80 markkas and those are listed below:

Youth Hostel Stadionin Maja at Pohj. Stadiontie 3B (tel: 496 071). Showers, self-service kitchen, or breakfast served. Between 25 and 45 markkas per person. Open all year.

Youth Hostel Satakuntatalo at Lapinrinne 1A (tel: 694 0311). Open 1 June to 31 August (ask for dormitory).

Youth Hostel Dipoli at Jämeräntaival 7, Espoo (tel: (90) 461 211). Open 1 June until 31 August.

The official room-finding service at Central Station is called *Hotellikeskus* (tel: 171 133). They attempt to find hotels or rooms in private houses at a price which fits your pocket.

For sleeping out (and God help you) try Hietaranta Beach, Sibelius Park or find a place in the parks around Olympia Stadium.

Camping Rastila, about 7 kilometres east of Helsinki (tel: 316 551). Open 15 May to 15 September. Camping fees around 18–45 markkas per person, per day. Cooking facilities, cafeteria, supermarket and sauna.

Helsinki: where to eat

With dinner in the student hostel costing the best part of 13 markkas you get the idea that it's best to head for the supermarket. (And even that's not cheap!) If you want to eat quickly and at a low cost you can find eating places called Baari, Grilli, Krouvi or Kahvila. Meal prices in the places listed below will come out between 20 and 30 markkas.

Carrols at Mannerheimintie 19, City Passage.

Go-Inn at Keskuskatu 6. Inexpensive, and quick service.

Hotelli Satakuntatalo at Lapinrinne 1A (tel: 694 0311). Open all the year. Lunch served between 11 a.m. and 2 p.m. and dinner from 5 p.m. to 8 p.m.

Helsinki: what to see and do

HELSINKI DESIGN CENTRE Kasarmikatu 19. Free. Displays the best in crafts and design in the country. Particularly interesting are the fabric designs.

ATENEUM ART GALLERY Kaivokatu 2. Fair collection of European masters, but fine collection of Finnish art from the last few centuries.

TAPIOLA GARDEN CITY This is one of the best designed living centres in Scandinavia. It shows you what suburbia can be like when someone puts his mind to creating a livable-in situation.

Much better than anything you'll see in England or America. Take a bus from the bus station, or walk – but it's nine kilometres from the centre of Helsinki.

SAUNA BATH The cheapest in town seems to be at the Olympia Stadium at Eläintarha. (Tram 3T or 3B from Central Station.) Costs about 15 markkas. Also a swimming pool at the stadium and in summer it's as good a place as any to meet people.

LINNANMÄKI Fun fair. Admission charge. Open May to mid-September. Get there on streetcars 7 or 8. For a little movement, try *Tivoli*, the discotheque in the middle of the park, open May through August. (Extra admission, but it may be worth it if you're looking for something.)

NATIONAL MUSEUM Mannerheimintie 34. It contains three sections. Prehistoric, historic, and ethnographic. It's also free on Tuesdays if you're looking for somewhere dry and warm.

Transport in Helsinki
The Helsinki bus and tram system is the way to get around. Cheapest way of doing it is to take advantage of the special offer of twenty-four hours of unlimited travel for less than 15 markkas. You can buy tickets aboard the vehicle. It'll pay off if you want to do a quick flash around the city.

A better deal, if you are interested in checking out Helsinki museums and sights, may be the *Helsinki Card*. It is available for one, two or three days. Prices, as we go to press, are 45, 60 and 70 markkas. No doubt it's more expensive by now. The card is available from the Helsinki Tourist Office.

Student discounts
Various museums, art collections, and theatres offer discounts to card holders. For full information check with:

FINNISH STUDENT TRAVEL SERVICE (FSTS), Travela Ltd at Mannerheimintie 5C, 00100 Helsinki 10 (tel: 90 624 101).

Addresses

Main post office (for poste restante) at Mannerheimintie 11, 00100 Helsinki 10.

American Express at TRAVEK Travel Bureau, Eteläranta 16, 00130 Helsinki 13 (tel: 171 900).

Finnish Student Travel Service (FSTS) at:
Kauppakatu 12, 40100 Jyräskylä 10 (tel: 941 17507).
Hallituskatu, 33, 90100 Oulu 10 (tel: 981 222 720).
Tuomiokirkonkatu 36, 33100 Tampere 10 (tel: 931 309 95).
Hämeenkatu 14, 20500 Turku 50 (tel: 921 335 815).

Helsinki City Tourist Office at Pohjoisesplanadi 19, 00100 Helsinki 10 (tel: 169 3757 and 174 088).

Finnish Travel Association at Mikonkatu 25, 00100 Helsinki 10 (tel: 170 868).

US Embassy at Itäinen Puistotie 14A, 00140 Helsinki 14 (tel: 171 931).

British Embassy at Uudenmaankatu 16–20, Helsinki 12 (tel: 647 922).

Hitchers' Tips and Comments...

If you're really hungry and down and out, go for the dried kippers which you can buy in supermarkets very cheaply. You can eat them straight away because they're precooked. Very nutritious.

If you want to spend a while in Lapland, walking around (the only real way to see it), buy a map or two in Rovaniemi to show you the many little country huts. Only the scale maps show them, but you need scale maps for walking anyway. The cost of the map is cancelled out by the fact it shows you where to get free accommodation and basic facilities, in return for which you are only asked to chop firewood and leave the place clean. If you've got good boots and gear you can have a real 'back to nature' trip inside the Arctic Circle.
Duncan S. Grey, Durham City, England

In-season fruit can be ridiculously cheap in Finland and Norway. You can fill yourself up for next to nothing.
Finnish forests abound with wild mushrooms and

toadstools. Many varieties make ultra-cheap and highly nutritious eating. *But take care – some are lethal! Check with the locals!*

Rural chain-stores like *Sokos* or *Osuuskauppa* in Finland (or *Slaget* in Norway), run a bargain of the week. The discount can be as much as 50 per cent. Keep your eyes open for some really good offers. *Adrian Park, Preston, England*

When in Helsinki, find out about the '3T' tram. It does a figure-of-eight about the city and the tourist office publishes a good guide that goes with the route. Rich types can actually take the tram, but the rest of us just walk the route. It's only five or six miles and takes in most sights. *Philip Attwool, Orpington, UK*

Re your ferry points. The difference in the Finnish language between a/ä is rather important! For example: Älä means 'don't', but ala means 'start'. Sälli means 'kid' and Salli is the woman's name 'Sally'. Näin is 'I saw', but Nain means 'I made love'.

By the way, there are two other ferry routes to Finland: from Travemünde (West Germany) to Helsinki (22 hours); from Gdansk (Poland) to Helsinki (36 hours).

Some tips: worth seeing and visiting are Åland Islands between Sweden and Finland. It is part of Finland, but everyone speaks Swedish there. The ferries during daytime go via Åland between Naantali – Kapellskär and Turku – Stockholm. It's cheap and the ferries are luxurious. *Finnish reader from Savonlinna.*

(Sorry mate, couldn't read your name. K.W.)

Cheap good meals can be obtained in the Helsinki University Hall. *K. M. Fitchet, Johannesburg, South Africa.*

Iceland

population	226,000
size	39,702 square miles
capital	Reykjavik, population 84,300
government	Republic
religion	Lutheran
language	Icelandic; English widely understood

currency   *Krona* One *krona* equals 100 *aurar*. Coins of 5, 10, 50
                  aurar, and 1, 5 *kronur*. Notes of 10, 50, 100, 500 *kronur*
                  (The old 100 *kronur* has been revalued to one new
                  krona. Be careful no one gives you old notes or coins)

Getting there can be expensive because of the distance. If you're
rich you can fly, but most people take the ferry to **Seydhisfjordhur**
from Scrabster, near Thurso, Scotland (about 800 kilometres) or
from Bergen, Norway (about 1000 kilometres). Both boats call at
Torshavn on the Faerøe Islands.

Alternatively, if you've got a cast-iron stomach, try hitching a
lift on an Icelandic fishing boat. Best ports to try are
Bremerhaven, Germany, or Grimsby, England. At Grimsby docks
ask at Danbrit, who are the agents for Icelandic vessels, if any
Icelandic boats are in port. While in the docks keep a close eye on
your stuff or it'll disappear. At the boat, chat up the watchman
who'll know if there's any chance of getting a ride. If so, it's
between you and the skipper. Things may be primitive aboard;
dirty, smelly, horrible food (the cook is the one who knows how to
boil water!) and the showers used to store nets. But the fishermen
are all good blokes. (Don't try to keep up with their drinking!) It
depends on the skipper as to whether you'll be asked to pay
towards your passage or work. Those boats that have sold their
catch in Europe will probably be heading straight home which
means there won't be much work to do anyway.

Anyone wanting to hitch home can try at either Grindavik or
Vestmannaeyjar, the two main Icelandic fishing ports. But be
warned that this could mean a six-week fishing trip in the Arctic
ocean with back-breaking work (like thirty-six hours at a stretch)
with maybe a storm thrown in. But as a deckhand you'd get a
percentage of the profits.

On arrival in Iceland you'll be confronted by immigration
officials who will insist that you have a return ticket to your
country of origin. If you don't have one, you'll be taken around to
the airline office to buy one. The ticket can usually be cashed in if
you decide to make other arrangements.

What to take

1 *Plenty of money*. Iceland is *very* expensive. Sweden is cheap by
comparison. You can get a slightly better rate of exchange by

changing money in a shop instead of in a bank. This way, you may also avoid the bank commission on cashing travellers' cheques.

2 *Warm clothing*. All the tourist blurbs say how warm it is in Iceland. What they mean is, it's warm for the latitude, which is just below the Arctic Circle. The weather is often wet and cold, particularly in the mountains. If there is a summer it will be in June–July, but even summer doesn't mean good weather. With luck you'll get so warm you have to take off one of your coats!

3 *A tent, and good sleeping-bag*. Because of costs, weather and the fact that you may be miles from civilization when night falls.

4 *Bottle of vodka*. Booze is extremely expensive, about four times the UK price. Icelanders like vodka. Scope here for good profit.

Where to sleep

Iceland has seven youth hostels, but two are so remote you can't reach them by hitching. Avoid hotels because of high prices, but do look for hotels which offer *svefnpokaplass*, which is a cheap deal (little more than a youth hostel) providing you bring your own sleeping-bag. The Edda Hotels, usually open only in summer, also sometimes offer *svefnpokaplass*. The Icelandic YHA distributes a leaflet listing these places, though it's sometimes out of date.

If you don't have a tent, you can sleep in farmers' barns. Most don't mind if you ask permission first, and guarantee not to smoke or use a stove (because of the hay).

In remote areas you find orange-coloured emergency huts for stranded travellers and shipwrecked sailors, complete with food, stove, fuel, bedding and radio transmitter. If you sleep in one of these places, *don't touch the supplies* unless you yourself are in a bad way, or you will be depriving someone else of his means of survival.

Where to eat

You will be on bread and cheese or cooking for yourself because restaurants are so expensive. Always carry plenty of food because it's often a couple of days hitching between villages. Shops close during the weekends so stock up on Fridays. If you want to eat out, try cafeterias, but even they are expensive.

Hitching

Hitching is pretty bad because the population is thinly spread and 40 per cent of Icelanders live in Reykjavik.

On the main road around the island the second car to come by will stop if the first didn't, but you may wait three hours for the *first* car. You do get long rides lasting all day, but more likely you'll get a ride ten kilometres to the next farm. On minor roads, just start walking and hope somebody decides to use that road that day.

You can't average much more than 50 kph in Iceland because apart from a stretch from Reykjavik to Selfoss, the roads are unmade and the track is often shared with a river bed, with plenty of ruts and boulders. Most vehicles are Land-Rovers or jeeps because ordinary cars can't take the bashing. Still, these conditions make Iceland interesting to hitch in.

What to see

In **Reykjavik**, don't miss the art galleries and museums, particularly the National Museum, which will give you an idea of Icelandic history, and the open-air Arbaer Folk Museum. At weekends the capital (and the whole island) is dead, so the citizens compensate by indulging in a certain amount of drinking. The deadliest drop is called *brennivin* (firewater) and you can consider yourself lucky if you can't afford it.

Thingvellir, 50 kilometres east of the capital, is where the Althing, the Icelandic parliament, was founded in AD 930. It's the oldest parliament in the world. Until 1800 the Althing met at the Logberg, where speakers stood on the clifftop to address the assembly below. See the Drowning Pool where adulteresses were thrown, and the Money Chasm where for decades idiots have thrown coins into the water. **Lake Thingvallavatn** is the largest in Iceland.

To the north is **Reykholt** where you can see steam springs. (Any place name with 'reyk' in it indicates that steam is present.)

In the north-west the **Vestfirdir Peninsula** boasts wild, untamed scenery, while at **Latrabjarg**, the most westerly point in Iceland, you can admire some of the highest cliffs in the world. Locals lower themselves on ropes down their faces to collect eggs. The northernmost part of Vestfirdir is uninhabited, the landscape untouched by man.

Akureyri, in the north, is Iceland's second largest town with 13,000 people. To the east is **Myvatn**, Iceland's fourth largest lake, famous for its volcanism, hot springs, boiling mud and weird rock formations that look so much like the moon that American astronauts were trained here. Careful where you put your feet because the mud is hot enough to cause severe scalds. Farther on is **Dettifoss**, Europe's highest waterfall, which is up a minor road and difficult to thumb to (a day's walk if you don't get a lift), but it's worth the trouble getting there.

In the south-east is **Vatnajokull**, Europe's largest glacier which takes up an eighth of Iceland. Immediately to the south is **Skaftafell National Park**, while south-west is **Hekla**, Iceland's most famous volcano, which last erupted in 1980.

Near **Lake Laugarvatn** is the original Geysir, now inactive. But nearby is another, called **Strokkur**, which spouts twice an hour. While in the area, try and see **Gullfoss Waterfall**.

The **Vestmann Islands** can be reached by ferry from the port of **Thorlakshofn**. The trip takes 3 hours. There is one inhabited island called **Heimaey**. Here stands the Vestmanns' only village, **Vestmannaeyjar**, which was partially destroyed in 1973 when a volcano erupted out of the ground at the edge of town. The new volcano is now about 600 feet high. It is still steaming and its rocks are hot to touch. If you climb to the crater, wear good boots as the cinders will cut shoes to pieces. Watch out for poisonous gas. You can't see it, but if you have trouble breathing, turn back. The neighbouring volcano is extinct and as it's the highest point on the island it affords a good view of the new island of **Surtsey** which rose from the sea during 1963–6.

★**Warning!** The interior of Iceland is pure wilderness and totally uninhabited. It's not advisable to go there unless you mount a full-scale expedition or join a (high-priced) tour which takes the proper equipment. If anything goes wrong you could be three days from the nearest telephone. If you plan a hike, leave details of your itinerary with the Tourist Office and report to them on your return so they know you're OK.

★**Warning!** Don't buy any more kronur than you need at the time. Most European banks won't touch them and even in Iceland itself you may have trouble converting them back to hard currency.

Addresses

Main post office (for poste restante) at Pósthusstraeti 5, Reykjavik.

American Express at Utsyn Tourist Agency, Austurstraeti 17, Reykjavik (tel: 26 611).

Tourist Information at Reykjanesbraut 6, Reykjavik (tel: 25 855).

US Embassy at Laufásvegur 21, Reykjavik (tel: 29 100).

British Embassy at Laufásvegur 49, Reykjavik (tel: 15 883 and 15 884).

Hitchers' Tips and Comments . . .

You failed to mention the beautiful scenery of the Snaeffels Peninsula and also the famous Snaeffels volcano, which was the starting point for Jules Verne's *Journey to the Centre of the Earth*. The volcano can be seen, on a clear day, from Reykjavik, even if you can't visit it. *Mark Naisbitt, Darlington, Durham, UK*

9 The Communist countries

Hitching in the Communist countries presents a whole lot of problems which many people would rather avoid. *To start with, you usually need visas to enter and with many of the countries that visa can be expensive, there being a basic rate to pay each day you remain in the country.*

Because of the hassle involved, it is advisable to check out visa requirements before you start on your trip, otherwise you might find yourself turned back from a border because you don't have the necessary documentation.

The last few years have seen travel restrictions in these areas eased considerably and the coming years will probably see things getting easier still.

To the best of my knowledge, no Communist country permits the import or export of their own currency.

★**Photography** Remember, in the Communist countries, to keep your camera pointed right away from military installations or anything which could be interpreted as such.

★**Drugs** If they catch you in the Communist countries it's goodbye world for a long, long time.

The following is a very brief rundown:

Albania

From a hitch-hiking point of view forget all about it. The Albanians aren't interested at this stage. If you want to pay a visit – and from all reports it's a fascinating place – you'll have to join up with a guided tour. Make inquiries at travel agencies.

Hitchers' Tips and Comments...

Anyone wanting to pay a visit to Albania should contact Regent Holidays (UK) Ltd, 13 Small Street, Bristol BS1 1DE (tel: 0272 211711) who are the sole accredited Albturist tour operators for the British Isles and the Commonwealth. It is not possible to go on your own. Even if it was permitted to hitch, things would be slow as the ownership of private cars is forbidden. Forget about any black-marketing here, there's no chance of selling anything to anyone. The locals are so unused to foreigners that they will stare at you in the street as if you were a man from Mars. When leaving, load up on cigarettes which are dead cheap. *Alan Barlow, Cheadle, UK*

Bulgaria

population	9,000,000
size	42,800 square miles
capital	Sofia, population 1,000,000
government	Socialist people's republic
religion	Eastern Orthodox mostly
language	Bulgarian; Russian widely spoken; some German; French and English understood
currency	*Lev* One *lev* equals 100 *stotinki*. Coins of 1, 2, 5, 10, 20, 50 *stotinki*, and of 1, 2, 5 *leva*. Notes of 1, 2, 5, 10, 20 *leva*

There's no problem entering Bulgaria. You don't need a visa if you are staying more than 30 hours and less than two months. If you're heading straight through the country in less than 30 hours you have to buy a transit visa. You can buy them at any Bulgarian embassy or consulate but they're no longer available at border crossing points.

Hitching is permitted in Bulgaria, but the authorities get uptight about people camping out. The law is that you only sack out in camping grounds (which are very cheap). If you do decide to sleep out, don't light a fire.

Important cities are **Plovdiv, Nessebur, Varna** and **Sofia**.

In five-thousand-year-old Sofia visit the Alexander Nevsky Cathedral and go down into the crypt to see the fabulous collection of old icons. Just as interesting, particularly if you're on your way to Turkey, are visits to some of Sofia's mosques. Try the Bouyuk Mosque. See also the great Archaeological Museum on Stamboliiski Boulevard with its incredible Vulchi Trun treasure.

Accommodation is expensive, so check with the tourist office for the latest on youth lodgings.

Addresses

Orbita, Bureau for International Youth Tourism at 76 Anton Ivanov Boulevard, Sofia.

State Tourist Information Office at 37 Dondukov Boulevard, Sofia.

US Embassy at 1 Alexander Stamboliiski Boulevard, Sofia (tel: 88 48 01).

British Embassy at 65–67 Boulevard Marshal Tolbukhin, Sofia (tel: 88 53 61).

Hitchers' Tips and Comments...

Be sure to get your passport stamped when you enter an eastern-bloc country. If you try and leave without an entry stamp you can really be up shit creek. *Jim Henderson, Regina, Canada*

The public transport is dead cheap – 2½ pence on Sofia's buses and trams, and about 1 pence per kilometre on the very clean trains. *Pete Fraser, Maggie Wilcock, Harlow, Essex, England*

Your information saying that no visa is required if you stay for less than two months only applies if your accommodation has been pre-booked and pre-paid.

Head gestures in Bulgaria are the reverse of ours – a nod means 'no', a headshake means 'yes'.

There are hard currency shops called *Corecom* – good, cheap places to pick up cigarettes to sell in Turkey. *Alan Barlow, Cheadle, UK*

Czechoslovakia

population	15,200,000
size	49,370 square miles
capital	Prague, population 1,400,000
government	Socialist federal republic
religion	Both Catholic and Protestant
language	There are two official languages: Czech (spoken in Bohemia and Moravia) and Slovak (spoken in Slovakia); younger people have all learnt Russian at school, though they may not like to speak it; German is widely spoken, more so the farther west you are, and especially among older people; English rarely understood
currency	*Koruna* 1 *koruna* equals 100 *paras*. Coins of 1, 2, 5, 10 *paras* and 1 *koruna*. Notes of 5, 10, 20, 50, 100, 500, 1000 *korunas*

To enter Czechoslovakia you must have a visa. The cost depends on your nationality. You don't have to obtain your visa in your country of origin. You can get it at any Czechoslovak embassy or consulate in any country, usually quite quickly. In London and Athens, for example, you normally get it while you wait. But remember, *you cannot get it at the Czechoslovak border*.

Unlike most countries, which have a set period for a tourist visa such as one or three months, Czechoslovakia gives you one for exactly the period you ask. So if you're not sure how long you want to stay, ask for the maximum time you're considering. The entry date you give doesn't matter as long as you enter within three months of the date the visa was issued. Once in the country, you are supposed to register with the police but if you stay in an hotel or camp, or book through Pragotur, they will do this for you.

All foreign tourists over the age of fifteen are obliged to exchange the minimum amount of hard currency into Czech money at the time of entering the country. You must change so much for every day of your visa. This cannot be changed back. (At the time of writing the amount was £8 per day, but check beforehand as the figure may change.) So, upon entering you must decide how long you want to stay. If it's for less time than stated on your visa, the visa will be shortened accordingly. It is possible to extend your visa while you are in the country.

Each year in July and August there are International Work Camps in Czechoslovakia. You work as an unpaid volunteer for two to three weeks, then stay for the rest of the month without the compulsory minimum currency exchange. You must apply through organizations in your home country. Write to CKM, Žitná 12, 1200 Prague 2, for details.

Where to sleep

Accommodation can be a hassle – everything is always full, including the youth hostels, many of which are only open in the peak of summer (even the hostels in Prague)! Hotels are expensive compared to other prices in Czechoslovakia because foreigners are charged a special tourist price. Prices vary according to grade (A, B or C) and locality. But the cheaper hotels are affordable, especially if there are two of you sharing. And you have to spend your money, anyway. If staying in hotels, expect to pay about half your daily exchange on accommodation. Beware of showers; if you have to pay extra for them they can cost a fortune. Much cheaper to take a shower in a railway station. CKM run some Junior Hotels which are much cheaper if you can ever find a vacancy. In Prague, Pragotur will find you a room in a private house for about the same price as an hotel.

Camping could be your best bet. You still pay an inflated price compared to the locals but it's much cheaper than hotels, and it's easier to find a camping spot than a room (though in Prague even the camps get full). There's a good atmosphere in the camps in summer with lots of Czechs and East Germans sitting around camp fires drinking and singing. Many camps also have bungalows for hire.

You are allowed to sleep in the open but you're not permitted to light a camp fire outside a camping ground. If you do, and get caught, you can be hit with a heavy fine. If you are not camping or sleeping out, try and book ahead, especially for Prague.

Where to eat

Eating out is cheap. Every eating place has a class (*skupina* I to IV). Cheapest are the class IVs which are usually stand-up buffets. At class III you can probably sit down and have waiter service. Class II is more like a Western restaurant but the prices aren't so high. Class I is expensive.

Prague eateries can get crowded. If you're not too fussy about what you want to eat, your best bet may be to go to one of the large buffets around Václavské náměstí and choose the shortest queue. And, if there are two of you, one can queue for the drinks while the other queues for the food!

A typical meal is soup (*polévky*) followed by pork (*vepřový*) with dumpling (*knedlík*) and Czech cabbage (like sauerkraut). And don't forget Czech beer – the best in the world and the cheapest drink you can buy. Česke Budějovice is the original home of Budvar (Budweiser) beer, and Plzeň of Pilsener beer.

Cukrárna (for cakes and sweets) tempt you wherever you turn and local ice cream (*zmrzlina*) is delicious.

Hitching

Hitching is tolerated throughout the country. But it's not all that easy due to the small size of the usually full cars. You'll make it easier for yourself if you hitch alone and with as small a pack as possible. Remember that you have to spend your £8 a day anyway, so don't hesitate to use the cheap public transport if the rides aren't forthcoming.

What to see

Czechoslovakia is a long, narrow country so it's best tackled in a lengthwise progression. You could enter from West Germany and visit **Karlovy Vary**, a popular spa town.

In **Prague** visit Hradčany Castle. From there you get a good view over the city. Architecture freaks will be particularly interested in the castle because it incorporates examples of just about every architectural style the city has ever known. Wander from here down across the beautiful Charles Bridge (*Karlov most*) and on through the old town to Old Town Square which is a good place to meet people. Have a look at the fabulous City Hall clock which gives a great, free clockwork show (what else!) on the hour. Walk on to the Jewish Quarter, where you can visit the cramped Jewish cemetery with graves layered on top of each other and see haunting reminders of the Nazi occupation in the drawings of children who were in the concentration camps.

Museums worth seeing include the National Gallery of Modern Art, the National Gallery, and the Museum of Asian, African and American Cultures.

The main attraction of **Brno**, the Moravian capital, is Špilberk Castle, with its notorious prison, used by the Hapsburgs and later by the Nazis. North of Brno is the **Moravian Karst** (Moravský Kras), a fascinating area of limestone caves. Ask for the information sheets in English which you can borrow at the entrance to each cave. From there head for **Slovakia**. The highlight for most people are the **High Tatras**, great mountains to walk in, though a bit crowded in peak summer, and you must keep to the marked tracks. Skiing in winter. South-west of the **Tatry** is the **Slovakian Paradise** (Slovenský Raj). You can walk through narrow limestone gorges and visit the **Dobšina** ice cave (no English translation available here). For all these areas of natural scenery good cheap tourist maps are available.

From Dobšina you can head north to Poland, east to the USSR, if you've managed to unravel the red tape, south to Hungary, or south-westwards to Austria via **Bratislava**, the Slovakian capital. Bratislava was once the Hungarian capital. It's not such an interesting city but worth a visit if you pass that way and want to splash out and use up your excess Czech currency. If you smuggle it out to Vienna, you'll only receive about a quarter of what you paid for it.

Addresses

CKM, Travel Bureau of the Czechoslovak Youth and Student Travel at Žitná 9 (tel: 29 85 89), and Jindřišská 28, Prague (tel: 26 85 07).

Čedok, State Tourist Office at Na Příkopě 18, Prague (tel: 22 42 51).

Čedok's Accommodation Service at Panská 5, Prague (tel: 22 70 04).

Pragotur at U Obecního domu 2, Prague (tel: 23 17 200).

Prague Information Office at Na Příkopě 20, Prague.

US Embassy at Trziste 15, Prague (tel: 53 66 41).

British Embassy at Thunovska 14, Prague 1 (tel: 53 33 47).

Hitchers' Tips and Comments...

Hitching in Czechoslovakia is OK, and for short distances usually faster than train or bus. The country is relatively cheap, but you are obliged to spend your daily exchange quota. I found youth hostels usually filled with school groups, so you must book in advance, whatever the IYH handbook says. You're allowed to camp in forests, but not in state parks. German is widely understood. Only some younger people speak English. *Ray Lampert, Calgary, Canada*

East Germany

It is possible to hitch from West Germany through the East to West Berlin but this must be done with one ride which you pick up at the border. Full details of this in the section on **West Germany**. My letters to the East Germans requesting information about their country and any regulations which may be in force about hitch-hiking were not answered. I don't think they like the idea.

Hitchers' Tips and Comments...

I find in most Communist countries you can only change back 50 per cent of the money you originally exchanged and only then with bank slips in hand to prove you changed the money in the first place. (Got that?) Best to change in small amounts so you don't get stuck with pockets full of East German marks, etc. *Jimmy Freedman, San Francisco, USA*

Hungary

population	10,700,000
size	35,900 square miles
capital	Budapest, population 2,000,000
government	Socialist people's republic
religion	Mostly Roman Catholic and Protestant

language   Hungarian; some German and English understood
                in tourist areas
currency   *Forint* One *forint* equals 100 *fillérs*. Coins of 10, 20,
                50 *fillérs*, and of 1, 2, 5, 10 and 20 *forints*. Notes of
                10, 20, 50, 100, 500, 1000 *forints*

Frontier formalities A visa is required except for nationals from
Austria, Finland and the socialist countries. A Hungarian tourist
visa is obtainable at road and air entry points or from the consular
sections of Hungarian embassies. No visas are issued on trains. It
is advisable to obtain a visa before arriving in Hungary, as there
may be delays of some hours before receiving the visa at the
border. Two photographs are needed with each visa application.

   Hitching is offically not permitted in Hungary, but there's plenty
of it and you'd be very unlucky to be stopped.

   Good places to visit are the **Lake Balaton** area, **Miskolc** and
Budapest.

   In Budapest see the Royal Castle, the ancient Church of
Matthias, the Fisherman's Bastion and the Gellert Hill Citadel.
Try the Museum of Fine Arts, the Hungarian National Museum
and the Hungarian Folkloric Centre. Consider, as you walk
around, that more than 30,000 buildings were wrecked in
Budapest during its vicious Second World War siege, and the work
which has gone into restoration.

   There are quite a few reasonably priced beds in the city. For
details check with the tourist office.

Addresses

Express Youth and Student Bureau, Szabadsag ter 16, 1051
Budapest V (tel: 317 777).

Tourist Office at Roosevelt ter 5, 1051 Budapest V (tel: 17 73 55).

TOURINFORM Information service by phone. Dial 17 9800.

US Embassy at V. Szabadsag ter 12, 1054 Budapest V (tel: 32 93
75).

British Embassy at Harmincad utcá 6, Budapest (tel: 18 28 88).

Hitchers' Tips and Comments...

I found hitching in Hungary OK, but if you get off the main roads take a train. They're cheap. But don't take an express. They're twice the price, half as interesting and only marginally faster. *Alan Thatcher, New Zealand*

If hostels and campsites are full at popular Hungarian destinations, you can try for accommodation in private houses. Some are registered with travel agencies, some simply have notices up outside the actual house. The rooms are reasonably priced. *József Böröcz, Budapest, Hungary*

The ISIC card is useful in Hungary where you can camp for around 50 pence a night each with the discount.

Budapest public transport must be the cheapest in Europe we reckon, with the metro only 1½ pence a ride, buses 2½ pence and trains 16 pence per 20 kilometres.

The pastry shops are as good as Austria's and one-sixth of the price. *Pete Fraser, Maggie Wilcock, Harlow, Essex, England*

Budapest's Keleti railway station is a good place to kip. It's clean and the police don't move you on until 4.30 a.m. *Mike Lowry, Edinburgh, Scotland*

If you come to Lake Balaton from Austria, don't hesitate to stop in Sopron. It's a town, not far from the border, with old, historic buildings, and good restaurants.

There's no compulsory exchange in Hungary and, if you keep the paper you get when you change your money, you can change it back to your own currency.

It's fairly difficult to find a student hostel in Budapest in summer. They are all overcrowded. But you can get a private room (through Express) for ten dollars a night. *A. Zale, Budapest, Hungary*

Poland

population 34,000,000
size 121,000 square miles

capital	Warsaw, population 1,450,000
government	Independent people's republic
religion	Roman Catholic
language	Polish; a little German and English understood
currency	*Zloty* One *zloty* equals 100 *groszy*. Coins of 5, 10, 20, 50 *groscy*, and of 1, 2, 5, 10, 20, 200 *zloty*. Notes of 20, 50, 100, 500, 1000 *zloty*

To enter Poland you need a valid passport and a tourist visa which costs around 300 zloty. If you're just passing through you have to buy a transit visa worth around 200 zloty which is valid for three days. To get the transit visa you have to show that you have any necessary entry visas for the neighbouring country. In addition you have to change £10 for each day of your stay in Poland. People who will be camping and can show that they belong to a camping club, and people with student cards, can change less. Write to the nearest Polish consulate or embassy for up-to-date info on visas and compulsory exchange.

As for hitch-hiking, it seems that the Poles are definitely on your side. The situation is best explained by Jerzy Gajewski from Krakow who sent in the following letter for the information of all hitchers who want to hit Poland:

'In Poland there are special hitch-hiking booklets with coupons to pay drivers. You buy them at the Polish Tourist Association shop for 40 zloty or in the sportsclubs or tourist offices. You go 2000 kilometres on the book and then buy a new one. The book is valid for one year.

When the holiday season is over the drivers send the coupons to Warsaw to the Auto-Stop Committee. Those who send the biggest numbers are awarded prizes. This idea was started 15 years ago and has proved a great success.' Jerzy adds: *'Right now I want to thank all the European drivers who took my friends and me in their cars.'*

Theoretically then, there'll be cars pranging into each other in their attempts to get to you first. Wouldn't you like to believe it . . .?

Important cities to visit are **Gdansk, Krakow** (the only major Polish city not destroyed in the Second World War) and, of course, **Warsaw**.

Warsaw was wrecked in the war, but you'd never know it as you wander around today. Many of the 'old' buildings you see have only been built since the war – based on the original plans which somehow survived the holocaust. See the lovely, restored streets of the Old Town, see the Historical Museum and National Museum. If you're a music buff you'll want to drop in on the Chopin Museum. Visit Castle Square and the Royal Castle. Have a look at the Heroes of the Warsaw Ghetto Movement – and contemplate what happened.

Even student accommodation is expensive in Warsaw. Get the latest info from student organizations and tourist offices.

Addresses

Polish Association of Youth Hostels at Chocimska 28, Warsaw.

Juventur, Youth Travel and Information, Jerozolimskie 32, Warsaw.

Almatur (Travel and Tourism Office of the Polish Students Association) at Ordynacka 9 and Krakowskie Przedmiescie 13, Warsaw.

Polish Tourist Association at Swietokrzyska 36, Warsaw.

US Embassy at Aleja Ujazdowskie 29–31, Warsaw (tel: 28 30 41).

British Embassy at Aleja Roz 1, Warsaw (tel: 28 10 01).

Hitchers' Tips and Comments . . .

As you can't hitch in East Germany, the cheapest way of getting from West Berlin to Poland is by taking a train to just over the Polish border. You should buy a return ticket to the West *in* the West because when you buy one in Poland you have to pay in western currency at an exorbitant exchange rate. (Internal journeys, to the border, can be paid in zloty.)

In Krakow see the marketplace, called Rynek Główny (Main Square). And don't miss the Wawel on its hill above the Vistula River. Up there you can see castles, churches, the tombs of the Polish kings and museums.

Tourist shops (called Pewex) sell goods for western currency. Good stuff, and very cheap.

Canteens, which are common in Polish cities, are highly recommended. You can have a hot, decent meal much cheaper than in a restaurant.

Hitching in Poland is great. Everybody does it: housewives, whole families, the lot. They don't put out a thumb, they just stand there, or wave at the cars. On the Warsaw to Krakow road there were about sixty people hitching, and in the 45 minutes we waited we saw one guy turn down five lifts! Not speaking Polish is a disadvantage in the rush to a car which stops, but we hitched a lift on a public bus with fare-paying passengers aboard. Poland is the place where all good hitchers go when they die!

The people are friendly and helpful, but keep away from the bureaucrats who spend hours filling in forms for everything and anything. *Jeff Hoyle and Mike Fullen, Bury, England*

Note *Several readers have written in to say that the Poles are interested in buying cheap pocket calculators. One guy claims he sold a calculator for 3000 zloty which cost only 30 DM in West Germany – 500 per cent profit! This year it's probably digital watches and electronic games. Anyone got any more hints along these lines? K.W.*

Romania

population	21,245,000
size	91,700 square miles
capital	Bucharest, population 1,700,000
government	Socialist people's republic
religion	Mainly Romanian Orthodox
language	Romanian, with English and French understood in tourist areas
currency	*Leu* One *leu* equals 100 *bani*. Coins of 5, 10, 15, 25 *bani*, and of 1, 3, 5 *lei*. Notes of 5, 10, 25, 50, 100 *lei*

Romania is easy to enter, but you must buy a tourist visa (check in London for current prices), and you must change £8 for each day you are in the country with a minimum of 3 days. Further, you cannot change back the money you have changed.

Hitching is permitted throughout the country, but the comment was added by the official I spoke with that: 'The population is not very familiar with this custom, so things might be a little slow.'

Important cities to visit are **Deva** (sample the brandy), **Brasov**, **Cluj** and **Bucharest**.

In Bucharest try to visit the Folk Art Museum and the Village Museum with its collection of genuine peasant houses which have been brought from all over the country and reconstructed. Stroll down the Calea Victoria, one of the main streets, for a taste of modern Bucharest, and for a more relaxed walk go into the marvellous Cismigiu Gardens where you'll have a good chance to meet up with students and other travellers.

Addresses

National Tourism Office at Boulevard Magheru 7, Bucharest.

BTTR Youth Tourist Office at Onesti 6–8, Bucharest.

American Embassy at Strade Tudor Argezhi 9, Bucharest (tel: 12 40 40).

British Embassy at Strade Jules Michelet 22–24, Bucharest (tel: 11 16 34).

Hitchers' Tips and Comments . . .

Hitching in Rumania is extremely hard and drivers who give lifts expect payment. Everyone I know who's been there says the same. Try the train. It's dead cheap. *Malcolm Clarke, London, UK*

It's foolish to change currency illegally in Iron Curtain countries because of police informers. But you *can* do it before you cross frontiers. A friend and I each exchanged £30 into Romanian lei at nearly three times the normal exchange rate at the Bureau de Change at Wien-Nord station, Vienna. We were still obliged to change the equivalent of $10 daily at the official rip-off rate and were careful to keep our Viennese lei concealed. With unofficially exchanged money only buy untraceable things, like food. *Charlie V., London, UK*

The Soviet Union

population	255,000,000
size	8,700,000 square miles
capital	Moscow
government	Union of socialist republics
religion	Officially atheist; varying degrees of toleration towards Russian Orthodox, Catholic, Protestant and Jewish congregations
language	Russian is the official and great unifying language, but there are more than 100 dialects used throughout the country; some English, German and French understood in larger cities
currency	*Rouble* One *rouble* equals 100 *kopecks*. Coins of 1, 2, 3, 5, 10, 15, 20, 50 *kopecks*, and 1 *rouble*. Notes of 1, 3, 5, 10, 25, 50, 100 *roubles*

Everyone I have ever met who has visited Russia has told me that the country is great and that the people are fantastic and that they want to go again. But when I've asked about the procedure for entering the country they've clammed up, not through lack of willingness to answer my question, but through pure confusion.

This is a quotation from a pamphlet issued by the Russian tourist organization, INTOURIST, which describes how people based in Britain get themselves a Russian tourist visa:

'Tourist, Transit and Business Visas are obtainable through travel agencies. Applications must be supported by:
1 a valid passport;
2 a completed visa application form.
Note: In Section 1 of the visa application form, the SURNAME should be underlined. In Section 6 ALL towns to be visited in the USSR should be entered together with dates of entry and exit, and purpose of journey.
3 three recent passport size photographs (approximately 1¾ × 1½ in or 4·5 × 4 cms) on a white background.

All documents and passport(s) must be submitted through the travel agency *not later than seven days* before date of entry into the USSR. In June, July, August and September, it is advisable to apply for visas as early as possible to avoid delay. *No charge is made for visas.*

If tourists wish, they may apply for a Soviet visa in person. In this case, in addition to the documents mentioned above, they should give the Soviet Consulate in London (5 Kensington Palace Gardens, London W8, tel: 229 3215/6, open Monday to Friday, 10 a.m. to 12.30 p.m.) a voucher from a travel agency with the number of INTOURIST (Moscow) confirmation on it.'

Got it? Right. Believing that some brave souls might still want to hitch-hike – presuming they think they can guarantee the dates of entry and exit to the towns they wish to visit – I wrote to INTOURIST asking if hitching was permitted in Russia. The answer didn't say yes or no, but went as follows: 'With reference to your letter . . . we would like to advise you that taking into consideration the distances in the USSR we do not encourage tourists to travel on a hitch-hiking basis.'

A later letter, which I wrote to INTOURIST asking about hitching, student hostels, etc., was answered like this: 'I am afraid that hitch-hiking is not permitted at all in the Soviet Union. Tourists must travel by air, rail or car. There are no hostels available to foreign tourists – they are accommodated in hotels, motels or camp sites. Camp sites are available to tourists travelling by car only, as they are often at some distance from railway stations, etc. There are no student concessions.'

An address to contact which may be able to offer you more hope than I can is:

SOVIET YOUTH TRAVEL BUREA (SPUTNIK), Chaussee Vorobyovskoe 15, Moscow, USSR.

For anyone thinging of making a quick jaunt into Russia from Finland (there are plenty of tours at a variety of prices), the following are a selection of addresses to contact:

FINNISH STUDENT TRAVEL SERVICE, Mannerheimintie 5C, 00100 Helsinki 10.

FINNISH TRAVEL ASSOCIATION, Mikonkatu 25, 00100 Helsinki 10.

FINLAND STEAMSHIP COMPANY, E. Ranta 8, Helsinki.

It's a pity that things are so difficult in Russia. It's the largest country in the world (more than twice the size of the USA) and has some fantastic cities and sites. Perhaps things will get easier soon.

Addresses (in case you make it)

Intourist Travel Office at 16 Marx Prospekt, Moscow.

US Embassy at Ulitsa Chaykovskovo 19–23, Moscow (tel: 252 24 51).

British Embassy at Naberezhnaya Morisa Toreza 14, Moscow (tel: 231 95 55).

Hitchers' Tips and Comments...

Excellent black market in Russia. Hard currency can be exchanged at four times the official rate, but you must spend it before leaving the country. They'll take anything – even Australian dollars. I also sold a brand-new pair of Levis for the equivalent of $200. Russian kids love printed T-shirts too. *Bob Sutherland, Christchurch, New Zealand*
    I keep saying it, but here I go again. Be ultra-careful in any black-market dealings. It can be a dangerous occupation. K.W.

Yugoslavia

population	22,000,000
size	98,766 square miles
capital	Belgrade, population 1,200,000
government	Socialist federal republic
religion	Greek Orthodox, Moslem, Catholic, Protestant
language	Serbo-Croat most widely used; some German and English understood
currency	*Dinar* One *dinar* equals 100 *paras*. Coins of 5, 10, 20, 25, 50 *paras*, and of 1, 2, 5, 10 *dinars*. Notes of 10, 20, 50, 100, 500, 1000 *dinars*

No trouble entering Yugoslavia. If you are travelling on a passport from a European country, you no longer need a visa. For anyone from outside Europe, a valid passport gets you a visa at your point of entry which will do you for 30 days. Check that things haven't changed before you head out.

Hitching is permitted and an accepted mode of transport amongst young Yugoslavs. Things get awfully tough, though, when you get into the outback mountainous country. Officially you are only supposed to camp in camp grounds, but you'd be unlucky to get picked up. If you do camp out, best not light a fire.

The most important cities and towns outside of **Belgrade** are **Zagreb, Sarajevo, Ljubljana, Skopje, Split, Mostar** and **Dubrovnik**.

In Belgrade just wander around and enjoy what I think is one of the better planned city centres in Europe. Visit the gardens and fortifications of Kalemegdan and see the confluence of the Sava and Danube rivers from high up in the park. While you're up there have a look at the dramatically presented War Museum which tells the history of Yugoslavia through its centuries of invasion and battle. See also the cathedral with its icons, the National Museum, and the Fresco Gallery with its fine collection of frescoes taken from ancient monasteries. In the evening wander down the street called Skadarlija, centre of what was once the old Bohemian part of Belgrade. It's a nice place to spend an hour and a good place to meet people, but be warned that restaurant prices there can be high.

Nearly all Yugoslav cities have youth hostels; and it's worth knowing that you can arrange accommodation in private homes.

Student ID card holders can get reductions on museum entry fees.

Addresses

Naromtravel (for youth travel) at Moše Pijade 12, 11000 Belgrade (tel: 339 030).

Tourist Information Office at main railway station or in the Terazije Street pedestrian underground passage.

US Embassy at Kneza Milosa 50, Belgrade (tel: 64 56 55).

British Embassy at Ulica Generala Zdanova 46, Belgrade (tel: 64 50 55).

Hitchers' Tips and Comments...

With reference to the Yugoslav coast route. I suggest people *don't* take it unless they have stacks of time. It's really fantastic scenery, especially towards the south, but it took me *three weeks* of hell-for-leather hitching. (I left a stack of leather behind, especially on the 69-km Senj to Karlobag stretch. I walked the whole way without a lift. My shoulder strap gave out and I had to use my tension strap as a replacement. Now my hip bones are a couple of centimetres narrower.) I'm not unique. I've heard similar reports from other travellers. *M. Pickersgill, South Africa*

It is illegal for Yugoslavs to pick up hitch-hikers. I was told this by several Yugoslavs.
 It is also illegal to take more than 1500 dinars out of Yugoslavia. *A Chaplin, Hatfield, Herts, UK*

If you have a portable stove, purchase your propane gas outside Yugoslavia as they don't sell it there. *Kate MacDonald, Aberdeen, Scotland*

Don't try kipping at the station in Belgrade. It closes from midnight – 3 a.m. for cleaning and you get no warning until they turn on the hoses. *Eric the Hippo, London, England*

Don't change too much money at once as they won't change it back, despite what it says on the exchange receipt.
 Coffee is the hottest black market item in Yugoslavia. In October 1983, a kilo could be sold for 1600 dinars, four times the price in Austria. The government forbids the import of coffee to save foreign exchange. *Alan Barlow, Cheadle, UK*

10 Morocco and North Africa

Morocco

population	17,300,000
size	174,471 square miles
capital	Rabat, population 360,000
government	Constitutional monarchy
religion	Moslem
language	Arabic; Spanish and French also official languages; some English and German spoken in tourist centres
currency	*Dirham* One *dirham* equals 100 *francs*. Coins of 5, 10, 20, 50 *francs*, and of 1, 5 *dirhams*. Notes of 5, 10, 50, 100 *dirhams*

Cheapest way to Africa is from Algeciras, in Spain, to Ceuta, which is the tiny Spanish colony just across from Gibraltar. The Algeciras–Tangier ferry is more expensive.

Tetouan, just a few kilometres from Ceuta, is becoming a favourite stopping place for hitchers on their way south. At the moment it's not particularly tourist-minded and is a good place to enjoy your first glimpse of a Moroccan city. Plenty of mosques, a fairly good market section, and OK people.

Tangier, 72 kilometres away, is an out-and-out tourist town and every Arab in it is chasing the fast buck. Nevertheless it's worth a day and if you go down into the *medina*, go to the Petit Socco (the small square) where you can sit in the cafés and talk with Arab students and other hitchers.

Ketema, up in the Rif Mountains, is promoted by the Moroccan tourist office as the ideal area for nature-lovers. So it is. But it's also where a great proportion of Morocco's grass is grown. To anybody thinking of buying a kilo, this book warns you strongly about the dangers of exporting the stuff. The Spanish officials at Algeciras do spot-checks on every boatload of tourists arriving. They do a lot of their checking on hitch-hikers. The ones they catch out get locked away for a few years.

Fez is an indispensable stop. One of the four imperial cities – the other three are Marrakesh, Rabat, and Meknes – it is actually three cities in one. The old city, Fes El Bali, is the one to head for. Here is one of the best market areas you'll find anywhere in the world; a tiny winding street some three kilometres long which probably hasn't changed much since the city was founded in AD 808. Scores of side streets lead off it creating such a maze that you can get lost by turning two corners. Deep in the *medina* you'll see people working at trades with implements as old as time; men hand-beating copper pots, sewing fine embroidery to kaftans, turning wood on string lathes worked with the toes, workers splattered with dazzling colours from the dye pots. Lots to see. Don't miss Fez!

Meknes, 60 kilometres west of Fez, although interesting, is a let-down. After Fez anywhere with the exception of Marrakesh is an anti-climax. But just north of the city are the ruins of the old Roman town of **Volubilis**.

Rabat is the capital of Morocco and has a fair amount to offer the wanderer. Linked by a bridge over the Bou Regreg to its sister city of **Sale** (once a pirate port), it has a good market area. See also the famous Tower of Hassan which was to have been part of the largest mosque in Islam, but was never finished, and the Mechouar, the Royal Palace.

Casablanca, like staid old Tangier, is no longer as rough as it was in the 1930s and 1940s when they made the great Humph Bogart movie. Nowadays it's a big bustling modern city and the main commercial centre in Morocco. But the old *medina* area is still intact and a delight to wander through.

Ask most people which is their favourite city in Morocco and you'll find it's a toss-up between Fez and **Marrakesh**. Marrakesh, called the 'pink city' because of the light which reflects from its ochre walls, has one great attraction which keeps visitors amused day after day and which has kept the Arabs amused for centuries. It's Djemma el Fna – the Place of the Dead – the great marketplace which in the morning handles most of the city's trading and where in the late afternoon jugglers, acrobats, snakecharmers, and storytellers come to entertain the crowds. See also the Koutoubia Mosque, with its 221-foot-high minaret and, just north of Djemma el Fna, the *medina* area which is nearly as good as the one in Fez.

Goulimime, way, way down south of Marrakesh, is where you see the famous Blue Men – desert nomads who have permanently blue-stained skin as a result of dye running from the robes they wear.

Beyond Goulimime, the roads get very rough and if you're hitching on for any great distance (and the distances between towns can be very great) try to get aboard a truck. They go longer.

Hitching in Morocco is OK – particularly if you're a man and woman travelling together. The Arabs – a happy easy-to-get-on-with bunch at any time – are very much taken by Western ladies, especially if they have long blonde hair.

For people who want to head east across towards Egypt, the coastal road is good most of the way, though you'll probably have trouble entering Algeria and Libya. Check on formalities *before* you try the trip.

Warning! As we go to press, there's a shooting war in southern Morocco. Take care!

★**Haggling** It can't be stressed too much that a price asked in Morocco is merely a manner of beginning a discussion as to the true value of the object. That goes for beds too. In the souks (the markets) the general rule for bargaining is to offer slightly less than one half of what the seller is asking and then act like crazy until you've agreed to pay slightly over half, and even then that will be too much. If you don't get a 30–40 per cent reduction, you can be sure that you're *really* being done! One of the best haggling techniques is to enter a shop in league with someone else. One of you expresses interest in the article, the other is non-committal. As the bargaining progresses, the non-committal one becomes more and more bored, insisting it's time to go. At crucial moments during the bargaining the one who's doing the buying pretends that he has to go to keep his friend happy. This act, if well performed, gets the price down with a speed which is in exact proportion to the amount of concern felt by the seller that he may lose his sale altogether.

Morocco: where to sleep

Sleeping in Morocco presents no problems. In many cities you can have a really good bed with room service and the works for 30 dirhams. Cheap and dirty places, of which there are plenty, rarely charge more than 10 dirhams – and even this is an arguable matter. I have heard of beds going for 5 dirhams – but they're not for me. I've stayed in plenty of 10-dirham hotels and, although sometimes they're fine, mostly they stink. Out on the roads, in the smaller towns like Ouezanne and Tetouan, you can find clean, first-class accommodation for 25 dirhams a head, while in the same places the cheap accommodation is *really* cheap! Prices in Marrakesh and Fez are going up as fast as tourists begin to discover Morocco and to counter this about the only hint that can be offered is to keep away from the tourist areas of the *casbahs* because hotels there are quite often *more* expensive than in European quarters.

Morocco: where to eat

How cheaply you can eat depends upon how strong your stomach is. Eat in the *casbah* where it is cheaper, of course, but you should take a little care in choosing your café. Go into something which doesn't look *too* filthy. Plenty of guys you meet in Morocco will tell you that *they're* never sick, but they might neglect to say that they've been living there for six months and that their stomachs are used to whatever it is stomachs get used to. Odds are that whatever you eat you're going to get a touch of diarrhoea, especially if you have a pampered American or English belly. Moroccan hygiene and European hygiene are two different things.

Prices are cheap. 15–20 dirhams should get you a good plateful of couscous with bread and a coke to wash it down. Out on the streets the little shishkebab braziers sell one or two kebabs with bread for a few dirhams. If you're really broke, buy a couple of those and get yourself some fruit from the market and you can eat for around 6 dirhams.

In the big cities the water is generally OK to drink, but out on the road, in the small villages, you can't be too sure.

Transport in Morocco

In Moroccan cities. don't worry about jumping a bus! They're cheap! If you decide to take inter-city transport, buses are cheaper than trains, but as with everything else in Morocco it's hard to establish the correct price. I once checked around Tangier to find how much a bus ticket was to Fez. I asked at three different places; the tourist office, the bus station, and at the bus itself. Each price quoted was different. I ended up hitching. If you do take a bus, try to get one of the 'peasant' buses. They're loaded with chickens, goats, and God-knows-what – and the Arabs are great travelling companions!

Addresses

Main post office (for poste restante) at Poste Principale, Rabat.

American Express, 26 Boulevard Mohammed El Hansali, Casablanca (tel: 636 61). 10 Avenue du Prince Moulay Abdallah, Tangier (tel: 382 46). 173 Avenue Mohammad V, Marrakesh (tel: 302 83).

Student Union of Morocco at 55 rue Zayanes, Agdal, Rabat.

Morocco Tourist Agency at 22 Avenue d'Alger, PO Box 19, Rabat (tel: 21252/53/54).

US Embassy at 2 Avenue de Marrakesh, Rabat (tel: 622 65).

British Embassy at 28 bis Avenue Allah Ben Abdallah, Rabat (tel: 314 03).

Because of tense political situations in some parts of North Africa, particularly Libya, it is advisable to be well informed before you enter those areas. Also, in Egypt, Algeria, and Libya, don't even pretend to point your camera at anything which looks vaguely military.

Hitchers' Tips and Comments ...

Take an extra watch or two if you're heading for Morocco, especially the very cheap but flashy kind you can pick up in the UK. It's a good investment. Just walk around with the watch you want to sell on your wrist. Eventually you'll be approached by a buyer who, after a lot of haggling, will give you double what you paid.

Watch out for thieves in Morocco. Once a Moroccan's set his sights on your wallet or something, he'll sit up all night, if need be, to pinch it. Lots of tales of people having sleeping-bags delicately cut open during the night and all possessions taken from inside. It's a way of life. *Clive Gill, Birchington, England*

Unless you look like an Arab I reckon you ought to stay out of Tangier. Hustler hassles are getting to be a real problem. But Fez is recommended to everyone. In fact, anywhere south is OK. Once away from tourist areas the Arabs are really nice and not out to screw you. *John Otis, Mankato, Minnesota, USA*

Fez is a hassle these days, too. But you've still got to see the place. K.W.

I was the victim of a rip-off in Casablanca and I want to warn all hitchers. A Moroccan kid approached me with 800 French francs, spun some story about not being able to change them at a bank because he didn't have a passport, and asked me to change them for him. To keep it short, I fell for it, and cashed about £90 in travellers cheques to meet the required amount of dirhams. I gave him the dirhams and then watched closely as he counted my 800 francs into my hand – seven one hundred franc notes and two fifties. Without any thanks he then pissed off. A few minutes later, in a café, I checked the francs. You've guessed! The two 50 franc notes were there OK, but the other seven notes were worthless rubbish from some Central African country, valued at about a quid each. The bastard did me out of £75! It didn't make me feel any better to learn that plenty of travellers who think they're doing someone a favour are being ripped off in the same way. Take care, folks! *J.L.T. (too embarrassed to give my name), UK*

Watch those friendly 'guides' in Morocco. A lot of them are professional pickpockets. *Rick Toohey, Atlanta, USA*

There is a great deal of traffic crossing the Sahara. Be sure to get lifts in vehicles with lots of passengers (more people to dig and push when you get stuck in the sand). *Barry Simmonds, Blackpool, UK*

Algeria

population	16,776,000
size	919,590 square miles
capital	Algiers, population 950,000
government	Independent republic under one-party military presidency
religion	Moslem
language	Arabic, with French widely spoken
currency	*Dinar* One *dinar* equals 100 *centimes*

Algiers is the capital of the country. See the old *casbah* area, the Mosque of Sidi Abd er Rahmane, the National Museum of Fine Arts with its collection of works by Arab artists, and the Moslem cemetery of the Marabout.

Anyone feeling like a 2000-kilometre trip into the desert might like to head to **Tamanrasset** which is due south of Algiers and the capital of the Tuareg nomads. For just a whiff of the sand and of an oasis town, try **Laghouat**, 416 kilometres south of Algiers and on fairly good roads all the way.

Constantine is probably the most striking city in Algeria – it's surrounded by a 500-foot-deep gorge. See the 600-foot-high Sidi M'Cid suspension bridge, one of the highest in the world, and the Palace of El Hadj Ahmed. Go into the Place de la Brèche in the centre of the city.

Addresses

US Embassy at Villa Mektoub, 4 Chemin Cheikh Bachir Brahimi, Algiers (tel: 60 14 15 through 29 or 60 36 70 through 72).

British Embassy at Residence Cassiopée, Bâtiment B, 7 Chemin des Glycines, Algiers (tel: 60 56 01).

Hitchers' Tips and Comments...

Pickpockets in Algeria are after passports. They sell them to forgers who then tailor them to the needs of would-be illegal immigrants. The pickpockets work in teams of three or four, often at crowded bus stations. Be *particularly careful* when getting on buses. Money belts are the only answer, and even they mightn't stop these bastards. *George Turner, Huddersfield, UK*

Tourists (except students) now *must* change 1000 dinar when entering Algeria, and at inflated official rates. *Rick Toohey, Atlanta, USA*
    I haven't been to North Africa (except Morocco) in some time, so can't attest to what's happening at borders re visas, compulsory money changing etc. Can't get much sense out of tourist offices either. Most don't even bother to answer my queries. But I can tell you this: hitchers' letters are contradictory. Someone will write in with a piece of info and then another letter will arrive dated two months later with a completely different description of what's going on. All you can do is find the latest information before leaving your base, and then update with other hitchers as you near your destination. The bureaucratic bullshit puzzle applies not only to North Africa, but also to Middle Eastern and Communist Bloc countries. K.W.

I found hitching good in Algeria. In the south you can get long lifts due to the great distances between main towns. Best lifts are on the trans-Saharan trucks. I managed to make it to Tamanrasset. At the service stations there, in the early morning or late afternoon, you can sometimes get a lift down to Niger, or even to the coast. Once you head inland in Algeria it is *important* that you carry at least two litres of water in a refillable container! *Simon Lingley, Uppingham, UK*

Tunisia

population	5,772,000
size	63,380 square miles
capital	Tunis, population 800,000
government	Independent state under one-party presidential regime
religion	Moslem
language	Arabic, with French widely spoken

currency   *Dinar* One *dinar* equals 1000 *millimes*. Coins of 1, 2,
                  5, 10, 20, 50, 100 *millimes*, and of ½, 1 *dinar*. Notes
                  of ½, 1, 5, 10, 20 *dinars*

There are ferry connections from Naples to Tunis at about £60 for
a single third-class fare and from Palermo to Tunis at about £50 for
a single third-class fare. Also from Marseilles for about £55. Ferry
bookings *out* of Tunisia can be very heavy. Try and book passage
back to Europe well in advance.

   Tunis, the capital, is a city of 800,000. Visit any of the old areas
for the real thing – though the tourists are ruining the place now.
Visit the Zeitouna Mosque and the Palace of Dar el Bey. For
historians, just a few kilometres from the centre of Tunis are the
ruins of **Carthage** which was defeated and destroyed by the
Romans in 146 BC.

   Sousse is fast becoming a tourist town, but is attractive
nevertheless. See the catacombs where 15,000 second- and
third-century Christians are buried. A few kilometres south is the
fortified town of **Monastir** with its renovated Ribat fortress, while
south again at **El Djem**, sitting alone on a plain, is the Colosseum
of El Djem, the largest Roman building in North Africa.

   Djerba is Homer's 'island of the lotus-eaters'. At the beautiful
capital of **Houmt Souk**, you can see sponge-divers plunging 50 feet
deep, using rock ballast.

   Kairouan, 60 kilometres inland from Sousse, is known as the
'mother of cities' and 'Kairouan the holy' for it is the sacred city of
Tunisia and amongst its 89 mosques is the Great Mosque of Sidi
Okba, the fourth most important in all of Islam. See also the Bir
Barouta Well, the waters of which are said to meet and mingle
with the waters of the holy well of Zemzem in Mecca, and the
souks, especially those of the carpet-makers.

   In **Dougga**, set in wild moorland to the west of Kairouan,
wander through ruins of almost complete Greek and Roman
towns.

   At **Matmata**, on the edge of the Sahara, three-quarters of the
9000 population live in caves. Locals are delighted to show you
through their troglodyte homes.

Addresses

US Embassy at 144 Avenue de la Liberté, Tunis (tel: 282 566 or 282 549 or 258 559).

British Embassy at 5 Place de la Victoire, Tunis (tel: 245 100).

★A cheap way of getting around is to share seats in a *louage*. This is a sort of long-distance taxi that can be flagged down like a bus as long as there's a spare seat going. They go all over the country and each town and village has its main *louage* stop. Passengers share costs. (Similar to the *dolmus* in Istanbul.)

Hitchers' Tips and Comments . . .

The *medina* in Tunis very touristy and it's getting harder to find bargains. Watch out for the following rip-off: you haggle with a dealer for something you like and agree on a price; then he produces a similar item and wraps it, saying (if you catch him at it) that the one you saw is a slightly damaged display item; later you find you've been given an inferior item.

Note that it's very easy to sell watches, blue jeans, etc., to the local boys.

Hitching is pretty good in Tunisia. Some drivers demand money for lifts but most don't, so there's never any need to pay. *Hugh Dunne, Dublin, Ireland*

Libya

population	2,444,000
size	697,358 square miles
capital	Tripoli (population 400,000) and Benghazi (population 250,000) are co-capitals
government	Proclaimed as the Libyan Arab Republic
religion	Moslem
language	Arabic; Italian widely understood

currency   *Dinar* One *dinar* equals 1000 *dirhams*

Libya is hard to enter. To even attempt to get a visa, you must have your passport translated into Arabic, a smallpox vaccination certificate and two passport photographs. Visas are not, repeat not, issued at the border. Full details from Libyan embassies or consulates.

Tripoli ('the shores of Tripoli' is relevant to the US Marines' action against the Libyan pirates) is a city of 400,000 people. Several good mosques to see, several interesting museums, plus the Arch of Marcus Aurelius which dates from AD 163. See the castle and the market of Suk-el-Mushir.

Close by (90 kilometres east along the coast road) you come to the ancient Roman city of **Leptis Magna**, one of the least-visited but best-preserved Roman cities in existence.

About 300 kilometres inland, through a stark desert landscape, you come to the oasis city of **Ghadames**, which sits right at the point where the territories of Tunisia, Algeria, and Libya converge. This is a Tuareg city, focal point of desert caravans, and one of the most fascinating in Africa. Strongly recommended to anyone searching for *real* Arab flavour.

As a startling contrast, **Benghazi**, which was savagely mauled in the Second World War, is a city of wide streets and with a completely modern aspect. Any students of the military (are there any left?) might like to visit the battlefields in the area surrounding the city or drop in on **Tobruk**, near the Egyptian border, which was the scene of a siege and terrible fighting during the desert war. In Benghazi itself, however, you can see the Royal Palace and the cathedral and search out shops which sell the famous Benghazi rugs.

Addresses

US Embassy at Garden City, Shari 'al Nsr, Tripoli (tel: 34 021 or 320 26). (American hitchers take note: as we go to press the US Embassy is closed.)

British Embassy at Sharia Gamal Abdul Nasser 30, Tripoli (tel: 31 191). (The British Embassy is closed at this moment, too!)

Egypt

population	37,233,000
size	386,660 square miles (including Sinai Peninsula)
capital	Cairo, population 4,500,000
government	Independent state under one-party presidential regime
religion	Moslem
language	Arabic, with English widely understood
currency	*Egyptian pound* One *pound* equals 100 *piastres*

You must buy a visa before you enter Egypt. Full details from Egyptian embassies or consulates.

Cairo is the big focal point of any Egyptian trip. This city of nearly 5,000,000 was founded in the tenth century but **Giza**, just a few kilometres out, is considerably older and the site of the famed Pyramids and the Sphinx. The Pyramid of Cheops is the largest of the three at Giza, standing 446 feet tall and having a base of 740 feet on each side. It covers 12 acres and contains more than 2 million blocks of stone, each weighing around 2½ tons. Visit the Tomb of Cheops, right in the centre of the mammoth. The Sphinx, near the Pyramids, was built at about the same time – 2700 BC. See, in Cairo itself, the Alabaster Mosque which has one of the most startling interiors you'll find in any religious building anywhere. Also in the Citadel area you can see the City of the Dead, a cemetery built like a miniature town. The Egyptian Antiquities Museum has the best collection of its type in the world, including the fantastic treasure removed from the tomb of Tutankhamun.

Alexandria, which was founded in 331 BC by Alexander the Great, was once the centre of both Greek and Egyptian culture. These days it's a busy port city. See Pompey's Pillar, the catacombs of Kom Al-Shoqafa (only rediscovered seventy-five years ago), the Greco-Roman Museum and the Ras-at-Tin Palace. West of Alexandria are the battlefields of **Alamein**, and east, **Rashid**, where the famous Rosetta Stone which gave scholars the clue to translating hieroglyphics was discovered in 1799.

The **Nile** trip is one of the most exciting you can undertake. There is plenty of traffic all the way down to **Luxor** and there's also the possibility of hitching rides on river transport. In and around Luxor, a town of 5000 people near the site of ancient **Thebes**, you can see a fantastic collection of buildings dating back to 1500 BC, many of them still in first-class condition even down to the paint on their walls. See the Valley of the Kings and the Valley of the Queens, the Karnak Temples, the Temple of Luxor, the Tombs of the Nobles, and the Funerary Temples of the Kings.

The beautiful *Abu Simbel Temple*, which was built by Rameses II 3000 years ago, is situated 256 kilometres south of **Aswan** which is 240 kilometres south of Luxor. The 400,000-ton temple has been cut into sections and relocated 200 feet up a mountainside to save it from being submerged in the Nile as a result of dam works. The area can only be reached by plane or boat. The return boat trip takes four days. Take your own food.

Addresses

US Embassy at Sharia Latin America 5, Cairo (tel: 28 219).

British Consulate at Ahmed Raghal Street, Garden City, Cairo (tel: 20 850).

Hitchers' Tips and Comments ...

I've just returned from a hitching trip in Egypt. Here's a few hints which might help fellow hitchers.

Hitching down the Nile is an unforgettable experience, but about two-thirds of all cars are registered as taxis – identifiable from the front by their yellow and orange licence plates. I got plenty of rides with private car owners, but many expected *baksheesh* for the service. You can feign incomprehension and walk off, or cough up the usually small sum they ask for. If you decide to pay you can decide if you're being had by remembering that the per capita income is around $500 per year (against about $5500 in the UK). (If you get fed up with the endless demands for money, just take the train, which is unbelievably cheap.)

The most pleasant way to visit the Valley of the Kings is not on an exorbitantly overpriced coach tour, nor by renting a bike (the area is like a furnace all year round), but by hiring a

donkey and a guide. To do this just go to the ferry that takes
you across the Nile and look like a tourist. The donkey-men
will pick you up quick enough. Bargain furiously and make
sure there are no hidden extras.

Water-purification tablets are an absolute must in Egypt.
Outside large towns the water usually comes straight from
the Nile. Nile waters are supposed to have life-giving
properties, but the stuff is lethal! [*Stick to bottled water
everywhere in Egypt, even in the cities. K.W.*]

Re currency, there's a rule that you must exchange a certain
amount of money every day you spend in Egypt, but it seems
to be a random amount depending on whether officials like
the look of your face. I found only two places where one could
exchange piastres back to foreign currency: Cairo airport (but
only if you have receipts to prove you changed it in the first
place); or on the black market at a loss of ten per cent.

To enter Egypt from Israel, first check that the border is
open! As a rough guide, it's supposed to be open from 8 or 9
a.m. to 6 p.m. Monday through Thursday, and 9 a.m. till noon
on Fridays. But there are religious holidays and other events
which can leave you kicking your heels by the border for
thirty-six hours or more. [*These times could change from
month to month. As Philip suggests, check before you get
there. K.W.*] Once you do get by the barbed wire allow three
hours for the processes of Israeli bureaucracy to take their
sluggish course.

This is *very* important: if you go to Israel and you want to
visit another Arab country (apart from Egypt) you should ask
the Israelis *not* to stamp your passport with an Israeli visa!
Philip Goddard, Cambridge, England

When entering Egypt from Israel, there's a wide
no-man's-land between the two borders which is crossed by
a special bus, so you have to hold back some Israeli money to
pay the fare or try your luck bribing the driver with cigarettes.
Keep your cool at all times on the Egyptian border. They try
and railroad you into changing $150 at very unfavourable
rates. Say you are only staying a few days and sometimes
you can get away with changing $100 or less. I saw one guy
talk his way through without paying anything by insisting he
was catching a boat from Alexandria the next day.

If you're taking a taxi to Cairo ignore the people who first approach you. There's a proper taxi stand where you can buy a ticket for around 6 pounds. Ignore any further demands from the driver for money. Pick a driver who doesn't look stoned. A burst tyre or two on the way is routine.

Egyptians will go to extraordinary lengths to get hold of your cash. Remember, a few quid to us is a week's wages for them. Never flash your money. Keep most of it hidden and only have a few pounds in your wallet.

It's OK to exchange your foreign currency in big shops in Cairo – they all offer about the same rate – but be careful you don't get ripped off.

When visiting the pyramids it's worth staying for the sound and light show in the evening – but make sure you go on a day when it's in English.

If you have a student card you get 50 per cent off train fares. Because of heavy bookings it's nearly always worth buying your ticket a few days before you wish to travel.

If you're going from Cairo to Luxor or Aswan it's a long journey and worth travelling '2nd class air-conditioned'. There's a big difference between plain 2nd class and 2nd class air-conditioned. I travelled 2nd class from Aswan to Cairo. The windows didn't shut, lights kept going out, people slept in the luggage racks, the train stopped at every station and we were pestered by beggars. (It was a twenty-hour journey!) Third class is worse!

At the Valley of the Kings in Luxor, don't hire a bloody bike! I did, and apart from getting lost, having a flat tyre, sunstroke, fighting loose handle-bars and suffering from exhaustion, I had a good time. You must buy your entrance tickets to the Valley when you first cross the Nile or you'll travel miles to some temple and they won't let you in because you haven't got a ticket. You also risk being sold tickets to temples or tombs closed for restoration. I reckon it's best to go by donkey with a guide. *Philip Newson, London, England*

When you're hot and tired in Cairo, go sit in the beautiful air-conditioned lounge of the Cairo Hilton. No one asks you to leave. At the equally luxurious Meridian Hotel you can taste the high life by spending about 4 Egyptian pounds and then sunbathe by their pool all day in perfect peace. This tip is mostly for girls who want a little privacy from ogling Egyptian eyes.

You can save lots of money when travelling in Egypt by buying a vacuum flask and sterilizing your own water – saves spending money on drinks.

Take something to combat mosquito bites, especially if you're allergic to them. Boy, did I suffer! *Carol Lyons, Northern Ireland*

Mosquito bites can cause you hell. Check at chemists or with doctors as to good insect repellents. Mosquitoes tend to bite at night when you're still and defenceless, so, if you're travelling in North Africa or the Middle East it's worth taking a mosquito net. It doesn't weigh much. K.W.

Best place to look for cheap rooms in Cairo is the Tahrir Square/Talaat Harb Street area. I found US dollars the best currency for changing on the black market. *Alan Thatcher, New Zealand*

Girls hitching in Egypt should be prepared. Egyptians think Western women are easy and that even married girls will bed-hop. They offer dinner, music, wine and hash and they expect favours in return! *Ester, Australia*

Don't bother hitching – the trains are dead cheap. I travelled third class which, although a bit uncomfortable, was great fun. The Egyptians are really friendly and hospitable, especially if you try learning some Arabic. You have to buy your ticket within half an hour before the train leaves.

Abu-Simbel: a boat (barge) leaves Aswan High Dam every Saturday morning bound for Abu-Simbel. It's mainly for Egyptians taking supplies to the Nubian village of Simbel (hence a bit rough), but there were plenty of young tourists. It takes around four days – remember to take food and especially water. The temples are really worth the visit. *Milton Stubbs, North Bailey, Durham, England*

11 Turkey and the Middle East

Turkey

population	46,000,000
size	301,381 square miles
capital	Ankara, population 2,500,000
government	Republic
religion	Moslem
language	Turkish; some English, French and German understood in large cities
currency	*Lira* One *lira* equals 100 *kurus*. Coins of 25, 50 *kurus*, and of 1, 2½, 5, 10 *lira*. Notes of 5, 10, 20, 50, 100, 500, 1000, 5000 *lira*

When you cross the Bosporus at Istanbul you've reached Asia. More than that, you are entering the area which archaeologists are now considering as the cradle of civilization, for in 1960, at **Hacilar** in the south-west of Turkey, a village was discovered which dates back to 6000 BC.

In a country where there is so much to see merely by wandering from any town to any town, the outstanding cities, after Istanbul, must be Izmir, Ankara and Konya. The two indispensable historical sites to visit are Troy and Ephesus.

Troy (or Truva) is just a few kilometres south of **Canakkale** and a dream for any student of history. Discovered in the nineteenth century by Heinrich Schliemann who used the writings of Homer in his efforts to locate it, Troy was previously considered only a legend. Excavations have now shown that no less than nine successive settlements were made on the site, the oldest dating back 5000 years, the most recent to 280 BC. Homer's Troy was on the seventh level – around 1200 BC.

Izmir, about a day's hitching from Troy and situated beautifully on the Aegean Sea, is known as the 'garden of the gods'. Dating from eleven centuries before Christ, its history has been so rough that there are not as many ancient remains to be explored as you

might think. It was destroyed in 600 BC and some time later
rebuilt by Alexander the Great, then in AD 178 was destroyed by
an earthquake and rebuilt by Marcus Aurelius. Then it was bashed
around by the Crusaders, and after that by internal strife and then
finally, between 1919 and 1922, it was occupied by the Greeks and
once more badly damaged. Ataturk, the greatest man in modern
Turkish history and first president of the republic, took it from the
Greeks in 1922 and reconstructed it. Things to see include
Ataturk's house, the Agora (the ancient Roman marketplace), the
Kadifekale Castle from which you have a tremendous view over
the city, and the Caravanserais, the ancient inns where the
caravans from the east rested during their journeys.

Three kilometres from **Seljuk** (where you can see the tomb of
the Apostle John) are the ruins of **Ephesus**. Dating from 2000 BC,
successive generations of Greeks, Romans and Turks have all left
memories of their stay. See the Arcadian Street, half a kilometre
long, once the main street in the old city. See the stadium where
the gladiators fought, see the gymnasiums, the Odeon, the Agora
and the gigantic theatre which can hold 24,500 people. Have a
look at the Cave of the Seven Sleepers where, legend tells us,
seven Christians and their dogs slept for 200 years and then awoke.
And seven kilometres away, on Mount Aladag, see the House of
the Virgin Mary where Mary is said to have lived after the death of
Christ. The water which runs beneath the house is supposed to
have healing properties and in 1963 the Pope declared the house a
place of pilgrimage.

At **Bodrum** you can see the castle with its tremendous collection
of artifacts raised from the ocean bed. Bodrum was once the home
of King Mausolus and here stood his famed Mausoleum, one of
the Seven Wonders of the World before it was destroyed in an
earthquake. (A second Wonder of the World stood near Ephesus.
It was the Temple of Artemis which was four times bigger than the
Parthenon. Now only a few columns stand. A third Wonder stood
on the Greek island of Rhodes – just a couple of hours by sea from
Marmaris – the Colossus of Rhodes.)

Marmaris, a semi-tourist town, makes a pleasant stop for a day.
Beautiful beaches to swim from and sleep on and ancient rock
tombs to visit.

Fethiye, yet another town so ancient that its origins are buried in
legend, has rock tombs much more spectacular than those at
Marmaris.

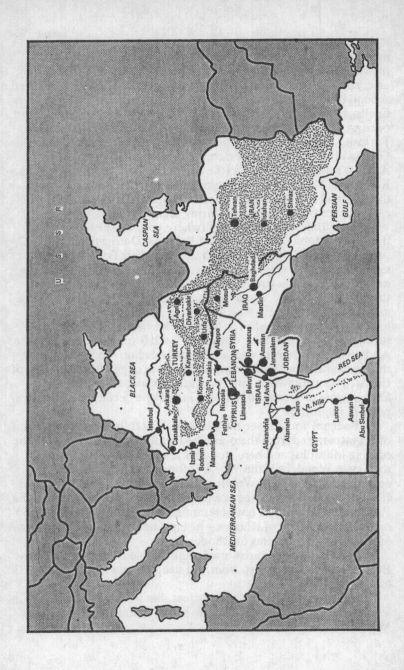

All along the Mediterranean coast lie dozens of villages and towns worth visiting, but it's when you start heading inland along the E24 that you end up in the *really* strange places – places where the inhabitants may not be used to seeing strangers. But, if you keep your cool and play it by ear you won't have much trouble.

Good cities to visit in this area of south-east Anatolia include **Urfa**, one of the oldest cities in the world, with its fantastic fortress and pools of mysterious holy water; **Mardin** (near the Syrian border) with its ancient monastery and nearby ruins of **Hasankeyf**, capital of the ancient kingdom of Eyyub, and **Diyarbakir** where the beautiful walls of the old city intrude amongst the more modern buildings and where you can see the Ulu Mosque, considered one of the greatest in Islam.

Up in East Anatolia, if you have the money and the time to go so far, you might want to visit **Agri**, the site of Mount Agri, or Ararat where, according to ancient writings, Noah's Ark is said to rest. And if you get that far, just 100 kilometres away are the borders of Russia and Iran.

Heading west again, back to something which you'll recognize as civilization, you can travel through **Malatya** (merely 3500 years old) on your way to **Kayseri**, known as the 'city of mausoleums'. Plenty to see in the way of mosques and monuments and a nice town to wander in.

Konya, south-west on Highway 73, is a city with its origins in prehistoric times. St Paul visited three times, making it an important centre for Christianity. Tremendous choice of sights to visit.

Ankara, 200 kilometres north of Konya on the E5, is a city of more than two million people and the capital of Turkey. The exact age of the city is not known though it probably dates from the third century BC. Amongst the many things to be seen are the Ankara Citadel, the Temple of Augustus, the Haci Bayram Mosque and the Anit-Kabir which is the Mausoleum of Ataturk. Also have a look at the Museum of Anatolian Civilizations, perhaps the best in the country.

Hitching in Turkey, though not as fast as in some countries, is not all that bad, though the farther east you go the less cars there are. But don't worry, you'll get used to waiting.

★**Camel wrestling** For one of the oddest sights you're likely to see anywhere, try to find yourself a real, live, genuine camel wrestling match. Mostly found in the Aegean region. You might try the town of Denizli, which is on the E24 when you turn in from the coast. Around this area you can also find *cock-fighting*.

★**Greasy wrestling** Those interested in watching the strong-arms indulging in the famous Turkish wrestling in which contestants are covered from head to foot with oil should stop off at Edirne, just over the Bulgarian border. It is one of the main centres for the sport.

★**Language** Not an easy one. But try these few words:
yes – *ev-et*   no – *hayir*
please – *lut-fen*   thanks – *tesh-ek-er-ed-erim*

★**Hitching** Sometimes in the more rural areas of Turkey you are expected to pay if you hitch. This idea of playing taxi seems to particularly appeal to Turkish truckies. So be careful, and if it happens haggle like hell!

★**For lady hitchers only** Sounds crazy to say it, but lots of ladies don't seem to realize that what gives in Europe or the States just ain't on when you're in the East. For instance, going bra-less under garments like light cotton Afghan shirts. In Istanbul you'll barely (so to speak) get away with it. Farther east you could be heading for trouble. Men and women are pretty well closeted from each other in less sophisticated areas of Asia and the sight of blatant bouncing boobies can be enough to make a local consider you a walking invitation.

Istanbul: where to sleep

You have to try hard to spend more than 1000–1500 lira for a bed in Istanbul. The cheapest areas are found on the European side of the city, up around *Sultanahmet,* which is the oldest section. The *Eminonu* section, behind the railway station, is also a good bet for centrally located and dirt-cheap hotels. Don't pay the first price on any room offered to you – bargain hard and you'll save about 10 per cent. Prices in better-class places are controlled by the government.

Istanbul: where to eat

Eat anywhere. 400 lira should give you a *big* meal! *Eminonu* is a good area for cheap cafés and restaurants. There's nothing more to be said on the matter – Turkey provides the cheapest eating in Europe.

For a nice breakfast, wander down to the Galata Bridge and have a freshly caught fish which will be grilled while you wait.

As to what you'll be eating in the cheap restaurants, don't worry too much. Make appropriate sign language and the waiter will take you into the kitchen so you can see what's cooking.

Lahmacun is like a pizza. *Kofte* is a meatball dish. *Balik* is fish. *Helva* is a sweet. *Siskebab* is a shishkebab. *Kahve* is coffee.

Istanbul: what to see and do

THE MOSQUES There are over twenty mosques in Istanbul, and if you have never visited one it's worth going. The main ones are the *Sultanahmet Mosque* (known as the Blue Mosque), *Saint Sophia* (a museum) and *Suleymaniye*.

DOLMABAHCE PALACE Built in 1854 it is a fine example of Turkish architecture mixed with European. The famous TOPKAPI PALACE is considered one of the great buildings of the world. It was started in the fourth century and continually added to until the nineteenth. It contains fabulous collections of jewels and porcelain.

KAPALI CARSI (The Covered or Grand Bazaar) is the world's most famous market. Once you could really pick up a bargain. These days you have to be a little more careful. But look carefully and haggle hard. You might do OK.

MISIR CARSISI is the Spice Bazaar, also known as the Egyptian Bazaar. It's covered, like the Grand Bazaar, though not nearly as big. But the best attraction is not the bazaar itself but the streets all around which are packed out with sellers flogging everything you can think of. I like it better than the Grand Bazaar – one reason being that there are very few tourists in the area (unlike the Grand Bazaar which is crawling with them); thus you can find a much better deal if you need to buy something. I've said it a couple of times already in this chapter but I'm saying it again: *bargain* for *everything*. *Never* accept the first price. Example: back in the preinflation days when a lira really *was* a lira, I found a little metal icon I really wanted. The junk seller who had it asked me 180 lira. I talked with him for fifteen minutes and offered him 20. He laughed and said he'd consider 150. I rolled around on the ground a bit and came up to 40. Then I couldn't budge him, so I left and came back an hour later. A bit more talking and he was down to 140 and I was up to 60. To cut it short, two visits and a lot of mirth later we agreed at 100. I'm sure, even so, a better bargainer would have got it for 75, but it was a lovely piece and I didn't want to risk losing it. But here's the sequel: next day in the Grand Bazaar I found another icon exactly the same. Asking price? 700 lira!

THE MUSEUM OF TURKISH AND ISLAMIC ART in the Suleymaniye Mosque building. See the incredible carpet collection. Also a beautiful collection of ancient books and manuscripts.

THE ARCHAEOLOGY MUSEUM is worth a visit to see the relics of ancient Troy and the tomb of Alexander the Great.

BOAT TRIP ON THE BOSPORUS Don't take any of the advertised tours. Go down to the Galata Bridge and pick your own tour on a regular ferry route. Plenty of trips to choose from and one lasting a couple of hours will cost you 50 lira return. Try the run to **Sariyer** which takes you by the old fortress of Rumelihisar and, opposite it on the right, the smaller fortress of Anadoluhisar. Ferry riding the Bosporus makes for one of the cheapest and most pleasant outings anywhere in Europe (or Asia, because the boats stop on the Asian side, too).

SULTANAHMET SQUARE Most hitchers and van travellers eventually find themselves in Sultanahmet. It's the great stopping place for people heading east and those coming from the east. This is where you can get route information for the big India trip, or pick up a van ride to Kabul or join an economy bus heading back to London. In Sultanahmet you can put up a notice in the *Puddin Shop* if you need to sell something to raise a bit of cash. But in Sultanahmet you can also get yourself in one hell of a lot of trouble. It's a weird place. It's just a stone's throw from the Blue Mosque and the Saint Sophia Museum and thus one of the most heavily populated tourist sites in Europe. But it's also one of the roughest joints in Europe. If someone asks if you want to buy dope tell him to get screwed, if he asks you to change money tell him to get screwed. If you do either of these things with someone who hasn't been vouched for as 100 per cent straight you're running an odds-on chance of doing business with a police informer – who'll be getting a nice little rake-off for dropping you in the shit. (The 'shit' in Turkey meaning about six years.) Otherwise an OK place. Cheap food, cheap rooms, cheap travel, lots of people and lots of information.

MOVIES Films are shown in original language with Turkish subtitles. Tickets are cheap. Student cards get you a 50 per cent discount at afternoon shows.

Warning! It's not only dope-peddlers, black-marketeers and police who cause you trouble in Sultanahmet. Keep an eye on some of your fellow-hitchers, too. Some of the freaks passing through are nasties. They keep alive by stealing anything from anyone stupid enough to leave stuff unguarded.

Transport in Istanbul
It's all cheap. Cheapest are the buses. Then comes the *dolmus* which can only be described as a communal taxi. It usually costs about 25 per cent more than the bus fare and runs on routes roughly the same as the bus. What you get for your 25 per cent extra is a quicker trip and much more comfort. Some of the *dolmus* cars have the word painted on them, but most look exactly like a taxi. Therefore you should always check before you get in whether it's a *dolmus* or a taxi. A taxi will cost you ten times the fare! If you *do* have to take a taxi, remember the old rule. Bargain! (Yes, even for taxis! They all have meters but they are never switched on.) Something under half the price you're quoted will be about right. If you feel like taking a trip out of the city, don't worry about the price of trains. They're dirt cheap.

Student discounts
Cut prices on most transport between cities, cut prices on ferry boats. Reduction at certain cinemas and theatres. (Theory and practice are two different things in Turkey – but try your luck anyway.) For information contact the youth and student travel information office:

INTRA-TUR, at Halaskargazi Caddesi 111, Harbiye, Istanbul (tel: 47 81 74).

TMTF, Babiali Caddesi 40, Cagaloglu-Istanbul (tel: 22 93 16).

Addresses

Main post office (for poste restante) at Büyük Postane, Istanbul.

American Express at Hilton Hotel, Istanbul (tel: 48 39 05).

Intra-Tur at Halaskargazi Caddesi 111, Harbiye, Istanbul (tel: 47 81 74).

Tourist Office at 57B Mesrutiyet Caddesi, Galatasaray, Istanbul (tel: 45 63 93).

US Consulate at 104 Mesrutiyet Caddesi, Istanbul (tel: 45 32 20).

British Consulate at Tepebasi, 34 Mesrutiyet Caddesi, Istanbul (tel: 44 75 40).

Hitchers' Tips and Comments ...

In Turkey, as you cross the border you are allowed to buy duty-free cigarettes and booze in special shops. These can be resold in the Grand Bazaar at almost double price. Some currencies can be changed on the black market at a rate of almost 25 per cent better than the quoted rate. To do the deal all you have to do is walk along one of the main streets looking like a tourist and you will be approached. Make sure you ask double what you are offered before dropping down to the real price, because all Turks like to bargain. *Phillip Bennett, London W11*

I want to make a point here I've hammered before. If you want to play the black market don't play it with someone who approaches you. Play it with someone you approach. That lessens the odds of that someone being a police informer (though it doesn't guarantee the fact). This approach to the black market, or to buy anything else which is slightly illegal, is particularly important in Turkey, Morocco and the Communist countries. See my comments about Sultanahmet Square. K.W.

Warning about Sultanahmet Square well taken. Also, I suggest a very strong warning to female hitchers in that country! Young English chap told me recently the cops cleaned out an entire fleabag near Sultanahmet Square and locked them all up for a week. No charges. No explanations. And many other such tales, especially against those unwise enough to camp in the open. *Unsigned, South Kensington, London*

Remember, if you get arrested anywhere for anything, it's the duty of your local consul to help you – that is, if he knows you've been arrested. Most countries will inform your consul if you're in a local prison, but some of the outback places don't bother. All you can do – if they won't let you near a phone – is to play it very cool and try to get a message out. While we're on the subject – if a cop at a station or a guard in a prison starts provoking you or roughing you up, don't fight back. If you do, that's the only excuse they need to bring in the heavies and draw the truncheons. Just keep smiling and if you can't do that try to keep your head and balls protected. K.W.

When entering Turkey your driver will get a special stamp in his passport which shows he brought in a car. Make sure you don't get the same stamp! If you do, you won't be able to leave because customs officials will think you've sold an imported car in Turkey. *Peter Nash, Chelmsford, England*

Istanbul. Point taken about Sultanahmet. For those wanting to sell duty-free stuff in the Grand Bazaar, Dunhills and whisky are the best sellers (100–150 per cent profit). *Marcel Thomas, Horndean, England*

Best places for lifts from Turkey to Afghanistan, Iran, Iraq, Saudi Arabia (not single girls!), Jordan and Syria are at the Mocamps. Try the Mocamp in Ankara, the BP-Camp at Adana and, best of all, Londra-Camp, Londra Asfalti, Bakirköy, Istanbul. Most nights you'll find 50 to 300 trucks waiting to head east. *Gundomar Uebel, West Berlin, Germany*

In Istanbul, avoid snapping photos of men with bears unless you want to pay a 'fee' under threat of a bear hug. *John Pilkington, Bristol, UK*

Don't doss anywhere in Turkey unless you're *sure* you won't be seen by the police or the army. They're strict about dossing. Even beaches are often searched. If caught you could be arrested which means a load of hassles, Turkish jails being no joke. On the other hand, camping sites are good and cheap in Turkey. If you're in Bodrum, try *Camping Ayaz* just outside town. Cleanest camping I've ever seen. Good place to recuperate if you've got food poisoning. *Tony Miller, Newcastle-upon-Tyne, England*

A lifesaver for me in Turkey was a simple roll of toilet paper. Turks don't seem to use it. Also take a couple of dozen anti-diarrhoea tablets. Odds are you're going to need them. *Jim Stafford, Dublin, Ireland*

I recommend fellow hitchers to consider a trip to the Black Sea Coast. It's unaffected by the evils of mass tourism. Sinop and Samsun are worth visiting. People don't seem to mind picking up hitchers, but there aren't that many cars. Buses and mini-buses are really cheap, though, and travelling on them is a great way to get to know the Turks. I've often been offered a meal and a bed. One last thing. The political situation in Turkey is more often than not unstable. Be very, very careful. Stay away from police, soldiers and drugs. I've heard sad things about people in trouble in Turkey. Take care with everything you do, even with things like talking about politics or wearing shorts outside of tourist areas! *Alfred Blaak, Koekange, Holland*

The Londra Trucking Camp is the place to hitch out of Istanbul. This is where the lorries to and from Europe stop. *Simon Lingley, Uppingham, UK*

Keep all your counterfoils from changing money. You can only change your money back at the border after US$20 expenses has been deducted for each day you spent in Turkey. *A. Chaplin, Hatfield, Herts, UK*

Several people had horror stories about what happened when they had a Turkish stamp in their passport. One West German had his rucksack turned inside out at the borders of Greece, Yugoslavia, Austria, Switzerland and his own country! *Eric the Hippo, London, England*

Visit Pamukkale, 15 kilometres north of Denizli. Here you can bathe at the Ozel Idare motel in the hot calcium springs, amongst Roman ruins where Cleopatra once bathed, or you can shower in the spectacular cascades nearby.

Cheap place to stay here is below the cascades in the village at Ali's Pension. Clean, and plenty of other travellers to meet as well.

We thought Turkey a great place, especially once out of Istanbul. The people are really friendly and just wouldn't stop helping us – giving us free food and drinks (and accommodation on many occasions) simply because they love to speak to foreigners. *Creb and Wez, Birmingham, England*

The Turkish black market rate is about 10 per cent above the official rate but definitely not worth it. It's likely you'll be approached in Istanbul. The blokes who offer to change also offer hash and are reputed to be plain-clothes police, so don't bother.

There's a strong demand for foreign booze and cigs that can be picked up in the hard currency shops at the border or in Bulgarian *Corecom* shops. Marlboro cigarettes are particularly popular. Don't change more money than you need, they won't change it back.

Hitching is very easy in Turkey but, if you get stuck, it's dark or the weather is bad, take the bus. They're dirt cheap, stop anywhere and go everywhere. If going south from Istanbul, get the boat to Yalova from the pier near the Galata Bridge. Don't let *Midnight Express* put you off from visiting Turkey. The Turks are the friendliest of people. I've even had the police set up a road block for me so I could get a lift and another policeman persuaded a bus driver to take me for a four-hour ride for nothing. Just keep away from drugs. *Alan Barlow, Cheadle, UK*

Cyprus

population	669,000
size	3572 square miles
capital	Nicosia, population 120,000
government	Republic
religion	Greek Orthodox and Moslem

language   Greek and Turkish, with English widely used
currency   *Cypriot pound* One *pound* equals 100 *cents*
             (previously 1000 *mils*)

Cypriot history is a succession of foreign invasions and domination. Current problems have arisen from the Cypriot mix of Greek and Turkish blood. To simplify a complex situation, Cyprus became independent after the British left in 1960. In 1974 the military junta ruling in Greece promoted a coup in Cyprus which provoked an invasion by Turkey, and resulted in a de facto division of the island between Turkish and Greek Cypriots. In 1983 the north declared itself an independent Turkish Federated State of Cyprus but, so far, only Turkey has recognized the state. *At the time of writing you may not cross from one part of the island to the other. Best check the situation before you visit.*

By air Cyprus is easily accessible from the Middle East and Europe. There are various shipping lines operating to Cyprus, connecting it with Piraeus (Greece) and the Middle East. In summer the service is frequent, but not in winter. For examples of fares, the Black Sea Shipping Company charges about C£53 from Piraeus for the cheapest class cabin, and the trip takes 38 hours. From Latakia in Syria it's around C£22 (cheapest class again), and takes about 8 hours. Sol Lines charge about C£40 from Piraeus to Limassol in spring and autumn, and about C£50 in summer, both deck class.

No visa is required for visitors from the British Commonwealth, USA and most of Western Europe. No jabs or malaria tablets needed. You're supposed to declare foreign currency if you have over US$500, and you may be asked to show that you have enough money for the time of your stay. Officially you can only take C£10 worth of Cypriot currency in or out of the country.

Where to sleep

Upon arrival immigration may insist that you have booked accommodation. So, if you know your arrival date, make a booking before you come for at least one night to satisfy them. If not, make a one-night booking when you arrive. Once you're over this hurdle, there are no official hassles and you can sleep where you like.

There are a few youth hostels for C£1 per night (sheets extra).

Note that Troodos hostel is open only in summer. Hotels are generally fairly expensive, but if you get the free hotel booklet from the tourist office and hunt around in it, especially in the 'Hotels without Star' and 'Guest Houses' sections, you'll find some singles for around C£4 to C£6, or half this price in Limassol. Larnaca is short on anything cheap. If you get stuck there, ask at the taxi office as they know a few crash pads, but bargain over the inflated prices.

There are three organized campsites, listed under 'Hotel Apartments' in the hotel booklet, which charge around C£1·50 per tent and C£0·30 per person per day.

Sleeping out is no problem, and seems to be accepted. As long as you're sensible and discreet you shouldn't have any hassles with anyone. The warm sunny weather suits the exercise (it rarely rains), except in the mountains where it can be cold.

Where to eat

Hunt out local haunts and avoid tourist traps, and you'll find good food at a realistic price. Cheapest dishes are usually things like moussaka, but be cautious with such meals as they are normally prepared once a week for the whole week. Try and find out how fresh the dish is and how it has been stored. Try the delicious fresh grapes in season. Local wine is cheap and plentiful.

Hitching

Hitching is good. Beware of being picket up by mini-buses then charged for the ride. If you are relying on the tourist office map, be warned that it hasn't been updated for some years during which time the road network has changed partly because the cease-fire line cuts through pre-existing roads.

What to see

Nicosia, with a population of 120,000, is the capital of the island. It is also, now, a divided city. See the excavated treasure in the Cyprus Museum. Through the middle of the town runs a line of barricades, guards and empty buildings.

Limassol is the second city of the island and although most of the old town is gone there is just enough left to give a whiff of what it must have been like. In the castle, Richard the Lionheart married Berengaria, and it was the same castle which was the headquarters of the Knights Templar and the Knights of St John. (There is a small zoo in the public gardens.)

Larnaca is said to have been founded by the grandson of Noah and has many religious associations, including the tomb of Lazarus who, according to legend, came to Cyprus after having been resurrected by Christ. Five kilometres outside Larnaca there is a very important monument of the Islamic world – the shrine of Hala Sultan who was a female relative of the prophet Mohammed.

Paphos and the west coast are less travelled than other parts. There are some fine mosaics in the House of Dionyssos. North of Paphos you find beaches, including Coral Bay and Polis. Between Paphos and Limassol is the birthplace of Aphrodite, **Petra tou Romiou**.

Inland are the mountains which offer, along with cooler temperatures, walking in summer and skiing in winter. There are numerous monasteries around the island. When the going gets hot, as it does in summer, check out the swimming beaches along the coast.

Turkish Cyprus Turkish Cyprus is accessible only from Turkey, or by direct flight from London. There are ferries all year round between Famagusta and Mersin, and in the high season there are additional ferries from both Mersin and Tasucu to Kyrenia. The Mersin–Famagusta ferry costs about £70 one way, including the steep port taxes. (Student discount available.)

According to the Cyprus government, it is illegal to enter Cyprus through any of the Turkish-controlled ports of entry though, of course, they have no means of stopping you. But, having entered Turkish Cyprus, you cannot cross to the rest of Cyprus.

Hitch-hiking is easy. Food is a bit more expensive than in Turkey.

Famagusta has a population of 38,000 and, before 1974, was the island's main port. Visit the old city and see the huge citadel identified with Othello's tower in Shakespeare's play.

Kyrenia is a small and very attractive seaside town with a beautiful old harbour fringed with cafés. It also boasts three castles. **St Hilarion**, which stands high above the city, is really spectacular and worth climbing up to see.

A really worthwhile expedition is to the ruined Gothic abbey of **Bellapais**, five kilometres from Kyrenia and open, in summer, from 7 a.m. to 6 p.m., in winter, from 8 a.m. to 5 p.m.

Nicosia (Turkish sector) In the fine old section visit the former Cathedral of Santa Sophia, now the Selimiye Mosque.

Addresses

American Express at A. L. Mantovani & Sons, 35–37 Evagoras Avenue, Nicosia (tel: 43777/78/79).

Tourist Bureau at 5 Princess Zena de Tyras Street, Nicosia (tel: 44264).

Tourist Bureau at 15 Spyrou Araouzus Street, Limassol (tel: 62756).

US Embassy at Therissos Street and Dositheos Street, Nicosia (tel: 65 151).

British Embassy at British High Commission, Alexander Pallis Street, PO Box 1978, Nicosia (tel: 73 131).

Hitchers' Tips and Comments...

If you go to Cyprus, it is impossible to cross from North Cyprus (Turkish) to South Cyprus (Greek) or vice versa. Also, if you go to North Cyprus, do not allow your passport to be stamped, otherwise you will not be allowed to enter Greece. This happened to us and we were deported from Rhodes when we arrived there from Marmaris, Turkey. That then causes problems getting back to Europe, unless you go through the Communist countries.

In Kyrenia, northern Cyprus, if going to the St Hilarion Castle (and it's worth a visit), get a lift all the way to the top. There is a military checkpoint half-way up the mountain road which stops walkers and only allows vehicles up to the castle.

The soldiers there, though, are friendly and helped us get a lift to the castle on a NATO bus. *Creb and Wez, Birmingham, England*

Warning! War and revolution are rife in the Middle East. If you are contemplating a trip to the area, keep yourself well informed on what is happening. The best way to do this is through your embassy or consulate. Visas are needed in many countries.

Following is a brief summary of what there is to see in the Middle East countries.

Syria

population	7,355,000
size	71,498 square miles
capital	Damascus, population 900,000
government	Republic
religion	Moslem
language	Arabic, a little French spoken
currency	*Syrian pound* One *pound* equals 100 *piastres*

Visas are necessary for everyone except those from Arab countries. Some nationalities (e.g., Australians and New Zealanders) may get their visas at the border but others (e.g., Americans and British) must obtain them from a Syrian consulate abroad. If intending to stay more than 15 days, you must report to the 'Direction de l'Immigration des Passeports et de la Nationalité' within 15 days of arrival. South Africans, Israelis, or people with an Israeli stamp in their passport, are refused entry. The border with Israel is closed and since 1967 Israel has occupied the Golan Heights.

There is a malaria risk from May through to October, and it's a good idea to have a cholera jab. Don't drink the tap water.

You can take up to 200 Syrian pounds into the country, and unlimited foreign currency which you are supposed to declare on arrival. You can take out local and foreign money up to the amount imported and declared.

Where to sleep

Syrian youth hostels cost about S£9·50 a night, including sheets
and cooking facilities (no meals are provided). Damascus Youth
Hostel is at Saleh el Ali Street 66, Mazra'a Square (tel: 45 95 40),
which is also the address of the Syrian Youth Hostels Association.
There are also hostels in Aleppo, Bosra, Der'a, Homs, Latakia
and Zabadani.

Cheap hotels are quite affordable, e.g., a double for around
S£40. For cheap hotels in Damascus start your search from the
Place des Martyrs and work towards the old city.

If you sleep out, be wary. It may be OK in some places, but
risky in others.

Where to eat

Eating in Syria is cheap compared to Jordan, so if you're heading
in that direction, eat out while you can afford it. When you sit
down for a meal, bread, olives, salad and pickles are free, so don't
order too much. If you have a sweet tooth you'll enjoy Syrian
pastry shops. Syria has nice fruit juice places where you can buy
freshly squeezed juice.

Hitching

Hitching is okay on the main roads. Sometimes, you even get free
rides in service cars. But hitching is not recommended for women
without a male companion. If you get stuck, buses are cheap (e.g.,
Hama–Damascus, 3½ hours, about S£10). But be warned that
they can get overcrowded and there may be a rush for the bus
when it pulls up. Hitching may be slower but it might be more
comfortable, too! Women hitchers might prefer to pay a bit more
for a less crowded bus. If not, be prepared to fight off wandering
hands.

What to see

Damascus (population of nearly a million), which dates back to
4000 BC, is the oldest continually inhabited city in the world. Its
Grand Bazaar is one of the great visits in the Middle East. See also
the Omayad Mosque with the tomb of St John the Baptist, the
Azem Palace, the National Museum and the tomb of Saladin.

Narrow back alleys around the old city are interesting. Much of the old wall and gates still stands. Everything to see in Damascus is within walking distance of the cheap hotel area and the youth hostel.

In **Aleppo**, second city of Syria, see the bazaars, the Museum of Aleppo, the Great Mosque and the Aleppo Citadel. Also, the ruined Convent of Simeon. There, fifteen centuries ago, St Simeon lived on the top of a pillar for twenty-seven years.

Palmyra, once the most important city in Syria, is now only a village. But there is much to be seen, including the ancient cemeteries with their weird decorations, and the Citadel of the Ma'anites.

Hama has huge old Roman waterwheels (*norias*) along the river Orontes, and a museum. Check out the back alleys and the sleazy Roman baths, but careful you don't get dragged inside – you may find *baksheesh* forcefully demanded from you.

Krak des Chevaliers – the Castle of the Knights – is the best-preserved Crusader castle in the Middle East. It saw tremendous battles before the Arabs took it in 1271. Complete with moat, dungeons (take a torch), drawbridge and all the rest, it's worth going out of your way to see it. But be warned that it's situated several kilometres off the main Tartus to Homs highway and difficult to reach by hitching. There is sporadic public transport, so best leave early so you can get back. The village below the castle seems unfriendly. Watch out for kids hurling rocks. If you miss the last bus down to the highway and someone offers to give you a ride down, they may expect payment.

Tartus is worth a visit if you want to check out a museum and a twelfth-century cathedral built by the Crusaders.

Latakia is a very ancient city which is now Syria's main port. As well as beaches, there are many ruins to see, including a Roman triumphal arch. North of the city is **Ras Shamra** where important excavations are being made.

Near the Jordanian border is **Bosra**, a second-century Roman city which later became an important Christian centre. Visit the sixth-century Byzantine Cathedral, the Roman baths, and Trajan's Palace.

Addresses

American Express at Chami Travel, Mouradi Building, Rue
Fardons, Damascus (tel: 11 16 52 or 11 95 53).

Student Office at IAESTE (Syrian committee), University of
Aleppo, Aleppo.

US Embassy at Chare (*Ave*) Mansour, Abu Rummanih,
Damascus (tel: 332 315).

British Embassy at 11 Kotob Building, 3rd floor, Mohammed
Kurd Ali Street, Malki Street, Damascus (tel: 332 561).

Hitchers' Tips and Comments...

In Damascus, you find cheap hotels in the El Mardja area near
the Grand Bazaar. Lots of military movement on the
Homs–Palmyra road. I don't advise hitching along it. Palmyra
worth the visit, even if you have to reach it by bus. Six square
miles of Roman ruins. Stay at The Camp Zenobia, or even in
the ruins. Aleppo was my favourite Syrian city. You find
cheap hotels in the area opposite the Tourist Office. *Simon
Lingley, Uppingham, UK*

Syrian visas can be bought at any consulate and the cost
depends on where you get it. You may need a letter of
introduction from your embassy. British embassies charge £6
in local currency at their rate of exchange for such letters.
Some nationalities are allowed to get their visas at the border
(the British are not among them). If you're in Syria for more
than 15 days, you have to get an exit visa from the police.
When applying for a visa, don't let on if you are Jewish or
you'll be turned down. People with 'obviously' Jewish names
probably won't get the visa anyway.

  The black market rate is 10 per cent above the official as in
Turkey. If you get stuck with Turkish liras, the black
marketeers outside the border post bank will take them at
more or less face value. Syrian banks won't touch them.

Make a point of learning Arab numbers, or shops and banks will cheat you. The black market is pretty open in Syria and there is little risk. In Damascus you can change money at the Souk el Hamadiyeh (US dollars preferred) and in Aleppo on Al Ayoubi Street at the clock tower, near the museum, and the tourist office. Don't bother trying to hitch out of Damascus to the south. It's a long walk and you'll end up among military installations. Instead, take a bus to Dera'a for four Syrian pounds from Bab Moussalla Square.

In Aleppo see the Citadel, the biggest in the Middle East. Krak des Chevaliers is hard to hitch to and badly signposted. Best to get a bus from Homs. The Arabic name of the Krak is Kalet Al Hosen which the locals are more likely to understand. Lastly, be careful in Syria about what you say. Don't ever admit to anyone that you have been in Israel or that you're going there, or even give mild approval of the place. Do not bring into the country any goods of Israeli manufacture, or Israeli money. If you do, it will be regarded as implicit evidence of having visited Israel or having Zionist sympathies. If they find you out, you'll be refused admittance to the country or deported. In line with this paranoia, do not hitch near anything military. Remember that the official line is that President Assad is the greatest man who ever lived, and you will be advised not to disagree with it at any time, including when talking with someone who slags the government. It's no exaggeration to say that there are secret police everywhere.

Iran

population	33,019,000
size	636,300 square miles
capital	Teheran, population 3,000,000
government	Republic
religion	Moslem
language	Persian
currency	*Rial* One *rial* equals 100 *dinars*

Warning! I have *no* information about the attitude of Iranian officials towards hitch-hikers since the revolution. If you get there, tread warily!

Teheran, with a population of 3,000,000 and at an altitude of 4000 feet, is the capital of Iran. See the bazaars and the museums. Visit the Mesjedeh Sepahsalar mosque, the only one still in use which non-Moslems may visit. See the Crown Jewels collection, including the largest uncut diamond in the world and the famous Peacock Throne. Just outside town, visit the ancient city of **Rai**, once the capital of Iran.

Isfahan is the home of the Mosque of Madreseh, the Palace of the Shahs and another good bazaar area.

Shiraz is known as 'the city of roses, nightingales and poets' and is just 64 kilometres south-west of **Persepolis**, which is the ruined capital of ancient Persia. Here you can see the tombs of Darius and Xerxes and the ruins of fantastic palaces. One of the big archaeological sites of the world.

Iraq

population	11,505,000
size	167,925 square miles
capital	Baghdad, population 2,000,000
government	Republic
religion	Moslem
language	Arabic
currency	*Dinar* One *dinar* equals 1000 *fils*

Warning! Iran and Iraq are at war. Avoid any discussion of the war and keep well away from the battle zone.

Baghdad is your genuine Arabian Nights city. See (from the outside unless you're a Moslem) the Kadhimain Mosque with its pure gold dome, the Abbassid Palace with its tremendous collection relating to the history of Islam, and visit the carpet market in the Covered Bazaar.

Babylon, ancient capital of the Babylonian empire and site of the Hanging Gardens of Babylon, one of the Seven Wonders of the World, is 88 kilometres south of Baghdad. See Nebuchadrezzar's Procession Street, the Lion of Babylon and the throne room.

Mosul once had a much better-known name – **Nineveh**. It sits on the west side of the Tigris River and has a million inhabitants. The ruins of Nineveh, which was destroyed in 612 BC, are on the east bank.

Addresses

US Embassy at Nidhal Street, Baghdad (tel: 961 38).

British Embassy at Sharia Salah ud-Din, Karkh, Baghdad (tel: 321 21).

Lebanon

population	3,100,000
size	4000 square miles
capital	Beirut, population 1,000,000
government	Republic
religion	Half Moslem, half Christian
language	Arabic, but English widely spoken
currency	*Lebanese pound* One *pound* equals 100 *piastres*

Warning! Check things out carefully before trying to enter Lebanon. It's a dangerous place. For full information contact Lebanon embassies or consulates.

Lebanon can be reached from Istanbul by sea, for about £50.

Beirut with a population of 1,000,000 is the capital, and can be very expensive if you're not careful. Things to see include the Al-Khodr Mosque where it is said St George slew the dragon, the National Museum and the Pigeon Grotto. To meet people, try the American University, the largest American educational complex outside the States. People from all over the world study there.

Baalbek, 56 kilometres north-east of Beirut, was the Heliopolis of the Greeks and Romans. Many of the ruins are equal to anything you can see in Rome. The Temple of Bacchus, built around AD 150, is outstanding.

Byblos is another ancient town, one so important to archaeologists that they have been excavating there since 1921, discovering successive layers of settlement dating back 7000 years. Plenty to see if you like examining rocks and ruins.

Addresses

US Embassy at Corniche at Rue Aiv Mreisseh, Beirut (tel: 361 800).

British Embassy at Avenue de Paris, Ras Beirut, Beirut (tel: 36 25 00).

Israel

population	3,371,000
size	7993 square miles
capital	Jerusalem. The diplomatic capital is Tel Aviv (population 400,000)
government	Republic
religion	Jewish
language	Hebrew, with English widely spoken
currency	*Shekel* One *shekel* equals 100 *agorots*. Coins of 10, 50 *agorots*, and of 1, 5, 10, 50 *shekels*. Notes of 50, 100, 500, 1000 *shekels*

Israel can be reached by sea from Piraeus (Greece), to Haifa for around £45 one way. It is possible to come by land from Egypt and from Jordan via the Allenby Bridge (the latter is possible if you have a permit issued in Amman but, due to the political instability of the region, the bridge may be closed at any time).

When you arrive in Israel, ask for the border stamp to be put on a separate piece of paper because most Arab and Moslem states will not allow entry if there's evidence of a visit to Israel in your passport. The initial stamp is valid for three months after which you're supposed to register. If you're going to Egypt and intend visiting other Arab states afterwards, don't get your Egyptian visa in Israel. It will say it was issued in Tel Aviv (a dead giveaway), and remember that the Egyptian stamp you'll receive at the border, if going overland, will also ban you from certain countries as it will state the name of the crossing point and show that you crossed from Israel.

Your luggage will very likely be searched on entry for bombs and guns. If entering from Jordan, you will definitely be searched. Do not leave your pack unattended anywhere. This is not so much a precaution against thieves but because it's all too easy to start a bomb scare.

Israel is expensive but you can save money on food by buying in the supermarkets where prices of basic food items are heavily subsidized. With inflation at over 200 per cent at the last count, don't change more money than required for immediate needs. Your shekels will lose 5 per cent of their value every week. Keep all exchange receipts in order to change your shekels back to hard currency. Prices on consumer goods, such as cassette recorders, radios and most electrical appliances, are high so a profit can be made on such goods if you bring them into the country to sell.

Hitching

Hitching is very good in Israel, particularly if you wear a green uniform and carry a gun. There are always a lot of soldiers on the road and drivers always give them priority. Your chances of getting a lift are vastly improved if you are a woman, or a man travelling with one. When hitching, don't use your thumb as in Europe. The gesture means 'fuck off'. Usually, the locals hitch by pointing at the ground with their forefingers. Unlike hitchers in other countries, Israelis do not spread themselves along the roadside but bunch together, usually at a bus stop. When a car stops, there'll be a free-for-all to get the seats. Just push your way in, though it may be difficult when carrying luggage. Remember, it'll be soldiers first. If you get stuck, buses are cheap.

Everything closes on the Jewish Sabbath, Friday sunset to Saturday sunset. All shops shut, buses stop running, museums close and there's little traffic on the roads. It's advisable not to doss out near borders or in the Occupied Territories (Gaza, West Bank, and Golan).

What to see

Jerusalem with its 400,000 inhabitants is the religious centre of Israel, and during its 4000-year-long history it has become a holy city for Jews, Moslems and Christians. In the Old City you can see the Church of the Holy Sepulchre, built on the traditional site of

Christ's crucifixion; the Garden of Gethsemane where Judas betrayed Christ; the mosque of the Dome of the Rock, Islam's third most important shrine after Mecca and Medina, where Mohammed ascended to heaven; and the Western or Wailing Wall, Judaism's most important site, which featured so prominently in the 1967 war. In the New City you can visit Mount Zion, the holy hill where King David is buried and where it is said Christ celebrated the Last Supper; the Israel Museum where you can see the Dead Sea Scrolls; Yad Vashem, the museum of the Nazi holocaust; and the Mea Shearim quarter, a world of its own where Orthodox Jews live exactly according to the laws of their religion. (Cheap beds can be found in the Old City.)

Just to the south of Jerusalem is **Bethlehem** where Christ is said to have been born. The Church of the Nativity marks the site.

Beersheba, the principal city in the Negev desert, is a good place to see Bedouins. Every Thursday morning they hold a market.

Masada is best reached from Beersheba. This great rock, which rises 1700 feet above the western shores of the Dead Sea, was the site of Herod's Palace and where the Zealots made their last stand against the Romans in AD 73. When the Romans finally took the fortress they found every man, woman and child had killed themselves rather than go into slavery.

The **Dead Sea** is the lowest point on earth (1312 feet). You'll have trouble swimming in it, let alone sinking, because of the high salt content. Don't swallow any of the water, it'll make you very sick. If you have any cuts, you'll soon know about them. Several beaches have showers to rinse off the salt.

Way down south, on the Red Sea, is the resort of **Eilat**. The town isn't much, but offshore are superb coral reefs. The best are some kilometres south of town in the Egyptian Sinai. (The Egyptian consulate in Eilat issues visas good for the Sinai.) Scuba equipment can be hired but, if you can't afford that, visit the Aquarium, which includes an underwater observatory 15 feet under the surface of the sea where marine life can be seen in its natural surroundings. There are several hostels in Eilat (official and otherwise) and a campsite, or you can doss on the beaches (watch out for thieves and rats).

Tel Aviv-Jaffa combined, make Israel's largest city. Jaffa, where Jonah is said to have been spewed out by the whale, was founded in 1500 BC. Adjoining Tel Aviv was founded in 1909. See the bazaars in the old city and the fine modern museums and galleries in the new.

North of **Haifa** is the old town of **Acre** (or Akke). Here you can see the city walls; the El-Jazza Mosque ('the Mosque of the Butcher') with Roman columns in the courtyard; 15 other mosques; the Crusaders' Subterranean City; and the Turkish Citadel which is now a museum of the Jewish Irgun resistance.

For details of working on *kibbutzim*, see the chapter **Working in Europe**.

Addresses

Main post office (for poste restante), Tel Aviv-Yafo Post Office, 8 Heharash, Tel Aviv.

American Express c/o Meditrad Ltd, 16 Ben Yehuda Street, Tel Aviv (tel: 546 54).

Israel Students' Tourist Association at 2 Pinsker Street, POB 4451, Tel Aviv (tel: 59 613).

Israel Students' Tourist Association at 8 Shmuel Hanagid Street, Jerusalem (tel: 28 298).

Israel Information Office at 7 Rehov Mendele, Tel Aviv (tel: 22 32 66).

US Embassy at 71 Hayarkon Street, Tel Aviv (tel: 654 338).

British Embassy at 192 Rehov Hayarkon, Tel Aviv (tel: 24 91 71).

Hitchers' Tips and Comments ...

Warning! People are coming to Israel without a return ticket and with prices high and jobs hard to find they're getting stuck here. Also, it seems that the British Embassy isn't feeling so charitable nowadays. *Chris Clarke, London*

A word of warning to anyone who wants to work in a kibbutz. Beware of some of the agencies who promise to fix everything up for you. If you're unlucky you may meet a shady operator who screws as much as he can out of you and when you arrive in Israel nobody wants to know about you. *Hugh Dunne, Dublin, Ireland*

In Israel try working on a moshav — like a kibbutz but you work for a farmer and you get paid a wage. *Creb and Wez, Birmingham, England*

Very expensive country. A cheap place to stay in Jerusalem is 'Mr A's Hostel', Old City, near Jaffa Gate.

It's preferable to work on a kibbutz as the life is easier. On the moshav you'll be working 10–11 hours per day and many of them are dead at night.

Eat self-service Felafel — pitta bread stuffed with salad and pickles. Don't get caught on the road or in a small place on the Sabbath day. No buses run and cars are few. The Sabbath is approximately 3 p.m. Friday to 3 p.m. Saturday. *K. M. Fitchet, Johannesburg, South Africa*

In Israel don't take your camera into a cinema. Security people may want to open it to check for hidden bombs — goodbye film! *Theo van Drunen, Oosterhout, Holland*

There is a weekly magazine called *This Week*, available from Information Offices. It gives information of where to eat, museums to see and maps of the large cities. *Martin Green, Nottingham, England*

Always keep enough money handy to pay the airport or port tax which is levied on departures from Israel. *A. Chaplin, Hatfield, Herts, UK*

Sleeping out in Jerusalem is very unwise, especially in Arab areas. I found the Hotel Zefonya great value. In Tiberias on the Sea of Galilee the Swiss Motel was the best value I've had anywhere. *Andrew Warmington, Cambridge, England*

If you intend to spend some time in Israel and your initial visa expires, your renewal visa must be stamped in your passport. Therefore, if you had any future plans of visiting Arab countries (except Egypt) forget it! You cannot enter them with the Israeli stamp.

The best area to look for work is Eilat. It's a tourist trap with hotels that nearly always need staff: chambermaids, kitchen staff, etc.

If you cannot get work in the hotels, go to the 'Peace Cafe' in the evening. It's a focal point for fellow travellers, the cheapest beer in town, and you often hear of work that's going. *Blondie, UK*

Jordan

population	2,700,000
size	37,738 square miles
capital	Amman, population 400,000
government	Monarchy
religion	Moslem
language	Arabic, some English and French spoken
currency	*Dinar* One *dinar* equals 1000 *fils*. Coins of 5, 10, 20, 50 and 100 *fils*. Notes of 500 *fils* and 1, 5, 10, 20 *dinars*. *Piastres* sometimes referred to instead of *fils*: 10 *fils* equal 1 *piastre*

The only relatively hassle-free way to thumb into Jordan is from Syria. The two countries are often not on the best of terms, but the border is normally open.

Part of Jordan, the West Bank, has been occupied by Israel since 1967. If you want to cross between Israel and Jordan, check out the constantly changing situation before you arrive in the Middle East, where it can be difficult to obtain reliable information.

The following is roughly the situation at the time of writing: if you have an Israeli stamp in your passport, you cannot enter Jordan. The Israelis used to put a stamp on a piece of paper into your passport instead of stamping the actual passport, but they seem to refuse to do this now. In Jordan you can apply for a permit to visit the West Bank, in Amman. This takes about a week to get and the only place you can cross is Allenby Bridge. Once on the West Bank there is nothing to stop you travelling anywhere in Israel but, if you want to re-enter Jordan, it may not be possible. Check it out first. If you get your Jordanian visa before entering Israel, it *may* be possible to enter Jordan but not to re-enter Israel.

Visas are best obtained in advance from a Jordanian embassy or consulate. The validity period varies.

Tap water should not be drunk. Hygiene is not as good as the modern surroundings may lead you to believe. There is still malaria in some parts. Obtain malaria tablets before you arrive, as they are difficult to obtain locally.

At present Jordan seems pretty safe to travel in but on the West Bank sporadic violence erupts, so keep an eye on the situation!

Where to sleep

There are no official youth hostels. Cheap hotels cost around
JD2500 a single or JD4000 a double. In Amman these are found in
the Balad or downtown area. It's cheapest to sleep on the roof, but
this is not recommended for females, as even European males
(especially those with blond hair) are sometimes groped during the
night. There are government rest houses near some tourist sites
but these are expensive. At Petra the Bedouins sometimes offer to
put you up in their caves. There is no accommodation at Jerash,
which is best visited as a day trip from Amman.

Jordan is not geared for camping, though there are some places
where you could pitch a tent. Sleeping out shouldn't be too much
of a problem, but it's not a good idea for women, nor in the north
from November to March when it rains.

Where to eat

Eating out is none too cheap in Jordan, especially when compared
to Syria. A lot of Jordan's food is imported. Search out the local
bakery for good, cheap bread, then hunt around the markets for
something to go with it. A cooker is worthwhile.

Alternatively, try the cheaper takeaways: *falafel* – small balls of
ground chickpeas served with salad in a sandwich (about 350 fils
each); *shawarma* – delicious slices of spitted spiced lamb. Pieces
are sliced off and wrapped in bread and cost about 250 fils each.
Two should fill you up.

Don't miss the fruit juice stalls in Amman.

Hitching

Hitching is generally good, though not recommended for women
without a male companion. Couples move fastest but, in front of a
vehicle, make sure the man sits between the driver and the
woman. It's cheap to catch a local bus from the centre of Amman
to a better hitching spot in the suburbs. The Desert Highway offers
easy hitching but the King's Highway, which is a more interesting
route, is difficult. (Petra can be time-consuming to get in and out
of from the Desert Highway.) People are generally friendly and
hospitable but, occasionally, ask for money. Buses are not a viable
alternative here. They are few and they are expensive.

The best map of the country is the Oxford, which includes a plan of Amman.

Carry your passport with you in the vicinity of Aqaba, where there are checkposts on the roads.

What to see

Amman is built on seven hills. It can be a confusing place to find your way around. Sixty years ago it was a desert village; now it is a modern town. Many businesses have moved from Beirut to Amman because of the war in Lebanon, which has caused a fast expansion of the city and spiralling prices. As is the case all over Jordan, a large proportion of the population are Palestinian refugees.

See the Roman Theatre which seats 6000 spectators, and the Costume and Folklore Museums beneath it. Go up to the Citadel to see the ruined Temple of Hercules, visit the Jordan Archaeological Museum and see the Circassian Guards outside the Basman Palace.

Jerash, just 30 kilometres north of Amman, has been called the Pompeii of the Middle East. Founded around 330 BC by Alexander the Great, it reached prominence in Roman times. Then, slowly, the sand piled up and it was all but forgotten until the 1920s when archaeologists went to work on the site. Plenty to see, including three theatres, two baths, innumerable churches and the remains of the huge Temple of Artemis.

Swimming in the **Dead Sea** is a unique experience. You cannot sink. In fact, it can be difficult to get your feet back on the bottom if you start floating. Best stick to the popular swimming spots – in places, the retreating level of the Dead Sea has exposed quicksand.

Thirty kilometres south of Amman is **Madaba**, known for its mosaics. East of Amman and out in the desert are quite a few castles, but for the hitcher they are difficult to reach. If you have the time to risk some slow hitching, the **King's Highway** south of Madaba offers spectacular scenery, a Crusader castle at **Kerak** and the Crusader fortress of **Shoubak**.

Petra, halfway between Amman and Aqaba, is a weird sight and, for 700 years – between the twelfth century and 1812 when it was accidentally rediscovered – it was truly a lost city. 'Rose-red Petra' (and it really is) was founded in 300 BC by the Nabataean

Arabs who took 500 years to carve it out of the solid rock of the mountains. Access is only by foot or hired horse from **Wadi Musa** through the dramatic **Siq**, a narrow chasm which made Petra so eminently defendable. After you've seen Petra you won't regret the desert journey you had to make to get there.

Aqaba is Jordan's port and is also doubling as a backdoor port for Iraq during its war with Iran. The town itself is unattractive – lots of litter, ships, hotels and development. The best parts of the beach are fenced in by the big hotels. Just across the bay is Eilat in Israel, so for security reasons swimming is not permitted after 6 p.m. It's worth travelling down the coast towards Saudi Arabia (you'll need your passport) and snorkelling among the fantastic coral. In this direction you'll also find the Aqaba Marine Science Station.

Addresses

Main post office in Amman is reliable for poste restante. Security check at door. No mail service to Israel.

American Express at International Traders, King Hussein Street, Amman (tel: 25072).

Student Office at IAESTE Office, Faculty of Engineering, University of Jordan, Amman (tel: 843 555 ext. 1789).

US Embassy at Jebel Amman, Amman (tel: 44 371).

British Embassy at Third Circle, Jebel Amman, Amman (tel: 412 61).

Hitchers' Tips and Comments...

Hitching good in Jordan due to friendly people. About 80 per cent of traffic on 'Desert Highway' are trucks. Petra *must* be visited. You can sleep with the Bedouins in the valley there – amazing experience. Not much in Amman. Cheap hotels are downtown near the Hasimi Mosque. *Simon Lingley, Uppingham, UK*

It's possible to cross from Jordan to Israel (though not the other way unless you have already come from Jordan and your visa is still valid) via the Allenby Bridge (King Hussein Bridge in Jordan). The trick is to ask to visit the West Bank which is part of Jordan under Israeli military occupation. To do this you must get a permit from the Ministry of the Interior in Amman, which is at the far end of King Hussein Street, a 40-minute walk from the centre. You must be there before 1 p.m. and you need a 50 fils revenue stamp (not a postage stamp) from the post office and one photo. Fill out some forms and wait between one and four days. It costs nothing, but don't say you are visiting Israel proper, only the West Bank, which includes East Jerusalem (the Old City). It's not possible to cross by foot. You must take a bus for 1 dinar or take a JETT bus from Amman for 2½ dinars. The checkpoint closes at 1 p.m. so it may be best to take the bus from Amman which starts at 6 a.m. From the Israeli side you may only take a taxi out of the customs post to either Jericho or Jerusalem. The price is negotiable. Anyone walking around in the Israeli border zone may be shot on sight, if he doesn't tread on a mine first. The Jordanians will let you back as long as there's no evidence of having visited Israel proper, but the Israelis may not let you cross back. And, of course, the whole thing may shut down at any time due to the tense situation in the Middle East. *Alan Barlow, Cheadle, UK*

12 Working in Europe

Members of EEC countries (i.e., Belgium, France, West
Germany, Italy, The Netherlands, Luxembourg, Denmark,
Ireland and the United Kingdom) can work in other EEC
countries without a work permit except in areas of public
administration but, otherwise, permits are usually required for
aliens. For example, a French girl trying to get employment in
Denmark would not need a work permit, but she must still obtain
a stamp on her passport from Danish immigration authorities
establishing actual residence in Denmark. If she wanted
employment in a country outside the EEC she would probably
need a work permit. For all that it should be noted that the theory
and the practice of a national of an EEC country working in
another EEC country are two different things. The tendency
seems to be for employers to favour their countrymen.
Theoretically you may have equal rights to the job, but when it
comes to the practicalities of the situation you run up against a
couple of barriers, the most obvious one being the language
problem.

A non-EEC member will almost certainly require a work permit
anywhere in Europe. Sometimes this permit has to be obtained by
the visitor before he enters the country in question, other times it
must be obtained by the visitor's employer after he has found a
job. The rules and regulations are generally so wound up in red
tape, and change so often, that the only sure way of finding out
complete details on the subject, as they apply at any particular
time, is to write to the nearest tourist agency in your own country
or the country in which you hope to work.

Presuming that most English-speaking people would be seeking
a job in England, the following addresses are offered. These
tourist agencies will give you the information you need or put you
in touch with the people who have the information.

Americans should write to the British Travel Offices at:

680 Fifth Avenue, New York, NY 10019.

John Hancock Center, Suite 2450, 875 N. Michigan Avenue,
Chicago IL 60611.
612 South Flower Street, Los Angeles, Calif. 90017.

Canadians should write to:
151 Bloor Street W, Suite 460, Toronto, Ontario M5S IT3.
602 West Hastings Street, Vancouver 2, BC.

Australians should write to:
171 Clarence Street, Sydney, NSW 2000.

New Zealanders to:
Box 3655, 97 Taranki Street, Wellington.

And South Africans to:
Union-Castle Building, 36 Loveday Street, PO Box 6256,
Johannesburg.
Union-Castle Building, 1st Floor, 51–55 St George's Street,
Cape Town.

Every day people arrive at English points of entry, hoping to find
work but without enough money in their pockets to support
themselves. Many of those people, unless they have a work permit
in their hands, are sent right back from where they came. These
work permits are getting harder and harder to find and generally
are only available to people who can fill jobs which British workers
can't. If you do get one it applies only to one specific job.

Check it all out before you leave home!

Useful guides published by Vacation-Work, 9 Park End Street,
Oxford OX1 1HJ, England, are: *Summer Jobs in Britain* and
Summer Jobs Abroad.

Warning! Beware of job-finding firms, particularly those which
guarantee you work in the world's most exotic corners after
they've received your £10 registration fee. Obviously not all – or
even most – job-finding firms are crooked, but during the last few
years there have been reports of fly-by-night operators who
advertise heavily for a week, rake in the loot and are never heard
of again.

The position – at the time of writing – is roughly this.

Austria

You must have a work permit to work. If you manage to contract for a job before entering the country your employer is supposed to apply for a work permit for you and then mail it to you. You then take it to the Austrian embassy in your area who will arrange a visa. If you find a job while passing through Austria then you have to front up to the local authorities and make application for a work permit from them. You don't need a permit to work as an *au pair*. There's often work available in hotels and in ski resorts. For fuller information students should contact:

Okista (Austrian Committee for International Educational Exchange), Türkenstrasse 4, 1090 Vienna, Austria.

Belgium

Work permits are needed for non-EEC members. However, unlike Austria where you are permitted to enter the country, seek a job and then apply for a permit, in Belgium you must have the job *before* you enter the country. Your employer will have applied for your permit and sent it to you and you will present it when you enter Belgium. For non-EEC members, work is hard to find.

Denmark

Work permits are no longer issued to nationals of non-EEC countries, except for a few marginal cases. EEC people can stay three months to look for a job after having first applied to local police for procedure for obtaining a residence permit. Students can try writing to:

Danish International Students Committee, 36 Skindergade, 1159 Copenhagen K, Denmark.

Finland

Work permits are needed before entering the country. Jobs are limited. For students, however, there is a fair chance of *au pair* work and also of entering the 'Family Scheme' programme where you live with a family, help with their daily work and also tutor them in the English language. For the latter there is free board and pocket money. Contact:

International Trainee Exchange of the Ministry of Labour,
Kalevankatu 16, PL 524, 00101 Helsinki 10, Finland.

France

Work permits are needed for non-EEC members. You can take it
as a basic rule that non-students *and* students must have a work
permit before they enter France. However, occasionally this rule is
relaxed and students (*only* students) are permitted to enter the
country, seek employment and after having found it make
application to the local Department of Work for a work permit.
When you make this application you will need the following
documents: (1) valid passport; (2) student identification card;
(3) a letter from your university or college establishing your
full-time student status; (4) a letter from your proposed employer
which will state his intention to employ you; (5) (if you are a
minor) a written permission from your parents allowing you to
enter France and work, witnessed by a member of a French
consulate or French embassy. Jobs are not easy to find but there is
some work available.

West Germany

Work permits are needed for non-EEC members. You may find
jobs available on factory assembly lines, on building projects, in
the hotel and catering trades . . . in short, in unskilled areas. If
you are bilingual you may find office work, but this is rarer. *Au
pair* work is available. To find work you should get in touch with:

Zentralstelle für Arbeitsvermittlung, Feuerbachstrasse 42, 0–6000
Frankfurt am Main, Germany.

This is a government labour agency through which trades and
businesses channel staff requests. The agency can put you in touch
with possible employers. It will also give you full information on
applying for a work permit.

Greece

Work permits are needed for non-EEC members *and* EEC
members who will probably get them if they are patient.

Information from any Greek National Tourist Office or, in Greece, from:

Ministry of Labour, 45 Piraeus Street, Athens.

Ireland

Work permit needed for non-EEC members, and if you enter the country with the stated intention of working, it must be shown at the border. You are supposed to arrange the job and have your employer apply for the permit.

Israel

As we go to press work permits must be obtained by your prospective employer before you enter the country, but contact the nearest Israel Tourist Office to make sure this remains true. The main work for young people is available on *kibbutzim*, or collective farms, for which you receive bed and board, the loan of work clothes and, maybe, about £10 per month pocket money. You may also receive free newspapers, cigarettes, aerogrammes, etc., depending on the *kibbutz*. You are expected to stay for at least a month. The work is, of course, mainly agricultural but sometimes in factories. The work will be boring, or dirty, or both, and basically you will do the work the *kibbutzniks* don't like but, in general, it is not too hard. You will meet volunteers from all over the world and probably make lasting friendships.

For full information you should write, before going, to the Israeli government/*kibbutz* representative office in your country or, when applying in Israel, contact any of the following *kibbutzim* organizations:

Ichud Hakevutzot Vehakibbutzim, Hayarkon Street 53A, Tel Aviv.
Hakibbutz Hameuchad, Soutin Street 27, Tel Aviv.
Hakibbutz Ha'artzi, Leonardo da Vinci Street 13, Tel Aviv.
Hakibbutz Hadati, Dubnov Street 7, Tel Aviv.

Or try the Israel Student Tourist Association, Ben Yehuda Street 109, Tel Aviv, Israel.

People with letters of recommendation from the *kibbutz* representative in their own country will get preference at the *kibbutz* offices. The offices will place you only on *kibbutzim* belonging to their own organization, so, if one office can't fix you up, try one of the others. You will have to pay a registration fee/ insurance premium of about £10, or show an insurance policy that covers you for accidents at work. Applying direct to a *kibbutz* is less certain. You will probably only get in if you know someone already there or if there is a shortage of volunteers.

For a whole book on *kibbutzim* try: *Kibbutz Volunteer* by John Bedford, published by Vacation-Work, 9 Park End Street, Oxford OX1 1HJ, England.

An alternative to *kibbutzim* is the *moshavim*, or cooperative farm. Work is harder and the hours are longer than on a *kibbutz*. You get paid about £140 worth of shekels a month, out of which you have to meet living expenses, so you won't get rich. The shekels are a drawback because it is difficult to convert them to hard currency. Your shekels rapidly lose their value with inflation in Israel at a couple of hundred per cent (and rising). How hard you work and your living conditions in general will depend on your farmer, and you will have more contact with the farmer than with other volunteers (it's the other way around on a *kibbutz*).

In Israel contact the Workers Moshavim Movement, Leonardo da Vinci Street 19, Tel Aviv.

There are opportunities for black work in the hotels and bars of Eilat, Jerusalem, and Tel Aviv. But there is a lot of competition from West Bank Arabs and the pay is bad, so you'll probably just make enough to live on.

Italy

Work permits not needed for EEC members. For others it is very difficult and you almost certainly can't take a job which could be satisfactorily filled by an Italian citizen. If you manage to find something your employer will have to get you a permit before you actually start working. For *au pairs* things are brighter. One address to inquire from about *au pair* work is:

Au Pairs–Italy, 46 The Rise, Sevenoaks, Kent TN13 1RJ.

Luxembourg

Work permits not needed by EEC members. Others may search for a job but before beginning work must have their employer apply for their permit.

Netherlands

Work permits not needed by EEC members. For others it is difficult. Also, you must have your work permit in hand as you enter the country. Not much work available, though some *au pair*. Students might manage to find something temporary by contacting:

Studenten Werkbureau Amsterdam, Koniginneweg 184a, Amsterdam.

Norway

Although some work is available in the fish processing and hotel and catering industries, the law requires you to have a work permit in hand before you arrive in Norway. After finding a job and making application for a permit to your nearest Norwegian embassy you may face a wait as long as three months before you get the piece of paper. Embassies can't find a job for you but they may be able to supply addresses of companies looking for staff.

Students interested in working on Norwegian farms and receiving room, board and pocket money, should contact:

Norwegian Committee for International Information and Youth Work, Akersgate 57, Oslo 1, Norway.

Portugal

Not a great deal of work about and, because of the low wage scale, if you do find something you can't earn enough to get ahead. The method of getting a work permit and a visa to go with it is complicated and must be applied for by the prospective employer.

Spain

Spain currently suffers a chronic unemployment problem, thus, for foreigners there's little work around outside the tourist industry.

However, it may be possible to find a job in resort areas. If you do, your employer should make application for your permit on your behalf. Legally you should have the permit before you actually begin working.

Students requiring information on vacation work should write to:

Spanish Union of Students, Bolsa Universitaria de Trabajo, Glorieta de Quevedo 8, Madrid 8.

Sweden

To work in Sweden you must have a permit, and get it before entering the country. To do so, you must have documented proof that you have a job and that you have somewhere to live.

For information write to:

International Association for the Exchange of Students for Technical Experience, Imperial College, London SW7.
   or:
Arbetsmarknadsstyrelsen, Fack, S-17199 Solna, Sweden.

Switzerland

Not much work available for foreigners and documentation must be arranged in advance. Even *au pairs* require work permits.

For good information about working in Europe you should buy the annual *Directory of Summer Jobs Abroad*, published by Vacation-Work, 9 Park End Street, Oxford. This excellent book gives up-to-date work permit and visa information plus long lists of companies and organizations seeking staff.

For people who want good, steady (rather than casual) work outside the British Isles, the best thing to do is to check the classified advertisements in London newspapers like the *Observer* and *The Times* or an international paper like the Paris edition of the *Herald Tribune*.

If you are in a particular country and in need of a job, one trick is to check out the local English language papers. They flourish where there are big tourist populations. For instance, in Spain there are at least four, all of which carry classified advertisements, some of which offer work. They are *Lookout* magazine which covers the Costa del Sol, and a rather strange little daily paper called the *Iberian Sun* which is available in most large cities, the *Costa Blanca News* covering the Costa Blanca and the *Majorca Daily Bulletin* covering the Balearics.

The type of work offered by advertisements in these papers is usually for secretaries or translators. Any girl who can type, take shorthand and who is completely fluent in a second language stands a chance of finding a job on the Continent. Any man who is fluent in a second language and who is a qualified professional worker stands a chance.

It's a good idea, when coming to Europe, to bring any documents you have proving your qualifications and experience in your field.

Many hitchers find their way into the movies as extras. Pay may be as much as £20 ($28) a day (considerably more if you can con someone into giving you a line to speak) and you might get work in a crowd scene for five to six days.

The main centres for film work at the moment are Madrid, Rome and London (London being well tied up by the unions).

You never know when this type of work is coming up. If you're interested, keep your ears open – there's usually someone in the hostels who knows what's happening.

Of course it's possible to find odd jobs in just about any European country if you're in the right place at the right time and if the employer takes a liking to you. For instance, in the summer there is limited (repeat *limited*) bar work available for pretty girls in most of the tourist resort areas – the Costa del Sol and Costa Brava in Spain, the Algarve and Costa do Sol area in Portugal, the French and Italian rivieras, etc. Also there is grape harvesting in southern France (Hérault) and southern Germany (Mosel valley) in September and October. Most of this work is of a very temporary nature and badly paid. You'll make enough to live on but not enough to build up your roll. You and your employer may be breaking the law, but you'll probably get away with it. (Don't write to me if you don't.)

There are other ways of picking up money. Plenty of hitchers make a living with their guitars either playing in the street or in clubs or restaurants where they receive food, a percentage of the take on drinks and/or tips.

Another way, particularly in Paris where the cops seem to be fairly easygoing towards down-and-outs, is to join up with pavement artists. Get yourself a packet of chalks and make a huge abstract on the pavement and wait hopefully for the pennies to fall. Of course if you're a trained artist who is capable of making really good chalk drawings, your chances of making some bread are tripled.

Some people carry silver wire and pliers in their pack and make simple jewellery to sell on sidewalks or in outdoor markets. Plenty of hitchers pick up objects in one country (e.g., beads in Morocco) to sell in the next. One hitcher makes £1 a time by cutting paper silhouettes of people or animals. Another makes simple puppets out of scrap found on the side of the road which he sells for as much as £3. I've seen a hitcher stage a quick magic show with handkerchiefs and lengths of rope while his wife passed a hat and kept an eye out for the police.

Straight-out begging is another way but the cops from any country are hard down on that. But if you're really broke you might be forced to do it. If so, be persistent and expect plenty of abuse. You might get enough for a feed which will fortify you enough so that you can think of another idea.

Luck.

Hitchers' Tips and Comments...

If you're down in Greece and Italy and in need of money or food make for a big port and approach one of the charter boats. They're always after crew, and even if you don't know about boats you can usually bluff your way to a job. You get free food, a lot of nautical miles, a few quid a week and a handful of blisters. Appearance isn't very important, but too much hair can lose you the better jobs.

It's nearly always possible to get a very temporary job as a kitchen porter (glorified pot washer) in both France and the UK without a permit. In small French cafés you usually get just food. In big hotels, a lot more work, but food *and* pay. In UK seaside towns in peak summer season cafés and hotels aren't too particular who works for them. You get money, food and sometimes a bed, which is good for a week's recuperation. Also in the UK fruit and potato picking jobs are available. Badly paid but good for a laugh and a kip.

Cheers and good hitching. *Clive Gill, Birchington, England*

By profession I am a charter boat skipper. My boat is moored at Monte Carlo. I noticed in your book a couple of references to working on charter boats. I'd like to point out to would-be 'sailors' that unless they have papers, work is very hard to find. Bluffing your way into a job, like Clive Gill did, will nine times out of ten lead to a black eye from an irate skipper who suddenly finds himself shorthanded because he's carrying a man who knows nothing about boats. Some skippers I've known have been so mad they've dumped the offender on deserted coastlines miles from civilization!

Anyway, if any readers are qualified and seriously interested, best places to hunt jobs are Antibes, Cannes, Beaulieu-sur-Mer, Monte Carlo (both old and new ports), Cros-de-Cagnes, Villeneuve-Loubet-Plage and La Napoule. April and May are the best times of the year, but also check with skippers during summer. Gibraltar is good from September onwards for boats sailing to the Caribbean and then on to the United States. *Captain M. J. Wiater, RNR, Monte Carlo, France*

For grape-picking in Germany, go to Bingen, a small town on the Rhine, south of Koblenz, and report to the local job centre. *Gregor Murphy, Paisley, Scotland*

Since I've taken to tramping these last few years I can give a couple of hints on how to keep going financially. Winter — December until April or May — is no time for travelling. But in Switzerland you can work these months in hotels or for ski-lifts. You get good sleeping quarters, time enough for a bit of skiing and you can save enough to tramp the other months of the year. The Swiss newspaper *Hotel-Revue* lists all open hotel jobs in the country . . . jobs like porter, chauffeur, etc. For ski-lift work it's a good idea to ask at ski-lift offices in each resort town. It's best to locate your job and sign a contract around October. (Then you can move down to Greece and lap up some sun before winter sets in and you have to start work.) Hotels and ski-lifts will arrange work permits — but step one is to find the job.

Aside from tramping it's fun and exciting to crew along on sailboats (if you've got a good stomach). It's possible to go to ports on the south coast of England (Ramsgate, Gosport, Cowes, Plymouth, Lymington) on weekends and bum rides. Or for the more adventurous, boats often leave Gosport for France, Spain and other Mediterranean ports. Often this leads to a job as a paid hand. A few summers ago I bummed lifts on boats for four months and ended up fifty quid ahead! *Steve Blume, Chicago, USA*

I've found if you're really broke a travelling circus is usually happy to pick you up. You get great food, a little money (lots of hard work!) and the chance to mix with truly fantastic people. I've done it twice and both times I just hated to leave. *James Daly, Dublin, Ireland*

For grape-picking work in Germany, go to Altzey, not far from Mainz, during the season. I got a fair wage plus free food and lodgings. *True Brit, Chelmsford, England*

The address you give for working in West Germany is no good unless you're a student writing from abroad. If you're already in Germany it is best to go to the local Arbeitsamt (Employment Office), the address of which can be found in the phone book. These offices have severely restricted opening hours and are staffed with hostile civil servants who are rude and unhelpful, and very often they don't like foreigners. Some will refuse to deal with you unless you speak in German. If your German is poor or non-existent you will probably get washing-up jobs, though you will do better if you have some sort of trade. Having got a job your problems are just beginning as you have to tackle the bureaucracy involved in getting a residence permit, without which you cannot have a Lohnsteuerkarte (tax card), without which you will pay the top rate of tax. At all stages deny having a religion unless you want to pay an extra church tax. If you find black work you will have none of this trouble. *Alan Barlow, Cheadle, UK*

Regarding work in Norway. Plenty of fruit-picking jobs around the Hardanger Fjord region. You can begin with strawberries in July, and continue with cherries, plums, apples and pears through September.

Some work on Crete, picking olives and oranges. Head up to the smaller villages around early November and start asking around. *Supertramp Schwarm, Eau Claire, Wi, USA*

Amsterdam. If stuck for work try the Heineken Brewery –
mostly donkey work.

Rotterdam. Try the dockyards. But pay is amazing,
depending on hours. It stinks, it's smelly and bloody hard
graft. *A. P. Kik, Middlesbrough, Teesside, UK*

13 Photography

Whether you're a serious amateur with a £200 SLR or a happy snapper with a £5 secondhand Instamatic, you'll probably be putting up with the extra weight of a camera in your pack to record your European hitch-trip.

For better pictures – especially if you've taken very few before – there are some simple hints you can follow:

1 Make sure you remove the lens cap before shooting. (If you don't you don't get any pictures!)

2 Keep your picture edges straight. Do this by lining up some vertical in the scene with the side of your viewfinder.

3 Don't jerk your camera when you shoot a picture or the snap will be blurred. You can avoid camera-shake by keeping one foot forward of the other and by holding the weight of the camera in the left hand so that the right is free to squeeze the shutter carefully. Practise squeezing the shutter when your camera is empty.

4 If you own a non-automatic camera with a built-in lightmeter and you know nothing about the operation of cameras and lightmeters, here are some very basic rules. (*a*) If you are snapping a general view with the sky in it, point your camera slightly down towards the ground so that you eliminate *most* of the sky from the meter eye. *Now* set your camera according to the maker's instructions. You do this because there is more light reflected from the sky than there is from the ground and, presumably, you want a correct exposure for the landscape. (*b*) If you want to photograph the sky (a sunset or cloud formation) or make a silhouette, then you disregard rule (*a*) and take your reading from the sky, usually to one side of the sun in case of sunrise and sunset pictures. (*c*) If you are taking pictures in the whitewashed villages of Spain, Italy, Greece etc., then remember that the white walls reflect more light

than the rest of the scene. If you aim your camera at an old lady sitting by a white wall, your meter will read the brightness of the wall and your old lady will come out too dark. What you must do is always take a reading from the subject you wish to photograph. If you can't go close enough to someone to measure the light on them, place your hand between six and nine inches in front of the camera meter eye so that the same light falls on your hand as on your subject, and take a reading from your own skin-tone.

5 If you own an automatic camera with no manual over-ride, the only control you have over exposure is via the ASA (or DIN) rating ring. If you think the general scene is reflecting more light than the subject you want exposed correctly, then try under-rating your film. For example, if you are using 100 ASA film and your ASA ring is set on 100 ASA, simply turn the ring back until it reads 50 ASA. The trick *might* work. (Don't forget to put it back in the right place for subsequent shots.) Only try it if you are using transparency film which needs critical exposure. If you're using negative film just leave the ring where it's supposed to be. The laboratory will probably make an automatic adjustment when they print your pictures.

6 If you're photographing sports, like skiing, car-racing, etc., remember that unless you have a sophisticated camera with very high speeds (1/500th of a second or better), you cannot stop action going directly across your viewfinder – it will be blurred. Try to position yourself so that the car or skier is travelling at an angle towards you. If you can't, pan your camera with the action as you take the picture.

7 If you're photographing people, don't be afraid to approach them for a close-up. Most people don't mind, or if they do they'll simply say no. (But Moslem Arabs have a habit of getting very angry about cameras. They believe that the camera is capturing their spirit as well as their image.)

8 Don't keep film in your pocket for any length of time. Your body warmth can affect its colour balance. Keep the film in its container and keep the container in a side-pocket of your pack where there is some air circulation. Keep colour film away from the sun.

9 Always load and unload your camera in the shade. If there is none, turn your back to the sun and unload in your own shadow.

This is to minimize the chance of light getting to the film and fogging it.

10 If you carry your camera in your pack, wrap it in a dry towel or shirt to protect it as much as possible from knocks and from car vibration which can loosen screws.

★**Film** Colour film prices in some countries are exorbitant. In Spain and France, for instance, they'll break your budget. Switzerland, Andorra and England are good places to buy film. In England, make sure you go to a discount place. Boots (the chemist shops) seem to offer a good deal. Major photo-shop chains are usually cheaper again. Always try and buy all the film you need in a large city where prices are competitive – outside the cities you can pay 20 per cent more. In Mediterranean countries never buy film anywhere except in a photo shop – if you do you'll be paying too much and it may have been sitting in the window in sunlight thus altering its colour balance. If you're broke buy out-of-date film *from camera shops only* (because they store film correctly). You can usually get it at half price! Look for the expiry dates on the side of the boxes and buy the films which have just gone over their dates. Always look at the date when you buy a film. If the film is out of date tell the salesman and ask for a discount.

14 Weights and measures

Miles/kilometres
A kilometre is roughly 6/10ths of a mile, so for a quick estimate multiply the number of kilometres by 6 and move the decimal point one place to the left (212 kilometres×6=1272. Insert decimal point one place to left=127·2 miles).

km	miles/km	miles
1·609	1	0·621
16·093	10	6·214
160·930	100	62·136
804·650	500	310·680
1609·300	1000	621·360

Pounds/kilograms
There are roughly 2·2 pounds to a kilogram.

kg	lb/kg	lb
0·453	1	2·205
0·907	2	4·409
1·360	3	6·614
1·814	4	8·818
2·268	5	11·023

Litres/gallons
For a rough calculation figure 4½ litres to the British imperial gallon. The American gallon is slightly less than 4 litres.

litres	gallons/litres	gallons
4·55	1	0·22
22·73	5	1·10
45·46	10	2·20

Pounds per square inch/kilograms per square centimetre

lb per sq in	kg per sq cm	lb per sq in	kg per sq cm
18	1·266	39	2·742
20	1·406	40	2·812
22	1·547	42	2·953
25	1·758	43	3·023
29	2·039	45	3·164
32	2·250	46	3·234
35	2·461	50	3·515
36	2·531	60	4·218

Equivalent sizes

women's clothing sizes

British	36	38	40	42	44	46
American	34	36	38	40	42	44
Continental	42	44	46	48	50	52

men's suits and overcoats

British and American	36	38	40	42	44	46
Continental	46	48	50	52	54	56

shirts

British and American	14	14½	15	15½	16	16½	17
Continental	36	37	38	39	41	42	43

stockings

British and American	8	8½	9	9½	10	10½
Continental	0	1	2	3	4	5

socks

British and American	9½	10	10½	11	11½
Continental	38/39	39/40	40/41	41/42	42/43

shoes

British and American	3	4	5	6	7	8	9	10
Continental	36	37	38	39	41	42	43	44

Continental glove sizes are the same as in Britain and America.

Fahrenheit/Centigrade

The general rule for the conversion of Centigrade into Fahrenheit is to multiply by 9/5ths and add 32. To translate Fahrenheit into Centigrade, subtract 32 and multiply by 5/9ths.

15 Language

The vocabulary in this language section has been kept as concise as possible for a very simple reason. When you can't speak a language and have no intention of learning it, the fewer words you have to play with the better. All you need are the basic words of survival and politeness. ('Thank you' is undoubtedly the first word you should memorize in any language.)

Even this ultra-simple list could cause you problems. Example? You're in Toledo and you want to go to Madrid, so you walk up to a fellow and say: '*Por favor, dónde está la carretera para Madrid*?' You say it so nicely that the fellow thinks you can speak Spanish, so he rattles off his answer: '*Pues, tiene que andar por la carretera unos dos kilómetros y medio más o menos, entonces tome Usted la primera bocacalle a la derecha . . . mire! si quiere le llevo en mi coche, es más sencillo!*' From there on in you'd better think awful fast because if this guy is in a hurry, odds are you're going to miss out on the ride up to the Madrid road which he just offered you!

The list has also been designed to help you on your way with emergencies and, as well, I hope you'll find enough words in here to allow you to carry on a bit of 'pidgin' smalltalk with just about anyone. Be patient!

French

English	French	pronounced
thank you	merci	*mair-see*
please	s'il vous plaît	*sil voo play*
good morning	bonjour	*bon-joor*
goodbye	au revoir	*oh re-vwahr*
yes	oui	*wee*
no	non	*noh*
I am . . .	je suis . . .	*jer swee*
are you going to . . .?	allez-vous vers . . .?	*allay voo ver*

English	French	pronounced
where is . . .?	où est . . .?	*oo eh*
the road to . . .	la route pour . . .	*la root poor*
the toilet	le lavabo	*lu la-va-boh*
the youth hostel	l'auberge de jeunesse	*ohberge de-jerness*
the station	la gare	*la gar*
I would like . . .	je voudrais . . .	*jer voo-dray*
to eat	manger	*mon-zhay*
a room	une chambre	*oon shombre*
how much?	combien?	*kohm-biyen*
when?	quand?	*kon*
left	gauche	*gohshe*
right	droit	*dwar*
straight ahead	tout droit	*too dwar*
yesterday	hier	*ee-yeh*
today	aujourd'hui	*oh-joor-dwee*
tomorrow	demain	*derman*
1	un	*urn*
2	deux	*der*
3	trois	*twah*
4	quatre	*catre*
5	cinq	*sank*
6	six	*sees*
7	sept	*set*
8	huit	*weet*
9	neuf	*nerf*
10	dix	*dees*
11	onze	*onz*
12	douze	*dooz*
13	treize	*traiz*
14	quatorze	*ka-torz*
15	quinze	*kanze*
16	seize	*seyz*
17	dix-sept	*dees-set*
18	dix-huit	*dees-weet*
19	dix-neuf	*dees-nerf*
20	vingt	*van*
30	trente	*trarnt*

English	French	pronounced
40	quarante	*kar-rarnt*
50	cinquante	*san-karnt*
60	soixante	*swah-sant*
70	soixante-dix	*swah-sant dees*
80	quatre-vingts	*catre van*
90	quatre-vingt-dix	*catre van dees*
100	cent	*sonn*
1000	mille	*meel*

Shopping

Apples – *pommes*. Aspirins – *aspirines*. Bananas – *bananes*.
Bandages – *pansements*. Beer – *bière*. Biscuits – *biscuits*. Blouse –
chemisier. Boots – *bottes*. Bread – *pain*. Cheese – *fromage*.
Chocolate – *chocolat*. Coffee – *café*. Dress – *robe*. Egg – *oeuf*. Fish
– *poisson*. Fruit – *fruit*. Jacket – *veston* (men's), *veste* (ladies').
Meat – *viande*. Milk – *lait*. Mineral water – *eau minérale*. Oranges
– *oranges*. Potatoes – *pommes de terre*. Salt – *sel*. Sandwich –
sandwich. Sausage – *saucisse*. Shirt – *chemise*. Shoes – *souliers*.
Skirt – *jupe*. Soup – *potage*. Socks – *chaussettes*. Sticking plaster –
sparadrap. Sugar – *sucre*. Sweater – *tricot*. Tea – *thé*. Trousers –
pantalon. Vegetables – *légumes*. Water – *eau*. Wine – *vin*.

German

English	German	pronounced
thank you	danke schön	*dan-ker-shun*
please	bitte	*bit-teh*
good morning	guten Tag	*goo-ten-targ*
goodbye	auf Wiedersehen	*ouf-weeder-zen*
yes	ja	*yah*
no	nein	*nine*
I am . . .	Ich bin . . .	*ik bin*
are you going to . . .?	gehen Sie nach . . .?	*gay-en-see nark*
where is . . .?	wo ist . . .?	*vo eest*
the road to . . .	der Weg nach . . .	*der veg nark*
the toilet	die Toilette	*de twarlet-tuh*
the youth hostel	die Jugendherberge	*de you-gend-er-berga*

English	German	pronounced
the station	der Bahnhof	der barn-hof
I would like . . .	Ich möchte . . .	ik mersh-ta
to eat	essen	ess-en
a room	ein Zimmer	ein tsimmer
how much?	wie viel?	vee-feel
when?	wann?	varn
left	links	leenks
right	rechts	reckts
straight ahead	geradeaus	gay-ray-day-ous
yesterday	gestern	guess-tern
today	heute	hoy-tuh
tomorrow	morgen	mor-gen
1	eins	eintz
2	zwei	tzvai
3	drei	dry
4	vier	feer
5	fünf	funf
6	sechs	zex
7	sieben	zee-ben
8	acht	arkt
9	neun	noyn
10	zehn	tzain
11	elf	elf
12	zwölf	tzwuhlf
13	dreizehn	drytzain
14	vierzehn	feertzain
15	fünfzehn	funfzain
16	sechzehn	zextzain
17	siebzehn	zeebtzain
18	achtzehn	arktzain
19	neunzehn	noyntzain
20	zwanzig	tzvahntzig
30	dreissig	dry-tzig
40	vierzig	feer-tzig
50	fünfzig	funf-tzig
60	sechzig	zex-tzig
70	siebzig	zeeb-tzig
80	achtzig	ark-tzig
90	neunzig	noyn-tzig

English	German	pronounced
100	hundert	*hoon-dert*
1000	tausend	*tow-sent*

Shopping

Apples – *Apfel*. Aspirins – *Aspirin*. Bananas – *Bananen*. Bandages – *Verbandszeug*. Beer – *Bier*. Biscuits – *Plätzchen*. Blouse – *Bluse*. Boots – *Stiefel*. Bread – *Brot*. Cheese – *Käse*. Chocolate – *Schokolade*. Coffee – *Kaffee*. Dress – *Kleid*. Egg – *Ei*. Fish – *Fische*. Fruit – *Obst*. Jacket – *Jacke*. Meat – *Fleisch*. Milk – *Milch*. Mineral water – *Mineralwasser*. Oranges – *Apfelsienen*. Potatoes – *Kartoffeln*. Salt – *Salz*. Sandwich – *belegtes Brötchen*. Sausage – *Wurst*. Shirt – *Hemd*. Shoes – *Schuhe*. Skirt – *Rock*. Soup – *Suppe*. Socks – *Socken*. Sticking plaster – *Heftpflaster*. Sugar – *Zucker*. Sweater – *Pullover*. Tea – *Tee*. Trousers – *Hosen*. Vegetables – *Gemüse*. Water – *Wasser*. Wine – *Wein*.

Spanish

English	Spanish	pronounced
thank you	gracias	*grar-thee-ahs*
please	por favor	*por fav-or*
hello	hola	*ol-ah*
goodbye	adiós	*ah-dee-os*
yes	sí	*see*
no	no	*noh*
I am . . .	yo soy . . .	*yo-soy*
are you going to . . .?	va usted a . . .?	*vah-oosted a*
where is . . .?	dónde está . . .?	*donday estah*
the road to . . .	la carretera para . . .	*lar car-ray-tera parah*
the toilet	el retrete	*el raytraytay*
the youth hostel	el albergue juvenil	*el al-ber-goh hoovay-neel*
the station	la estación	*la ay-star-thee-on*
I would like . . .	querría . . .	*kerr-eeya*
to eat	comer	*com-mayr*

English	Spanish	pronounced
a room	una habitación	*oona ahbee-tah-thee-on*
how much?	cuánto?	*kwon-toe*
when?	cuándo?	*kwon-doe*
left	izquierda	*eeth-key-air-dah*
right	derecha	*day-ray-cha*
straight ahead	todo derecho	*toh-doh day-ray-choh*
yesterday	ayer	*a-yer*
today	hoy	*oy*
tomorrow	mañana	*marn-yar-nar*
1	uno	*oo-no*
2	dos	*dos*
3	tres	*tress*
4	cuatro	*kwat-tro*
5	cinco	*thin-ko*
6	seis	*sais*
7	siete	*see-ay-tay*
8	ocho	*o-choh*
9	nueve	*noo-ay-vay*
10	diez	*dee-eth*
11	once	*on-thay*
12	doce	*do-thay*
13	trece	*tray-thay*
14	catorce	*ca-tor-thay*
15	quince	*keen-thay*
16	dieciseis	*dee-eth-ee-sais*
17	diecisiete	*dee-eth-ee-see-ay-tay*
18	dieciocho	*dee-eth-ee-o-choh*
19	diecinueve	*dee-eth-ee-noo-ay-vay*
20	veinte	*vain-tay*
30	treinta	*train-ta*
40	cuarenta	*kwa-renta*
50	cincuenta	*thin-kwenta*
60	sesenta	*say-senta*
70	setenta	*say-tenta*
80	ochenta	*o-chenta*
90	noventa	*no-venta*
100	cien	*thee-en*

English	Spanish	pronounced
500	quinientos	keen-nee-entos
1000	mil	meel

Shopping
Apples – *manzanas*. Aspirins – *aspirinas*. Bananas – *plátanos*.
Bandages – *vendajes*. Beer – *cerveza*. Biscuits – *galletas*. Blouse –
blusa. Boots – *botas*. Bread – *pan*. Cheese – *queso*. Chocolate –
chocolate. Coffee – *café*. Dress – *vestido*. Egg – *huevo*. Fish –
pescado. Fruit – *fruta*. Jacket – *chaqueta*. Meat – *carne*. Milk –
leche. Mineral water – *agua mineral*. Oranges – *naranjas*. Potatoes
– *patatas*. Salt – *sal*. Sandwich – *bocadillo*. Sausage – *Salchicha*.
Shirt – *camisa*. Shoes – *zapatos*. Skirt – *falda*. Soup – *sopa*. Socks –
calcetines. Sticking plaster – *esparadrapo*. Sugar – *azúcar*. Sweater
– *suéter*. Tea – *té*. Trousers – *pantalones*. Vegetables – *verduras*.
Water – *agua*. Wine – *vino*.

Italian

English	Italian	pronounced
thank you	grazie	*grah-tzyeh*
please	per piacere	*pairr pee-ah-chay-ary*
good morning	buon giorno	*bwon-dior-no*
goodbye	arrivederci	*ar-reev-e-derch-ee*
yes	si	*see*
no	no	*noh*
I am . . .	io sono . . .	*yo sohno*
are you going to . . .?	va lei a . . .?	*vah lay-ee a*
where is . . .?	dov'è . . .?	*doh-vay*
the road to . . .	l'autostrada . . .	*l'otoh-stra-dah*
the toilet	il gabinetto	*eel ga-bee-naytoh*
the youth hostel	l'albergo per giovani	*l'albairgo per joh-vah-nee*
the station	la stazione	*la stah-tzyohnay*
I would like . . .	vorrei . . .	*vorr-ay-ee*
to eat	mangiare	*mahn-diah-ray*
a room	una camera	*oona kah-may-rah*
how much?	quanto?	*kwan-toh*

English	Italian	pronounced
when?	quando?	kwan-doh
left	sinistra	see-nee-strah
right	destra	dess-trah
straight ahead	tutto diretto	too-toh dee-ret-toh
yesterday	ieri	ee-yay-ree
today	oggi	oh-djee
tomorrow	domani	doh-mar-nee
1	uno	oo-no
2	due	doo-ay
3	tre	tray
4	quattro	kwat-tro
5	cinque	cheen-kway
6	sei	say-ee
7	sette	set-tay
8	otto	aw-toh
9	nove	noh-vay
10	dieci	dee-ay-chee
11	undici	oon-dee-chee
12	dodici	doh-dee-chee
13	tredici	tray-dee-chee
14	quattordici	kwat-torr-dee-chee
15	quindici	kween-dee-chee
16	sedici	say-dee-chee
17	diciassette	deeh-cheeah-set-tay
18	diciotto	dee-chiot-toh
19	diciannove	dee-cheeah-noh-vay
20	venti	vayn-tee
30	trenta	trayn-ta
40	quaranta	kwah-rahn-ta
50	cinquanta	cheen-kwahn-ta
60	sessanta	sais-sarn-ta
70	settanta	set-tan-ta
80	ottanta	ot-tan-ta
90	novanta	no-van-ta
100	cento	chayn-to
1000	mille	mee-lay

Shopping
Apples – *mele*. Aspirins – *aspirina*. Bananas – *banane*. Bandages –

fascia. Beer – *birra*. Biscuits – *biscotti*. Blouse – *blusa*. Boots – *stivali*. Bread – *pane*. Cheese – *formaggio*. Chocolate – *cioccolata*. Coffee – *caffè*. Dress – *abito*. Egg – *uovo*. Fish – *pesce*. Fruit – *frutta*. Jacket – *giacchetta*. Meat – *carne*. Milk – *latte*. Mineral water – *acqua minerale*. Oranges – *aranci*. Potatoes – *patate*. Salt – *sale*. Sandwich – *panino*. Sausage – *salsiccia*. Shirt – *camicia*. Shoes – *scarpe*. Skirt – *gonna*. Soup – *zuppa*. Socks – *calzini*. Sticking plaster – *cerotto*. Sugar – *zucchero*. Sweater – *maglione*. Tea – *tè*. Trousers – *calzoni*. Vegetables – *legumi*. Water – *acqua*. Wine – *vino*.

Dutch

English	Dutch	pronounced
thank you	dank U	*dahnk yu*
please	alstublieft	*als-too-bleeft*
hello	hallo	*hah-loh*
goodbye	daag	*dahk*
yes	ja	*yah*
no	nee	*nay*
I am . . .	ik ben . . .	*ick ben*
are you going to . . .?	gaat U naar . . .?	*haht yu nahr*
where is . . .?	waar is . . .?	*vahr iss*
the road to . . .	de weg nar . . .	*der veg nahr*
the toilet	het toilet	*het twa-let*
the youth hostel	de jeugdherberg	*der yugd-hair-berk*
the station	het station	*het sta-si-on*
I would like . . .	ik wil graag . . .	*ick vil grahg*
to eat	eten	*ay-ten*
a room	een kamer	*ayn ka-mer*
how much?	hoe veel?	*hu vehl*
when?	wanneer?	*wannair*
left	links	*links*
right	rechts	*rekts*
straight ahead	rechtdoor	*rekts-door*
yesterday	gisteren	*hist-erun*
today	vandaag	*fan-dak*
tomorrow	morgen	*morghen*
1	één	*ayn*
2	twee	*tvay*

English	Dutch	pronounced
3	drie	*dree*
4	vier	*feer*
5	vijf	*fife*
6	zes	*zess*
7	zeven	*zeh-ven*
8	acht	*ahkht*
9	negen	*neh-khen*
10	tien	*teen*
11	elf	*aylf*
12	twaalf	*twahlf*
13	dertien	*dehr-teen*
14	veertien	*feer-teen*
15	vijftien	*fife-teen*
16	zestien	*zess-teen*
17	zeventien	*zeh-ven-teen*
18	achttien	*ahkht-teen*
18	negentien	*neh-khen-teen*
20	twintig	*tvintihk*
30	dertig	*dare-tihk*
40	veertig	*fare-tihk*
50	vijftig	*fife-tihk*
60	zestig	*zess-tihk*
70	zeventig	*zeh-ven-tihk*
80	tachtig	*tahk-tihk*
90	negentig	*neh-khen-tihk*
100	honderd	*hohn-dert*
1000	duizend	*doy-zent*

Shopping

Apples – *appels*. Aspirins – *aspirines*. Bananas – *bananen*.
Bandages – *verband*. Beer – *bier*. Biscuits – *koekjes*. Blouse –
bloes. Boots – *laarzen*. Bread – *brood*. Cheese – *kaas*. Chocolate –
chocolade. Coffee – *koffie*. Dress – *jurk*. Egg – *ei*. Fish – *vis*. Fruit
– *fruit*. Jacket – *jack*. Meat – *vlees*. Milk – *melk*. Mineral water –
mineraal water. Oranges – *sinaasappelen*. Potatoes – *aardappelen*.
Salt – *zout*. Sandwich – *belegd broodje*. Sausage – *worst*. Shirt –
overhemd. Shoes – *schoenen*. Skirt – *rok*. Socks – *sokken*. Soup –
soep. Sticking plaster – *hechtpleister*. Sugar – *suiker*. Sweater –

trui. Tea – *thee*. Trousers – *broek*. Vegetables – *groenten*. Water – *water*. Wine – *wijn*.

Swedish

English	Swedish	pronounced
thank you	tack	*tahck*
please	var snäll och	*vahr snel ok*
hello	hallo	*hal-loh*
goodbye	adjö	*ah-yuh*
yes	ja	*yaw*
no	nej	*nay*
I am . . .	jag är . . .	*yawg air*
are you going to. . . ?	resar ni. . . ?	*ray-sahr nee*
where is. . . ?	var är. . . ?	*vahr ehr*
the road to . . .	vägen . . .	*vay-gen*
the toilet	toaletten	*toh-ah-let-ten*
the youth hostel	yungdomshär-bärge	*yung-dums-hair-bahr-yeh*
the station	järnvägssta-tionen	*yehern-vehgs-stah-shoh-nehn*
I would like . . .	jag vill ha . . .	*yawg veel hah*
to eat	att äta	*aht-air-tah*
a room	ett rum	*eht room*
how much?	hur mycket?	*huhr mew-keht*
when?	när?	*nehr*
left	vänster	*vehn-stehr*
right	höger	*huh-gehr*
straight ahead	rakt fram	*rakt fram*
yesterday	i gár	*ee gohr*
today	i dag	*ee dak*
tomorrow	i morgon	*ee mohr-gohn*
1	ett	*et*
2	två	*tvoh*
3	tre	*treh*
4	fyra	*few-rah*
5	fem	*fem*
6	sex	*sex*
7	sju	*shew*
8	åtta	*oht-tah*

English	Swedish	pronounced
9	nio	nee-yoh
10	tio	tee-yoh
11	elva	ehl-vah
12	tolv	tohlv
13	tretton	treht-ton
14	fjorton	fyohr-ton
15	femton	fem-ton
16	sexton	sex-ton
17	sjutton	shew-ton
18	arton	air-ton
19	nitton	nit-ton
20	tjugo	tshu-goh
30	trettio	treht-tyee
40	fyrtio	fur-tyee
50	femtio	fem-tyee
60	sextio	sex-tyee
70	sjuttio	shew-tyee
80	åttio	oht-tyee
90	nittio	nit-tyee
100	ett hundra	et hun-dra
1000	ett tusen	et too-sen

Shopping
Apples – *äppler*. Aspirins – *aspirin*. Bananas – *bananer*. Bandages – *bindel*. Beer – *ö*. Biscuits – *kex*. Blouse – *blus*. Boots – *stövlar*. Bread – *bröd*. Cheese – *ost*. Chocolate – *chokolad*. Coffee – *kaffe*. Dress – *klänning*. Egg – *ägg*. Fish – *fisk*. Fruit – *frukt*. Jacket – *jacka*. Meat – *kött*. Milk – *mjölk*. Mineral water – *mineralvatten*. Oranges – *apelsiner*. Potatoes – *potatis*. Salt – *salt*. Sandwich – *smörgås*. Sausage – *korv*. Shirt – *skjorter*. Shoes – *skorna*. Skirt – *kjol*. Socks – *strumpor*. Soup – *soppa*. Sugar – *socker*. Sweater – *sveater*. Tea – *té*. Trousers – *byxor*. Vegetables – *gronsäker*. Water – *vatten*. Wine – *vin*.

Calendar 1985

January

S	M	T	W	T	F	S
		1	2	3	4	5
6	7	8	9	10	11	12
13	14	15	16	17	18	19
20	21	22	23	24	25	26
27	28	29	30	31		

February

S	M	T	W	T	F	S
					1	2
3	4	5	6	7	8	9
10	11	12	13	14	15	16
17	18	19	20	21	22	23
24	25	26	27	28		

March

S	M	T	W	T	F	S
					1	2
3	4	5	6	7	8	9
10	11	12	13	14	15	16
17	18	19	20	21	22	23
24	25	26	27	28	29	30
31						

April

S	M	T	W	T	F	S
	1	2	3	4	5	6
7	8	9	10	11	12	13
14	15	16	17	18	19	20
21	22	23	24	25	26	27
28	29	30				

May

S	M	T	W	T	F	S
			1	2	3	4
5	6	7	8	9	10	11
12	13	14	15	16	17	18
19	20	21	22	23	24	25
26	27	28	29	30	31	

June

S	M	T	W	T	F	S
						1
2	3	4	5	6	7	8
9	10	11	12	13	14	15
16	17	18	19	20	21	22
23	24	25	26	27	28	29
30						

July

S	M	T	W	T	F	S
	1	2	3	4	5	6
7	8	9	10	11	12	13
14	15	16	17	18	19	20
21	22	23	24	25	26	27
28	29	30	31			

August

S	M	T	W	T	F	S
				1	2	3
4	5	6	7	8	9	10
11	12	13	14	15	16	17
18	19	20	21	22	23	24
25	26	27	28	29	30	31

September

S	M	T	W	T	F	S
1	2	3	4	5	6	7
8	9	10	11	12	13	14
15	16	17	18	19	20	21
22	23	24	25	26	27	28
29	30					

October

S	M	T	W	T	F	S
		1	2	3	4	5
6	7	8	9	10	11	12
13	14	15	16	17	18	19
20	21	22	23	24	25	26
27	28	29	30	31		

November

S	M	T	W	T	F	S
					1	2
3	4	5	6	7	8	9
10	11	12	13	14	15	16
17	18	19	20	21	22	23
24	25	26	27	28	29	30

December

S	M	T	W	T	F	S
1	2	3	4	5	6	7
8	9	10	11	12	13	14
15	16	17	18	19	20	21
22	23	24	25	26	27	28
29	30	31				

(Thanks to Martin Doran of Derry, Northern Ireland, for suggesting this calendar!)

Calendar 1986

January
S	M	T	W	T	F	S
			1	2	3	4
5	6	7	8	9	10	11
12	13	14	15	16	17	18
19	20	21	22	23	24	25
26	27	28	29	30	31	

February
S	M	T	W	T	F	S
						1
2	3	4	5	6	7	8
9	10	11	12	13	14	15
16	17	18	19	20	21	22
23	24	25	26	27	28	

March
S	M	T	W	T	F	S
						1
2	3	4	5	6	7	8
9	10	11	12	13	14	15
16	17	18	19	20	21	22
23	24	25	26	27	28	29
30	31					

April
S	M	T	W	T	F	S
		1	2	3	4	5
6	7	8	9	10	11	12
13	14	15	16	17	18	19
20	21	22	23	24	25	26
27	28	29	30			

May
S	M	T	W	T	F	S
				1	2	3
4	5	6	7	8	9	10
11	12	13	14	15	16	17
18	19	20	21	22	23	24
25	26	27	28	29	30	31

June
S	M	T	W	T	F	S
1	2	3	4	5	6	7
8	9	10	11	12	13	14
15	16	17	18	19	20	21
22	23	24	25	26	27	28
29	30					

July
S	M	T	W	T	F	S
		1	2	3	4	5
6	7	8	9	10	11	12
13	14	15	16	17	18	19
20	21	22	23	24	25	26
27	28	29	30	31		

August
S	M	T	W	T	F	S
					1	2
3	4	5	6	7	8	9
10	11	12	13	14	15	16
17	18	19	20	21	22	23
24	25	26	27	28	29	30
31						

September
S	M	T	W	T	F	S
	1	2	3	4	5	6
7	8	9	10	11	12	13
14	15	16	17	18	19	20
21	22	23	24	25	26	27
28	29	30				

October
S	M	T	W	T	F	S
			1	2	3	4
5	6	7	8	9	10	11
12	13	14	15	16	17	18
19	20	21	22	23	24	25
26	27	28	29	30	31	

November
S	M	T	W	T	F	S
						1
2	3	4	5	6	7	8
9	10	11	12	13	14	15
16	17	18	19	20	21	22
23	24	25	26	27	28	29
30						

December
S	M	T	W	T	F	S
	1	2	3	4	5	6
7	8	9	10	11	12	13
14	15	16	17	18	19	20
21	22	23	24	25	26	27
28	29	30	31